C0-AYG-997

THE LIFE CYCLE:

Perspectives and Commentary

Paul Cameron

distributed by
DABOR SCIENCE PUBLICATIONS
Oceanside, New York 11572

43296

Copyright © 1977 by
Paul Cameron

Library of Congress Cataloging in Publication Data

Cameron, Paul.
  The life cycle.

  1. Developmental psychology.   I.   Title.
BF713.C35   155   77-16675
ISBN   0-89561-057-4

A Marvin Bernstein Book

Printed in the United States of America

Contents

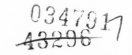
034791
43296

Foreword

This is a somewhat unusual text in that it "covers" the life-cycle broadform but does not attempt to "touch down" in every area in which a substantive body of knowledge exists. Theory is admixed with specific research examples. These liabilities are to some degree compensated for by only presenting those areas in which the author has demonstrated some research expertise. I hope the reader will glean some of the fun of the enterprise from its pages.

PAUL CAMERON

Foreword

This is a somewhat unusual text in that it "covers" the life-cycle broadform but does not attempt to "touch down" in every area in which a substantive body of knowledge exists. Theory is admixed with specific research examples. These liabilities are to some degree compensated for by only presenting those areas in which the author has demonstrated some research expertise. I hope the reader will glean some of the fun of the enterprise from its pages.

PAUL CAMERON

1

THE LIFE-SPAN IN PERSPECTIVE

Mankind shares a few common experiences including being born, getting older as long as one lives, and dying. Just about anything that goes on during "getting older" and the circumstances of both birth and death vary as a function of the culture in which one becomes a person and the philosophies to which one is subjected. Being counted a member of the human community varies from the relatively generous "at conception" of the Roman Catholics and Chinese to the rather niggardly "8 days from birth" of the Ghanaese. Death is regarded by some as "all she wrote," by others as the beginning of a life of bliss, horror, or boredom, and by yet others as a transformation of persons into rocks or spirits that may aid or interfere with the lives of the breathing.

In between the conferral and removal of human membership, a person is subject to extensive age-, sexual-, and often, social class-grading and consequent treatment. While every social system can usefully be regarded as an intricate dynamism of competing and complementary forces, it is worthwhile to sort social systems along a continuum from an economic perspective as it usually involves and influences (perhaps even subsumes) most of the other perspectives. The various social systems valuate the age — groupings differently, as depicted in Figure 1.1. At the food-gathering or savage stage of development, the skills, knowledge and strength of the middle-aged make them, overall, the most useful members of society. The old, as long as they are not infirm (and infrequently even if they are), are the carriers of the cultural traditions, stories,

FIGURE 1.1

Comparative Valuation Placed Upon Persons, Slaves, and Industrial
Workers by Sex

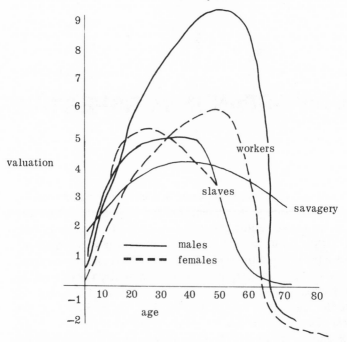

and histories of the people as well as useful members of the society
from an economic standpoint. As such they often fall behind the
middle-aged in overall status. The strength and endurance of young
adults makes them more useful than preadults who are in turn more
highly valued than children.

With the onset of barbarism and slavery, the world of man is
bifurcated into the owned and the owners. Among slaves, depending upon the kinds of tasks to be performed, the middle-aged
usually command the higher price in light of their skills and ability
to direct and lead, the old are of value as house servants and
minders of the lighter tasks, and young adults furnish much of the
brawn. Children sometimes compete with the old for the meeting of
light tasks, but disease and accident limit their use values, leading
to the well-known adage "a slave in hand is worth two fooling
around in the bushes." In the ruling or owning class, social status

often rose with age until death or senility intervened. While in primitive times all persons' influence on society ceased with demise, from barbarism onward, for the owning classes, a will or legacy often allowed an owner to "live on" in restrictions regarding his property. While old slaves inevitably slowly declined in value, an old owner, depending on his holdings, might increase in social status and the attentions paid him. The sex-differentiations made during savagery, under which women enjoyed an equal or nearly equal status to men, changed markedly to sexual discrimination with the onset of property ownership, especially within the owning class. During the slavery period in the United States a female generally brought about as much as a male at auction, with value peaking around her early, and attractive child-bearing years. Males sustained their top value from young adulthood through middle age. In the owning classes, a wife often commanded maximal status while she enjoyed the sexual attentions of the husband, which declined as her male progeny attained adulthood. The wife within the owning class was often relegated to a rather inferior status by the rule of primogeniture. As the owning classes always constitute a numerically small minority, Figure 1 depicts the value of the producers.

As indicated above, Figure 1.1 is drawn for slaves from their sale value; for industrial workers from the salaries paid to the sexes as well as from the proportion of the sexes that participate in the labor force which also determines their respective valuations. It could well be argued that, as a class, females under industrialism have been valued too highly relative to males, as seen in Figure 1.1, since many females today, for most of their lives, act as housewives (or domestics) — a relatively low paying job in our society. With the onset of industrialism, a new phenomenon appeared on the world scene — negative valuation. In primitive societies living at subsistence levels, old or handicapped persons were often "disposed of" by various methods before they constituted a "burden" on the system. With the exception of capitalist Germany under the Third Reich, industrialized countries support the old rather than "disposing" of them. Every person so supported constitutes an economic burden on the system (in the United States, circa 1975, annual social security pension payments averaged about $1,500 a year). Every female born is potentially a greater burden on the system than a male because females live so much longer and "sap" societal resources for a greater proportion of their lives. From an efficiency standpoint, industrialism is thus presented with three basic choices:

1) set an age beyond which workers will not be permitted to exist,

2) eliminate all but males (which would have rather disastrous effects upon the continuation of the race and the sale of cosmetics), or

3) draw more females into the productive process for a longer period of their lives.

The choice that has been made is evident in Table 1.1 in which countries that are relatively undeveloped are compared with those more highly developed. As the "heart" of the labor force consists of the middle-aged, the best indicant of the direction of the evolution of industrialism available to us is revealed in the sixth column of Table 1.1. This column, which effectively excludes differences in the age compositions of societies, reveals that females are of considerably greater worth in the more industrialized nations. On the average, males are worth about 300% more than females in the less developed lands, but only about 50% more in the developed lands. With the further incorporation of females into the labor force, near equality of the sexes is to be expected. However, unless females have the "decency" to emulate their male counterparts by shortening their life-span and achieving equal off-the-job-due-to-illness rates, it appears likely that society will continue to be more appreciative of males. Figure 1.2 suggests that the United States is "in step" with the median degree of such incorporation. Obviously forces other than industrialism are acting here. Generally those countries that suffered severe male losses in World War II have accelerated rates of female labor force participation; and the ideologic preachments of the Communist nations are associated with elevated rates.

While the main line choice has been the third female-incorporating alternative, there is no small consideration of the first. At this writing, it appears that there is something of a "swell" toward the acceptance of at least some aspects of life-shortening — especially toward those old persons who are costing large sums to maintain in intensive care wards. Where such a campaign will lead

TABLE 1.1

Sexual Composition of the Labor Force as a Function of Industrialism

Per cent in labor force

per capita consumption of energy in pounds of coal*	# of countries	TOTAL POPULATION				AGED OVER 15				AGED 45-49			
		MALE		FEMALE		MALE		FEMALE		MALE		FEMALE	
		range	Md	range	Md	range	Md	range	Md	range	Md	range	Md
<4,000	21	44-62	52	3-34	13	76-94	84	6-64	21	88-99	95	5-61	23
4,000⟩	15	52-63	59	20-48	38	74-84	80.5	27-64	45.5	91-98	96.5	20-81	62.5
difference			7		25		-3.5		24.5		1.5		39.5

Brazil, Chile, Colombia, Costa Rica, Ecuador, El Salvador, Ghana, Greece, Guatemala, India, Korea, Liberia, Mexico, Nicaragua, Panama, Paraguay, Spain, Tunisia, Turkey, Uruguay, Yugoslavia vs. Australia, Bulgaria, Finland, France, E. Germany, Hungary, Ireland, Japan, Luxembourg, New Zealand, Poland, Romania, Sweden, USSR, United Kingdom**.

SOURCE: *Statistical Abstract of the United States, 1970.
         **United Nations Demographic Yearbook, 1972.

is problematic, but a "negative valuation" is a heavy burden in any society. In a social system where cost accounting vies with the Biblical God's "sparrow count," the setting of a firm age of "permanent retirement" is far from "out of the question."

BIFURCATION OF WORK AND PLAY

Little or no distinction between work and play was made in savagery. Everyone did both. As soon as they could be productively useful, children were incorporated into the economic life of the community. With the evolution of culture into barbarism and then into industrialism a harder line was drawn between the two. Within barbarism the upper classes tended to "play," the slaves "worked" and the freemen both worked and played. The distinction grew much sharper under capitalism. "Work is when you are getting *paid* to do something, play is when you get to do what you want." The requirement that only paid work is "real" work has resulted in females' housework not being counted in the gross national product even though it is in many senses of the word, work.

Whereas in savagery, work and play tended to be evenly distributed over the life-span, in industrialism work is bunched in the middle and play toward the end. Children, teenagers, and even young adults are deliberately excluded from work — they are to spend their hours at play or in school. The old are also excluded from work. The young play/learn to fill the time until they can work; the old to fill their time until demise.

There are a number of possible disadvantages to such a discontinuous cultural pattern. What effect does the "squandering" of so much time have upon the young? Is "killing time" a reasonable or adequate way to prepare youth to assume a productive role? How do many of the rather trivial things the young do in our society (e.g., cheerleading, football playing, "hanging out," "cruising around") relate to their becoming genuinely productive members of society? In a time when the young are, if anything, larger, healthier, and more knowledgeable than in preceding eras, they are generally cast in the role of "bums." When schooling ends, "bummery" is also to end, and a switch to a "grindstone mentality" occurs. It could easily be argued that indolence provides a poor preparation for productivity. In the middle of life, a productive orientation is to take over — and, if a job is found and retained, take over it does. One of the more common complaints of adults in our society is the press of day-to-day living coupled with a lack of time and opportunity to play (see the "annoyances" paper in this volume).

Even as indolence appears to be poor preparation for productivity, so productivity appears inadequate preparation for leisure. After a productive middle life, the adult is set adrift to play away his remaining years. Play/work/play — a series in which the preceding segment ill equips the traveler. Entry into each segment constitutes a strain on the ability of the person to adapt.

Is this pattern necessary? If some modest inefficiencies were permitted, the answer would have to be "no." There are 215 million people in the United States and about 90 million in the labor force. Assuming a 40-hour week from each of the 90-million it appears that our society requires about 3.6 trillion man-hours of labor/week to function. If all the able-bodied over the age of 12, were employed we would have a potential labor force of about 145 million people who would have to work an average of 25 hours a week to meet society's needs. Were teenagers to start off at 15 hours or two days of work a week, and were the old to taper off their contribution to as little as 8 hours or one day a week, the middle members of the life-span would not have to work more than about 30 hours or 3 to 4 days a week. We know that work *feels* good after a period of leisure, and we also know that leisure *feels* best after work. Spending some time doing work "freshens" one's leisure, and vice versa. But all work or all play gets to be a bloody drag. A common complaint of the young and old is their enforced leisure, similarly the "workers" complain of their lack of leisure. Were we to rationalize the system, we could grant the middle segment more leisure and the ends of the life-span more work — quite possibly a more happy arrangement for all.

Industrialism (or capitalism) initially utilized persons across the life-span from about the age of five. But, over the years, the efficiency-seeking properties of the system eliminated child labor and began to nibble at the labor of the old. A shrinkage of the useful (i.e., employable) life-span for workers continues at this writing: young adult participation in the labor force is being eroded by their increasing enrollment in higher education and old adult participation is being reduced both by the lowering of "official" retirement ages and by payment of bonuses to retire early in many heavily-automated industries to permit the permanent "retirement" of their job-role. Not all industrialized countries have proceeded at the same pace, nor settled on the same retirement ages. Some have officialized retirement as early as age 55 (e.g., Japan) while others have brought selected retirees back into the labor force in time of shortage (e.g., the USSR). But the general tendency of industrialized societies to efficiently utilize labor power acts to "trim" the labor force participation proportion of the males (Table 1.2) even as it swells the proportion for females (Figure 2).

While the inefficiencies associated with the utilization of younger and older workers are minor (and for that matter somewhat debatable), even as less efficient machinery and processes are discarded as a function of the capitalist efficiency ethic, this also becomes the fate of old workers in the aggregate. The phenomenon can be observed in the United States in Table 1.3.

FIGURE 1.2

Female Labor Force Participation Rates in Per cent, United States 1920-1960

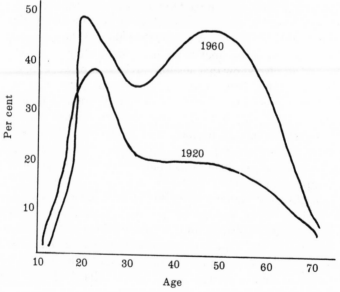

TABLE 1.2

Percent of Males in the Labor Force: Circa 1950

TYPE OF COUNTRY	n	age <14	15-19	20-24	25-54	55-64	65+
industrialized	21	4	72	91	97	86	38
semi-industrialized	30	13	70	92	96	89	61
agricultural	21	24	78	91	96	92	70

SOURCE: United Nations Demographic Yearbook, 1972, p.12

TABLE 1.3

Percentage of Younger and Older Persons in the Labor Foce, U.S.

age	14-19		65+	
	male	female	male	female
1890	50	25	68	8
1900	62	27	63	8
1920	52	28	56	7
1930	40	23	54	7
1940	35	19	42	6
1950	40	23	41	8
1960	-	-	32	11
1970	-	-	25	10

From a humanistic standpoint, the older person, who works in the valley of the shadow and sees his mortality evaporating not too many paces ahead, might well be considered to deserve the greatest benefits. The Turkish custom of serving the oldest first as they are closer to death smacks of such a spirit. From this perspective, when comfort or honor is to be bestowed, the older ought to be the prime recipients; when danger threatens, the youngest ought to enjoy the greatest security as they have the most life to lose.

THE AGE PARAMETERS OF ADULTHOOD AND YOUTH

During savagery, births and deaths were not recorded and obviously birthday parties were neglected. A general time of birth placed a person in a cohort and he was treated as a cohort member across the life-span. During the barbaric period, worthy members of the ruling class had their birthdays and deaths noted and/or celebrated. Births of the ruling class were first recorded in the Western world in England in 1538 to keep inheritances accurate. (Deaths were recorded for the same reason.) Birth registration did not become general and compulsory in England until over 300 years later, in 1874. Until recently, most persons could claim to be just about any age (with a consequent influence upon longevity); a person's age was not the important information it is today. People were often treated as they appeared and performed (Shakespeare divided the life-span into seven functional parts without reference to age). While persons have never had the luxury of being "only as old as they felt," their age always being tempered by how old "others thought they were," today one's age is carefully recorded and noted and one is "as old as he can *prove*."

It appears that once society has gone to the trouble to accurately index something, that measurement is put to use. Age has moved beyond generalities, such as Aristotle's ("men are strongest from 30 to 35") to exactitude (one can vote in the United States on his eighteenth birthday, but not the day before). Generally, functionalism has fallen before ageism. A hearty 60-year-old slave might well command a decent price, a like-aged industrial worker would probably go unhired. Politicians have had much to do with stabilizing the age associated with various landmarks. Bismarck, in

Germany, fixed upon 65 as the correct age of retirement and in 1935 the United States Social Security system concurred. Depending on the country or state, persons can drive motorcycles or motor bikes in their early teens, pilot automobiles in their late teens, contract debts, marry, and vote at age 18. Most modern countries accord nearly full rights of citizens to those in their late teens, but are also exacting increasing adult responsibilities from them.

In the far East (Korea, China, Japan), a person is considered a "youth" until age 32, "middle aged" until age 40, and "old" from age 40 to age 60 (a new cycle starts at age 61). Social researchers have been slow to arrive upon a like consensus regarding just when a person becomes an adult, middle-aged, or aged. One investigator will utilize post-36-year olds and characterize the group as "old," another will call the same group "aged," and yet another "middle-aged." Similarly, samples of college students are called "young adults," "teenagers," or "adolescents." Our linguistic community has determined what the parameters of sex are (just about no one would have trouble identifying whether a person was of one sex or another well over 99.9% of the time. Hermaphrodites "spoil" the symmetry of the convention, however. Nature is arbitrarily "parcelized" by mankind, and since she deals in varieties of what one terms "continua," there are always "kickers" in any classificatory system), and scientists, along with the rest of society, utilize the distinction profitably. It would be reasonable to determine what the linguistic community has done with the age parameters at the various terms of age status (as a starting point at least).

Two studies touch on the question of how adulthood is divided. In 1965, Neugarten, Moore, and Lowe attempted to contact a 2% sample of households in randomly-selected housing tracts (failure rate was unreported) and ended up interviewing 50 men and 43 women whom they called "middle-aged." Respondents were asked at what age a person was "a young woman," etc. as per column 1 in Table 1.4. Most responded with a single age or a narrow age range and the investigators sorted out a range into which they felt a majority of the responses fell. The per cent of the respondents' answers that fell within the age ranges in Table 1.4 ranged from 57 to 89, with a median of 83. The investigators also reported three other samples of varying sizes and ages totaling 150 persons from whom "essentially the same patterns emerged in each set of data."

Cameron (1969) asked 253 males and 318 females ranging in age from 11 to 100 — about half obtained via a random phone survey and half gotten via a face-to-face quota sample — the following: "Although everyone uses the term 'young adult,' 'middle-aged,' 'old,' and 'aged,' we don't know what ages are included in most peoples' use of the word. What ages do you think of when you hear or use the words 'young adult'? That is, what's the youngest a person can be and still be a 'young adult'? The oldest he can be?" and so forth for the categories listed in the second column of Table 1.4. The agreement between the different investigators employing different methodologies, utilizing different samples at different times is high — as one could reasonably expect of well-taught and enforced standards in the linguistic community. Cameron noted a tendency for females and older people to provide somewhat higher parameters for each category (e.g., the inter-quartile range for older males giving estimates of the beginnings of old age was 57.5-70, for the corresponding females it was 65-75). Neither study provides a model of scientific rectitude. The Neugarten et al. report is vague as to what led to the selection of precisely those parameters reported and the degree of agreement with these parameters by the other 150 persons interviewed.

TABLE 1.4

Age Parameters of Young Adulthood, Middle Age, Old, and Aged

Neugarten et al.		ages indicated	Cameron
a young man	18-22	18-25	young adult
a young woman	18-24		
a middle-aged man	40-50	40-55	middle-aged
a middle-aged woman	40-50		
an old man	65-75	65-79	old
an old woman	60-75		
		80+	aged

The Cameron study was performed on a rather hodgepodge sample. It would be "nice" if it could be said that the weaknesses of the one study were complemented by the strengths of the other — it can't.

The major fault of the Cameron study was its lack of known representativeness of sample. But unlike the difficulty stemming from inferring the attitudinal stance of a population from a sample of questionnable representativeness, when it comes to matters linguistic, a mixed sample is probably quite close to a representative sample in generalizing to the population. The chief function of language is to communicate and persons of a linguistic community must use terms to mean the same thing or communication will be curtailed. While our linguistic community permits considerable diversity of attitudes, no community tolerates diversity of meanings. Therefore the linguistic community "enforces" conformity of term-usage upon all its members. As the Cameron effort was more systematic than the Neugarten et al. effort and directed specifically to the determination of age parameters, it appears to provide the best estimates we have at this time.

PROPORTIONS OF THE GENERATIONS IN THE POPULATION

Over a period of time, the proportion of old persons in the population of industrialized countries has increased. Figure 1.3 presents the age distributions in the United States and Great Britain circa 1850 and 1950. It should be noted that the trend is for the population to move from a pyramidal to a rectangular distribution. The same phenomenon is occurring in the relatively nonindustrialized world — so the effect cannot be attributed to industrialism *per se*. In 1970, there were about 154 million persons aged 60 or older living in the industrialized world, compared to 137 million in the less industrialized countries. It has been estimated that in the year 2000 there will be 231 million over-59-year olds in the industrialized areas and 354 million in the less industrialized countries.

Put another way, in the developed nations a 33% overall increase in population is expected, with a 50% increase in the older group. In the less industrialized countries the increases are expected to be 98% and 158% (Beattie, 1975). No one is sure when or if a population becomes "top heavy."

FIGURE 1.3

Age Distributions in the United States and Great Britain
circa 1950 vs. circa 1850

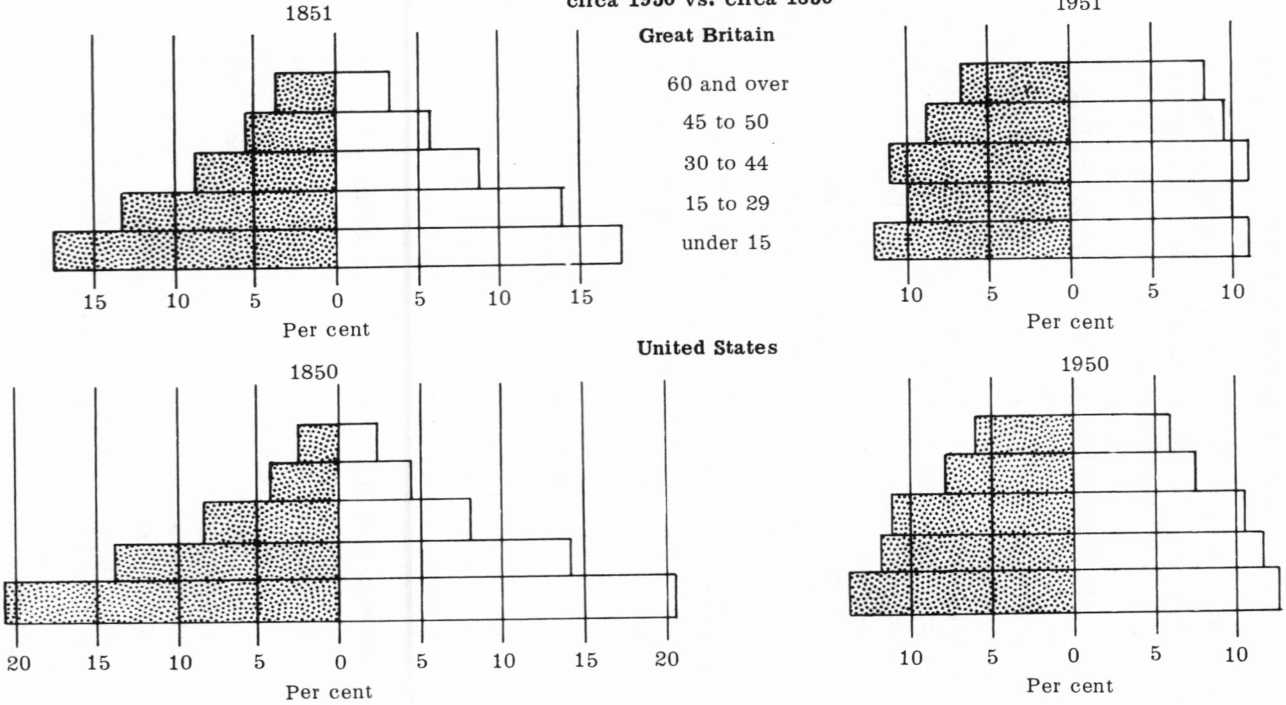

Great Britain

60 and over

45 to 50

30 to 44

15 to 29

under 15

United States

SOURCE: Sheldon, 1960, p. 31.

If old people were not shunted out of the labor force, most of them could probably more than "carry their own economic weight." So far in man's history of social organizations, only agrarianism utilizes the labor of the old with any "vigor" (see Table 2) and only the USSR has recalled retired workers to any appreciable degree. When children were, relative to the population, plentiful, society was relatively indifferent to their nuture. Today, industrialized nations are often characterized as "child centered" — certainly the care shown children appears to have expanded as their relative proportion declined. In the same vein, it appears that when the old were few in number they were more highly valued, and now that they exist in substantial numbers . . .

"CURING PLASTIC CEMENT" vs. "THE LEAKY SIEVE"

Half a millennium ago, St. Ignatius contended that if given charge of a child until 7 years of age, subsequent attempts to change the child's course would be fruitless. While not religiously inclined, social science currently resonates with the saint's notion. Freud and his followers have amassed instances of aberrations that appear traceable to some childhood trauma and they argue that basic personality is largely "set" by the age of 3 or 4. Psychologists have asserted that intelligence, creativity, willingness to delay gratification and more must be shaped while the child is quite young, lest all opportunity at modification be lost. "Head start," nursery school, and Sesame Street are but some of the dues that educators have paid to the notion that early cognitive training is a necessary condition for later development. "Eggshell parenting" is another "buy-in." Every child-parent interchange is important, and who knows when a given event will not only "stick" with the child, but possibly "set the dye" for future development? "One trail" models of learning, beliefs that "we never really forget anything," and stage theories in general provide further buttressing of the notion.

Currently the human infant is treated as though he were a piece of slowly curing plastic cement. Things just naturally "stick," and once they "cure in" form the base for any future development. Concern and planning are the key concepts invoked when interacting with such a being. If anything, one is to err toward providing information or experiences too early rather than too late.

There is another, perhaps more ancient, view of human development. From it, the infant is seen as a "leaky sieve" through which information and experiences pour. Only a little of the volume is retained. That which sticks and partially clogs the hole, does so almost haphazardly so that while development occurs, it happens in fits and starts and things that once stuck often get washed away again. Retention is the exception rather than the rule. Casual parenting ("if you show them a good time the best bet is that they'll forget it, likewise if something bad happens") follows from such a perspective. Education based on such a vantage point emphasizes repetition. Early training is seen more as a time-filler than a deadly serious game. "Forgetting" is the key concept in learning theory, and developmental psychology proceeds to emphasize the post-childhood period of life. There is "plenty of time to catch up" with the other children, because even if the others have tried hard, probably they will be only a little ahead. While no one would deny that some mighty impressive things go on in childhood, children are so much more like "nurds" than persons (one is born human, but learns to be a person), that casual directing is less apt to prove frustrating to the child or to the teacher. As more and more sticks, the child gets more and more competent, and a greater volume of new things will stick more rapidly. The posited development is sketched in Figure 1.4. As humans age they are able to handle and assimilate more information until some point toward the end of the life span when things start getting unstuck and the holes larger as they head back toward the sieve-end of things.

FIGURE 1.4

DEVELOPMENT ALONG THE PLASTIC CEMENT — LEAKY SIEVE CONTINUUM

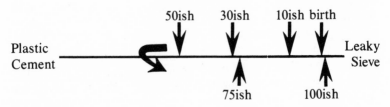

While the sophisticated reader has already been exposed to the plastic cement model, a pretty fair case can be made for the "leaky sieve." First, as anyone who has tried to study and retain knows, even adults "leak." While some of all experiences "stick," the learning of a mass of information is hard work. Parents know that if you tell a child to do something, the child will have to be reminded again . . . and again.

In motor-skill development a number of studies jibe with a "leaky" pattern. If infants of the same age are separated into those who are and those who are not allowed to walk, climb stairs, or what have you; then you allow the second group to have at it — surprise — in a few days or even hours the second group "catches up." In a classic study, some children were taught typing starting in the second grade. For a few hours a week through the sixth grade they pounded away. At the beginning of the sixth grade, some children who had not had typing were introduced to it. In a few months the groups were indistinguishable in error rate or typing speed. Anyone who has taught a musical instrument to children could provide countless examples of the same phenomenon (yes, it is true that it is a rare virtuoso who was not started out quite young — the very young do learn something, but then very few virtuosos are produced in any music education program).

The general rule that rather little is retainable per unit of time earlier in life has been shown fairly consistently with various kinds of tasks (see Figure 1.5 for age vs. nonsense syllables and lines of poetry). During World War II, the United States armed forces were able to take unschooled "backwoods types," send them to school for a few weeks or months, and bring them "up to snuff" relative to other certifiably educated cannon fodder. Similarly, only a few weeks of specialized training in a foreign language is required to make the normal adult equivalent or superior to those who studied the foreign language through high school. Generally, in the school systems over the United States very little new material is introduced from grades 3 through 8. Review, review, and more review is the rule. No matter what the subject, the first few months following summer vacation have to be spent reminding the young scholars of their past achievements.

From a general socialization standpoint, most children who are reared in orphanages, foster homes, or even rather "bad" situations turn out "OK." While it is an advantage to be reared by two parents in an intact, loving home, many murderers and mental patients come from just such ideal settings. Overall, it appears fair to say that no matter what the criterion, a group of children reared under bleak conditions will, on the average, only be about 10% worse off than a batch of children grown under superb circumstances. More than enough for a "statistically significant difference," but unkind nonetheless to the "plastic cement" notion. Further support for the "sieve" is provided by the life outcomes of people labeled retarded as children. As adults they are often indistinguishable from their fellows. The monumental failure of "head start" programs to deliver appreciably smarter children to the door of kindergarten is well known. Rare is the instance when "head started" children do not start kindergarten somewhat ahead. But similarly rare is the retention of their advantage more than a few months into the school year. The same can be said of "follow through" and a host of such "enrichment" programs. It is very hard to enrich a sieve — and for the effort expended, modest results are, at best, to be expected. If it is even "doable," it takes about 5 or 10 times more effort to teach a task to a 5-year-old that is "easy" for a 10-year old. Kagan and Klein (1973) list more evidence of the kinds I have enumerated, and although they construe it within a Kantian "inbuilt mechanisms maturing" framework, by far the bulk of it can be accounted for by the "maturing sieve." The more a human knows of socially relevant material, the more advanced socially relevant material he can assimilate. One can, with overwhelming effort, make a 5-year old as knowledgeable as the typical 6-year old. A 5-year old who knows as much as a typical 6-year old might have an IQ of 120 — but he would still be an extremely ignorant being (would you want your daughter to marry one?). And if you reduce the effort, within a year or so he will undoubtedly be in-line with other 6 ½-year olds (and maybe lose his ulcers). Shades of the Scandinavian countries that start children reading at age 7 and, *surprise:* their children not only read as well as ours who start at age 6, but *far* fewer have reading disabilities. Pressure on a sieve is costly to those applying the pressure, and potentially rather frustrating to the sieve. In agreement with Paul Goodman, it appears probable that we could delay formal education until age 8, or 9, or even 10. If we want our children to know as much by age 18 as they do today, we can be rather confident that such could be accomplished — and probably with fewer "educational casualties."

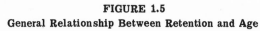

FIGURE 1.5
General Relationship Between Retention and Age

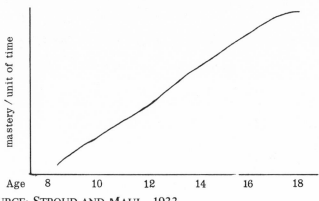

SOURCE: STROUD AND MAUL, 1933

LIFE EXPECTANCY

One of the more interesting and practical tricks from the statisticians' bag is the probable life expectancy of each of us. One often hears that the average Roman lived to the ripe old age of 25 or 30 or thereabouts and one conjures up a Rome filled with rather youngish types, sexually sparkling and warlike to boot. While such a Rome would be a novelist's delight, this picture is rather removed from reality. If we were to travel back to ancient Rome we would probably notice little difference in the age composition of the populace from that of our own. Age then meant much the same thing as it does to us, and an "old" person then would probably be "old" today. The actuarial notion of the "average life-span" in which survival of all those born-live statistic was simply not thought of. Table 1.5 compares the expected years of life by sex in India (which in 1950 would be close to ancient Rome in life expectancy), Brazil, and the United States. Clearly, while life expectancy at birth has changed toward the dramatically longer, a middle-aged person in India has perhaps 12 statistical years less to live than a similarly-aged American. An old Indian "misses" even fewer years. The dramatic change has been in infant mortality rates; older people have benefited to a modest degree from the advances of medicine.

Put another way, one of every 415 Indians born alive lives to age 85 (.24%) as compared to one of every 130 Americans (.74%).

TABLE 1.5

Expected Years of Life, by Sex in Various Countries

		birth		age 40		age 70	
		male	female	male	female	male	female
India	1950	32	32	21	21	7	8
	1951–60	42	41	22	22	8	9
Brazil	1950	50	56	25	31	8	11
U. S.	1950	67	73	31	36	10	12

SOURCE: United Nations Demographic Yearbook, 1956, 1972

The same general pattern is evidenced in the life expectancy for the United States over the past 70 years. Table 1.6 summarizes the trends for Caucasians in the United States. You will note that modern medicine has disproportionately favored females (Tables 1.5 and 1.6). As might be expected, the female-saving properties of modern medicine have dramatically increased the female proportion of the population.

TABLE 1.6

Expectation of Life in the U. S. at Particular Ages Since 1900

age	0	10	20	45	65	70	75	80
			males					
circa 1900	48	51	42	24	12	9	7	5
1940	63	57	48	26	12	9	7	5
1950	66	60	50	27	13	10	8	6
1960	68	60	50	27	13	10	8	6
1970	68		50	28	13	10		
			females					
1900	51	52	44	26	12	10	7	6
1940	67	61	51	29	14	11	8	6
1950	72	64	55	31	15	12	9	7
1960	74	66	56	33	16	12	9	7
1970	76		57	34	17	13		

In the "good old days," males constituted a majority of the populace, but within the past generation the scale has tipped to the female side (Table 1.7). As females participate to a greater extent in the labor force, (particularly if they share the hazardous occupations equally with males — about 15,000 workers, almost all male, are killed in industrial accidents each year in the United States, additionally over 100,000 deaths are attributable to occupational diseases and about 400,000 new cases of disabling job-related diseases are logged each year. Thus millions probably have their lives appreciably shortened by the various substances to which they are subjected and injuries, not to mention the yearly "average" of 12,000 deaths and 25,000 serious wounds that males have experienced in the various United States military ventures over the past 35 years) we will discover to what degree the "strains" associated with employment affect their life expectancy. Then too, perhaps the phenomenon of medical advances disproportionately aiding the female is a quirk of time, and male medical problems will be graced for some period in the future.

TABLE 1.7

Sex Ratio of Population By Age Over Time

males

	1910	1920	1930	1940	1950	1960	1970
All Ages	52	51	50	50	50	49	49
<15	50	50	51	51	51	51	51
15-24	50	49	49	50	49	50	50
25-44	52	51	50	50	49	49	49
45-64	53	54	52	51	50	49	48
65+	50	50	50	49	48	46	43

SOURCE: Statistical Abstract of the United States, 1970, no. 24, p. 24.

REFERENCES

Apter, D.E. *Ghana in Transition*. New York: Atheneum, 1968.

Beattie, W.M., Jr. Discussion. *The Gerontologist*, 1975, *Part II*, 15, 39-40.

Bromley, O.B. *The Psychology of Human Aging*. Middlesex, England: Penguin, 1974, see p. 66 where the author suggests that euthanasia might satisfy the " . . . demand for a rational use of limited resources."

Cameron, P., Age parameters of young adult, middle aged, old-aged. *Journal of Gerontology*, 1969, *24*, 201-202.

Carleton, G.W. *The Suppressed Book about Slavery*. New York: New York Times, 1968.

Engels, F. *Origin of the Family, Private Property, and the State*. New York: International Publishers, 1968.

Kagan, J. and Klein, R.E. Cross-cultural perspectives on early development. *American Psychologist*, 1973, *28*, 947-961.

Neugarten, B.L. and Moore, J.W., and Lowe, J.C., Age Norms, age constraints, and adult socialization. *American Journal of Sociology*, 1965, *70*, 710-717.

Palmore, E.B. and Manton, D. Modernization and Status of the aged: international correlations. *Journal of Gerontology,* 1974, *29,* 205-210.

Statistical Abstract of the United States 1970, pp. 71, 212, 330.

Stroud, J.B. and Maul, R. The influence of age upon learning and retention of poetry and nonsense syllables. *Journal of Genetic Psychology,* 1933, *42,* 242-250.

VALUES, NEEDS, AND WANTS ACROSS THE LIFE-SPAN
WITH DONNA BROWN AND DIANA DEMAREE

What do Americans value? Answering of the question has ranged from the entertaining social psychological commentary of Tocqueville to the sophisticated questionnaires of contemporary psychologists. When value is discussed at the level of "national character" so many variables are brought into play and substantive information of so many sorts is required that different investigators arrive at differing conclusions with ease. The domain of value subsumes so vast a content that it can be "sliced" innumerable ways from a multitude of philosophical perspectives (Lepley, 1949).

The widely-employed values questionnaires were generated from various philosophic systematizings of "value." Yet they all (Handy, 1970) share a design feature that promotes reservations regarding their results. Each but *samples* the value domain. Whether 6 aspects or "realms" of value (as with the Allport-Vernon-Lindzey 1951 Scale) or 18 (as with the Rokeach, 1968) are employed, many aspects of value are not addressed by the questionnaire, opening the possibility that had more or all of the aspects been included the results would be different. The Allport-Vernon-Lindzey Scale, for instance, yields a relative score for each of 6 realms of value. Scores inform that a person apparently prefers dealing with, say, religion to aesthetics and the relations of each to the other 4 "aspects" of the scale. As the scores on these aspects are only relative to each other and not to the entire domain of value, no matter what the scores, one cannot say whether religion figures large or small in the given person's value system.

Another difficulty with value questionnaires lies with systematization *per se.* No matter how incisive a given systematization, if it employs different concepts or terms than those employed in ordinary discourse, or, perhaps even more awkwardly, common terms representing other than common referents, the differences introduce a degree of uncertainty into the results of questionnaires based upon it. The uncertainty stems from the question of adequacy both of accurate translation from the formulation to ordinary discourse by the questionnaire developers, and the responding of the questionnaire takers. The questionnaire writers and systemizers are of comparable professional level and undoubtedly communicate with a relatively high degree of accuracy (though many reservations are expressed about particular "translations," see Handy, 1970). Ordinary members of the linguistic community would appear less apt both to employ and know how to respond to questions regarding unusual constructions of the value domain. The same questionnaire-response "phenotype" undoubtedly hides an abundance of "genotypic" meanings.

From one point of view it might be argued that the linguistic community determines to what the concept of "value" will refer, and probably has a "natural" (that is "ordinarily common") way of dividing the conceptual domain into subareas or subdomains. If this is the case, then an important way of studying the "values" of a population would be to determine how persons *use* the concept "value" and what the "natural" categorization of the value domain for this population is. While such a program lacks the charm of elegant theory or sophisticated methodology, it certainly provides a potentially worthwhile point of view. As by far the majority of research into the domain of value has proceeded from rather "hard" or "fixed" philosophical positions, an investigation that proceeded along the above "ordinary discourse" lines might well be expected to generate an informative alternative set of information.

An idealized representative model that appears to most adequately generate a "natural" categorization of the concep "value" would require open-ended questioning regarding what is valued,

1) of a representative sample of the population,
2) by a representative sample of the population,
3) with recorded responses sorted by a representative sample of the population,
4) into a set of categories devised *post hoc* from examination of the recorded responses by a representative sample of the population.

The same model would, of course, apply to the generation of a "natural" categorization of the concepts "want" and "need." This is a report on an attempt to generate a "natural" categorization of the terms value, want, and need for members of United States society and the weightings placed on the various categories across the life-span.

Method

As ours was an unfunded, exploratory investigation, our method approximated the idealized model. The questionnaire was introduced by informing the subject that we were engaged in a university project out of the psychology department and consisted of the following 6 items:

"What are the two most important things in *your* life — what two things do *you* value the most?"

"What do you think are the two most important things in life for *people in general?* In other words, what two things do people value the most?"

"What two things do *you* need the most?"

"What two things do *people in general* need the most?"

"What two things do *you* want the most?"

"What two things do *people in general* want the most?"

We also asked for the age, sex, race, and occupation of the head of the household for each subject. Order of administration of questions was reversed every other interview.

The *sample* was drawn from two urban areas, Detroit, Michigan and Evansville, Indiana. In Detroit the questionnaire was administered to 91 classrooms serviced by 15 substitute teachers (6 were Negro) yielding 2,960 subjects aged 10 to 19 who filled out the questionnaire at their desks. About 10% of the questionnaires were unusuable due to sloppiness, misunderstanding of instructions, or incomplete answering. A systematic phone sample with multiple starts and 2 call-backs on different days and different times utilizing the Detroit metropolitan phone book was carried out yielding 2, 877 households in which the first person answering was interviewed. One hundred nineteen contacts refused to cooperate (a rejection rate of less than 5%) while approximately 25% of the phone numbers attempted yielded no answer (the phone would appear to ring, and was rung 2 more times as per the design, but there is no way to determine whether the number "actually" exists shy of asking the phone company — which, incidentally, claimed to be unable to provide an answer). "No answers" were substituted for with the next following residential number. In Evansville, the same systematic phone sample with multiple starts was employed yielding 925 contacts and 63 refusals (rejection rate of less than 7%). The sample fell short of the representative ideal in a number of particulars including the sampling from only 2 urban areas, the nonrandom selection of schoolrooms, the nonrandom manner in which the population is represented in the phone book (although because phone numbers are constantly changing we interviewed a number of persons at unlisted numbers, and 93% of the dwelling units in these Standard Metropolitan Areas have phones of which about 75% are listed), and the nonrandom way in which the phone is answered (females and younger persons appear more apt to answer a phone). The strength of the sample lies in its size. Further, even though the sampling was haphazard-systematic and not random, while the 1960 Census estimated the proportion of Negroes in the Detroit Standard Metropolitan Area at 15% and the 1970 Census estimated the proportion of Negroes and other minority races at 22% we garnered 18% Negro in-class and 19% on-phone in 1968-69 and appear to have fortuitously arrived at a reasonably representative sample of the population of Detroit. Contact with so many members of the linguistic community allows considerable confidence in the possibility of generation of a "natural categorization." Further, the correspondence between our sample's proportion of Negro respondents *vis-a-vis* the Census estimate of the proportion of Negroes, coupled with the "reasonable appearing" relationship between the proportion of persons employed in higher and lower status occupations (see Table 1) and the size of the sample, encourages some degree of confidence in the weightings placed on the categories by the various age-groups.

The *interviewers* were trained college student volunteers who received credit toward course work for participation (86 in Detroit, 42 in Evansville). College students fail to represent the general population in a number of particulars among which are their lower age, their overrepresentation of the professional-business class, their greater education, and, presumably, their greater sophistica-

43296

tion in the use of language. These nonrepresentativenesses constitute deficiencies, the weight of which is open to some question. While their greater sophistication in the use of language might be regarded as an asset in an investigation of this sort, their age and class differences appear relatively serious deficiencies. The category "creator/discoverers" consisted of a panel of 12 students and the first 2 authors. Basically the group met and discussed the various responses and hammered-out classification of responses. The basic philosophy of the undertaking was to group those responses that seemed to fall together with no "forcing" and to permit as many categories as might be required. Forty categories were set-up initially, and by the end of the study had grown to over 75; however, only 23 categories garnered 1 or more of the responses.

The *coders* were the authors and 12 and 6 students at Detroit and Evansville, respectively.

The 23 *categories* with sample responses were:

Category	Sample Responses
family	"my children's happiness," "my parents," "my spouse," "my grandchildren"
friendship	"having lots of friends," "friends," "companions to do things with"
formal education	"getting a good education," "getting a H.S. diploma (degree)"
happiness	"being happy," "having fun in life," "having a good time"
material goods	"a new bike," "a nice house," "nice things"
career	"having a good job," "being employed," "working at an interesting job"
bodily requirements	"getting enough food, drink, sleep, etc."
religion	"living for Jesus, God, Mohammed, etc.," "going to church"
self-actualization	"understanding myself," "developing myself," "knowing more about myself"
sex	"getting plenty of nooky," "having a boy friend, girl friend"

0347917

informal education	"knowing more about the world," "understanding people"
freedom	"living in a free country," "being able to do what I want"
prestige	"having people look up to you," "others admiring you"
money	only scored for "money"
health	"health," "good health," "being healthy"
love	only scored for "love"
life	only scored for "life"
nothing	only scored for "nothing"
peace	only scored for "peace"
security	only scored for "security"
pets	"having a pet," "my pet," "my dog, cat, etc."
financial security	"having enough money," "being wealthy"
peace of mind	only scored for "peace of mind"

Coding agreement (for a sample of 120 responses) averaged 94% in Detroit and 92% in Evansville. Occupational status was coded (after Caplow, 1954) as "higher" if the head of the household was a professional, business owner or manager, or independently wealthy and "lower" if the person worked as a clerk, salesperson, factory operative, etc., or was unemployed. Thus the "owner" of a beauty salon would be counted as "higher" but her employees as "lower," a schoolteacher as "higher" but her secretary as "lower." The interrater agreement for this "2-levels" scheme was just shy of 100%.

Raw data from the schoolrooms and phone interviewers were examined for comparability. Each age-sex-race-occupational level group from the schoolrooms was compared with its counterpart from the phone sample for each of the 23 categories (i.e., there were 23 categories x 2 series x 2 occupational levels x 2 races x 9 ages equals 1,656 comparisons). Only a handful of differences that appeared strikingly different turned up and the data was combined. Part of the lack of difference probably stems from the similarities between a subject's writing out an answer to a printed question and an interviewer's recording a subject's verbal answer to a verbal question. In the first instance a person is coding his response into understandable English, while in the second, the "essence" of a communication is recorded (just about no one could take down responses verbatim — the "ohs" and "ahs" are left out, and, of course, even greater trimming and consolidation of responses occurs before the "pen hits the paper"). Neither the writing-subject nor the writing-interviewer desires to "fill the page" with an answer.

Results

The distribution of the sample by age (after Cameron, 1969), sex, race, and occupational or social class is displayed in Table 1.8 (all subjects who neglected to provide complete information are excluded). The self-reported values, wants, and needs and appraisals of the generalized other's values, wants, and needs are summarized across age-groups in Table 1.9. Considering each age-group of equal weight in arriving at a "national average," responses falling in the "top ten" most frequently nominated for each age group are summarized by median percentage in Table 1.10.

TABLE 1.8

Racial, Generational, Sexual, and Socioeconomic Distribution of the Sample

	under 13	13-17	young adult	26-39	middle-aged	56-64	old	total
White Higher Status Females	143	393	109	181	211	68	66	1171
White Lower Status Females	423	548	198	248	375	128	162	2082
White Higher Status Males	140	178	38	86	90	37	39	608
White Lower Status Males	373	352	131	108	126	62	64	1216
Negro Higher Status Females	13	19	8	14	15	5	2	76
Negro Lower Status Females	133	140	38	57	94	35	22	519
Negro Higher Status Males	11	11	3	12	9	1		47
Negro Lower Status Males	94	144	23	35	33	15	20	364
Total	1330	1785	548	741	953	351	375	6083

TABLE 1.9

Self-Reported Values, Needs and Wants by Generation
(absolute number of respondents nominating is followed by percent in parentheses)

OWN VALUES

Generation, Age	under 13	13-17	young adult	26-39	middle-aged	56-64	old
N	1488 (%)	1957 (%)	592 (%)	721 (%)	982 (%)	376 (%)	405 (%)
family	603(40.5)	540(27.6)	327(55.2)	619(85.8)	662(70.3)	90(23.9)	83(20.5)
money	296(19.9)	418(21.4)	96(16.2)	66(9.2)	78(8.3)	26(6.9)	40(9.9)
health	110(7.4)	65(3.3)	64(10.8)	158(21.9)	347(36.8)	150(39.9)	159(39.3)
friendship	153(10.3)	434(22.2)	60(10.1)	39(5.4)	57(6.1)	35(9.3)	40(9.9)
formal education	388(26.1)	335(17.1)	32(5.4)	13(1.8)	9(0.9)	10(2.7)	6(1.5)
happiness	104(7.0)	227(11.6)	111(18.8)	86(11.9)	117(12.4)	44(11.7)	42(10.4)
love	83(5.6)	336(17.2)	67(11.3)	47(6.5)	50(5.3)	10(2.7)	16(3.9)
material goods	188(12.6)	139(7.1)	52(8.8)	68(9.4)	70(7.4)	21(5.6)	40(9.9)
life	129(8.7)	264(13.5)	41(6.9)	24(3.3)	45(4.8)	18(4.8)	20(4.9)
career	85(5.7)	134(6.8)	60(10.1)	59(8.2)	67(7.1)	22(5.9)	17(4.2)
bodily requirements	116(7.8)	79(4.0)	11(1.9)	32(4.4)	42(4.5)	16(4.3)	14(3.5)
religion	38(2.6)	57(2.9)	35(5.9)	81(11.2)	127(13.5)	73(19.4)	64(15.8)
self-actualization	66(4.4)	98(5.0)	48(8.1)	36(4.9)	39(4.1)	13(3.5)	18(4.4)
sex	77(5.2)	179(9.1)	27(4.6)	4(0.5)	3(0.3)		1(0.2)
nothing	85(5.7)	108(5.5)	16(2.7)	18(2.5)	30(3.2)	14(3.7)	24(5.9)
peace	53(3.6)	110(5.6)	19(3.2)	16(2.2)	40(4.2)	15(3.9)	23(5.7)
security	8(0.5)	17(0.9)	21(3.5)	32(4.4)	51(5.4)	15(3.9)	13(3.2)
informal education	33(2.2)	35(1.8)	19(3.2)	9(1.2)	29(3.1)	11(2.9)	12(2.9)
pets	97(6.5)	37(1.9)	2(0.3)	1(0.1)		2(0.5)	
freedom	13(0.9)	61(3.1)	18(3.0)	18(2.5)	21(2.2)	10(2.7)	4(0.9)
financial security	16(1.2)	15(0.8)	5(0.8)	12(1.7)	18(1.9)	14(3.7)	7(1.7)

JUDGMENT OF OTHER VALUES

Generation, Age	under 13	13-17	young adult	26-39	middle-aged	56-64	old
money	533(35.8)	926(47.3)	222(37.5)	232(32.2)	295(30.0)	96(25.5)	104(25.7)
family	275(18.5)	315(16.1)	169(28.5)	261(36.2)	272(27.7)	71(18.9)	95(23.4)
health	141(9.5)	57(2.9)	67(11.3)	145(20.1)	325(33.1)	138(36.7)	122(30.1)
love	228(15.3)	45(2.3)	74(12.5)	54(7.5)	54(5.5)	15(4.0)	20(4.9)
life	263(17.7)	347(17.7)	44(7.4)	38(5.3)	49(5.0)	20(5.3)	23(5.7)
happiness	76(5.1)	197(10.1)	120(20.3)	108(15.0)	131(13.3)	61(16.2)	56(13.8)
material goods	192(12.9)	127(6.5)	71(12.0)	107(14.8)	94(9.6)	44(11.7)	46(11.4)
bodily requirements	348(23.4)	105(5.4)	14(2.4)	34(4.7)	36(3.7)	17(4.5)	10(2.5)
career	166(11.2)	192(9.8)	49(8.3)	66(9.2)	66(6.7)	29(7.7)	26(6.4)
friendship	90(6.0)	255(13.0)	44(7.4)	43(6.0)	57(5.8)	28(7.4)	41(10.1)
peace	106(7.1)	162(8.3)	24(4.0)	25(3.5)	49(4.9)	23(6.1)	27(6.7)
nothing	90(6.0)	100(5.1)	19(3.2)	28(3.9)	43(4.4)	32(8.5)	31(7.7)
formal education	132(8.9)	114(5.8)	10(1.7)	18(2.5)	23(2.3)	13(3.4)	14(3.5)
self-actualization	40(2.7)	95(4.8)	49(8.3)	52(7.2)	58(5.9)	11(2.9)	25(6.2)
religion	41(2.8)	23(1.2)	22(3.7)	43(6.0)	81(8.2)	35(9.3)	47(11.6)
security	6(0.47)	25(1.3)	48(8.1)	70(9.7)	69(7.0)	11(2.9)	7(1.7)
prestige	6(0.40)	83(4.2)	35(5.9)	40(5.5)	39(3.9)	8(2.1)	12(2.9)
freedom	22(1.5)	82(4.2)	12(2.0)	19(2.6)	22(2.2)	11(2.9)	10(2.5)
sex	32(2.2)	103(5.2)	9(1.5)	4(0.6)	10(1.0)	2(0.05)	0(0.0)
financial security	4(0.26)	22(1.1)	7(1.1)	16(2.2)	20(2.0)	12(3.2)	3(0.7)
informal education	18(1.2)	28(1.4)	11(1.8)	12(1.7)	19(1.9)	8(2.1)	13(3.2)

Generation, Age	under 13 (%)	13-17 (%)	young adult (%)	26-39 (%)	middle-aged (%)	56-64 (%)	old (%)
N	1488	1957	592	721	982	376	405
money	383(25.7)	601(30.7)	197(33.3)	228(31.6)	275(28.0)	90(23.9)	111(27.4)
love	150(10.1)	550(28.1)	162(27.4)	174(24.1)	162(16.5)	43(11.4)	42(10.4)
bodily requirements	559(37.6)	274(14.0)	47(7.9)	78(10.8)	79(8.0)	51(13.6)	44(10.9)
material goods	372(25.0)	210(10.7)	63(11.5)	100(13.9)	132(13.4)	42(11.2)	48(11.8)
formal education	304(20.4)	390(19.9)	32(5.4)	26(3.6)	28(2.9)	9(2.4)	8(1.9)
family	321(21.6)	195(10.0)	66(11.1)	104(14.4)	114(11.6)	35(9.3)	44(10.4)
friendship	156(10.5)	332(17.0)	75(12.7)	55(7.6)	73(7.4)	34(9.0)	55(13.6)
health	70(4.7)	45(2.3)	50(8.4)	108(14.9)	290(29.5)	130(34.6)	142(35.1)
nothing	123(8.3)	182(9.3)	57(9.6)	66(9.2)	129(13.1)	56(14.9)	92(22.7)
religion	29(1.9)	50(2.6)	19(3.2)	60(8.3)	92(9.4)	40(10.6)	35(8.6)
happiness	45(3.0)	134(6.8)	67(11.3)	67(9.3)	82(8.4)	35(9.3)	35(8.6)
self-actualization	40(2.7)	135(6.9)	52(8.8)	54(7.5)	70(7.1)	18(4.8)	8(1.9)
career	57(3.6)	151(7.7)	36(6.0)	36(4.9)	52(5.3)	21(5.6)	10(2.5)
informal education	43(2.9)	108(5.5)	52(8.8)	45(6.2)	50(5.1)	13(3.4)	12(2.9)
security	3(0.2)	50(2.6)	68(11.5)	101(14.0)	106(10.8)	45(11.9)	25(6.2)
peace	43(2.9)	84(4.3)	18(3.0)	22(3.0)	39(3.9)	17(4.5)	15(3.7)
sex	61(4.1)	137(7.0)	17(2.9)	4(0.5)	3(0.3)		1(0.2)
life	41(2.8)	48(2.5)	3(0.5)	4(0.5)	7(0.7)	4(1.6)	8(1.9)
financial security	6(0.4)	11(0.6)	10(1.7)	28(3.9)	31(3.2)	12(3.2)	13(3.2)
freedom	8(0.5)	43(2.2)	19(3.2)	8(1.1)	14(1.4)	2(0.8)	6(1.5)
peace of mind		13(0.7)	8(1.4)	21(2.9)	19(1.9)	11(2.9)	5(1.2)

OWN WANTS

Generation, Age	under 13	13-17	young adult	26-39	middle-aged	56-64	old
money	488(32.8)	620(31.7)	111(18.8)	123(17.0)	150(15.3)	54(14.4)	62(15.3)
material goods	607(40.7)	328(16.8)	81(13.7)	93(12.9)	116(11.8)	39(10.4)	32(7.9)
family	242(16.3)	234(12.0)	141(23.8)	209(29.0)	204(20.8)	67(17.8)	70(17.3)
happiness	89(6.0)	269(13.7)	179(30.2)	187(25.9)	266(27.1)	71(18.9)	74(18.3)
health	45(3.0)	47(2.4)	63(10.6)	171(23.7)	364(37.1)	156(41.5)	184(45.4)
love	109(7.3)	398(20.3)	80(13.5)	84(11.6)	66(6.7)	20(5.3)	24(5.9)
peace	150(10.1)	237(12.1)	42(7.1)	75(10.4)	136(13.8)	52(13.8)	67(16.5)
nothing	154(10.3)	191(9.8)	25(4.2)	48(6.6)	79(8.0)	42(11.2)	57(14.1)
formal education	201(13.5)	256(13.1)	34(5.7)	35(4.8)	24(2.4)	6(1.6)	4(0.9)
friendship	124(8.3)	249(12.7)	38(6.4)	40(5.5)	57(5.8)	30(7.9)	45(11.1)
career	97(6.5)	214(10.9)	87(14.7)	58(8.0)	52(5.3)	22(5.9)	5(1.2)
bodily requirements	144(9.7)	72(3.7)	16(2.7)	21(2.9)	23(2.3)	9(2.4)	12(3.0)
self-actualization	42(2.8)	109(5.6)	49(8.3)	47(6.5)	56(5.7)	8(2.1)	18(4.4)
sex	82(5.5)	168(8.6)	21(3.5)	0(0.0)	1(0.1)	0(0.0)	0(0.0)
security	1(0.06)	321(16.4)	54(9.1)	75(10.4)	95(9.7)	35(9.3)	24(5.9)
life	47(3.2)	73(3.7)	8(1.4)	16(2.2)	22(2.2)	8(2.1)	13(3.2)
pets	131(8.8)	22(1.1)	1(0.2)	0(0.0)	0(0.0)	0(0.0)	1(0.2)
informal education	18(1.2)	55(2.8)	23(3.9)	14(1.9)	31(3.2)	7(1.9)	5(1.2)
freedom	24(1.6)	58(2.9)	13(2.2)	11(1.5)	16(1.6)	8(2.1)	10(2.5)
religion	12(0.8)	23(1.2)	8(1.4)	31(4.3)	38(3.9)	15(3.9)	20(4.9)
financial security	10(0.7)	26(1.3)	15(2.5)	23(3.2)	27(2.7)	13(3.5)	13(3.2)
prestige	8(0.5)	44(2.2)	19(3.2)	15(2.1)	22(2.2)	12(3.2)	12(2.9)
peace of mind	5(0.3)	14(0.7)	9(1.5)	23(3.2)	25(2.5)	13(3.5)	12(2.9)

JUDGMENT OF OTHERS' WANTS

Generation, Age	under 13	13-17	young adult	26-39	middle-aged	56-64	old
money	828(55.6)	1264(64.6)	292(49.3)	291(40.3)	385(39.2)	140(37.2)	161(41.6)
material goods	432(29.0)	215(10.9)	86(14.5)	106(14.7)	47(4.8)	71(18.9)	65(16.8)
peace	271(18.2)	274(14.0)	34(5.7)	76(10.5)	132(13.5)	53(14.0)	62(16.0)
happiness	81(5.4)	208(10.6)	139(23.5)	164(22.7)	217(22.0)	72(19.1)	69(17.8)
love	165(11.0)	353(18.0)	66(11.1)	72(9.9)	73(7.4)	23(6.1)	24(6.2)
family	161(10.8)	145(7.4)	56(9.5)	77(10.7)	114(11.6)	34(9.0)	36(9.3)
health	36(2.4)	36(1.8)	42(7.0)	117(16.2)	190(19.3)	93(24.7)	105(27.1)
career	101(6.8)	177(9.0)	64(10.8)	60(8.3)	81(8.2)	20(5.3)	25(6.4)
bodily requirements	252(16.9)	118(6.0)	19(3.2)	23(3.2)	27(2.7)	19(5.0)	16(4.1)
nothing	109(7.3)	156(7.9)	23(3.9)	45(6.2)	53(5.4)	32(8.5)	44(11.4)
friendship	98(6.6)	173(8.8)	31(5.2)	42(5.8)	46(4.7)	20(5.3)	15(3.9)
prestige	15(1.0)	128(6.5)	73(12.3)	67(9.3)	51(5.2)	20(5.3)	11(2.8)
self-actualization	24(1.6)	53(2.7)	40(6.8)	46(6.4)	39(3.9)	7(1.9)	10(2.6)
freedom	47(3.2)	73(3.7)	10(1.7)	20(2.8)	19(1.9)	10(2.7)	9(2.3)
life	59(3.9)	77(3.9)	5(0.8)	18(2.5)	13(1.3)	5(1.3)	2(0.5)
sex	48(3.2)	109(5.6)	12(2.0)	1(0.1)	1(0.1)	1(0.2)	1(0.2)
formal education	59(3.9)	55(2.8)	7(1.1)	14(1.9)	23(2.3)	6(1.6)	10(2.6)
security	5(0.3)	22(1.1)	67(11.3)	86(11.9)	108(10.9)	24(6.4)	26(6.7)
financial security	23(1.5)	38(1.9)	13(2.2)	27(3.7)	37(3.8)	17(4.5)	12(3.1)
pets	15(1.0)	45(2.3)	17(2.9)	5(0.7)	15(1.5)	5(1.3)	4(1.0)
informal education	8(0.5)	36(1.8)	15(2.5)	24(3.3)	16(1.6)	13(3.5)	7(1.8)
religion	15(1.0)	11(0.6)	6(1.0)	14(1.9)	18(1.8)	12(3.2)	9(2.3)

JUDGMENT OF OTHERS' NEEDS

Generation, Age	under 13	13-17	young adult	26-39	middle-aged	56-64	old
money	493(33.1)	662(33.8)	169(28.5)	219(30.4)	272(27.6)	103(27.4)	111(27.4)
bodily requirements	813(54.6)	454(23.2)	68(11.5)	88(12.2)	130(13.2)	78(20.7)	48(11.8)
love	263(17.6)	719(36.7)	179(30.2)	176(24.4)	189(19.2)	56(14.9)	45(11.1)
friendship	133(8.9)	334(17.1)	105(17.7)	86(11.9)	102(10.4)	44(11.7)	52(12.8)
material goods	287(19.3)	146(7.5)	34(5.7)	64(8.9)	90(9.2)	39(10.4)	42(10.4)
health	87(5.8)	56(2.9)	39(6.6)	110(15.2)	235(23.9)	86(22.9)	91(22.5)
informal education	49(3.3)	121(6.2)	62(10.5)	102(14.1)	108(10.9)	27(7.2)	40(9.9)
career	142(9.5)	166(8.5)	35(5.9)	37(5.1)	66(6.7)	24(6.4)	40(9.9)
formal education	115(7.7)	205(10.5)	26(4.4)	33(4.6)	46(4.7)	13(3.5)	27(6.7)
happiness	40(2.7)	129(6.6)	75(12.7)	54(7.5)	74(7.5)	33(8.8)	27(6.7)
peace	110(7.4)	140(7.2)	35(5.9)	27(3.7)	47(4.9)	20(5.3)	21(5.2)
self-actualization	29(1.9)	125(6.4)	48(8.1)	66(9.2)	85(8.6)	28(7.4)	15(3.7)
nothing	65(4.4)	115(5.9)	33(5.6)	38(5.3)	55(5.6)	24(6.4)	48(11.8)
security	13(0.9)	52(2.6)	89(15.0)	107(14.8)	119(12.1)	33(8.8)	30(7.4)
religion	43(2.9)	60(3.1)	34(5.7)	71(9.8)	100(10.2)	51(13.6)	45(11.1)
family	81(5.4)	98(5.0)	29(4.9)	45(6.2)	60(6.1)	27(7.2)	21(5.2)
financial security	21(1.4)	16(0.8)	17(2.9)	25(3.5)	31(3.2)	14(3.7)	14(3.5)
sex	26(1.7)	66(3.4)	13(2.2)	3(0.4)	8(0.8)	5(1.3)	4(0.9)
life	39(2.6)	35(1.8)	6(1.0)	9(1.2)	8(0.8)	5(1.3)	5(1.2)
freedom	19(1.3)	35(1.8)	10(1.7)	14(1.9)	12(1.2)	1(0.3)	7(1.7)
prestige	2(0.1)	39(1.9)	9(1.5)	11(1.5)	9(0.9)	2(0.5)	3(0.7)
peace of mind	1(0.06)	2(0.1)	10(1.7)	19(2.6)	19(1.9)	6(1.6)	6(1.5)

TABLE 1.10

Median Percentage Across the Life-Span Associated With Values, Needs, and Wants

values	Md %	needs	Md %	wants	Md %
family	41	money	28	health	24
health	22	love	17	happiness	19
happiness	12	health	15	family	18
religion	11	friendship	13	money	17
friendship/money	10	material/goods/security	12	material goods	13
material goods	9	bodily requirements/ family/nothing	11	peace	12
career	7	happiness	9	nothing	10
love	6	religion	8	security	9
life	5	self-actualization	7	friendship	8
self-actualization/ peace/nothing/bodily requirements/security	4	informal education/career	5	love/career	7
freedom/formal education informal education	3	formal education/peace	4	self-actualization	6
financial security	2	financial security	3	formal education	5
sex	1	life	2	religion	4
pets	0	peace of mind/freedom	1	peace of mind/bodily requirements/financial security	3
		sex	0	freedom/life/prestige/ informal education	2
				sex/pets	0

Table 1.11 summarizes the per cent of responses reported in common for the 6 dimensions. The mean percentage overlap between the self-reported values, needs, and wants averaged 21.7%. The mean overlap between own vs. other's values, needs, and wants was 27.8%.

A question that the data can partially answer is "do persons in the sample differ in some systematic way in their frequency of nomination of one of the 23 responses for the domains of value, need, and want as a function of their sex, status, or race?" To answer the question, first each response's (e.g., "family") frequency for each cell formed by the age, sex, race, and status variable was noted for each metropolitan area (see Table 1.12 for an example for the domain "own needs" and response "career" for Detroit). It should be noted that the Negro-white differences are actually Negro-white differences in Detroit, the Evansville sample provided so few Negroes (less than 30) that they were excluded from analysis. For purposes of analysis each cell was considered an independent test of any given difference. Then, to compare females to males for difference, the proportions of female vs. male nominations for that response "holding age, social status, and race constant" by comparing first white females of high status under the age of 13 with white males of high status under the age of 13 then proceeding to the next cell (13-17-year olds) for a like comparison, and then to the next cell (18-25-year olds) and so forth until 25 comparisons for the city of Detroit had been made (cells with no respondents provided, of course, no comparison), then the same analysis was performed for Evansville (11 comparisons could be made) for a total of 36 comparisons in which 24 of the comparisons' males more frequently nominated "career" than females; sign test probability equals .033. This procedure appeared the most reasonable and conservative considering the large numbers involved. All of those comparisons that exhibited a probability of less than .05 are reported in Table 1.13. Combination of the Evansville and Detroit data in this way tended to reduce the number of differences that would be reported as "in general" when, in fact, they came from only one city. In general, the number of significant differences was reduced by a factor of one-fourth by utilizing this procedure. As there were 414 comparisons, about 21 differences would have been expected by chance. Of the 69 comparisons along the variable "social class" we would have expected 3 or 4 differences by chance while we recorded 9; for the variable "sex" we recorded 10; while for "race" we recorded 27.

In Table 1.14, an analysis similar to the above was performed for differences between self-reported values, needs, and wants and judgements of the generalized other's values, needs, and wants. As we wanted to compare self-nominations to nominations about the generalized other, it appeared appropriate to compare each age-group's frequency of nomination of a given response (e.g. prestige) for self as compared to its frequency of nomination of the same response for the generalized other. Thus 7 comparisons were available (sex, race, and social status were thus "held constant") as compared to the 28 comparisons available in the preceding analysis. Each response-comparison in which 7 out of 7 comparisons fell in the same direction (i.e., "prestige" was more frequently nominated as something the generalized other wanted than the self-wanted) is recorded in Table 1.14.

Discussion

As employed in ordinary discourse, "value" and "need" appear distinctive descriptive concepts (after Ossorio, 1966). That is, one's values bear no necessary relationship to one's needs; they are, so to speak, orthogonally related. A person's value system has no necessary bearing on his need system. Both "value" and "need" however, appear necessarily related to "want." A person's wants often stem from his needs or values. While definitions of the 3 concepts are legion (e.g., Lepley, 1949) our work with their ordinary usage then emboldens us to attempt to approximate the definitions as they appear to be commonly employed.

According to Gosling (1962), and we concur, a person can be said to need something if:

1) its absence places him in a state of pathology
2) its absence intensifies or prolongs a state of pathology, or,
3) its absence maintains a state of pathology.

A person, it would appear, can be said to positively value something if:

1) A good degree of effort is (or would be) expended to obtain (or maintain) it, and/or

2) he derives (or would derive) substantial pleasure or satisfaction or escapes from substantial discomfort or displeasure on account of it.

Interests appear a subset of value. However, being interested in a thing informs that a person would expend some, but not a great deal, of energy or substance to be near or about a thing. Further, that he would derive some pleasure, or, more probably, be relieved of the displeasure of unrequited curiosity or unfulfilled desire to orient *vis-a-vis* a thing.

A person may be said to want something because:

1) he needs it, and/or
2) he values it, and/or
3) it satisfies cognitive imperatives, or "value judgments" e.g., "do X, lest you go to hell," "peace is better than war," "cognitive consistency is requisite to sound thinking," "I believe K, therefore I want Z," "people in my culture all wear clothes, therefore I want to wear clothes," etc.

Values-Needs-Wants Across the Life-Span The course of self-reported values across the life-span traced a complex pattern. The "basic" or "animalistic" aspects of man's existence might be considered to be indexed by the categories "bodily requirements," "life," "material Goods," "money," "pets," and "health." Clearly the first 5 evidenced themselves most frequently in the early part, while they declined at the apparent expense of "health" toward the end of the life-span. Frequency of nomination of the categories "formal education," "material goods," "bodily requirements," and "pets" peaked in the pre-adolescents. The "Disney ethic" regarding animals appears hale and hearty in the United States circa 1970. The categories that peaked during the teenage years were "money," "friendship," "love," "life," "sex," "peace," and "freedom." The life-love-sex trinity seems to "mesh" with the Freudian emphasis placed on the sexual component of the "life-force." "Family" declined while "friendship" reached its peak — a finding in line with the accepted lore on adolescence, abandonment of family for peer attachments. "Happiness," "career," and "self-actualization" peaked in young adulthood "Family" value was also on the "incline." The 26-39-year olds featured the height of "family" value. Almost half of all nonidiosyncratic responses fell into the "family" category. These are the years of progeny rearing, and progeny make their mark on the value system. In apparent harmony with the shrinkage of family at the expense of peer attachments in the teen years, "friendship" reached its nadir at this point in the life-span. "Security" was the only peak and "formal education" the only trough in middle age. If "security" and "financial security" are combined, the 56-64 age-group and middle-aged group were essentially equivalent along the security dimension. Low points for "money", "love," "material goods," and "self-actualization" and the apex of "financial security," "religion," and "health" were reached for the 56-64 age-group. The old exhibited further decline in "family," "happiness," and "career," and some possibility of upturns in "money," "material goods," "nothing," and "peace."

Marx (1961) argued that the need for money was the dominant and overriding need in a capitalist society. His contention does not fare ill in light of self-reported needs. Only toward the end of the life-span does the claimed need for "health" surpass "money."

"Money" as a value peaked in the early part of the life-span, as a need it stays essentially constant, and, overall, was claimed to be needed about 2 or 3 times as frequently as it was valued. "Love" traced the same pattern across the life-span as a value and as a need, but being more frequently reported as a need than a value. "Material goods" traced the same pattern in both the need and value domains, but was only somewhat more emphasized as a need than a value. "Formal education," "health," "sex," "peace," and "self-actualization" all traced the same life-span patterns as needs and values and captured about the same frequencies of nomination. "Family" was valued highly and peaked as a value in the 26-39 age-group. As a need, "family" was moderately claimed to be needed and peaked in childhood and remained constant thereafter. "Happiness" was considerably more frequently claimed to be valued than needed in the early part of the life-span, but the frequency of nominations remained about the same after young adulthood. "Life," "career," "religion," and "freedom" traced the same value and need profile across the life-span, but were consistently more frequently nominated as values than as needs. One of the most noteworthy differences concerns the category "nothing." As a response, "nothing" terminated that part of the questioning.

As such it was probably employed at times as an indirect refusal to answer. However, comparison of the frequency of nomination of "nothing" in the value and need domains suggests that it was a meaningful category in-the-main. About 5% of the responses regarding personal values were "nothing" — it verges on impossible for a person to literally value "nothing," although at times persons may exist for whom no particular value stands out from the set of values so that the value domain appears a level field. For the need domain the frequency of "nothing" responses approximately 10% and gradually rose until middle age and then rose more rapidly to 23% in old age. If the responses are to be taken somewhat literally, *about one-fifth of old people claimed that they were getting from life what was necessary to keep them from a state of pathology.* That an upturn occurs toward the end of the life-span may bespeak of a more philosophical acceptance of life, or even perhaps, that some significant fraction of the old consider that they have gotten what is necessary out of life and are going to their " . . . rest with a good grace as an olive falls in season . . . " (Marcus Aurelius in *Meditations*). Of course it is also possible to be pessimistic about this figure — about 4 out of 5 old persons apparently live with an anticipation of pathology — our social system has "freed" only one-fifth from such concern. A comparison with past and present social system's old persons' responses would probably prove most interesting.

What respondents claimed to want was related to what they claimed to value and need. If we consider the "top ten" most frequently nominated values and needs in relationship to the "top ten" most frequently nominated wants, for preadolescents 6 of the 10 wants are more frequently nominated as needs than values, the same holds for teenagers, but at young adulthood the value system seems to become dominant over the need system and remains so until demise (if we consider the most frequently nominated want as counting 10 points, the next-most frequently nominated as counting 9 points, and the lowest frequency as counting 1 point, then preadolescents' wants "score" 32 points need vs. 23 points value; adolescents' 36 need vs. 19 value; young adults' 39 value vs. 16 need; 26-39 year olds' 30 value vs. 25 need; middle-aged 35 value vs. 20 need; 56-64-year olds' 30 value vs. 25 need; and the old 35 value vs. 20 need). Generally, the same pattern for values, needs, and wants by category is used by each age-group.

Though generally the case for the *generation's* responses taken as a whole, the correlations between *individual's* self-reported values, needs, and wants was rather modest (see Table 1.11). The same relationship obtained for judgments of the generalized others' values, needs, and wants. However, there are exceptions. For instance, "security" peaked on the values array in middle age, peaked on the needs array on the 26-39-age group, and peaked as a want in the teen years.

TABLE 1.11

Percentage of Response Communality

	Others' Values	Own Needs	Others' Needs	Own Wants	Others' Wants
Own Values	26.8	21.2	16.7	20.1	13.3
Others' Values		18.1	19.2	17.6	21.0
Own Needs		29	29.8	23.8	19.5
Others' Needs				18.9	21.0
Own Wants					26.8

The frequency with which persons claimed to want something bore no certain relationship to the frequency with which they claimed to value or need that thing. With the exception of pre-adolescence, persons claimed to want health more frequently than they claimed to need it, and after adolescence, to want health more frequently than they claimed to value it. "Love" was consistently more frequently claimed as a need than as a want, and more frequently nominated as a want than a value. "Happiness," on the other hand, was more frequently nominated as a want, then next-most frequently nominated as a value, and least frequently nominated as a need. "Religion" was most frequently nominated as a value, then as a need, and last as a want. "Prestige" only appeared as a want (only a handful of persons claimed prestige as an important value or need). "Peace" was more frequently nominated as a want than a value or need.

TABLE 1.12
"Career" - Detroit
Claimed Own Needs

| Group | Preadolescents | Adolescents | Young Adults | | Middle-Aged | | Old |
	under 13	13-17	18-25	26-39	40-55	56-64	65+
White Females Higher SES	2/272 .7%	23/748 3.1%	6/150 4.0%	0/230 -----	4/278 1.4%	1/84 1.2%	0/84 ----
White Females Lower SES	7/830 .8%	21/1038 2.0%	3/312 1.0%	2/354 .6%	9/554 1.6%	5/160 3.1%	0/194 0%
White Males Higher SES	5/268 1.9%	13/372 3.5%	0/46 0%	7/104 6.7%	3/120 2.5%	1/42 2.4%	1/48 2.1%
White Males Lower SES	15/742 2.0%	41/686 6.0%	11/218 5.0%	6/152 3.9%	7/178 3.9%	2/88 2.3%	0/96 0%
Negro Females Higher SES	1/26 3.8%	2/38 5.3%	2/16 12.5%	0/28 0%	0/30 0%	0/10 0%	0/4 0%
Negro Females Lower SES	9/263 3.4%	10/280 3.6%	1/178 1.3%	5/114 4.4%	12/188 6.4%	0/70 0%	0/43 0%
Negro Males Higher SES	1/22 4.5%	2/21 9.5%	0/6 0%	2/24 8.3%	1/18 5.6%	0/2 0%	0 0%
Negro Males Lower SES	6/188 3.2%	24/288 8.3%	4/46 8.7%	3/69 4.3%	2/66 3.0%	3/29 10.3%	1/40 2/5%

Sex, Social-Class, and Racial Differences The sex differences that emerged (Table 1.13) appear generally interpretable in terms of the roles of the sexes in our society as soon as we "buy" the assumption that a higher frequency of nomination by one sex means that, that sex values the category more than the sex that gave a lower frequency of nomination for that category. Females are considered more "love" and males more "sex" oriented. Further, females are the socializers of our society so their emphasis on "friendship" and "family" appear well placed. Similarly the male's emphasis is on "career." The only curiosity is females' more frequent nomination of "peace." Just what is meant by "peace" in this context is somewhat uncertain. Perhaps "absence of war and conflict" was meant in line with the romantic notions that preceded giving the franchise to females to "provide a corrective, peaceful influence on world politics." On the other hand its higher incidence among females might relate to greater personal turmoil or even a request for quietness.

The social class differences (Table 1.13) were relatively few, and somehow reasonable. Persons with less money in our social system might well orient toward material goods, money and bodily requirements. Unfortunately, *post hoc* explanations always appear reasonable — certainly many would have contended that those with more money might well want money to a greater degree than those with less of it.

The surprise in the sex-social class-race differences lies with race. Of 56 statistically-significant differences, 37 or two-thirds occurred as racial. The number of statistically-significant differences that might be expected by chance would approximate 7 for sex, 7 for social class, and 7 for race. While all of the differences between the social classes and sexes might well have turned up by chance, the same cannot be said of the racial differences.

If the frequency of nomination differences speak to "mentalities," and as usually employed in both the philosophical and psychological literature this would appear to be the case, then the Negro mentality is rather different from the white mentality. Probably the Negro-white difference in mentality is greater than the higher-lower social class difference in mentality, or the male-female difference. If one assumes that the number of differences in category-nomination reflects the number of differences in mental-

TABLE 1.13

Racial,* Sexual, and Social Class Differences in Self-Reported and Judgments-of-the-Generalized-Other's Values, Needs, and Wants

THE GENERALIZED-OTHER

"White" vs. Negro			Male vs. Female			Higher vs. Lower Social Class (indexed by occupation)		
Values	**Needs**	**Wants**	**Values**	**Needs**	**Wants**	**Values**	**Needs**	**Wants**
W>N religion	W>N happiness	W>N happiness			F>M peace		L>H material goods	L>H money
W>N happiness	W>N prestige	W>N prestige					L>H money	L>H bodily requirements
W>N prestige	W>N health	W>N peace						
W>N health	W>N friendship	W>N friendship						
W>N self-actualization	W>N sex							
W>N friendship	W>N love							
	W>N education							

SELF-REPORT

"White" vs. Negro			Male vs. Female			Higher vs. Lower Social Class		
Values	**Needs**	**Wants**	**Values**	**Needs**	**Wants**	**Values**	**Needs**	**Wants**
W>N pets	W>N happiness	W>N peace	M>F money	F>M love	F>M peace	L>H bodily requirements	L>H bodily requirements	L>H bodily requirements
W>N peace	W>N sex	W>N happiness	F>M family	M>F career	M>F sex	L>H material goods		L>H money
W>N happiness		W>N sex		M>F career	F>M friendship			L>H material goods
	W>N security	W>N religion			F>M love			
	W>N self-act.	W>N health			M>F career			
	W>N friendship	N>W bodily requirements						
	W>N love	W>N security						
	N>W career	W>N self-actualization						
		W>N love						
		W>N nothing						

* racial difference from the Detroit sample only

W>N means that white more frequently than negroes utilized this response

M>F means that males more frequently than females utilized this response

H>L means that higher social class more frequently than lower social class utilized this response

ity, then the racial difference is about triple that of the sex or social class difference. Gottlieb (1969) questionnaired 3,602 members of the Job Corps who were high school dropouts and compared their responses with those of 737 high schoolers in regard to the value they placed on kinds and aspects of employment opportunities. While he generally employed a closed-ended questionnaire and was primarily interested in job-related values rather than values *per se,* one of his noteworthy findings was the larger difference in response frequencies between Negroes and whites as compared with differences between the dropouts or nondropouts. Our results, and to some degree Gottlieb's, lend support to those who have been contending that there is a "black experience" rather distinct from the "white experience" (e.g., Carmichael, Malcom X). The analysis was performed with an eye to consistency irrespective of age. When you bifurcate data, you rather expect an approximate "balancing-out" — if males more frequently than females score higher on 3 categories, then it is reasonable to expect females to score higher on approximately 3 categories. Inspection of Table 1.13 shows that with 2 exceptions, whites "outnominated" Negroes on the 37 differences. Obviously the Negro nominations went elsewhere, but between the white and Negro "left-over nominations" a scattered array presented itself. White responses were more "bunched" perhaps indicating stereotype of response or mental set.

Self vs. Generalized Other If the differences between self-reported and judgments of others are taken as an index, then the generalized other is viewed as rather more "coarse" than the self. Others want prestige to a considerably greater extent than the self. Others also want security (and pets) more than the self. Others less frequently than the self want "family" and "religion" (both rather meritorious desires) and more frequently than the self want "money" and "material goods" (both rather crass desires). The generalized other suffers in comparison with the self in being rather greedy and grasping of power while self is more attuned to the higher or more noble thing in life. Generally, it would appear that Americans are not suffering from the belief that "most people are pretty noble compared to me." *Au contraire,* the self "rises above the moral dearth about him." Comparison with the members of other cultures would be interesting in this regard. Logically one could aspire to the same level of moral excellence he believed existed about him or feel equivalent to others as well as feeling rather "above it all." Graft might well find easier expression in societies where it is generally believed that most are considerably more corrupt than oneself ("I can take quite a bit before I sink to the level of most of my contemporaries").

TABLE 1.14

DIFFERENCES IN FREQUENCY OF SELF-NOMINATED VS. GENERALIZED-OTHER NOMINATED RESPONSES

Self-Nomination more Frequent than Generalized-Other Nominated

Values	Needs	Wants
Family	Family	Family
Pets	Material Things	Self-Actualization
	Happiness	Religion
	Nothing	Nothing
	Peace-of-Mind	Peace-ofMind

Generalized-Other Nominated more Frequently than Self-Nominated

Money	Love	Money
Life	Maintenance Needs	Maintenance Needs
Maintenance Needs	Peace	Pets
Peace	Prestige	Prestige
Prestige	Informal Education	
	Religion	

There are a number of widely-employed procedures that attempt to assess the attitudes of a person by what he "projects" to others. Such procedures range from the use of dolls "this is the child doll, this is the father doll," etc. to estimating what "others" would think about a particular event. Presumably the person largely "projects" his own attitudes as the attitudes of others. How much of a person's estimates of how "others" feel about something are projections of his own feelings and how much involves reality-appraising? The present investigation provides a limited test of this question. The correlations that would correspond to "overlaps" (Table 4) of about 25% would range around .50. Inspection of the self vs. other judgments for values, needs, and wants suggests that the correspondence between the collective self-reports of the generations and the collective judgments of the generations about the generalized other is higher than the self-report/generalized other-judgment correspondence (e.g., the rho correlation coefficient between young adults' self-reported values and judgments of the generalized other's values is .84 which would correspond to an overlap of about 70%). We here have evidence that while the correspondence between what one reports about oneself and judges to be true of the generalized other is substantial, the correspondence between the self-reports of the members of a generation and the judgments of that generation about the generalized other *taken as a whole* (that is, treating the generation as though it were an individual) is much more substantial. In this case, judgments of the collectivity are considerably more interrelated than judgments of individuals comprising the collectivity. To the degree that correspondence between judgments reveals "projection," individuals "project" considerably less than generations do (although how a generation *could* "project" is unclear). The greater degree of correspondence between generational self-reports and other judgments vs. individual's self-reports and other judgments suggests the possibility that theoreticians have noted the general correspondence between, say, what young adults claim to value and what they seem to believe others value. The noticing of this relationship might have led to a kind of logical short-circuit, viz "if young adults generally X, then this young adult Xs." Allport has been fierce in his insistence that there is no necessarily logical relationship between the outcomes of grouped data and individual outcomes (1968). Grouping data is one way of "handling it" intellectually, and perhaps these "generalities" are the most substantive information that the social sciences can provide and dispense. However, dealing with grouped data can often result in a logical "short circuit," and the present results lend weight to the possibility that such a circuit occurred in thinking about "projection" of the kind under discussion. In any case, it is puzzling that the "projection" concept should prove more efficacious to "explain" generational than individual similarities when psychological dynamisms are theoretically adopted and administered by individuals.

Cross-Cultural Comparison Cross-cultural or cross-national administration of the questionnaire ought to have some bearing on delineating the differences between the persons inhabiting various societies. Two of my students, Mark Gunn and Mary Lynane

Guenthner, visited Madrid, Spain in 1971 and administered a Spanish translation of the present questionnaire to a convenience sample of 109 nationals. About 60% of those contacted refused to provide a complete interview. Responses that captured 5% or more of the responses are presented in Table 1.15. Conclusions about national differences are hardly warranted considering the small size of the Spanish sample. However, the large number of similarities in frequency of response-category nomination between the American and Spanish samples suggests that they share a common linguistic and/or cultural tradition, and/or the course of human life influences ones values, needs, and wants somewhat

TABLE 1.15

MADRID, SPAIN, 1971

Own Values

Young Adults	%	26-39	%	Middle-Aged	%	56-64	%
N 67		25		11		6	
Love	34	Health	32	Health	45	Family	50
Health	28	Money	24	Love	45	Health	33
Career	24	Love	16	Money	27	Friendship	33
Money	22	Family	16	Bodily			
Self-Actualization	15	Career	12	Requirements	18		
Family	13	Religion	8				
Friendship	6						

Own Needs

Love	42	Health	40	Health	45	Health	67
Health	40	Money	32	Money	45		
Money	31	Love	24	Love	18		
Self-Actualization	10	Career	20	Peace	18		
Family	6	Sex	8				
Peace	6						
Friendship	6						

Own Wants

Family	24	Family	48	Family	73	Health	50
Love	24	Health	24	Money	27	Family	33
Money	18	Money	16	Career	18		
Health	16	Career	12				
Career	12						
Peace	7						
Happiness	6						

irrespective of culture. Members of both societies nominated "money" with equivalent frequency. Relative to the American sample the Spanish appear definitely more "health" and generally more "love" oriented. Americans appear more "happiness" oriented. "Family" tended to be more frequently nominated by Americans as a value, by Spaniards as a want. In an investigation somewhat similar to the present, in which about a thousand American and Scottish teenagers were asked the open-ended question "what are the two most important things in life," Scots nominated "health" as a value 5 times more frequently than Americans (Cameron and Robertson, 1970). In the present investigation the ratio is about 3:1, Spanish to American. Perhaps Europeans experience health concerns to a greater degree than Americans. More European countries will have to be polled to determine the validity of this notion. The Scot-American teen study reported that Scots, about twice as frequently as Americans, nominated "happiness" while in the present investigation Americans out-nominated Spaniards on "happiness" about 3:1. Similarly, in the teenage study, Americans nominated "love" more frequently than Scots in a ratio of about 4:1, compared to the present somewhat greater frequency of "love" as a nomination by Spaniards. Scots less frequently than American teenagers, nominated "family" as a value, even as Americans apparently nominate "family" as a value more frequently than Spaniards; however, the American-Scot ratio of nomination was about 1½:1 as compared to the present approximately 5:1. Aside from these, a potentially more significant difference was hinted at. A little over 2% of the responses of the Spanish subjects involved an expression of concern over the well-being of mankind and/or a desire to serve mankind. Of over 10,000 responses of Americans, literally only two handfuls of such responses occurred. Perhaps we are observing merely a difference in expression — perhaps both groups harbor an equivalent beneficient concern for the race, but Spaniards are taught to express it. Or perhaps both groups harbor an equivalent indifference toward the race, but Spaniards are taught to say such "politenesses." Somehow, however, one would be more comforted if some significant fraction of the United States sample had bothered to engage in such "politeness" instead of coming across as dwelling in highly self-serving worlds. One is reminded of Allport's conclusion in his study of the college students of 10 nations conducted two decades ago that " . . . American students were the most self-centered, the most "privitistic" in value. They desired above all else a rich, full life for themselves, and showed little concern for . . . the fate of mankind" (1968).

One is further almost compelled to note the "weird" pet-preoccupation on the part of the United States sample. The probable "kinky" nature of this relationship has been noted before for personal mental health (Cameron and Mattson, 1972) but needs to be further explored as a possible social aberration.

Issues of Methodologic Concern The domain of "value" (or "need" or "want") can be "sliced" an almost infinite number of ways in the same manner in which the cognitive or affective domains can. It is a relatively easy matter to demonstrate that one can structure aspects of personality without reference to Freud (e.g., Skinner), or historical evolution without reference to Marx (e.g., Pareto). Any domain or "parcelling of the world-stuff" that the linguistic community has devised/invented (and this includes, of course, all the components of the linguistic system), can be compartmentalized and/or divided into a large number of parts or aspects from one point of view, and compartmentalized and/or divided into an equally large number of parts of aspects from another perspective, *ad infinitum*, limited only by the inventiveness of man. But what *can* be done, and what *has* been done are separated by a number of considerations, among which are: (a) it takes time and effort for an "inventor" to develop and publicize his particular systematization; (b) it takes time and effort for the audience to whom he directs his appeal to learn and apply his system; (c) "known" systems are more cherished than new systems because of: (1) the effort required to learn the new system, and (2) the "known" system often has its components reified in the mentality of its users. It takes considerable effort to "snap" the intellectual "fetters" imposed by the "known" system to be able to appraise the efficacy of the new system. Thus "what is" in the way of intellectual partitionings is certainly less diversified than what "could be."

Values. There are a large number of systematizations of the value domain. We will neglect consideration of many of these because: (1) some have not yet resulted in scales or questionnaires which are widely employed (e.g., Kluckhorn and Strodtbeck, 1961); (2) some bear upon a particular valuation of aspects of value (e.g., Piaget and Kolberg appear to admire "motivational intent" value judgments rather than "damage wrought" value judgments and address themselves to the development of this desired orientation); (3) some were designed to assist vocational choice (e.g., the Kuder and Strong Interest Scales); and (4) some are designed to reflect politico-life-style differences (e.g., von Mering, 1961, Catton, 1954). Even with this reduction a substantial number of parcelizations of the value domain that compete for the same attention as our efforts remain. Among these we will consider Morris' (1956), Allport-Vernon-Lindzey's (1951), Symonds' (1936), and Rokeach's (1968).

One must first be struck with the sheer diversity of these categorizations. With rather infrequent exception, the number of partitions and the names and/or description of these partitions are generally theorist/scale-designer specific. That is, there is relatively little duplication of what theorists consider "important." Symonds claimed that his scale "exhausts the scope of most people's interests" while Rokeach modestly suggests the revamping of Christianity on the basis of research with his scale (1970)! The major categorizations for each theorist under consideration are listed in Table 1.16 (the Allport-Vernon-Lindzey and Morris scales involve more extensive descriptions of their variables, the Symonds and Rokeach stand as they were designed and utilized).

The four scales appear to separate into two kinds — the Allport-Vernon-Lindzey/Morris and Symonds/Rokeach. The first kind approaches the domain of values from a universe-of-discourse-exhausting framework, while the second fixates upon selected "counters" within the possible array (although, of course, both Symonds and Rokeach appear to regard their sets of "counters" as rather exhaustive). One-word or one-line categories (including our own) are characterized by considerably more ambiguity than the more elaborate categorizations (the first kind). Do persons ranking the Rokeach "family security" have either the Symonds' "money" or our category of "family" in mind when they utilize it? Is the Rokeach "self-respect" related in some way to our "self-actualization" or Symonds' "mental hygiene"? While there is an extensive literature of how people across the life-span have scored on the 6 subscales of the Allport-Vernon-Lindzey, how these scores relate to changes of emphases in personal values across the life-span is obscure. The many score of articles employing the Allport-Vernon-Lindzey permit generalizing about the course of scores on this instrument across the life-span, and the many additional articles that are certain to appear in the coming years will enable refinements in this regard. But in the last analysis, reasonable generalizations will center about "scores on this test" as a function of whatever independent variables are selected for study, but essentially no more about "the value system in-general" or "values in-general" than today. Adding other scales, with their results, would appear as likely to obfuscate as clarify the study of values. The Symonds, Morris and Rokeach scales have generated their own bodies of information about "scores on this test," but the meaning of this information is considerably more ambiguous than some (e.g., Rokeach, 1970) would have us believe. Each scale can justifiably be confronted with the questions: (a) why does it address values from *this point of view,* and (b) why does it *stop with* 6 (Allport-Vernon-Lindzey), 15 (Symonds), 18 (Rokeach) . . . etc. *partitioning* of the value-domain from its point of view? The prospect of creating a "super test" by combining all of the "counters" from each commonly utilized test would be questionable both from the standpoint of subject time and reliability of score and why one should stop with only the inclusion of the popular scales. As questionable would be the meaning of the scores themselves (if Rokeach's "family security" ranked much lower than Symonds' "home and family," what would that mean?).

The sheer addition of counters is not the advancement the study of values needs, the profession is quite aware that the number of counters in common and professional discourse is very large indeed. Instead, we need to know which counters are of sufficient psychological import that they should be included in a scale to study values (or needs or wants or interests, etc.) The human mind boggles at the, say, rank ordering of 2,000 counters. Clearly some relatively limited number of counters is required for orderly understandable investigation. The method adopted here generates, in

TABLE 1.16

COMPARISON OF THE "BASIC" VALUES NOMINATED BY SELECTED THEORISTS

Symonds	Rokeach	Allport–Vernon–Lindzey	Morris
Health	A World at Peace	Theoretical (Truth)	Preserve the best that man has attained
Sex Adjustment	Family Security	Economic (Usefulness)	Cultivate Independece of persons and
Home and Family	Freedom	Aesthetic (Beauty)	Control the self stoically/things
Courtesy and Manners	Happiness	Social (Helping Others)	Show sympathetic concern for others
Attractiveness	Self-respect	Political (Power)	Experience festivity and solitude in alternation
Social Adjustment	Wisdom	Religious (Mystical)	Act and enjoy life through group participation
Morals	Equality		Constantly master changing conditions
Philosophy of Life	National Security		Integrate action, enjoyment, contemplation
Safety	A Sense of Accomplishment		Live with wholesome, carefree enjoyment
Money	A Comfortable Life		Wait in quiet receptivity
Daily Schedule	Salvation		Medidate on the inner life
Civic Affairs	True Friendship		Chance adventuresome deeds
Recreation	Inner Harmony		Obey the cosmic purpose
Mental Hygiene	Mature Love		
Study Habits	A World of Beauty		
	Social Recognition		
	Pleasure		
	An Exciting Life		

our opinion, both a manageable and understandable set of counters.

While we did not directly inquire regarding the value *systems* of our respondents, it does not appear unreasonable to regard the relative frequencies/category (or counter) as being rather close approximations of the normative value systems of the age-groups. While there were constraints placed on the relative frequencies by asking respondents for the "top two" values, it does not appear wildly unreasonable (though knowledgeable men would differ) to regard the percentage parameters as comparable. If we were to do so, then "family" would be thrice as valued to 26-39-year olds as to teenagers, while "friendship" was 4 times as valued to teenagers as to the 26-39-year olds. The ratio of the parameters within and between groups also bears note. For the under 13-year olds, the family is about 4 times as important as friends, for the teen years the family is somewhat more important than friends (perhaps 27.6/22.2 or about 20% more important?), while in the 26-39-year olds the family is 16 times more important, and in the old the family is about twice as important.

There is considerably more "charm" and intellectual satisfaction to, say, such a weighting for the teen years, than interpretations of a few, rather ambiguous items, arguing for somewhat the same point, namely that teenagers, even though they are strongly influenced by peers, still place more importance on family than peer relationships (e.g., Gold and Douvan, 1969), or that after a much stronger emphasis on family relationships in the middle years, old people start to reemphasize friendship (e.g., Atchley, 1972). "Career" would then be twice as important to young adults as to the old, "health" 10 times as important to the old as to teenagers. While the level of measurement was nominal, as we are addressing "the generalized old person," the "generalized teenager" etc., treating the various parameters as though they were ratio data appears about as reasonable a way to proceed as may exist (even were the subjects to be asked, "How much more important to you is education than money?" or to compare their values now as, say, middle-aged persons with what they were when they were teenagers, the resultant data would present about as many problems in terms of additivity etc.). As the questions were open-ended a "true zero point" did exist.

One, if not the final, test of an approach is what one can practically do with it. If we regard the data as representative of the data that might be generated by the United States population, and apply the assumptions that would enable us to manipulate the comparisons between age-groups, then some "propaganda problems" might become somewhat more possible of solution. For instance, it has been the intention of the federal government to discourage smoking among teenagers, but this propaganda effort has had scant success. As the current propaganda effort emphasizes "health," we might well expect that it would be about 10 times more effective in getting old persons to quit smoking than teenagers, while a campaign that emphasized that a person who smoked would be loved less or would have his portion of "love" endangered would be about 4 times more efficacious in appealing to the sensibilities of teenagers. In addition to propaganda efforts, this information might prove useful in determining the kinds of governmental programs various age-groups might find desirable.

Needs Relative to the number and variety of scales and "partitionings" of the domain of value, the domain of need is "underworked." Some discussion of "basic" needs occurs in comparative psychology, but at the human level of analysis, the armchair generations of Murray (1938), Maslow (1955), Fromm (2956) and Ossorio (1966) appear the most elaborate widely-employed categorizations extant. A summary of the basic needs posited by these theorists is presented in Table 1.17 (Murray has at various times proposed over 40 needs, but they are so scattered through his writings the 20 most frequently-referred to are listed). While each theorist's usage of and/or definition of the "counters" in his system is somewhat different, for convenience and because the meanings of the concepts represented by the "counters" overlap, a parallel structure is presented in Table 1.17. and 1.9 enable comparison between our relatively "ordinary discourse" display of needs and these theorist's needs. There is, of course, quite a difference between asking for a report of what one considers the "basic needs of human kind" (to which these theorists addressed themselves) and asking a population what "they and/or others need." However, there is reason to look for similarity in the two sets of "counters" within each systematization. Our category "informal education" appears to subsume much of what the four theorists agree upon as

TABLE 1.17

FUNDAMENTAL OR BASIC NEEDS POSITED BY MURRAY, MASLOW, FROMM, AND OSSORIO

Murray	Maslow	Fromm	Ossorio
Order/Understanding	Cognitive understanding	Frame of reference	Order and meaning
Affiliation	Belongingness and love	Rootedness	Love
Autonomy		Transcendence	
Harmavoidance/	Safety (Avoidance of harm)		
infavoidance		Relatedness	
		Identity	
Achievement	Self-actualization		Self-actualization
Sex/Sentience	Physiological (Food, water)		
			Security
Aggression			
Abasement			
Counteraction			
Dependence			
Deference			
Dominance			
Exhibition			
Nurturance			
Play			
Rejection			
Succorance			

"understanding-order" while "belongingness-love" might be distributed between our "love," "friendship," and "family." "Self-actualization," "physiological," and "security" appear very close to identical "counters" within the systems. But most of Murray's and some of Maslow's and Fromm's needs appear to be "orphans." Whether the presence of "orphans" within one's systematization of the domain of needs is a fault is arguable. Certainly we cannot argue that the "counters" in our systematization merely "fell out of" the linguistic system, even though this was our intent. But ours would, by its very consensually-constructed nature, be much more likely to approximate this "ideal."

Wants. Discussion and theorization about wants has generally been handled in terms of either values and/or needs. The linguistic-logical analysis of Ossorio (1966) suggested that this was inappropriate and misleading. Our results lend credence to his charge. "Happiness" ranked second in frequency of nomination as a want over the life-span (Table 1.10), but considerably lower as a need or value. Similarly, "money" ranked first as a need, but fifth as a value and fourth as a want. A theorist who studied only values (or needs, or wants) and proceeded from his results to predict psychological processes would necessarily be ignoring important realms of information. For instance, the TAT supposedly indexes the needs of respondents. If it does index needs, then systems (e.g., McClelland, 1961) built upon responses to the TAT ought to be considerably less efficacious in predicting events of psychological import than they would have been if values and wants also had been taken into account. As what people want influences their behavior to a greater degree than what they value or need (Ossorio, 1966), if one were to attempt to predict behavior from the study of only one realm, wants would be the domain of choice. But if prediction or understanding of behavior or psychological state or process are among the goals of psychology, then attention to the three domains ought to meet more success than attention to any one.

The methodology we have followed here satisfies many of the criticisms that have been directed against systematizations of the value or need domains. First, and perhaps most importantly, instead of partitioning the domains with recourse to a preconceived (and quite possibly idiosyncratic) systematization, we attempted to permit our respondents to generate the categories. Handy (1970) notes that von Mering (1961), by performing all of the categorization of the responses of his relatively uneducated sample of persons, might very possibly have injected a sophistication that did not exist in the data and might be rejected by the subjects themselves. Our method of coding would appear to satisfy this objection to a considerable degree. While others have recognized the intellectual necessity of putting some limit on the number of counters in their systems, ours is the only one that generated one or two-word categories in a relatively nonarbitrary way (although Morris adopted some of the same procedures by having his students criticize and add to his counters). The concept "arbitrary" connotes both idiosyncracy and "willy-nilly-ness." In a sense, all partitionings and limits stemming from the order that man imposes on the universe are arbitrary in a "willy-nilly" way. But when an initially arbitrary concept is adopted by the linguistic community, it loses its idiosyncratic overtone (in a fashion similar to the adoption of the .05 level of confidence by users of inferential statistical techniques). In the present case, by imposing a 1% frequency-of-nomination-level on retention of a category, the linguistic community "participated in" and "endorsed" with its nominations, the non-idiosyncratic nature of the limitation. Murray, Rokeach, or Symonds appear to have limited their counters largely as a function of the inventor's convenience or imagination.

We have reported an alternative way of "going about doing science" in the realm of values, needs, and wants, that, for want of a better characterization might be called the "ordinary discourse" method. Time will indicate whether ours is more useful than, or merely supplementary to, the other major approaches.

REFERENCES

Allport, G.W., Vernon, P.E. and Lindzey, G. *A Study of Values*. Boston: Houghton Mifflin, 1951.

Allport, G. W. *The person in psychology*. Boston: Beacon, 1968.

Atchley, R.C. *The social forces in later life*. Belmont, California: Wadsworth, 1972.

Cameron, P. and Robertson, D. R. A comparison of the cultural values of Scot and U. S. children. *International Journal of Psychology,* 1970, *5*, 135-139.

Cameron, P. Age parameters of young adult, middle aged, old and aged. *Journal of Gerontology,* 1969, *24,* 201-202.

Cameron, P. and Mattson, M. Psychological correlates of pet ownership. Psychological Reports, 1972, *30,* 286.

Caplow, T. *The sociology of work.* Minneapolis: University of Minnesota Press, 1954.

Catton, W. R. Jr. Exploring techniques for measuring human values. *American Sociological Review,* 1954, *19,* 71-97.

Fromm, E. *The art of loving.* New York: Harper & Rowe, 1956.

Gold, M. and Douvan, E. *Adolescent development: readings in research and theory.* Boston: Allyn Bacon, 1969.

Gosling, J. Mental causes and fear. *Mind.* 1962, *71,* 289-306.

Gottlieb, D. Poor youth: a study in forced alienation, *Journal of Social Issues,* 1969, *25,* 91-120.

Handy, R. *The measurement of values.* St. Louis: Warren Green, 1970.

Lepley, R., ed. *Value: a cooperative inquiry.* New York: Columbia University Press, 1949.

Maslow, A.H. Deficiency motivation and growth motivation. In M.R. Jones, ed., *Nebraska symposium on motivation.* Lincoln, Nebraska: University of Nebraska Press, 1955.

McClelland, D.C. *The achieving society.* Princeton, New Jersey: Van Nostrand, 1961.

Morris, H.A. *Varieties of human value.* Chicago: University of Chicago Press, 1956.

Murray, H. A. *Explorations in personality.* New York: Oxford University Press, 1938.

Ossorio, P. *Persons.* Los Angeles: Linguistic Research Institute, 1966.

Rokeach, M. *Beliefs, attitudes, and values.* San Francisco: Jossey-Bass, 1968.

Rokeach, M. Faith, hope, bigotry. *Psychology Today,* 1970, *3,* 33-58.

Symonds, P. M. Life problems and interests of adults. *Teachers College Record, 1936, 38,* 144-151.

Von Mering, O. *A grammar of human values.* Pittsburgh.

WHAT ANNOYS AMERICANS: 1920'S VS. 1970'S

with James Devlin and Bill Cox

Around the country various municipalities are enacting laws against smoking in public places and the issue has been broached for the United States as a whole in the Congress. Just how annoying is the smoking of others? How annoying is exposure to "second hand tobacco smoke" within the universe of annoyances? As the United States surgeon general has proclaimed smoking a hazard to health (January 11, 1971) in the face of various epidemiological studies that suggest a health effect (Cameron, 1967, 1969, and 1973), the issue is of more than academic interest.

A cataloging of common annoyances of the United States population has not been published since Cason (1930). As he found "missing the spittoon" and "smelly feet" common complaints in upstate New York, and times have changed, a new catalogue would appear useful. In the present research we attempted to provide evidence on both issues.

Method

Two studies were performed. The first, carried out from 1970 through 1971, involved the systematic phoning of persons with listed phone numbers in seven urban areas in the United States. The second, performed in the fall of 1971, featured the area sampling of persons in Louisville and Owensboro, Kentucky. In the first study, 1,488 adults were interviewed from the following communities in order of numbers of respondents "contributed": Evansville, Louisville, Los Angeles, St. Petersburg. Chicago, Denver, and Detroit. Approximately 25% of numbers originally chosen were not contacted and 8% of chosen respondents refused to cooperate. The interview included the following items: ". . . we all have things that annoy us in day-to-day living, and we'd like to know what two things annoy you most in day-to-day living? After the subject had responded he was then asked, "what is your reaction when someone smokes around you and he's fairly close by, such as in an elevator, or restaurant, or bus? Would you say it was: (1) the most pleasant thing you generally encounter around other people, (2) very pleasant, (3) pleasant, (4) o.k., it doesn't affect you one way or the other, (5) annoying, (6) very annoying, or (7) the

most annoying thing you generally encounter around other people?" Order of presentation was reversed for every other call.
Generally little coding of the first question was required with 90 of
the respondents choosing superordinate categories identical to
those reported in Table 1.18. "Daily pressures" was the only interpretive category and included complaints about schedule constraints and absolute demands upon the respondent. In the second
study, 172 adults were interviewed by a smoker with a 45% rejection
rate. The interviewer asked the respondent "What aspect or feature of day-to-day existence do you most (regard as): (1) disap-
prove, (2) dislike, (3) find objection to, (4) despicable/horrible,
(5) abhorrent/abominable/atrocious, (6) bothersome, (7) disturbing, (8) irksome/irks/bugs, (9) annoying, (10) irritating/gets on
your nerves, (11) exasperating, (12) infuriating/incensing
revolting/enraging, (13) intolerable?" The purposes of this study
were three: (a) to provide some comparison with phone-generated
responses, (b) to locate the concept "annoy" within the domain of
"negative orientation concepts," and (c) see what effect the presence of a smoker had upon responses. While respondents tended to
use superordinate categories as in the first study, about three times
the amount of interpretive coding was required.

Results

The results of the first study regarding annoyances are summarized in Table 1.18 by sex as there were no systematic age or
location differences. X_2 comparisons indicated that males and
females differed in the frequency with which they nominated "bad
drivers (ing)," "job/boss," "phone calls," "children," "salesmen,"
and "housework." Results of reactions to the "secondhand tobacco smoke" item are summarized in Table 1.19 by sex and
whether respondent was a smoker. Female smokers were more
tolerant of second hand tobacco smoke than male smokers ($X^2 =$
6.97; df= 2; $P<.05$) while the opposite was the case for nonsmokers ($X^2 =$ 16.2; df= 3; $P<.01$).

The results of the second study regarding annoyances and more
affectively negative orientations are summarized in Table 1.20. The
"strongly held objection to" column summarizes the reactions to
items 4, 5, 7, 12, and 13. In Tables 1.18 and 1.20 the percentages

refer to the total set of responses and thus do not add to 100 because of idiosyncratic answers. Inspection of Tables 1.18 and 1.20 suggests a moderate degree of communality of response, but clear differences as a function of interviewer and/or mode of interview are evident.

Discussion

Second hand tobacco smoke appears to be rather annoying to the adult population of the United States. In the phone survey (Table 1.18) it ranked among the top 10 most frequently nominated annoyances. In the door-to-door survey it ranked 22nd as an annoyance and was only mentioned twice in the "strongly held objection to" category. When directly queried, about 40% of the adult population reported it as an annoyance with smokers reporting considerably less frequent annoyance than nonsmokers. As about 40% of the adult population smokes we have evidence in the present study that this proportion of the population is matched by the proportion of adults which is annoyed by the practice. As the overwhelming majority of children object to secondhand tobacco smoke (Cameron, 1972) it appears fair to say that the majority of the United States population is annoyed by secondhand tobacco smoke.

The strength with which most person's aversion to secondhand tobacco smoke is held is apparently rather weak. The correlation between powerful aversions and weak or moderate aversions (Table 1.20) is modest at best. While we are unaware of a way to translate either annoyances or powerful aversions into the kinds of actions persons would take to alleviate their "suffering," our results would hardly seem to indicate that smokers need fear for their lives. On the other hand, politicians might well find that passing "no smoking" laws would provide no small amount of "cash" in their political "bank."

In our exploration of the life-span reactions to secondhand tobacco smoke we have unearthed evidence to suggest that the period of life in which such smoke is most aversive is childhood. The teen years usher in a more "accepting/tolerant" attitude which persists until demise. But the smoking of a partner adversely affects date selection (Cameron and Hudson, 1973), disturbs mar-

TABLE 1.18

MOST FREQUENTLY NOMINATED ANNOYANCES

males	n	%	females	n	%
bad drivers	65	16*	phone calls	180	17*
noise	62	16	noise	179	17
phone calls	50	12	children	134	12*
job, boss	33	8*	bad drivers	91	8
children	27	7	salesmen	51	5*
inflation/prices/taxes	22	5	secondhand tobacco smoke	47	4
daily pressures	21	5	daily pressures	36	3
Vietnam	14	3	pet problems	36	3
bad manners	14	3	housework	31	3*
secondhand tobacco smoke	13	3	bad manners	30	3
cheaters/liars	13	3	inflation/prices/taxes	28	3
pollution	11	3	being interrupted	28	3
sickness	9	2	Vietnam	18	2
being interrupted	5	1	pollution	17	2
crime	4	1	cheaters/liars	15	1
know-it-alls	3	1	sickness	11	1
spouse	3	1	mechanical things not working	11	1
pet problems	4	1	know-it-alls	10	1
			crime	8	1

91 90

*Statiscally significantly different at the .05 level.

TABLE 1.19

ATTITUDES TOWARD SECONDHAND TOBACCO SMOKE

	males				females			
	smokers		nonsmokers		smokers		nonsmokers	
	n	%	n	%	n	%	n	%
most annoying			15	7	4	1	93	13
very annoying	6	3	21	10	13	4	138	19
annoying	36	19	61	29	42	12	198	27
o.k.	134	73	108	52	275	81	302	41
pleasant	6	3	3	1	3	1	1	
very pleasant	1	1			1			
most pleasant							1	

TABLE 1.20

THINGS TO WHICH A NEGATIVE ORIENTATION IS HELD: ANNOYANCES
VS. STRONGLY HELD OBJECTION

	annoyances		strongly held objection to		
	n	%		n	%
bad drivers(ing)	65	14	crime	35	8
noise	56	12	war	35	8
pollution	40	9	pollution	27	6
inflation	37	8	politics	26	6
children	37	8	phonies	22	5
telephone calls	31	7	ignorance	21	5
housework	28	6	drugs	17	4
phonies	26	6	welfare	16	4
politicians	25	6	civil disobedience	16	4
salesmen	24	5	government	15	3
daily pressures	23	5	children	15	3
war	22	5	pornography	13	3
ignorance	17	4	inflation	12	3
commercials	17	4	depersonalization	11	3
pet problems	16	4	job/boss	11	3
financial	15	3	bad manners	9	2
morals	15	3	financial	8	2
job/boss	15	3	news media	8	2
drug usage	13	3	pet problems	8	2
undependable people	12	3	police	7	2
secondhand tobacco			noise	7	2
smoke	11	3	oppresive authorities	7	2
hippies	11	3	bad drivers	5	1
depersonalization	11	3			

riages (Cameron, Hooks, Gifford, Carter, Coats, and Ankner, 1975), and troubles the parent-child relationship (Cameron, 1972). The social-psychological mechanism by which something so roundly condemned in childhood becomes not only acceptable but also participated in might well serve as a model of drug-acquisition/usage in general.

The relationship between phone-generated annoyances and face-to-face generated annoyances is rather substantial (Table 1.18 vs. Table 1.20). "Phone calls" were about twice as frequently nominated as annoyances in the phone survey — a reasonable difference. We would rather expect a phone call to more frequently remind persons of the annoying value of a call than a face-to-face interview. The appearance of "phonies," "politicians," "ignorance," etc. on the one listing and not the other is more troubling. It may be that people are more apt to display idiosyncracy in a face-to-face interview.

The listings in Tables 1.18 and 1.20 of "what annoys Americans" appears far more representative of today's society than that generated by Cason in 1928. In fact, comparison of his list with ours suggests almost no overlap (see Table 1.21 which lists the "top 20" of Cason's annoyances). If his survey was reasonably representative of the feelings of the populace of his time and ours is similarly representative, then the United States has changed almost completely "aversion-wise" in the space of 40 years. Whatever the degree of the "generation gap," it would either appear that it should be much wider than it is and/or people have changed dramatically.

The importance of locating the concept "annoying" within the domain of "negative concepts" is pointed-up in Table 1.20. Many of the nation's pollsters have asked questions regarding how people feel about something and then proceeded to call for sweeping changes of one sort or another. As the set of responses we generated in reaction to "abhor" bore almost no relationship to the set generated by "annoy," considerable caution in applying results of such polls is called for.

TABLE 1.21

THE TWENTY "TOP" ANNOYANCES: CIRCA 1930
(in descending order of frequency)

the odor of dirty feet
a person coughing in my face
to see or hear an animal being harshly treated by a person
to see or hear a child being harshly treated by an older person
a person cheating in a game
a dirty bed
the odor of a bad breath
to see a person at the table spitting out food
to find a hair in food that I am eating
to see a person blow his (or her) nose without using a handkerchief
to see a person's nose running
to see stains of tobacco juice around a man's mouth
to hear a mosquito near me when I am trying to go to sleep
the odorous condition of another person's body
to find some dirt in food that I am eating
to see an intoxicated woman
a dirty wash basin
a young person showing disrespect for a much older person
to see a woman spit in public
a religious hypocrite

REFERENCES

Cameron, P. The presence of pets and smoking as correlates of perceived disease. *Journal of Allergy,* 1967, *40,* 12-15.

Cameron, P., Kostin, J. S., Zaks, J. M., Wolfe, J. H., Tighe, G., Oselett, B., Stocker, R., and Winton, J. The health of smokers' and nonsmokers' children. *Journal of Allergy,*, 1969, *43,* 336-341.

Cameron, P. Secondhand tobacco smoke: children's reactions. *Journal of School Health,* 1972, *42,* 280-284.

Cameron, P. and Hudson, D. Teenager's attitudes towards a date's smoking. *Adolescence,* 1972, *8,* 433-438.

Cameron, P. and Robertson, D. Effect of home environment tobacco smoke on family health. *Journal of Applied Psychology,* 1973, *57,* 142-147.

Cameron, P., Hooks, W. A., Gifford, G. F., Carter, L., Coats, D., and Ankner, J. The effect of tobacco smoking upon spouse relationships. *Paper presented at Southeastern Psychological Association,* Atlanta, March 28, 1975.

Cason, H. Common annoyances: a psychological survey of everyday aversions and irritations. *Psychological Monographs,* 1930, *40,* no. 182, 1-218.

2

LIFE SATISFACTION AND AFFECTIVITY

Our first question each day is whether to go on living. One of the prime considerations in the raging argument that attends our emergence from the sheets is our life-satisfaction. If things have been going ill, we are more likely to "pull the plug" than if they are going smoothly. Further, we have to judge what there is to look forward to — current misery is more tolerable if a pleasant event awaits a passage of time. Is there some relatively invariant pattern of life-satisfaction associated with aging that transcends cultures? Is there some idiosyncratic pattern that occurs within industrialized cultures? Answering these questions is far from easy. First, there are cultural changes occurring almost yearly that may be influential in a person's assessment of happiness at any given point in the life-cycle. For instance, Medicare and Medicaid may have favorably affected old persons' life-satisfaction, and the current tendency toward childlessness may be negatively affecting younger adults' happiness. At this writing, an economic recession is "in progress." Probably the happiness of many members of society is lowered as a consequence.

Cultural change, life-tasks, and rewards within a culture as a function of position in the life-cycle, circumstance, chance, decisions made in the past (whether or not to marry, to take one job or another), as well as age, affect life-satisfaction. Untangling their several effects and extracting the effect of age *per se* is no mean task. There is probably no "correct" strategy in the pursuit of truth in the matter. Any longitudinal study will necessarily be contaminated by the cultural and historic changes that affect the life-satisfaction of the subjects under study. It could happen, for instance, that one might find young adulthood to be the "happiest time of life" for a given cohort. But if that cohort spent post-young adulthood involved in wars and/or economic depressions, what interpretation should be put on our results? The linguistic meaning of "main line," frequently-invoked concepts such as "happiness" change very slowly. But in industrial societies where the content of what goes into making one happy frequently undergoes changes (possession of a television or smoking pot were once quite beyond ken) it is conceivable that the meaning of a concept might shift somewhat from cohort to cohort. Thus it is possible, though still, thankfully remote, that declared "happiness" by older cohorts might have a slightly different meaning than the same degree of happiness reported by younger cohorts.

Cross-sectional studies run periodically over a period of time would help to sensitize us to possible cultural changes/influences. Since the effects of age must be studied across a large span of time, no one study, or for that matter, set of studies, will "settle the issue."

A number of independent variables appear to fluctuate along with or influence happiness. Marital status, economic standing, educational attainment, health, children, and age all seem to require inclusion here. We are not sure which way the relationship between life-satisfaction and these variables operates. Being married usually is associated with greater happiness than being single. But do happier people attract mates more readily and/or does the status of marriage effect a change toward greater happiness? And the possible effects of marriage presumably vary as a function of when one arrives at "bliss." Married 14-year olds may be less happy than singles while the opposite may obtain for 24-year olds.

Overlooking the state of knowledge regarding life-satisfaction, three tasks await exploration:

1) Undoubtedly *the* most important factor in life-satisfaction is the determination of a person to be happy. *Happiness is an achievement*, perhaps the, and certainly one of the, greatest achievements of living. No one, to my knowledge, has inves-

tigated the effort that the various age-groups expend to maintain happiness.

2) Life-satisfaction needs to be "componentized." That is, the various facets of living that go into influencing life toward a more or less pleasant course need explication. Health, confidants, money, etc. have been involved as "prime" components. The relative value of each needs parameterization.

3) Longitudinal studies need to be performed. Are happy children tomorrow's happy adults? Are teenage wallflowers the mental patients of the future?

We have arrived at a point in our understanding of the issue when more studies of age differences are probably unnecessary. We know little about the above three questions — and need to know more.

EGO-STRENGTH AND HAPPINESS OF THE AGED

Are the aged blissful or regretful? Is youth the "prime of life?" Or, to put the question another way, "Which is the happiest period of life?" Although informal speculations attempting to answer these questions abound, to the author's knowledge only seven studies bearing on this issue have been attempted and each falls short in some respect of providing an answer in which one can place much confidence. The present study seeks to aid in the answering of the above questions.

Materials and Methods

Three kinds of aged (over 59-years old) samples were compared with a younger (aged 18 to 40) sample along the dimension of "morale-happiness." The three aged populations were:

1) Those who maintained their own homes,

2) those hospitalized, and

3) those residing in a cooperative "golden years" apartment.

The four subsamples were drawn from the city of Boulder, Colorado. The residential aged and young subsamples were obtained by a random area-sampling technique encompassing all of the city (the residential aged had a mean age of 70.05, S.D. = 8.48; its socioeconomic status (SES) as measured by a weighted average ranging from 5 (high) to 1 (low) and incorporating educational level, occupational status, and last year's income = 2.52; the young had a mean age of 30.10, S.D. = 6.03; SES = 3.26). The hospitalized aged were randomly drawn from those aged able to cooperate in two hospitals (mean age = 80.32, S.D. = 9.14; SES = 1.98); and the cooperative apartment dwellers were randomly selected from the total population of a federally-sponsored, church-related institution (mean age = 72.24, S.D. = 7.12; SES = 2.11). Socioeconomically the subsamples differed significantly (F = 8.73; df = 3354; <0.001: *post hoc t* tests indicated that the young had a higher status than the residential aged (t = 5.01; <0.001), hospitalized aged (t = 7.17; <0.001), and cooperative apartment aged (t = 6.73; <0.01) while the residential aged tended to enjoy a higher status than the hospitalized (t = 2.27; <0.03) and cooperative apartment (t = 1.84; <.10) aged with the latter two groups essentially equal in status (t = 5.77; <0.01) and cooperative apartment (t = 4.21; <0.01) aged, while the latter two subsamples did not differ in age (t = 1.41; NS). All Ss were Caucasian.

Canter's (1965) short form of the Barron Ego-Strength Scale (Barron, 1953) was used as an estimate of ego-strength. The Barron Scale has successfully separated the mentally disturbed from normal individuals (Taft, 1957; Tamkin and Klett, 1957: Gottesman, 1959; Grosz and Levitt, 1959; Silverman, 1963).

It is possible to conceptualize overall "happiness" as consisting of a preponderance of moods of happiness over moods of sadness. For an estimate of subsample happiness one might sample the moods of members of each subsample and compare the subsamples' happy, neutral, or sad moods. Part of "consciousness sampling" (Cameron, 1966) was employed to this end. The Ss in each subsample were asked to characterize their affective state over the last half hour as "happy," "neutral," or "sad." To guard against the possibility that "happiness" and "sadness" meant different things to the various subsamples, the Zazlow Picture Sequence Scale, which consists of 13 still-frames from a motion picture in which the actor and actress progress from affectionate regard to brutality was administered. The Ss were asked to point to the frames where "happiness ends" and "sadness begins." It was assumed that groups to whom "happiness" and "sadness" meant the same thing would locate their "ending" and "beginning" at the same locations on the Zazlow Scale.

The interviewers were paid college students, ten of each sex. The S refusal rate was 5%. Females constituted about 75% of respondents in each of the four subsamples.

A total of 320 Ss, approximately half aged and half young, were administered consciousness sampling. Approximately half of the Ss were randomly selected to take the ego-strength and/or the Zazlow Scale(s). The above tests were administered as follows: (1) equally often within hour intervals from 8:00 a.m. to 8:00 p.m. to control for time-of-day bias; (2) equally often by male and female interviewers to control for sex-of-interviewer bias; (3) by each administrator to Ss in each of the four subsamples to control for idiosyncratic influences of interviewers; and (4) by interviewers ignorant of the aims of the study to guard against experimenter-hypotheses/formation bias (Rosenthal, 1963). All sampling took place on the 4th and 5th of April, 1966.

Results

"Do the aged enjoy a higher, lower, or equal ego-strength as compared to younger adults?" is the first question considered. Table 1 summarizes the mean ego-strength scores of the four subsamples. As the value of the one-way analysis of variance was great enough to have occurred by chance with slight probability, a series of *post hoc t* tests was performed to clarify the relationships. Ego-strength of the aged appears definitely below that of the young for each of the three aged subsamples. The hospitalized aged also showed a tendency to lower ego-strength than the other aged subsamples. A scattergram for each aged subsample's distribution of scores revealed no tendency for age to correlate further with ego-strength score. Two multiple regression analyses (performed with and without the addition of the hospitalized aged to the S pool) both indicated that age accounted for about 22% and socioeconomic factors for about 8% of the variance (R = 0.55).

The second question posed was "Are the aged more, less, or equally content with their lot (i.e., 'happy') as compared to younger adults?" All subsamples reported more "happy moods than "sad" ones (the young subsample reported 79 happy, 68 neutral, and 12 sad moods; the residential aged reported 41, 31, and 7 respectively; the hospitalized aged reported 15, 20, and 6; and the cooperative aged 20, 13, and 4; $X^2 = 3.97$; df = 6; NS). That "happiness" and "sadness" meant much the same thing to the subsamples was evidenced by statistically insignificant differences between the subsamples in their mean locations of "happiness ends" and "sadness begins" on the Zazlow Scale.

TABLE 2.1

Mean Ego-Strength Score of the Four Subsamples

Subsample	N	Mean	S.D.	t_a
Young	75	34.41	4.95	$t_{1,2} = 3.77$; $p < 0.001$
Old, residents	33	30.09	6.97	$t_{1,3} = 6.03$; $p < 0.001$
Old, hospitalized	22	27.14	5.07	$t_{1,4} = 3.35$; $p < 0.001$
Old, cooperative	17	29.94	5.03	$t_{2,3} = 1.78$; $p < 0.15$
				$t_{2,4} = 0.08$; NS
				$t_{3,4} = 1.72$; $p < 0.15$

$F = 7.187$; df = 3/139; $p < 0.001$.

Discussion

The results seem to indicate that the ego-strength of the aged is below that of the young while "happiness," in a more limited sense, is equal for the two groups. These findings seem to directly contradict only three studies. Cumming, Henry, Dean, McCaffrey, and Cassetta (1961a) administered a four-item dichotomously-scored questionnaire to 211 50-to-70-year-old Ss. They concluded, in line with the Cumming-Henry theory, that disengagement produces happiness and that happiness increases with age after 65. Two years later they repeated the same measure on 156 of the original Ss and found what they considered to be weak confirmatory evidence for the conclusion of the first study. Cumming, Henry and Parlagreco (1961b) administered the same four-item questionnaire to 186 Ss between the ages of 60 and 89 and concluded that after age 65 happiness increase with age. Finally, Meltzer (1963) asked 257 Ss ranging in age from 19 to 77 years whether they had had their "share of happiness" and found that the percentage of "yes" responses increased with age. Clearly the decline or equilibrium of affective tone and ego-strength indicated by the present study does not fit into the Cumming and Henry prediction of increased "happiness" with age. Although the present study was cross-sectional in design, and thus does not actually measure change, the same is true of the above studies with the exception of the longitudinal part of the Cumming et al. (1961a) study. Since this longitudinal study was of short duration, and had an attrition of about 25% of the original sample, its findings are rather tenuous. Further, as the Cumming et al. studies used samples whose lower age range was never below 50, even though the theory presumes to compare the aged with the young, one cannot be sure that if young adults had been sampled the results would have been favorable to the theory. Meltzer's (1963) study used a wider age range, but one's "share of happiness" might reasonably be expected to increase with age, while any retrospective judgment is subject to considerable question (Mason, 1954).

Four studies are harmonious in varying degrees with the present study. Morgan (1937) requested retrospective judgment of 300 aged individuals (all 65 or over) as to what the happiest time or period of their life was. The modal response was the middle adult years. Landis (1942) asked the same question of a larger sample (450) of the same kind of Ss and got the same results. If we regard their "happiness" as the "ego-strength" of the present study, some support is found for their conclusions. Gardner (1949) tried much the same thing but specifically asked the Ss to compare their happiness now with that which they had during middle age ($n = 193$; age range $= 60$-90 years). A majority reported themselves as happy today as they were while in their middle years. It is conceivable that the economic depression had more to do with the results of the Morgan and Landis studies than the age of their Ss, since many of them undoubtedly underwent deprivation for the preceding 10 to 12 years. The Gardner study seems to have, in effect, asked the Ss to skip over the depression years and this might partially account for his results.

Mason (1954) utilized a more indeterminate technique. She had a Q-sort questionnaire with one item that could be answered yes or no. The older group (n = 90; mean age = 60 years) answered "yes" significantly more frequently than the younger group (n = 30; mean age = 35 years) to the statement "I don't enjoy living as much as I used to." Here, although we would not wish to make an issue of a one-item finding, the domain of ego-strength (or morale, see below) seems more involved and could be construed as consonant with the present study's finding of decreased ego-strength with age. These four studies are subject to all the criticisms laid against retrospective judgments, especially that it is entirely possible that a person could not make a valid retrospective appraisal. With the well known tendency for memories to become selective toward pleasantness it is further possible that the Ss are comparing rosy memories with less rosy reality in the Morgan, Landis, and Mason studies, although this explanation falls short of accounting for the Gardner findings.

The meanings associated with the use of the word "morale" largely comprise those meanings associated with the more oft-used professionally "ego-strength" (i.e. *Webster's* (1961) defines morale as " . . . a state of individual psychological well-being and buoyancy . . . derived from a sense of purpose and usefulness, and confidence . . ." while English and English (1958) define ego-strength as " . . .adjustment in general . . . resoluteness or character strength . . .") Four practicing psychologists, Ronald Johnson, Peter Ossorio, Donald Weatherly, and Martin Mayman, agreed that the meaning-domains of "morale" and "ego-strength" largely overlapped and were asked to critically examine the Barron Scale for appropriateness as a measure of "morale." They all, independently, judged the Barron Scale suitable for the measurement of morale. The order of mean ego-strength is as one would expect if ego-strength were related to morale (i.e., felt competency). The aged who maintain their own homes, and consequently meet successfully the same challenges as the young (i.e., salesmen, landscapers, etc.) have the highest "morale." Those who have surrendered some degree of their independence to cooperative living and thus have withdrawn from many confrontations with life are the next lowest in morale; while those who have given up almost all of their independence for hospital care have the lowest morale. Of further interest, the ratio of "happiness" to "sadness" is lowest for the hospitalized aged. The probability of both measurements of the domain of "happiness-morale-ego-strength" yielding lowest values for the hospitalized aged is $(\frac{1}{4})^2$; $p<0.062$. The latter finding is suggestive that the hospitalized aged are least apt to typify the aged population as a whole along this dimension.

Summary

The Barron Ego-Strength Scale, the Zazlow Picture Sequence Scale, and part of "consciousness sampling" were administered to four populations — young adults, aged adults maintaining their own residences, hospitalized aged, and aged cooperative apartment dwellers. Evidence was presented that indicates (1) the aged possess lower ego-strength (construed as morale) than the young; (2) the normal aged are as happy as the young; and (3) the terms "happiness" and "sadness" mean much the same thing to the young and the old.

REFERENCES

Barron, F. An ego-strength scale which predicts response to psychotherapy. *Journal of Consulting Psychology,* 1953, *17,* 327-333.

Cameron, P. Age as a determinant of differences in non-intellective psychological dimensions. Unpublished Doctoral dissertation, University of Colorado, 1966.

Canter, A. A brief note on shortening Barron's ego-strength scale. *Journal of Clinical Psychology,* 1965, *21,* 285-286.

Cummings, E., Henry, W. E., Dean, L. R., McCaffrey, I., and Cassetta, R. The issue of successful aging. Chapter 3 in: Cummings, E., and Henry, W. E., ed., *Growing Old.* New York: Basic Books, 1961. pp. 128-142.

Cummings, E., Henry, W. E., and Parlagreco, M. L. The very old. Chapter 6 in: Cummings, E., Henry, W. E., ed., *Growing Old.* New York: Basic Books, 1961. pp 201-209.

English, H. B. and English, A. C. *A comprehensive dictionary of psychological and psychoanalytical terms.* New York: Longmans, Green, 1958.

Gardner, L. P. Attitudes and activities of the middle aged and aged. *Geriatrics,* 1949, *4,* 33-50.

Gottesman, I. I. More contruct validation of the ego-strength scale. Journal of Consulting Psychology, 1959, *23,* 342-346.

Grosz, H. J. and Levitt, E. E. The effects of hypnotically-induced anxiety on the manifest anxiety scale and the Barron ego-strength scale. Journal of Abnormal and Social Psychology,1959, *59,* 281-283.

Landis, J. T. What is the happiest period in life? *School and Society,* 1942, *55,* 643-645.

Mason, E. P. Some factors in self-judgments. *Journal of Clinical Psychology*, 1954, *10*, 336-340.

Meltzer, H. Age differences in happiness and life adjustments of workers. *Journal of Gerontology*, 1963, *18*, 66-70.

Morgan, C. M. The attitudes and adjustments of recipients of old age assistance in upstate and metropolitan New York. *Archives of Psychology*, 1937, *214*, 131-381.

Rosenthan, R. On the society psychology of the psychological experiment: the experimenter's hypothesis as unintended determinant of experimental results. *American Scientist*, 1963, *51*, 268-283.

Silverman, J. The validity of the Barron ego-strength scale in an individual form. *Journal of Consulting Psychology*, 1963, *27*, 532-533.

Taft, R. The validity of the Barron ego-strength scale and the Welsh anxiety index. *Journal of Consulting Psychology*, 1957, *27*, 247-249.

Tamkin, A. S. and Klett, C. J. Barron's ego-strength scale: a replication of an evaluation of its construct validity. *Journal of Consulting Psychology*, 1957, *21*, 412.

STEREOTYPES ABOUT GENERATIONAL FUN AND HAPPINESS VS. SELF-APPRAISED FUN AND HAPPINESS

What is the happiest time of life? Which period of the life-span do the members of our culture believe to be the happiest? Various investigators have studied self-appraisals of persons of differing ages and have arrived at widely divergent conclusions. Cumming and Henry (1961), and Meltzer (1963) reported results that suggest that happiness *increases* with age or at least toward the end of the life-span: Mason (1954) presented data that suggest that happiness *decreases* with age; and Cameron (1967), Gardner (1949), Landis (1942), and Morgan (1937) submitted results that suggest that happiness is largely *invariant* across the adult life-span. To date, no one appears to have investigated what the various generations *believe* about the various generations' happiness. The present study was undertaken to add more evidence bearing on the self-appraisal happiness controversy and provide a beginning toward answering the question of beliefs regarding generational happiness.

"How happy is your life?" is a "state of being" question (Ossorio, 1966). Unlike moods, which are relative to a person's usual affective state and which are heavily affected by immediately prior circumstances, a person's appraisal of his "overall" quality of existence takes in broader considerations. To answer this question a person must judge: (1) how "far" he could "go" and where he's "at" relative to others in his society, and (2) how things are "going" for him relative to his personal life history. The theoretic structure upon which this paper is based holds that persons who are permanently socially-disadvantaged (and for purposes of argument, we will assume that this would include women, Negroes, those of lower social status) or permanently socially-advantaged (i.e., men, whites, those of higher social status) can be expected to adjust their happiness-unhappiness appraisal to the "way things are and reasonably could be" for members of their social situation. Thus a woman can be expected to adjust her "potential" to the fact of male-sex preference, a Negro his "limit" to the fact of white preference and so forth. Besides this adjustment, a person must also appraise how well things are relative to his life history (thus a wealthy person might find the news of inheriting $5,000 quite distressing, while a poor person might "leap for joy").

On these "person theory" grounds (Ossorio, 1966), we would expect the generalized Negro, or generalized woman, or generalized youth, etc., to appraise his happiness as being at about the same level as any other class of generalized other. This has been demonstrated to be the case for the malformed, for instance (Cameron, Van Hoeck, Weiss, and Kostin, 1971). Exceptions to this rule should come about only when persons comprising some class (women, Negroes) feel that their potential or what "could be" is being unjustly-unreasonably thwarted by some outside-themselves agency. As long as this class of persons does not believe that its potential is being unjustly-unreasonably crimped, the "objective" social situation could be expected to have no effect upon the class' appraisals of happiness, even if, in fact, it were being unjustly-unreasonably discriminated against. Likewise, if a class of persons believes that it is being discriminated against unfairly, even if the "objective" social situation is not unfairly-unreasonably discriminatory, we can expect the class to feel less happy. Unless and until a large minority or majority of Negroes or women believe that "given an equal chance, which is socially-practically possible, I would be able to do just as well as whites or men," the self-appraisals of the persons in this class could not be expected to differ appreciably from other classes of persons. There is a good deal of formal and informal evidence that most women today believe that men "deserve" their higher status for one reason (or "excuse") or another, ("men are better trained," "men are naturally less emotional," etc.). Consequently, we would expect little if any difference in happiness between the sexes in our society. If, on the other hand, "women's liberation" or similar movements or circumstances can persuade a large minority or majority of women to believe that they are unjustly-unreasonably discriminated against, we would then expect some difference between the reported happiness of men and women in our society.

The two factors — membership in social class and personal life history — are probably not equally weighted in arriving at an appraisal of happiness. One's social class is probably "ground" and personal life history "figure" in the judgment. In the following study, the generations — young adults, middle-aged, and old were compared for self-appraised happiness. While there is little doubt that the old are in many ways discriminated against in our society (Bromley, 1966), it is uncertain that the old regard this discrimination as unjust or unreasonable in-the-main. In fact, if they have been thoroughly socialized, we would expect today's old to have had a history of discriminating against the old of their day and to look upon their current treatment or status as "natural."

Subjects, Interview, and Questionnaire

Subjects. In order to determine which ages should be included in the generations "young adult," "middle-aged," and "old," a pilot study was conducted which empirically established that, linguistically speaking, persons are young adults aged 18 to 25 inclusive, middle-aged from 40 to 55, and old from 65 to 79 (Cameron, 1969). Desiring to represent these age groups as adequately as possible, and realizing that there might be sex differences in the results, six strict area samples of the city of Detroit (excluding the inner city), for Caucasians only, were performed; 317 white subjects were approached at home at least twice to assure a low rejection rate and paid $2 for the interview. Through a system of almost unlimited callbacks, we ended up with 19 rejections (i.e., a rejection rate of <6%). Interviewers were 12 trained, paid college students. Slightly over 50% of the data were recalled and verified both to clarify ambiguities, or correct mistakes, and to assure that no "dry labbing" had occurred.

Interview. Subject was approached by asking him to fill out a questionnaire concerning his beliefs about adults. He was assured anonymity, asked to fill out the interview in another part of the residence; then, when finished to seal the interview in an envelope provided for the purpose. The interviewer: (1) induced the subject to cooperate, (2) delivered the materials, and (3) answered any questions that the subject might have (there were relatively few). Whenever asked questions about the questionnaire, the interviewer read the question aloud for the respondent, and in a few cases provided minor definitional clarification. When leaving, the interviewer induced the subject to record his phone number on the envelope, and when outside, recorded the address. Whenever a subject had neglected to answer any question(s), a person other than the interviewer reinterviewed the subject by phone or in person and requested completion. The data were thus made over 99% complete. Each interviewer interviewed an equal number of males and females evenly distributed over the three age groups to control for any idiosyncratic interviewer-affects. Half of the subjects in each sample were administered the "opinions" part of the questionnaire first, and the other half the "self-report" part first.

Questionnaire. Subjects were asked to compare the generations and rate themselves along the following six dimensions. The questionnarie was introduced — "How do you believe the three age groups (young adults, middle-aged, and old) compare in:
  1) over-all happiness? _____ are the happiest _____ are the least happy
  2) opportunities for happiness? _____ have the most opportunities _____ have the fewest opportunities.
  3) opportunities for fun? _____ have the most opportunities _____ have the fewest opportunities.
  4) desire for fun? _____ want fun most _____ want fun least.
  5) desire for happiness? _____ want happiness most _____ want happiness least.
The self-report part of the questionnaire was a mirror of the

above, consisting of a Likert scale (above average, average, below average) introduced — "How would you compare yourself with all other adults of your sex in:

1) over all happiness?
2) opportunities for happiness?
3) opportunities for fun?
4) desire for fun?
5) desire for happiness?

Subject was also asked his age, sex, his income to the nearest $500 for the past year, and the highest grade he completed in formal schooling. Socioeconomic Status (SES) was computed by multiplying the number associated with income (e.g., 1 = under $5,000; 2 = $5,000-$7,999; 3 = $8,000-$11,999; 4 = $12,000+) by 2 and adding it to the number associated with education (1 = completed less than 8th grade; 2 = 8th-11th; 3 = high school diploma; 4 = some college; 5 = B.A.; 6 = M.A.; 7 = Ph.D.). All analyses broke SES into two levels, those scoring 9 or higher and those scoring 8 or less.

The mean ages of the samples were 21.0 for the young adults, 48.2 for the middle-aged, and 70.2 for the old. SES levels were 8.89, 9.39, and 6.02, respectively (educational levels were 3.52, 3.25, and 2.49 with the young and middle-aged thus falling between the "high school diploma" and "some college" categories, while the old fell between the "8th-11th" and "high school diploma" categories; for income the groups averaged 2.68, 3.10, and 1.79 with the young thus averaging under $8,000 a year; the middle-aged over $8,000; and the old under $5,000).

Beliefs and Self-Reports of the Generations

Beliefs of the generations. A three-way fixed-effects analysis of variance (generation × sex × socioeconomic status) uncovered only one significant main-effects difference in the opinions of the social classes (higher socioeconomic status persons tended to more frequently regard the "happiest" generation as the old) and none for generation or sex. The middle-aged were most frequently believed to be the happiest, young adults were believed the happiest next-most frequently, and the old were believed to be the happiest least frequently. Under our system of scoring responses were the generations believed to be equally happy; each would have scored giving a point for most, 2 points for second-most, and 3 for least. Instead, the middle-aged scored 527, young adults 633, and the old 742. Young adults were believed to have the most opportunities for happiness (with a score of 471), the middle-aged the next-most (587), and the old fewest (844). The young were believed to have the most opportunities for fun (391), the middle-aged the next most (627), and the old the fewest (884). The young were believed to have the greatest desire for fun (391), the middle-aged next-most (666), and the old least desire (877). The middle-aged (558) and the young (587) were believed the least desirious (757).

Self-reports of the generations. The generations did not differ in their reported happiness. All three generations' mean estimates were above the "average" level which would be represented by a score of "2"; young adults' mean was 2.4; the middle-ageds' mean was 2.3; and the olds' was 2.4. Both sexes' mean was 2.4, while the higher socioeconomic status persons' mean was 2.5 compared to 2.3 for those of lower social status. Only the main effect of social class was statistically significant ($F = 8.87$; $p < .01$).

Neither the generations nor sexes significantly differed in their appraisals of opportunities for happiness. Young adults' and the olds' mean was 2.4; the middle-ageds' 2.3; males' 2.4; females' 2.3; and higher social status persons' 2.4 compared to lower social status persons' 2.3 (which tended to be statistically significant, $F = 3.74$; $p < .06$).

The generations, sexes, and social classes did not differ statistically-significantly in their appraisals of opportunities for fun. Young adults' mean was 2.4; middle-ageds' 2.2; and the olds' 2.1; males' was 2.3; and females' 2.1. The higher social class persons averaged 2.3 and the lower social class persons averaged 2.1. There were tendencies ($p < .10$) for both the sex and social class differences to be statistically significant.

The generations differed in their professed desire for fun. The young mean of 2.6 differed significantly from the middle-ageds' 2.3 or the olds' 2.2 ($F = 8.41$; $p < .01$). Males scored at 2.4; females at 2.3, and the higher socioeconomic class at 2.4 vs. 2.3 for the lower socioeconomic class.

Young adults claimed to possess a greater desire for happiness.

The young adult mean was 2.7, the middle-aged mean 2.5, the old 2.4 ($F = 6.21 p < .01$). Both sexes' mean was 2.5; the higher social class' 2.6 and the lower social class' was 2.5. Clearly "happiness" was desired more than "fun" for the generations, sexes, and social classes (overall $t = 65.1; p < .001$).

Stereotypes

The stereotypes of the members of our culture in regard to the generations are kind to the middle-aged. While the young are believed to receive more opportunities for happiness while possessing an equivalent desire for happiness as the middle-aged, the middle-aged are believed to *achieve* more happiness than the young. The old are seen as having relatively fewer opportunities for happiness and, for that matter, relatively low desire for happiness. Yet the old are believed to *achieve* happiness beyond their opportunities and at about the same level as their desire (i.e. achieve 742 compared to desiring 757). The young, on the other hand, are believed to have a high desire for happiness, and the most opportunities for happiness, yet are believed to *fail to achieve* happiness to the degree of their desire (i.e., they achieve 633 in the face of opportunities of 587 and desire of 587). Clearly the middle-aged are doing "better" than they have desire or opportunity for. Just as clearly, the young are believed to be "blowing it." Our culture looks unfavorably at persons who do less well than their opportunities provide — especially if the persons themselves desire the outcome of the opportunities. A person's happiness is an achievement wrest from his personal life history, his appraisals of others at or near his "station in life," and his circumstances (or opportunities). In this instance, the young are seen as falling short of the happiness they have coming given their opportunities. As such the young probably incur some disapprobation as a consequence.

In spite of the strength of the stereotypes (as indexed by their consistency across generations); the self-reported happiness of the generations did not differ. As those of higher social class are more advantaged in our social system, their belief in their greater happiness indicates a realistic attunement to reality. Those of higher social class could have believed that they achieve more happiness because they "try harder," but such was clearly not the case.

Instead they attributed their greater happiness to greater opportunity.

Conclusions

Previous research into generational happiness permits no easy summary of findings. Some investigators have concluded that adult persons become happier as a consequence of age after the fifth decade (Cumming and Henry's monograph, 1961, presents three such studies). Meltzer (1963) has reported data that could be construed as supporting the notion that adult persons become less happy with age. Finally, a number of studies have reported evidence that suggests that happiness remains relatively constant across the life-span (Cameron, 1967); Gardner, 1949; Landis, 1942; Morgan, 1937). The present results lend weight to the concept that happiness of adults is unaffected by age *per se* in our culture.

Age was related to responses to the question "taking things all together, how would you say things are these days — would you say you're happy, pretty happy, or not too happy these days?" In area samples totaling 4,466 persons (Bradburn and Capolovitz, 1965; Gurin, Veroff, and Feld, 1960). The proportion of persons choosing "very happy" declined, that choosing "not too happy" increased and the proportion choosing "pretty happy" remained constant with age. It is unfortunate that these otherwise informative studies hinged on a question in which the differential age-response rates might be linked to its construal as an appraisal of *things* (i.e., the life-situation) rather than a judgment of life-satisfaction. In both studies this item followed and preceded questions regarding the state of "things" in the past and future. Thus aside from the possible linguistic ambiguity of the responses (was "not too happy" construed as "unhappy" or "not excessively happy"?), the results may be accounted for in large part as appraisals of degree of satisfaction with the environmental surround as a function of age. If an investigator wants to know about life-satisfaction, it would seem appropriate to ask about it directly at some point in the questionnaire rather than "inferring" it from a single ambiguous item (neither study permitted subjects to characterize themselves as unhappy). As linguistically-responsible, multi-item questionnaires of life-satisfaction are possible (e.g., Cameron et al., 1971), it is indeed regrettable that such well-carried-out studies should permit no unequivocal interpretation of their results.

The lack of sexual or generational differences in self-reported happiness suggests that, at this time, for the city of Detroit at least, neither sexual nor generational discrimination is apt to provide pressure for social change. On the other hand, the lower happiness of the lower social class in our sample does suggest that some pressure for social change may come from this quarter.

REFERENCES

Bradburn, N., and Caplovitz, D. *Reports on happiness*. Chicago: Aldine, 1965.

Bromley, D. B. *The psychology of human aging*. Baltimore: Pelican, 1966.

Cameron, P. Ego-strength and happiness of the aged. *Journal of Gerontology*, 1967, *22*, 199-202.

Cameron, P. Age parameters of young adults, middle-aged, old, and aged. Journal of Gerontology, 1969, *24*, 201-202.

Cameron, P., Van Hoock, D., Weiss, N., and Kostin, M. Happiness or life satisfaction of the malformed. *Preceedings, Seventy-Ninth Annual Convention, American Psychological Association*, 1971, 641-642.

Cumming, E., and Henry, W. E. *Growing Old*. New York: Basic Books, 1961.

Gardner, L. P. Attitudes and activities of the middle aged and aged. *Geriatrics*, 1949, *4*, 33-50.

Gurin, G., Veroff, J., and Fold, S. *Americans view their mental health*. New York: Basic Books, 1960.

Landis, J. T. What is the happiest period in life? *School and Society*, 1942, *55*, 643-655.

Mason, E. P. Some factors in self-judgments. *Journal of Clinical Psychology*, 1954, *10*, 336-340.

Meltzer, H. Age differences in happiness and life adjustments of workers. *Journal of Gerontology*, 1963, *18*, 66-70.

Morgan, C. M. The attitudes and adjustments of recipients of old age assistance in upstate and metropolitan New York. *Archives of Psychology*, 1937, *214*, 131-381.

Ossorio, P. G. *Persons*, Los Angeles: Linguistic Research Institute, 1966.

THE LIFE-SATISFACTION OF NONNORMAL PERSONS
with Donna Gnadinger Titus,
John Kostin, and Marilyn Kostin

How much do the handicapped enjoy life? Are mental retardates as happy as normals? While empirical studies bearing on such questions are few (Cameron, Van Hoeck, Weiss, and Kostin, 1971; Gruhn and Krause, 1968), both lay and professional opinion has it that defective people enjoy their existence considerably less than normals (Titley, 1969). This opinion has led to broad-based support for the abortion and/or infanticide of defective children in the Western world. Normals appear to reason that "if they don't look as good as I do, and/or aren't as intelligent as I am, how *could* they be as happy?" Yet it is a rare person who is not relatively deficient in a number of respects compared to his peers. Some of us are not very attractive physically, others lack some socially valued skills or knowledge. Most "normals" learn to adjust to or cope with their deficits — they manage to enjoy life no matter or in spite of their lot. Perhaps the defective manage to enjoy life using the same psychological mechanism.

Happiness is a "state of being" concept (Ossorio, 1966). Unlike moods, which are relative to a person's usual affective state and which are heavily influenced by immediately prior circumstances, a persons' appraisal of his "overall" quality of existence takes in broader considerations. To answer questions of happiness a person must judge (a) how "far" he could go and where he's "at" relative to others in his society and (b) how things are "going" for him relative to his history. We would contend that persons who are permanently disadvantaged socially in our society (this would include women, nonwhites, handicapped, those of lower social status) can be expected to adjust their appraisal of life-satisfaction to the "way things are and reasonably could be" for members of their social status. That is, one's membership in a fixed social status category *per se* ought to have no influence on how satisfying one finds his life. Three studies were performed to test this proposition.

Method

Study I

Subjects. One hundred and forty-four physically defective persons were convenience sampled, with one-third coming from the outpatient clinics and one-third coming from the inpatients of two Detroit hospitals. The remaining third came from the student body of Wayne State University. The handicapped were matched with a normal control as to sex, approximate age, and status (i.e., outpatient, inpatient, or student). Where possible, inpatient controls were matched as to length of hospitalization. An additional seven student normals were acquired and retained in the analysis. Two-thirds of the sample were male. The handicapped sample was composed of 64 with paralysis, 37 with a muscular difficulty, 16 with a deformed limb, 12 with a lost limb or missing member, 11 who were blind, and 4 with a hearing impairment. The questionnaire was read to those who because of blindness or palsy, could not write. In such cases, their controls were also administered the questionnaire orally.

Questionnaire. The respondent gave his age, sex, race, and family income last year (under $5,000, $5,000-$9,999; $10,000-$15,000, over $15,000). He was then asked: (a) How much do you like people in general? (not at all, very little, somewhat, considerably, very much); (b) How much do you think that people in general like you? (same responses as above); (c) These days my life is (just great, more than satisfactory, satisfactory, less than satisfactory, just miserable); (d) What was your mood during the past half-hour? (happy, neutral, sad); (e) How has your life been so far? (very difficult, difficult, average, easy, very easy); (f) How do you expect life to be in the future? (same responses as above); (g) Have you ever contemplated suicide? (yes, no); (h) How many times?_____; (i) Have you contemplated suicide in the past month? (yes, no); (j) Do you find life frustrating? (never, infrequently, sometimes, frequently, constantly); (k) How much do you look forward to next month? (very much, considerably, somewhat, very little, not at all); and (l) To me religion is (very important, important, of small importance, unimportant, very unimportant).

Study II

Subjects. The Sample in this study consisted of 46 physically handicapped persons from the Kentucky School for the Blind and Kentucky Industry for the Blind, with a few coming from the community at large. These Ss were matched regarding sex, race, and approximate age with normals in the community. The study had to be terminated before 2 of the handicapped could be matched, so controls numbered 44.

Questionnaire. The questionnaire was identical to that of the first study with the addition of "When did you become handicapped?" to index the possible psychological differences between congenital and acquired defect.

Study III

Subjects. The Louisville Parochial School System provided four classrooms of retarded (mean IQ = 70.8; age range = 6-19 with a mean of 13 years) children. Children who were in any way physically deformed or who were nonCaucasian were excluded from the sample. Remaining children were divided by sex, and 20 retarded boys and 20 retarded girls were randomly selected to participate. As parental cooperation was expected to be of lower quality for normals, a pool of 21 normal boys and 28 normal girls was selected to provide controls. Eventually complete results were obtained on 20 controls (the subset of 40 controls did not differ statistically significantly on any of the dimensions on which we obtained data from the initial set of 48).

Because of the doubtful validity of questioning retarded children regarding their happiness, each child was observed twice in two situations (in class and at recess). Raters familiarized themselves with the children and established the normalcy of their presence in these situations. Then, unbeknownst to the children, those children who had been selected were observed individually, utilizing a systematic procedure to determine which child would be observed for a given minute. Each child was observed for a one-minute segment of time and then later for another one-minute segment in that situation, in each instance being rated as to whether he appeared to be "happy," "neutral," or "unhappy" over that minute in that situation.

Ratings were made independently by two raters — one familiar with the general thrust of the study and the other ignorant of our aims. While the two raters averaged 97.7% agreement in their characterizations of the transient moods of the children, without exception, when the raters differed, the "ignorant" rater's judgments tended to elevate the happiness estimate of the retardates relative to the normals. While there was a very high degree of agreement, the "knowledgeable" rater tended to become a victim of the "bend over backwards" phenomenon. Thus, if there is a bias in our results, and it is obviously slight, it falls in a direction that would tend to disconfirm our hypotheses rather than confirming them.

Teachers answered: (a) "How would you personally rate this child's intellectual ability?" (much below average, below average, average, above average, much above average); (b) "How would you rate this child's social adjustment?" (extremely disturbed, moderately disturbed, average adjustment, above average adjustment, unusually well adjusted); and (c) "How would you rate this child's general level of happiness?" (always or almost always unhappy, more often unhappy than happy, equal periods or amounts of happiness and unhappiness, more often happy than unhappy, always or almost always happy). Further, they answered yes or no to the following items regarding each child: (a) "sees the bright side of things" and (b) "seems as happy as most children." Parents of the children were asked to answer the same questions.

Results

Study I

Three-way fixed-effects analyses of variance (age × sex × condition of administration) indicated that there was no difference in mode of administration — whether orally administered or self-administered — for any of the dependent variables assessed with a Likert Scale format.

The malformed ss were older than the normals, ranging in age from 12 to 81 with a mean age of 38 versus a range of 14 to 76 and an average of 30 for the normals ($t = 3.57$, $p < .01$). Normals had a higher income level. The lowest income level was occupied by 16%

Table 2.2

INTERCORRELATION MATRIX FOR NORMALS AND HANDICAPPED

Handicapped	Normals												
	1	2	3	4	5	6	7	8	9	10	11	12	13
1. Age		-.15	-.08	-.01	-.07	.16	.05	.06	.18*	.01	-.08	.08	.22**
2. Income level	-.41**		.12	.14	.11	-.07	.17*	.10	.06	φ	.09	-.07	φ
3. Degree of liking of generalized other	-.11	.03		.63**	.54**	.33**	.33**	.30**	.22**	.34**	.36**	.45**	.32**
4. Degree of appraised liking by generalized other	-.20*	.15	.48**		.54**	.49**	.35**	.41**	.22**	.29**	.32**	.36**	.27**
5. Degree of satisfaction with life	-.21*	.34**	.22**	.30**		.50**	.38**	.44**	.28**	.34**	.44**	.43**	.23**
6. Mood (unhappy to happy)	φ	.05	.35**	.31**	.41**		.27**	.34**	.21*	.21*	.24**	.37**	.25**
7. Appraised ease of life	-.08	.10	.07	-.04	.17*	.10		.45**	.31**	.23**	.44**	.27**	.14
8. Expected ease of life	-.05	.12	.02	.03	.46**	.29**	.48**		.25**	.34**	.34**	.29**	.11
9. Whether S had ever contemplated suicide[a]	.20*	-.11	.25**	.11	.11	.15	φ	.12		.30**	.27**	.16	-.22**
10. Whether S had contemplated suicide in past month[a]	.11	-.11	.04	-.05	.21*	.11	-.10	.14	.29**		.30**	.27**	.11
11. How nonfrustrating S found life	.10	φ	.13	.18*	.29**	.14	.09	.32**	.22**	φ		.41**	.12
12. How much S looked forward to next month	-.22**	.03	.25**	.07	.28**	.27**	.26**	.31**	.16	.13	.29**		.18*
13. Claimed value of religion	-.02	-.01	.28**	.27**	φ	.10	-.11	-.20	.22**	.01	.04	.10	

[a] 1 = yes; 2 = no.
* p < .05.
** p < .01.

of the handicapped versus 8% of the normals, while the highest income level was occupied by 35% of the normals versus 12% of the handicapped. For purposes of analysis, the lowest two levels of income were considered low and the highest two levels considered high. Type of deformity (e.g., blind, deaf) was not systematically related to the psychological dimensions of the study.

Happiness of Life. A series of three-way fixed-effects analyses of variance tests (age x income level x sex x presence or absence of handicap) indicated that income was the only statistically significant main effect ($F = 5.27, df = 1/283, p < .03$). The mean for higher social status was 3.17, for lower social status, 2.68. Similar analyses indicated that income level was the only statistically significant main effect regarding degree of looking forward to next month ($F = 6.20; df = 1.283, p < .02$), with those of higher status registering a mean of 3.75 and those of lower status, 3.63. The same series of tests indicated that income level was the only statistically significant main effect in degree of reported life frustration ($F = 3.91, df = 1/283, p < .05$). Lower income status normals averaged 2.78; higher income normals, 3.40; and higher income handicapped, 2.92. Mood over the past half-hour did not differ for handicapped and normals ($X^2 = 2.74; df = 2, ns$). The correlation matrix for normals and handicapped is presented in Table 1.

Difficulty of Life. Analyses of variance indicated that income level ($F = 4.98, df = 1.283, p < .04$) and presence or absence of handicap ($F = 3.99, df = 1/283, p < .05$) were significant main effects. The means for the subsamples were 2.64 for lower income normals, 2.48 for lower income handicapped, 3.18 for higher income normals, and 2.56 for higher income handicapped. Expected difficulty of life traced the same pattern (the analysis outcomes were almost identical; the means were 2.74, 2.05, 3.07, and 2.58, respectively).

Suicide. Frequency of contemplation of suicide was found to be unrelated to sex, age, or income level but was related to presence or absence of handicap. Ninety-eight normals reported never having contemplated suicide, while 54 reported one or more such contemplations. The corresponding figures for the handicapped were 111 and 33 ($X^2 = 5.3$, $df = 1$, $p < .05$). Reported frequency of having contemplated suicide in the past month and number of times that Ss claimed to have attempted suicide in the past five years were unrelated to presence or absence of handicap. Seven of the normals and six of the handicapped reported having contemplated suicide in the past month.

Affect from and toward the Generalized Other and Religiosity. The handicapped claimed to like the generalized other to a greater degree than normals did ($X^2 = 10.4$, $df = 3$, $p < .05$), and females claimed to like the generalized other more than males did ($X^2 = 8.8$, $df = 3$, $p < .05$). The handicapped also claimed to feel more liked by the generalized other ($X^2 = 12.1$, $df = 3$, $p < .01$). Analyses of variance indicated that there were age, sex, racial, and handicapped-normal differences in religiosity. For the normals, claimed importance of religion was positively related to age ($r = .22$, $p < .02$), while females claimed to value religion more than males ($F = 9.21$, $df = 1/263$, $p < .01$), and blacks tended to claim more importance for religion than whites ($f = 3.29$, $df = 1/263$, $p < .10$). For the handicapped, only the sex difference emerged. Religion was claimed to be "very important" to 23 normals versus 41 handicapped, "important" to 67 normals versus 70 handicapped, "of small importance" to 26 versus 25, "unimportant" to 21 versus 6, and "very unimportant" to 14 versus 2. Clearly, the handicapped claimed to value religion more than normals did ($X^2 = 22.3$, $df = 4$, $p < .001$).

Study II

No differences between the 11 handicapped who had had their defect since birth and the 35 who had acquired their defect along any of the dimensions of the study were uncovered. The "mood over the past half-hour" dimension of life satisfaction tended to evidence greater happiness among the handicapped than normals, while tendencies for the handicapped to claim greater affection from and toward the generalized other were also found (all chi-squares associated with these tendencies were less than 2.0). A median test indicated that the handicapped claimed to value religion more ($X^2 = 5.1$, $df = 1$, $p < .03$). One of the normals and one of the handicapped claimed to have attempted suicide in the past five years. Thirteen of the handicapped and 12 of the normals claimed to have contemplated suicide (11 of the handicapped once, 2 of the handicapped twice; for the normals nine had once, two had twice, and one had thrice). None had contemplated suicide in the last month. No statistically significant income level differences along any of the dimensions were uncovered.

Study III

The two independent Os' categorizations were almost statistically identical. The first O's classifications of affect in the academic setting yielded a difference between the male retardates and normals favoring the greater happiness of the former ($X^2 = 8.0, df = 2, p < .02$). The same relationship tended to hold for the recess situation ($X^2 = 4.64, df = 2, p < .10$). The second O characterized the male retardates as more frequently happy in both the academic ($X^2 = 8.26, df = 2, p < .001$) and recess ($X^2 = 8.26, df = 2, p < .001$) situations. No significant differences between the distribution of characterizations within either situation for the females were found.

Teachers responded no to "sees the bright side of things" regarding 7 retarded versus 4 normal males and 12 retarded versus 3 normal females. Parents responded no to the same item regarding 6 retarded versus 7 normal males and 11 retarded versus 6 normal females. Only the difference between the teachers' responses regarding the females was statistically significant ($X^2 = 6.82, df = 1, p < .01$). Teachers responded no to "seems as happy as most children" regarding 5 retarded versus 4 normal boys and 9 retarded versus 6 normal girls. Parental answers ran three versus one and five versus one, respectively.

On the rating scale concerning intelligence, a three-way fixed-effects repeated-measures analysis of variance (retarded versus normal, male versus female, and teacher versus parental ratings) indicated that all three main effects were statistically significant. Normals were rated higher in intelligence than retardates were, males were rated higher than females, and parents rated their child higher than the teachers did. For social adjustment, the main effects of teacher versus parental ratings and retarded versus normal were statistically significant. Normals were rated as more socially adjusted, while parents gave a higher rating to their child than the teachers did. Parents rated their child happier than the teachers did ($F = 7.38, df = 176, p < .01$,) and retardates were rated as happier than normals ($F = 4.38, df = 176, p < .04$), with almost all of the variance contributed by the males.

Discussion

From a commonsense standpoint, appraisals of life satisfaction should be related to degree of frequency of frustration in life, attempts to remove oneself from life (i.e., suicide), general mood, and degree of looking forward to both the immediate and remote future. When a person says that he is frustrated, he is declaring that he *feels* thwarted by conditions as he finds them. Frustration includes both components of personal morale and the difficulty of the objective situation. A person can *be* thwarted in attaining a goal and not become frustrated in the face of considerable adversity. Conversely, a person can become frustrated because of circumstances that would provoke bare notice on the part of most persons. Thus, appraised difficulty of a circumstance ought, all things being equal, to be related to frustration. (In Table 2.2, only the correlation coefficient for normals was statistically significant, although the handicapped Ss' correlation tended in the same direction.) Further, general morale or life satisfaction ought to be related to lack of frustration with life (which held for both normals and handicapped in Table 2.2). Our findings would seem consistent with negative correlations between reported happiness, (a) reported anxiety (Wilson, 1960), and (b) reported worry (Gurin, Veroff, and Feld, 1960).

The general mood of a person ought to be related to his life-satisfaction. Life can be conceptualized as a series of moods. More frequent moods of happiness ought to be associated with more enjoyment of the life process; conversely, more frequent moods of unhappiness ought to be associated with less life-satisfaction. Clearly, for both the normal and handicapped, such was the case (see Table 2.2). Wessman and Ricks (1966) have reported that young adults' affective states correlate with their generalized state of well-being.

The positive correlations between appraised liking of and liking by the generalized other for both the handicapped and normals (see

Table 2.2) echoes one of the strongest findings in the research on correlates of happiness — namely, that happiness had been found to relate to successful involvement with people (Wilson, 1967).

That these happiness-related variables with few exceptions intercorrelated significantly with each other for both samples suggests that (a) the usage of the linguistic system is similar for the two samples; (b) the psychological mechanisms of normals are much like those of the handicapped; and (c) we were assessing the same underlying universe of discourse, namely, life-satisfaction, for both.

In Study I, appraised life-satisfaction was positively related to income level in harmony with major studies of the issue (Bradburn and Caplovitz, 1965; Cameron, 1972; Cantril, 1965; Gurin et al., 1960). Life-satisfaction was unrelated to age, which is consonant with some research (Cameron, 1967, 1972), while others have reported a negative relationship between age and their index of happiness in adult life (Bradburn and Caplovitz, 1965; Gurin et al., 1960). There were no sex differences, a finding noted by most researchers in the area (Wilson, 1967). Income level was the only significant variable related to life-frustration and degree of looking forward to the future, while quality of mood was unrelated to any of the variables under consideration. In Study II, none of the variables, including income level, was found to be related to life-satisfaction, life-frustration, or degree of looking forward to the future, while a tendency for the handicapped to have more affectively pleasant moods was uncovered. Both studies uncovered no evidence of a difference between the handicapped and normals in self-reported life-satisfaction or its linguistic relatives.

In the first study, higher income level was associated with judging one's life as less difficult. Such an appraisal would appear judicious — money often softens life's blows in our culture. The handicapped judged their lives as more difficult and likely to stay that way as compared to normals' judgments. In a society that is built for "normals," in which the operation of machines assumes normality, etc., the appraisals of both the handicapped and the normal appear veridical. In Study II, the lack of difference between the appraisals of the handicapped and normals is most likely accounted for by the small numbers involved. However, while the Detroit handicapped were generally "living in the real world" and thus subject to the raw edge of their defect, the Louisville handicapped generally lived in relatively "shielded" environments. Both of the institutions for the blind were specifically designed for persons with defects of that nature. Possibly interactions with their environment were no more difficult than that of normals.

In the first study, the handicapped and females averaged a higher degree of liking for the generalized other, while the handicapped claimed to feel more liked by the generalized other; the handicapped tended in the same direction in the second study. Other studies using the same scale have reported that females claim a greater degree of liking for the generalized other as compared to males (Cameron, Conrad, Kirkpatrick, and Bateen, 1966; Cameron and Mattson, 1972), while the finding was not replicated in another investigation (Cameron, Frank, Lifter, and Morrisey, 1971). One investigation has reportd that blacks claim to feel liked by the generalized other to a greater degree than whites claim to feel liked (Cameron et al., 1971). That the handicapped, who are lower on the social scale than normals, should share greater liking for the generalized other with females, who likewise possess a lower social status, and also share a greater claimed liking from the generalized other with blacks, who are of lower status, may be significant. Perhaps the socially disadvantaged seek and obtain more interpersonal involvement as a psychological shield against the burden of their position.

Both studies found evidence that the handicapped place more value on religion. Both women and blacks appear to value religion more than men or whites (Cameron, 1969). Social commentators have noted the compensatory value of religion for those occupying an oppressed or inferior social rank for millenia.

There would appear to be three ways to find out about the happiness of a person. He could be asked, which would be the easiest way but it is subject to lack of candor; persons who know him well could be asked, which would result in responses that might be either dishonest or mistaken; and he might be watched, which would result in ratings that might be mistaken and/or based on falsification of typical behavior on the part of the subject. In Study III, the two last methods were employed. Interestingly, the observational results tended to agree with the rating results. The retarded boys' means regarding happiness were higher than the normals' for both parental and teacher ratings. Likewise, the retarded males appeared to be more affectively happy in class and at recess. For the females, retardate versus normal ratings and retardate versus normal affective tone yielded no differences. Of interest, if one compares the female controls' affective tone with the male controls' affective tone in the classroom, the girls were happier (for the two Os, the chi-squares were both over 15.0 and significant at the .001 level). The slight difference between the male and female retardates in class falls in the same direction. For many years the classroom has been characterized as more congenial to the fair sex by educators and noneducators alike. Both males and females, retardate or normal, were happier at recess than in class.

The rating scale results appear reasonable. Parents were more generous in the rating of their children along all three dimensions as compared to teachers. Parents have more psychological investment in their children than teachers, and they could reasonably be expected to regard their child in at least a little better light than a teacher. Yet both parents and teachers agreed that the retardates were less intelligent than normals. Both teachers' and parents' mean rankings of the retardates placed their intelligence at below average. For normals, ratings tended to place them between "average" and "above average" on the scale. Ratings of social adjustment favored the normals to a slight degree. The retardates' average rating fell just below the "average" point, while the normals' fell about the same distance above the "average" point. The crucial variable from the standpoint of the present investigation was the "happiness" scale. Here, both normals' and retardates' averages fell at a point approaching the "more often happy than unhappy" designation. We would regard the statistically higher ratings given to the retardates along this dimension as due to obtaining an unusually happy group of retarded males. Both parents and teachers were able to make apparently veridical judgments regarding the intelligence of their children, and that fact would seem to validate their appraisals of the happiness of the same children.

We began this series of investigations to seek empirical evidence bearing on the issue of whether membership in a fixed social status category affects life-satisfaction. The three studies yielded the same finding: no systematic difference in life-satisfaction between persons who are members of fixed social statuses. The investigation by Gruhn and Krause (1968), which compared the life-satisfaction of 73 handicapped East German high school children with normal controls, reported the same lack of difference. Not finding a difference is not the same thing as establishing that there is no difference. Yet, because our procedures indexed the difference in happiness between persons of varying incomes in our social system, and the intercorrelations and tendencies within each study generally corresponded with what is known to be true of life-satisfaction, the lack of difference between the persons of fixed social categories appears to reflect "the way things are." That handicapped persons more frequently judged and reported their lives as more difficult lends credibility to their reports of life-satisfaction.

A person's appraised happiness is the resultant of two factors. First, he must take into account his current position in the social status matrix. Within this matrix there appear to be two kinds of statuses: those that are fixed and those that are flexible. While no status is immutably fixed (there have been periods in man's history when race was apparently not a status-conferring attribute), it would appear that sex, generation, race, and presence or absence of handicap constitute attributes that result in categorization in fixed statuses at the present time. Employment status, marital status, and wealth appear to constitute attributes that locate one along flexible status dimensions. While one cannot change his class within fixed-status dimensions (sex-change operations not withstanding), a person can change his class within flexible dimensions. Second, he must consider the events of his personal life history. How "things have been going" recently affect a person's judgment of contemporary happiness. These two factors — membership in social classes and personal life history — are probably not equally weighted in arriving at an appraisal of life satisfaction. One's fixed social statuses are probably "ground," while one's recent life history (which would, of course, include much regarding success along flexible dimensions are "figure" in the calculation. Fixed social-class memberships must be "lived with." One of the major achievements of persons in any society is wresting happiness from "the way things are." A person can aspire to change his class along the "flexible" dimensions, but if he is to successfully function he must first learn to accept his fixed statuses and work out his salvation within them.

If we accept that the social statuses of women, blacks, and the handicapped have sufficient psychological buttressing in the social consciousness to be considered "fixed social statuses," then we would expect the generalized woman, or generalized black, or generalized handicapped person to appraise his happiness as being at about the same level as any other class of generalized other. That is, he will essentially "ignore" his fixed-class liabilities or assets in his appraisal of life satisfaction.

Exceptions to this rule should occur only when persons comprising some class feel that their potential for happiness or what "could be" is being unjustly or unreasonably thwarted by some outside-themselves agency. As long as this class of persons does not believe that its potential is being unjustly or unreasonably crimped, the "objective" social situation could be expected to have no effect on the class' appraisals of happiness, even if, in fact, it were being unjustly or unreasonably discriminated against. Likewise, if a class of persons believes that it is being discriminated against unfairly, even if the "objective" social situation is not unfairly or unreasonably discriminatory, we can expect the class to feel less happy. Most handicapped persons appear to believe that their handicap rends them less socially useful, and therefore discrimination is acceptable. Those of lower wealth in our social system appear less satisfied with existence, and as such, they may be only a few psychological steps away from dramatic intrusion into social functioning.

REFERENCES

Bradburn, N. M. and Caplovitz, D. *Reports on happiness*. Chicago: Aldine, 1965.

Cameron, P. Ego strength and happiness of the aged. *Journal of Gerontology*, 1967, *22*, 199-202.

Cameron, P. Valued aspects of religion to Negroes and whites. *Proceedings of the Seventy-Seventh Annual Convention of the American Psychological Association*, 1969, *5*, 741-742. (Summary)

Cameron, P. The generation gap: Which generation is believed to have the most fun and happiness and how do the generations rate themselves on desire for fun and happiness? *The Gerontologist*, 1972, *12*, 120-190.

Cameron, P., Conrad, C., Kirkpatrick, D. D. and Bateen, R. J. Pet ownership and sex as determinants of stated affect toward others and estimates of others' regard of self. *Psychological Reports*, 1966, *19*, 884-886.

Cameron, P., Frank F. D., Lifter, M. L. and Morrisey, P. *Personality differences between typical urban Negroes and whites. Journal of Negro Education*, 1971, *40*, 66-75.

Cameron, P., and Mattson, M. Psychological correlates of pet ownership. *Psychological Reports*, 1972, *30*, 286.

Cameron, P., Van Hoeck, D., Weiss, N. and Kostin, M. Happiness or life satisfaction of the malformed. *Proceedings of the Seventy-Ninth Annual Convention of the American Psychological Association*, 1971, *6*, 641-642. (Summary)

Cantril, H. *The pattern of human concerns*. New Brunswick, N. J.: Rutgers University Press, 1965.

Gruhn, H. and Krause, S. Zum Sozialverhalten Korperlick auffallinger Kinder und Jugenlicher. *Probleme und Ergebnisse der Psychologie*, 1968, *23*, 73-86.

Gurin, G., Veroff, J. and Feld, S. *Americans view their mental health*. Ann Arbor: University of Michigan Survey Research Center, 1960.

Ossorio, P. G. *Persons*. Los Angeles, Calif.: Linguistic Research Institute, 1966.

Titley, R. W. Imaginations about the disabled. *Social Science and Medicine*, 1969, *3*, 29-38.

Wessman, A. E. and Ricks, D. F. *Mood and personality*. New York: Holt, Rinehart and Winston, 1966.

Wilson, W. R. An attempt to determine some correlates and dimensions of hedonic tone. Unpublished doctoral dissertation, Northwestern University, 1960.

Wilson, W. R. Correlates of avowed happiness. *Psychological Bulletin*, 1967, *67*, 294-306.

MOOD AS AN INDICANT OF HAPPINESS: AGE, SEX, SOCIAL CLASS, AND SITUATIONAL DIFFERENCES

What is the "happiest time of life?" Professional and lay stereotypes saddle the old with the least happiness (Cameron, 1972). Various investigations have been construed as supporting the stereotype while other research has been interpreted as demonstrating that happiness is invariant across the life-span.

Affectivity is an important component in the calculation of a person's happiness (of life-satisfaction). In ordinary discourse, affectivity is a continuum with mood anchoring one and emotion the other end. Persons, at all waking moments, are in an affective state. While not continually experiencing an emotion, persons are always experiencing a mood which locates somewhere along the pleasant-unpleasant continuum.

Affectivity bears a unique relationship to life-satisfaction. While both life-satisfaction and the state of a person's affect are subsets of the concept "attitude" (Ossorio, 1966), the conceptual linkage between them is considerably closer than between either and any other attitude. Although life-satisfaction is related to other states, one's typical state of affectivity is involved in appraisal of life-satisfaction more than any other state.

Emotions affect life-satisfaction. "Triumph" and "joy" would be expected to contribute toward elevating while "melancholy" and "sorrow" would contribute toward depressing life-satisfaction. But the effect of an emotion upon life-satisfaction is modified by the mood the person had or was in when the event that precipitated the emotion occurred, even as an emotion affects the quality of mood one finds oneself in. Mood is the underlay or stage upon which emotions play. A "good mood" can "cancel out" the psychological force of an unpleasant event of modest import while a "bad mood" can magnify the psychological impact of an unpleasant event to some degree. While both mood and emotion contribute to a person's affective state, mood, because of its constancy, plays the most influential role in setting his affective tone.

Thus an important component of happiness is the proportion of pleasant as opposed to unpleasant moods in a person's life. A person or class of persons (as females, old people) who experience greater life-satisfaction than another, would generally be expected either to be more frequently in (or experience more intense) pleasant moods and/or less frequently in (or experience less intense) unpleasant moods than the other. Considerations other than mood-tone can evaluate or depress a person's life-satisfaction (statuses, successes/failures, and emotions also enter in; see Cameron, Titus, Kostin, and Kostin, 1973). However, generally for persons, and especially for classes of persons, mood is most directly related to life-satisfaction.

We judge the pleasantness of situations from the distribution of kinds of affective displays that persons evidence in them. Weddings are "happy" events in large measure because the persons occupying that situation display (and presumably would report) pleasant affect. Death-row is an "unhappy" situation because the persons inhabiting that situation display unpleasant affect to a greater degree than persons-in-general across situations. Similarly, a "happy" person is one that displays more than the typical amount of pleasant affective state relative to the amount of pleasant affect usually displayed by persons occupying his situation and/or engaged in his type of activities (one could be a "happy" or morose executioner). This "general rule" is, of course, at times rendered inappropriate by the person who "fakes" pleasant affect indiscriminately and by others who through various philosophical/ psychological commitments (as stoicism) learn to adjust their "happiness" to more modest (or immodest) frequencies of positive affect. Due to the general rule, however, it is sensible to inquire as to whether a person, a sex, a generation, or a situation is "happier" or more pleasant than another.

Application of the general rule is difficult as so many considerations need to be taken into account to arrive at the calculation of life-satisfaction for a class of persons (as males), and somewhat less difficult when applied to a person. While we often have or can arrange to have enough contact with a person in enough different situations and/or activities to judge his happiness from his moods, it is considerably more difficult to systematically gather evidence as to a sex's or generation's happiness from their moods. While many members of the linguistic community undoubtedly know how to go about determining, say, the happiness of the generations from examination of their moods in various situations, "time and effort" act as formidable barriers to such an undertaking. This paper reports the first large-scale *in vivo* (as opposed to retrospective account) assessment of mood as a function of age, sex, social class, and situation.

Some of the questions such an inquiry can shed light upon include "are women more affective than men" and "is the time spent at work less pleasant than time spent elsewhere?" As emotions interact with mood, if women are more emotional than men, this emotionality might well be expected to generate one or more of the following:

(a) women's mood fluctuates more than men's,
(b) women experience more happy/pleasant moods than men,
(c) women experience more unhappy/unpleasant moods than men, and
(d) women's moods are more intense than men's.

A cross-sectional *in vivo* sample of moods can bear upon "b", "c", and "d" while a longitudinal *in vivo* sample would be required to address "a." As one of the more consistent empirical findings is the lack of a sex difference in life-satisfaction (Wilson, 1967), if women were found to experience more frequent happy/pleasant moods, then they ought also to experience more frequent unhappy/ unpleasant moods (or perhaps more intense unpleasant moods, or less intense pleasant moods) to "balance out" their affect relative to men's. At least since Marx (1846, cited in Fromm, 1961), the work situation has been decried for its supposed lack of charm in capitalist society. If the work situation is less pleasant than other common situations, one ought to find either: (a) a higher frequency of unhappy moods, and/or (b) a lower frequency of happy moods, andor (c) a greater intensity of unhappy moods, and/or a lower intensity of happy moods at work than in situations-in-general. Similarly, as those of higher social status have consistently reported greater life-satisfaction than those of lower social status (Wilson, 1967), we would expect persons of higher status to report more frequent pleasant/happy moods (or more intense pleasant moods) and/or less frequent unhappy/unpleasant moods (or less intensity of same) than persons of lower status. A cross-sectional *in vivo* assessment of moods can bear upon all of these possibilities.

Method

Five separate studies involving 6707 respondents were performed. All but the third study utilized an identical item "how would you characterize your mood of the last half hour? (happy, neutral, sad)." In the first two studies, if he were happy or sad the subject was additionally asked "how intense was your mood over the last half hour? (very, moderately, somewhat, barely)." The third study, conducted over 10 weeks of an introductory psychology class, utilized the item changed to "your mood or impulse of the last instant." All at-home interviews were conducted as part of strict area samples, at-school interviews via systematically-selected classes from participating schools, at-work interviews via a total convenience sample of persons who happened to work where interviewers did, while at-leisure-recreation samples were gotten via interviewing every k^{TH} person in a systematically-chosen situation. Time-of-day was controlled-for by conducting a third of the interviews in the morning, a third in the afternoon, and a third in the evening (8 a.m. through 8 p.m.); however the at-work sample was *ad lib* and the at-school samples were drawn across the school day. Table 2.3 summarizes the locations and characteristics of the studies. About half of the sample in each study was female; rejection rates for the studies ranged from 1% (for the first study) to 11% (for the fourth); the first study was conducted in 1966 the last in 1972. In the third (college student) study, subjects were addition-ally asked: (a) were you mainly thinking about satisfying your own or another's interests? (b) were you thinking about: (1) how others were regarding/evaluating you? (2) religion? (3) sex? (4) the past, present, or future? (c) (if thinking about a person) was he your or the opposite sex? (d) how or to what degree were your thoughts tied to the situation at hand? (completely [about the class, or classmates, etc.], remotely [about school or schooling], unrelated [unrelated to any consideration of the class, the topics of the class, etc.]) and (e) to complete the Cameron Religious Dimensions, the Barron Ego-Strength, and Eysenck Personality Scales. In the fifth study, subjects were classified as higher status if the head of the household was a professional, bourgeois, or person of some au-thority (i.e., foreman, police chief) and lower status if other (i.e., factory operative, clerk).

Results

We found no systematic time-of-day, locational, or religious differences along the dimension of mood. Therefore the life-span results are presented by age-groups (after Cameron, 1969) in Table 2.4 In the last two rows of Table 2.4, the average percentage across situations is presented (i.e., $\frac{\Sigma \%}{M}$). With the possible exception of the 4- to 7-year-olds, inspection of Table 2.4 reveals no age differences in frequency of pleasant or unpleasant mood. A sex difference appears, however. If we regard the frequency of each sex's neutrality within each of the four situations (i.e., school, work, home, leisure) within each of the 10 age-groupings as a test of affectivity, in 24 of 35 untied comparisons, the male frequency of reporting neutrality of mood was higher (sign test $p < .05$). If male and female responses across situations are summed separately for comparison, males averaged 43% happy-pleasant, 49% neutral, and 8% unhappy-unpleasant, while females averaged 46% happy, 44% neutral and 10% unhappy (X^2 corrected for continuity = 12.34; $df = 2$; $p < .01$).

Situationally, if we regard each cell formed by the ten ages and two sexes as 20 tests of affect-in-situation, we note that in 17 of 20 instances, the highest frequency of happy mood occurred at leisure (combinatorial $p < .001$), while 12 of the lowest frequencies of unhappiness were reported at leisure (combinatorial $p < .02$). There was little to choose between the other (school, work, home) situations. Happy-pleasant mood predominated over unhappy-unpleasant mood in a ratio of about 5:1.

The affective tone displayed by the higher and lower social classes in the fifth study is presented by situation and sex in Table 2.5. Usual X^2 analyses ($2\,df$) for the four comparisons between the social classes yield values of 3.79 (NS) for higher and lower social class males at leisure, 4.33 (NS) for females at leisure, 1.02 (NS) for males at nonleisure, and 3.91 (NS) for females at nonleisure. Since higher-status persons have been demonstrated to show higher life-satisfaction than lower-status persons (Wilson, 1967), they ought, on theoretical grounds, to be expected to experience more frequent happy and/or less frequent unhappy mood than lower-status persons. It thus is reasonable to look at the observed distribution of upper-status subject's mood as the *expected* distribution of the mood of lower-status subjects. Since a relatively large N is necessary to constitute such an expected distribution, the four subgroups in Table 2.5 were combined and chi-square was calculated for the observed mood distribution of lower-status subjects, using the mood distribution of upper-status subjects as the theoretical distribution. This resulted in a chi-square value of 22.78, which, with 2 df, is significant at the .001 level. Those of lower status reported less pleasant affect than those of higher social status.

Table 2.3. Characteristics of the Five Studies.

Study	Location	Type of Sample	Type of Subjects	n and Settings	Mood of	Other Measurements
1	Boulder, CO	area	adults 18-40; over 59	320 at home	last half hour and intensity	contents of consciousness; various personality scales
2	Menomonie, WI	area; random schoolrooms; every kth person in sit.	aged 4 – 21	510 at school; 133 at home; 49 at church; 25 lover's lane; 52 recreation	last half hour and intensity	contents of consciousness
3	Detroit	convenience	college students	187 in class	last instant (21 times each)	contents of consciousness; various personality scales
4	Los Angeles, Louisville, Evansville, Detroit, Denver	area; every kth person in sit., all in-sit., convenience	aged 7 – 103	1721 at home; 1438 at work; 742 at leisure; 477 at school	last half hour	contents of consciousness
5	Glenwood Springs; near San Francisco	area; every kth person in situation	aged 8 – 97	462 at home; 391 at leisure; 13 at work; 18 at school	last half hour	contents of consciousness; occupation of head of household

Table 2.4. Moods: By Age and Situation.

Age	4-7			8-11			12,13			14,15			16,17			18-25			26-39			40-55			56-64			65+		
Mood [a]	H	N	U	H	N	U	H	N	U	H	N	U	H	N	U	H	N	U	H	N	U	H	N	U	H	N	U	H	N	U
At school																														
Male n	19	5	∅	71	67	12	40	54	4	39	42	1	17	29	1															
Male %	79	21	∅	47	45	8	41	55	4	48	51	1	33	56	1															
Female n	37	1	∅	59	67	10	49	59	9	32	28	5	22	22	5															
Female %	98	∅	3	43	49	7	42	50	8	49	43	8	46	41	8															
At home																														
Male n	6	1	2	16	5	2	9	11	1	8	6	1	6	9	2	110	141	20	102	104	24	91	112	24	[c]	[c]	[c]	14	5	[c]
Male %	67	11	22	70	22	9	43	52	5	53	40	7	35	53	12	41	52	7	44	45	10	41[b]	49[b]	11[b]	[c]	[c]	[c]	51	11	[c]
Female n	9	3	2	24	13	1	9	9	4	6	3	3	10	6	6	147	160	41	130	176	26	128	131	26	32	43	15	41	41	10
Female %	64	21	14	63	34	3	41	41	18	50	25	25	46	27	27	42	46	12	39	53	8	45[b]	46[b]	8[b]	36	48	15	45	45	10
At work																														
Male n													2	2	∅	87	98	∅	84	159	36	69	101	15	13	22	10	2	3	1
Male %													50	50	∅	39	44	∅	33	62	16	38	55	6	36	61	6	33	50	17
Female n													6	6	2	108	98	14	49	53	14	42	67	8	7	12	∅	2	6	∅
Female %													43	43	14	45	40	7	42	45	13	36	57	7	37	63	∅	25	75	∅
At leisure																														
Male n	1	∅	∅	13	12	1	13	9	6	12	11	2	32	24	2	94	95	5	46	34	7	32	21	7	5	2	5	8	7	∅
Male %	100	∅	∅	47	52	4	47	32	21	48	44	8	53	39	8	46	47	8	53	39	8	55	36	10	72	28	9	53	47	∅
Female n	4	∅	∅	22	12	3	13	12	∅	17	14	4	34	21	4	102	76	8	71	41	6	28	17	5	8	2	∅	10	6	2
Female %	100	∅	∅	47	47	6	52	48	∅	49	40	11	54	33	11	53	40	10	41	36	5	56	34	10	80	20	∅	56	33	11
Overall average of moods across situations																														
Male %	82	11	7	54	40	7	44	46	10	50	48	5	43	50	8	36	57	7	43	49	8	45	47	8	48	49	3	43	49	8
Female %	87	7	6	51	43	5	45	50	9	49	39	15	47	38	17	46	45	8	47	44	9	46	46	9	51	44	6	42	51	7

[a] Moods: H = Happy; N = Neutral; U = Unhappy.   [b] younger adults (aged 18 to 40).   [c] older adults (aged over 59).

Table 2.6. (Study 5)—Higher and Lower Socioeconomic Groups' Affect by Sex and Situation.

Situation		Males Happy	Males Neutral	Males Unhappy	Females Happy	Females Neutral	Females Unhappy	Males Happy	Males Neutral	Males Unhappy	Females Happy	Females Neutral	Females Unhappy
Higher class	N	47	19	5	54	33	4	28	30	8	41	24	9
	%	66	27	7	59	36	4	42	45	12	55	32	12
Lower class	N	98	77	13	92	91	15	41	34	8	67	75	20
	%	52	41	7	46	46	8	49	41	10	41	46	12

Table 4. (Study 2)—Intensity of Last Half Hour's Affect.

Affect Degree of Affect		Happy Barely	Happy Somewhat	Happy Moderately	Happy Very	Unhappy Barely	Unhappy Somewhat	Unhappy Moderately	Unhappy Very
Children, Teen-Agers	N	11	134	111	193	14	23	12	18
	%	2	30	25	43	21	34	18	26
Adults	N	2	23	81	35	2	8	10	7
	%	1	16	57	25	7	30	37	26

Table 2.7. (Study 3)—Correlations Between Frequency of Happy, Neutral, and Unhappy Mood In-Class and Other Variables.

Frequency of Thinking	Thinking About Religion	Thinking About Sex	Thinking About Others	Thinking About the Opposite Sex	Self-Serving Orientation	Other-Serving Orientation	Barron Ego-Strength Scale	Eysenck Neuroticism Scale
Happy	.05	.29***	.19*	.49***	.15*	-.06	-.08	-.09
Neutral	-.09	-.21**	.05	-.31***	-.14	.22**	.02	.05
Unhappy	.22**	.15*	.04	.04	.17*	.03	-.04	.16*

	Cameron Religious Proclivity Scale	Thinking About the Past	Thinking About the Present	Thinking About the Future	Thoughts Situationally Tied	Moderately Tied	Untied	Happy Mood	Unhappy Mood
Happy	-.17*	.17*	-.22**	.11	-.23**	.17*	.12	-.41***	-.35***
Neutral	.03	-.27***	.32***	-.24**	.05	-.27***	.03	.01	
Unhappy	.08	.05	-.09	.19*	-.06	.15*	-.07		

*p<.05. **p<.01. ***p<.001.

Intensity of affect for the subjects in the first two studies is reported in Table 2.5. For our sample of children and teenagers, happy mood was reported as more intense than unhappy mood ($X^2 = 34.3$; $df = 3$; $p < .001$). The intensity of adult unhappy mood did not differ from the children's ($X^2 = 2.7$; $df = 3$; NS), while children reported more intensity of happy mood than adults ($X^2 = 45.5$, $df = 3$; $p < .001$). Adults of both sexes and all age levels reported a median of "moderate intensity" for pleasant and unpleasant moods.

The correlations between frequency of happy, neutral, and unhappy mood in-class and the other variables in Study 3 are reported in Table 2.7. Religious proclivity negatively correlated with frequency of happy mood, the Barron Ego-Strength Scale, was uncorrelated with frequency of kind of mood, while the Eysenck Neuroticism Scale score was related to frequency of neutral mood, while both frequency of pleasant and unpleasant mood were related to frequency of contemplation of the past and future. Frequency of pleasant and unpleasant mood was related to thinking about other than the situation at hand. Frequency of thinking about religion was related to frequency of unhappy mood; frequency of thinking about sex to frequency of both happy and unhappy mood and negatively related to frequency of neutral mood. Frequency of thinking both about others and the opposite-sex-other was positively related to frequency of happy mood, while frequency of a self-serving orientation or attitude was related both to frequencies of happy and unhappy mood. Frequency of happy and frequency of unhappy mood were unrelated, but frequency of both was negatively related to frequency of neutral mood.

Marital Status and Race

For Study 4, 11% of our respondents were black. "Happy" mood was reported by 41% of whites vs. 33% of blacks, "neutral" mood by 50% of whites vs. 60% of blacks and "unhappy" by 10% of whites vs. 7% of blacks. No race difference in over-all affective tone was indicated ($X^2 = 3.2$; $df = 2$; NS); however, blacks less frequently than whites indicated nonneutral mood ($X^2 = 9.1$; $df = 1$; $p < .001$).

Marital status tended to be differentially associated with kind of mood. Application of the X^2 statistic revealed no statistically significant difference between the distribution of mood of the married/unmarried/divorced - separated - widowed. However, if Bradburn's (1969) uggestion of computing an affective "balance" is approximated with our data by subtracting percentage of unpleasant mood from percentage of pleasant mood for whites and blacks separately for Studies 4 and 5, then the data indicates that the married were "happiest" and the divorced-separated-widowed least "happy" for all but one of the four comparisons (combinatorial $p < .001$ for whites in Study 4 the differences were 33, 30, and 29 for married, unmarried, divorced, etc.; in Study 5 they were 45, 45, 23; for blacks in Study 4 the differences were 29, 28, 0 and in Study 5, 25, 17, and 0).

Discussion

Are the old less happy than the young adults? If the conclusions of the authors of two large-scale studies are accepted, the answer is "yes" (Bradburn and Caplovitz, 1965; Gurin, Veroff, and Feld, 1960). These studies and their conclusions are widely cited and highly regarded across the social sciences (Wilson [1967] points to them as models of research). Clearly their conclusions are at variance with our results which suggest that there is no age difference in generalized happiness as indexed by mood.

Examination of the Gurin et al. and Bradburn and Caplovitz studies suggests that inadequacies of analysis led to their conclusions. In both efforts univariate analyses yielded the following: (a) age negatively correlated with reported happiness, (b) income level correlated with happiness, and (c) educational level correlated with happiness. An age by income by educational level multivariate analysis would therefore have been in order. Gurin et al. refer to a 2-variate (2 levels of income by 3 levels of education) in a tabular supplement not included in the book that indicated education is associated with greater happiness with income controlled. As the average generational educational level has risen with the years, even this conclusion might have been seriously tempered had age been simultaneously controlled. The *only* 3-variate analysis reported or referred to is presented by Bradburn and Capolvitz (3 levels of age by 2 levels of income by 2 levels of education). For the higher level of income, the median value for the two levels of education reporting that they were "not too happy" ran 9.5% for those under the age of 40, 9% for those 40 to 59, and 8% for those 60 or over. For the lower-income level, the corresponding medians ran 13.5%, 22.5% and 26% (neither of the other two responses to their "general happiness" question is reported or referred to — presumably inclusion would not have appreciably affected the results). Further, while the majority of those less than age 60 had higher education and higher income in the rating scheme, 76% of those 60 or older had lower education and lower income. While neither set of investigators reported further multivariate analyses of these demographic variables, it appears likely that income, and possibly to a considerably lesser degree, education accounted for all of the age differences. The two recent large-sample studies of reported happiness in which age and social status were included in a multivariate analysis found substantial social class, but no age differences (Bradburn, 1969; Cameron, 1972). Further analysis of the Gurin et al. and Bradburn and Caplovitz data would appear in order especially in light of Bradburn's claim (1969) that even though the 3-variate analyses eliminated age as an independent variable affecting happiness in his latest study, the Bradburn and Caplovitz effort, even with income and education controlled showed " . . . some independent negative effects of age on psychological well-being among persons over sixty-five."

Investigation of the stereotypes that the general population holds regarding happiness and age has indicated that adults of all ages, of both sexes, and varied social class believe that the old is the least happy generation (Cameron, 1972). This stereotypic belief, combined with attitudes of antipathy toward the old, prepares members of our society to accept biased statements about the old as long as they are derogatory. For instance,

> . . . younger people have their futures ahead of them and feel they have higher stakes in life. . . . their aspirations and expectations are higher. Older people, conversely, have their lives largely behind them; they are unhappier . . . (Gurin et al., 1960).

Here a truism, younger persons have more future, is coupled with an apparent stereotype regarding which generation is more desirous of life.

> . . . [O]lder people . . . have achieved acceptance of themselves .
> . . But this achievement occurs at the cost of resignation and
> apathy, and lower happiness and gratification. . . . That older
> people tend to be less happy is not surprising — in a period of
> decline and growing limitation of gratification, we would ex-
> pect to find less happiness (Gurin et al., 1960).

Even when their own results suggest that the old might be happier
or better-adjusted, a depreciating reason is generated to explain the
outcome. " . . .[O]lder people show some tendency to worry less
than younger people. These . . . findings may be viewed as a
reflection of lower aspiration, withdrawal, or resignation" (Gurin et
al. 1960). Such "explanations" do not necessarily follow from any
results that the investigators generated; instead appeal is made to a
kind of "common knowledge." While speculative, it is not difficult
to imagine that such attitudes contribute to the apparently more
frequent "administrative termination" of the lives of old people in
hospital (Cameron, 1973).

When investigators talk about two variables being correlated in a
casual sense, they necessarily imply "all other things being equal"
(Ossorio, 1966). The old may, in fact, be less happy as a class, but
this does not warrant saying that age and happiness are negatively
correlated unless other significant variables have been controlled.
It is one thing to empirically determine that the old persons in a
given social system are less happy than younger persons and quite
another to claim that age *per se* is the important variable. If old
persons were, on the average, less economically well-off than
younger people, one would have to control for this economic
difference and still find a negative relationship to begin to arrive at a
conclusion of an intrinsic relationship between age and happiness.
Investigators who uncover an empirical relationship and then assume casual correlations might well be suspected of undue haste.

An investigation bearing on generational happiness was reported
by Cantril in 1965. A total of 18,653 persons residing in 14 counties
was interviewed regarding a number of variables. The question
with most bearing on happiness was preceded by two questions
concerning what the person wanted in order to be happy and what

would make him unhappy. Then the subject was shown a ladder and asked.

> . . . the top of the ladder represents the best possible life for you and the bottom represents the worst possible life for you. Where on the ladder do you feel you personally stand at this time?

This item taps more than the conceptual domain "happiness," including components of achievement, fortune, and adjustment to circumstances. However, it assesses the "happiness" domain in large measure. In his overall summary, Cantril summarizes the position on the ladder into which persons of various ages fell. For those aged 29 or less, the frequency of those who gave themselves a low rating on the ladder was 28%, for those 30 to 49 it was 29%, and for those 50 and over 25%. The percentage of those who gave a high rating to themselves for the corresponding groups was 24, 22, and 29. Age differences were small, and, if anything, tended to favor the happiness of older subjects. The United States of America sample was additionally asked about life-satisfaction *per se*. Cantril alludes to analyses that indicated that the results of this item essentially parallel those obtained with the ladder question with estimates varying little by age, but considerably and positively with economic status.

In a questionnaire study of 385 handicapped and normal persons ranging in age from 12 to 81 in which they were asked to characterize their life as being "just great," "more than satisfactory," "satisfactory," "less than satisfactory," or "just miserable," no age or sex, but the usual social-class differences in degree of satisfaction were found (Cameron et al., 1973). Additional items inquiring into contemplations of suicide, amount of frustration, and degree of looking forward to the future were generally unrelated to age but evidenced social-class differences.

Taken together, the empirical literature would seem most satisfactorily construed as suggesting no casual relationship between life-satisfaction or happiness and age *per se*. Each of the larger studies that has come to a differing conclusion appears deficient in some important respect so that its results do not contradict compellingly the notion that age and happiness are unrelated. All of the above investigators agree that social class is positively related to life-satisfaction and it would appear that economic variables account for the lion's share of demographic differences.

Affectivity: Age, Sex, Race, Marital Status, and Social Class

Some (e.g., Hurlock, 1967) have suggested that preadolescents and early adolescents are more emotional than either children or persons in their late teens. "Common opinion" appears to regard children and teenagers as more emotional than adults. Our results (Table 2.6) suggest that the proportion of pleasant-neutral-unpleasant moods does not vary systematically by age after early childhood. However, the intensity claimed by children and teenagers for pleasant mood was greater than that claimed by adults. Hurlock's suggestion gains no support from our results, while "common opinion" receives the limited support of the intensity-difference. Inspection of Table 2.4 suggests that at about the age 12 or 13 the "typical" adult pattern of reporting approximately equally frequent pleasant and neutral mood emerges.

Our results provide support for the notion that females in our culture are more emotional than males. While we found no evidence that female moods are more intense than male's, we did find that nonneutral moods were more often reported by females. In harmony with expectations that greater affectivity by females ought to display itself on both ends of the affective continuum to "balance out" to a functional equivalency for males and females, females reported both more frequent pleasant and unpleasant moods than males. Our results suggest that, while a sex difference in affectivity does exist, it is modest.

Mood differences across situations were examined by kind (i.e., pleasant/neutral/unpleasant) of mood while intensity of and changeability of mood in-situation was not indexed. The Marxist-related situation was not indexed. The Marxist-related contention that the job is a particularly uncharming place received no support from our investigation. Being "at leisure" was associated with more charm than being elsewhere but the "elsewheres" failed to differ from each other in affective tone.

Stereotypically, blacks are "known" for their emotionality at religious meetings and attraction for "action" kinds of entertainment. The lower affectivity we found for the blacks of our sample is at variance with this stereotype. While our sample of blacks was modest, and we are dealing with verbal report, when we applied the "balancing" computation to married, single, and divorced/separated blacks, the pattern was the same as for whites and in harmony with the same bulk of research on marital state life-satisfaction differences. Further research is indicated.

Almost all research has indicated that, other things being equal, married people report greater life-satisfaction than single people, who in turn report greater happiness than the divorced/separated/widowed (Bradburn, 1969). Our results for kind of mood tended to fall in the same direction. As "half an hour's worth" of mood is only a small component of life-satisfaction, probably we would be expecting too much of mood to find the same pattern with such a limited sample of people. As we did not index intensity or changeability of mood, future research might well proceed along these lines.

The question of the typical affective state of persons in our culture was addressed by Flugel in 1925. Nine adults cooperated for 30 days, going through their everyday activities while keeping a record of their mood, hopefully recording within the hour after each change of mood. Among the results that he reported was the finding that, overall, 50% of the moods were characterized as pleasureable, 28% as neutral, and 22% as displeasurable. Our overall results suggest that about 45% of half-hour moods are pleasant, 47% neutral, and 9% unpleasant. Both studies agree that there are more pleasant than unpleasant moods. In Flugel's study, the ratio was about 2½:1, while in the present it was about 5:1. From a linguistic standpoint, it would seem that neutral moods would almost have to be more frequent than either happy or unhappy moods. "Happy" and "unhappy" are the ends of a continuum which necessarily contrast with the middle and each other. "Happy" would lose its communicative value if it dominated reported mood. From this standpoint, our results regarding relative frequency of mood would appear to be closer to the "true" values than Flugel's, but our frequency of "pleasant" is probably still too large.

While Bradburn (1969) reported a lack of correlation between frequency of incidence of pleasant and unpleasant affect, his results' dependency on retrospective accounts (into which memory and attention enter heavily) contrasts unfavorably with our *in vivo* procedure. Carried out *in vivo*, at least one can contend that people claim to feel *X;* carried out retrospectively one can only contend that if people noticed, and now remember, they claim *X* occurred.

Frequency of happy mood was negatively-related to religious proclivity, while frequency of thinking about religion was positively correlated with frequency of moods of unhappiness (Table 2.7). While quite modest, these correlations fall in a direction opposite to the usual positive relationship between religiosity and life-satisfaction (Wilson, 1967). Cantril (1965) for instance, reported a .18 correlation between life-satisfaction and the claimed importance of religion. Cameron et al. (1973) reported a correlation of .23 between the same variables. The Eysenck Neuroticism Scale was negatively correlated with frequency of happy moods, as one might well expect of a neuroticism scale. However, the Barron Ego-Strength Scale was not correlated with frequencies of mood, even though it and the Eysenck appear to be tapping the same general personality domain and employ the same "yes/no" pencil and paper technique.

Sex appears to both warm and chill the hearts of college students (Table 2.7) The frequency of both happy and unhappy moods was related to the infrequency of thinking about sex. The same mixture obtained with frequency of thinking about the self or the contemplation of what others thought about one. Last, it appears that affectivity was related to thinking about something other than class and classroom activities — an unpleasant note on which to end for a teacher.

REFERENCES

Bradburn, N. M. *The structure of psychological well-being*. Chicago: Aldine, 1969.

Bradburn, N. M. and Caplovitz, D. *Reports on happiness*. Chicago: Aldine, 2965.

Cameron, P. Age parameters of young adult, middle-aged, old and aged. Journal of Gerontology, 1969, *24*, 201-202.

Cameron, P. The generation gap: Which generation is believed to have the most fun and happiness and how do the generations rate themselves on desire for fun and happiness? *Gerontologist*, 1972, *12*, 120-123.

Cameron, P. Marxian theory vis-a-vis suicide and convenience killing. Paper presented at Midwestern Psychological Association meeting, Chicago, 1973.

Cameron, P., Titus, D., Kostin, J. and Kostin, M. The life-satisfaction of nonnormal persons. *Journal of Consulting Psychology*, 1973, *41*, 207-214.

Cantril, H. *The pattern of human concerns*. Rutgers University Press, New Brunswick, New Jersey, 1965.

Flugel, J. C. A quantitative study of feelings and emotion in everyday life. *British Journal of Psychology*, 1925, *15*, 318-355.

Gurin, G., Veroff, J. and Feld, S. *Americans view their mental health*. Ann Arbor: University of Michigan Survey Research Center, 1960.

Hurlock, E. *Adolescent development*. New York: McGraw-Hill, 1967.

Marx, K. *Economic and philosophic essays of 1846*. In E. Fromm, *Marx's concept of man*. New York: Ungar, 1961.

Ossorio, P. G. *Persons*. Los Angelex: Linguistic Research Institute, 1966.

Wilson, W. Correlates of avowed happiness. *Psychologial Bulletin*, 1967, *67*, 294-306.

EMOTIONALITY ACROSS THE LIFE-SPAN

Affectivity as a function of age has received modest attention in the life-span literature. Some (Dean, 1962; Friedman and Granick, 1963) have argued that affectivity declines with age, others that it increases with age (e.g., Linden and Courtney, 1953). Rounding out the possibilities, an argument for invariancy of affect across the life-span has been forwarded (Schuster, 1952).

Some, usually speaking from the psychoanalytic orientation, reify affectivity, placing "it" within the individual. It is even argued that affectivity "wears out" with age (e.g., Lakin and Eisdorfer's (1962) ". . . aging . . . associated with a decline in affective 'energy', " or Dean's (1962) ". . . a . . . decline in the capacity for affective response.") Others have argued that entering into an emotional state is generally contingent upon an individual's discovering himself in a situation in which an emotional response is socially "called for" (Ossorio, 1976). From this point of view emotionality does not reside in the person, but depends upon his reaction to the kind of social situation within which he performs. Ossorio (1976) particularly notes that a person may or may not *feel* emotional while acting emotionally — that is feeling emotional is neither a sufficient nor necessary component of emotional behavior. The studies of Schachter in which physiological functioning was disturbed with drugs while situations were created that "called for" emotional response (Schachter and Singer, 1962; Schachter and Wheeler, 1962) appear to buttress Ossorio's contentions.

Recently, Cameron (1975) proposed that dealing with the superordinate concept "affectivity" might not be as useful as following ordinary discourse and bifurcating affectivity into mood and emotion. He argued that mood and emotion could best be regarded as interrelated but separable events, and that each deserved separate investigation as to frequency and kind across the life-span.

Reported research on affectivity to date ignores linguistic niceties and "mixes" mood and emotion indiscriminately (e.g., The Clyde Mood Scale (1960) lumps such concepts as "rebellious," "furious," "nagging" while the Nowlis (1956) effort conglomerates "glum," "discouraged," "lazy," and "impulsive." The present investigation sought to explore:

1) how persons in our linguistic community use the concept "emotion";
2) whether the frequency of reporting oneself as being in an emotional state varied with age;
3) whether there are sex differences in frequency of reporting oneself as being in an emotional state; and
4) what the members of our culture believe regarding sex differences in emotionality.

Method

One thousand two hundred and five persons aged 10 to 87, 399 male and 806 female, were interrupted in the situations at-home (n=794), at-work (n=52), and at-leisure (n=359) in 12 locations across the United States (Los Angeles, Boulder, Colorado, seven locations in Maryland, two locations in West Virginia, and Palm Beach, Florida.) Area sampling was employed in 7 locations (for the at-home sample) and systematic convenience sampling in the rest. Overall rejection rate was less than 27%. In the first wave of sampling (n=459) subjects were approached without warning and asked: (1) are you presently experiencing an emotion? (joy, anger, etc.)? (Y/N) (2) If so, what emotion are you experiencing? (3) what "triggered" the emotion? (4) when was the last time you experienced an emotion? (few minutes ago/within the hour/few hours ago/within the day/yesterday/few days ago/within the week/month or so ago/year or so ago), (5) how often do you experience an emotion? (hourly/more than 3 times per day about 3 times per day/about 2 times per day/daily/more than 3 times per week/about twice a week/more than 3 times per month/about twice a month/ monthly/a few times a year/never) and (6) what was your mood of the past half hour? (pleasant/happy/neutral/unpleasant/unhappy)? The second wave of sampling added the questions "which sex is more emotional, males or females?" and "which sex displays its emotions more frequently, males or females?" The sex, marital status, years of such status, number of children, occupational status of the head of the household, and the race of the respondent were also recorded. The first wave took place in the winter-spring 1974, the second in summer 1975. The first featured about half male and half female interviewers and the second 2 female interviewers.

Results

It should first be noted that the two waves of interviewing generated similar results in regard to differences, estimates, and the like with but a rather glaring exception — the incidence of reporting being in an emotional state averaged about 40% in the first wave and about 60% in the second. As we noted, there was no sex-of-interviewer difference in the first wave, perhaps the second-wave results were due to the season, and/or the higher rejection rate. As the data of the second were all collected by the same 2 young women, precise parameterizing of this dimension awaits further research. The rest of the findings are made the more "solid" by the two-wave similarity.

Emotionality Across the Life-Span Table 2.8 provides evidence of declining reportage of emotion as a function of age for both males ($X^2 = 11.2$, df = 4; $P < .05$) and females ($X^2 > 50$; df = 4; $p < .001$).

TABLE 2.8

REPORTED EMOTIONALITY AS A FUNCTION OF AGE AND SEX

age		10-17		Y.A.		26-39		M.A.		56-64		old	
sex		Male	Fem	Male	Fem	Male	Fem	Male	Fem	Male	Fem	Male	Fem
experiencing	yes	11	43	91	147	75	152	28	67	5	16	6	16
an emotion?	no	13	23	50	101	68	142	35	61	8	22	9	16

However, both the teen-child age group and the older segments of the life-span could stand some "fleshing out" in terms of numbers of respondents. The incidence and kind of pleasant and unpleasant emotions (Table 2.9) was proportionately similar across the life-span with the exception of young adulthood when the rule of approximately an equal number of pleasant to unpleasant emotions was "broken." In young adulthood approximately twice as many pleasant as unpleasant emotions were reported.

TABLE 2.9

FREQUENCY AND KIND OF EMOTION REPORTED AS A FUNCTION OF AGE AND SEX

age	10-17		Y. A.		26-39		M. A.		56-64		old	
	Male	Fem	Male	Fem	Male	Fem	Male	Fem	Male	Fem	Male	Fem
positive emotions												
joy/happiness	5	14	34	52	17	38	4	14		6	2	5
amusement			1	3	2	5		2				
gratitude								1				
love	2		7	5		3	2	2				
enthusiasm				2		1						
peacefulness		1	8	9	1	13	1	5	1	2		1
affectively neutral or un-classified emotions												
excitement			1	5	3	4	2	2				
sexual desire			1		3	1	1					
life-livingness	2	1	2	5	3	2		1	2			
wonder			2		6	5		3				1
negative emotions												
anger	2	4	3	13	3	9	2	7		1	1	2
sadness/depression	5	8	7	7	3	14	8	5		3		
anxiety/nervousness/confusion		3	4	16	5	31	1	9		4		3
fear			1	2	3	1		3	1			
boredom			2	4	3	3		3				
silly/foolish				3	3	1		1				
hunger				1	1		2					
pain			1	1	1	1	2			1	1	
irritable		1	1	2		2						1

Estimates of "last time I experienced an emotion" and "frequency with which I experience emotions" traced the same pattern as actual emotion as reported-in-experiencing — that is a "hump" in the 18- through 39-year-old age groups. Median estimates by the age groups for "last time experienced" were "within a day" for teenagers, "few hours ago" for young adults and the 26-39-year olds, "within a day" for the middle-aged, and "yesterday" for the older groups. Median estimates for "frequency of experiencing an emotion" were "about twice a day" for teenagers; "more than 3 times a day" for young adults; "about 3 times a day" for 26-39-year olds; "about twice a day" for middle-aged and 56-64 year olds; and "about twice a week" for the old.

The relative independence of mood and emotion are pointed up by the affective tone of the mood of the past half hour as summarized in Table 2.10. Mood traced a relatively constant pattern across the life-span.

TABLE 2.10

RELATIONSHIP OF MOOD AND EMOTION

	Mood		
	happy/pleasant	neutral	unhappy/unpleasant
n= emotion	472	183	66
pleasant	192 (41%)	17 (9%)	6 (11%)
unpleasant	69 (15%)	68 (37%)	43 (65%)
?	43 (9%)	12 (7%)	1 (2%)
no emotion	168 (36%)	86 (47%)	16 (24%)

Sex differences We found no sex differences in frequency of reported emotion. When the sexes are compared in their *estimates* of either the "last time" or "how frequently" they experienced/experience an emotion, males provided lower estimates. Both sexes opined that: (1) females are more emotional than males and (2) females are more apt to display emotion.

Young adulthood appears to be the "brightest" time of life from an emotionality standpoint (and is also *the* time to think about others — see the "How Human Oriented is the Mind Across the Life-Span?" article in this volume). If the age differences reveal developmental processes, post-young adulthood must be rather a "downer." From a ratio of twice as many pleasant to unpleasant emotions to "even-steven" might be a bit of a shock.

Discussion

The major findings of the present investigation are the lack of a sex difference coupled with an age difference in emotionality. We arrived at these findings utilizing rather inelegant methodology. Our knowledge about emotionality has stemmed from psychologists either: (1) constructing closed-ended questionnaires about affectivity (typically retrospective estimates at that) or (2) reading the tea leaves of the Rorschach or TAT. In the cloak of sophistication ("How often do you find yourself feeling _____?" "very often," "fairly often," "sometimes, but not too often," "hardly ever," "never?" (Dean, 1962) or "During the past few weeks did you ever feel (1) pleased about having accomplished something? (2) that things were going your way? (3) bored? (4) upset because someone criticized you?" (Bradburn, 1969) the profession has generated results that verge upon the unintelligible. While there is nothing wrong, per se with elegance, there is something correct about clear questions asked of representative samples of persons.

There is no need to indulge in the gratuitous "let's index hormonal levels to account for our results." Since males as frequently as females are provided with social reasons to react emotionally, our results fit the Ossorian (1966) model of emotionality. The next question that arises is "do the old less frequently inhabit situations that call for an emotional response and/or have the old more frequently chosen not to react to a situation in an emotional manner?" Since most of the situations that "call for" an emotional reaction involve interaction with other persons, the lower rate of social interaction by the old may account for our finding (e.g., the old may react emotionally as often as the young given the same circumstances, but if such circumstances are more frequently experienced by the young, then they would "be more emotional.") It also appears that many older persons have adopted a more stoic attitude toward life — "I used to get upset, but now I don't let it phase me." While we do not have direct evidence as to the relative contribution of either explanation, both appear potentially operative.

In the only large-scale investigation of mood *in vivo* published to date (Cameron, 1975), pleasant mood was reported about 47% of and unpleasant mood about 8% of the time. In the present investigation, pleasant mood was reported about 67% and unpleasant mood about 10% of the time. While the ratio of pleasant to unpleasant mood appears about 6 to 7 to 1 in both studies, the parameters of these events were substantially different, particularly to the pleasant end of the continuum. Both studies found females less frequently than males reporting a "neutral" mood. Separate treatment of the concepts "mood" and "emotion" within the domain of affect appears quite reasonable, particularly so as knowing the quality of one enables only a "better guess" as to the state of the other.

Overall, persons in our society appear as apt to be in an emotional state as not at any given instant. Estimates of emotionality are definitely to the "low side" of our *in vivo* findings. The utility of actual sampling vs. estimates is pointed up by our findings regarding emotionality as a function of age. While our *in vivo* procedure produced evidence that the old are less frequently emotional, their estimates of emotionality would make them appear even less emotional than they tested.

REFERENCES

Bradburn, N.M. *The structure of psychological well-being*. Chicago: Aldine, 1969.

Cameron, P. Mood as an indicant of happiness: age, sex, social class and situational differences. *Journal of Gerontology*. 1975, *30*, 216-224.

Dean, L.R. Aging and the decline of affect. *Journal of Gerontology*, 1962, *17*, 440-445.

Friedman, A.S. and Granick, S. A note on anger and aggression in old age. *Journal of Gerontology*, 1963, *18*, 283-285.

Lakin, M. and Eisdorfer, C. Affective expression among the aged. *Journal of Projective Techniques*, 1960, *24*, 403-408.

Linden, M. E. and Courtney, D. The human life cycle and its interruptions. American Journal of Psychiatry, 1953, *109*, 906-915.

Nowlis, V. Research with the mood adjective check list. In S. S. Tomkins and C. E. Izard, eds, *Affect, cognition, and personality.* New York: Springer, 1965, pp. 72-87.

Ossorio, P. *Persons,* Los Angeles: Linguistic Research Institute, 1966.

Schachter, S. and Wheeler, L. Epinephrine, chlorpromazine, and amusement. *Journal of Abnormal and Social Psychology,* 1962, *65,* 121-128.

Schachter, S. and Singer, J. E. Cognitive, social and physiological determinants of emotional state. *Psychological Review,* 1962, 69, 379-399.

Schuster, D. B. A psychological study of a 106-year-old man. *American Journal of Psychiatry,* 1952, *109,* 112-119.

3

TEMPORALITY ACROSS THE LIFE-SPAN

with

Darius Bahador, Department of Psychology, Jundi Shapur University, Ahwaz, Iran

K. G. Desai, School of Psychology, Education and Philosophy, University of Gujart, Ahmedabad, India

G. Dremel

Theorists ranging from Aristotle to Piaget have commented on temporality in humankind. Some analysts have maintained that the degree and quality of future-orientation constitutes one of the best single indices of mental health (e.g., Adler (1925), Allport (1950), and May (1958); others that present-orientedness constitutes a hallmark of mental health (Buhler, 1968). Aristotle held that old humans dwell on the past, and Piaget appears to argue that the ability to engage in planful future-thinking commences in adolescence.

Theoreticians appear able to agree that time has at least four significant dimensions — past, present, future, and extension. "Past" refers to some period removed from the present in which events have already occurred, the present to some portion of time in which things have "just occurred" and are occurring, and the future to that part of time which has yet to be and in which events are yet to occur. The "extension" dimension refers to the "distance" in time-units that an event is (or will be) from the present (so many days, hours, years, millenia, etc. ago or to come). While there are some senses in which the "present" might refer to years-worth of time (e.g., the present policy), in ordinary discourse, "present" appears to refer to some small segment of the immediate past, with the "immediate" not ordinarily encompassing hours but rather minutes of time.

"Temporality" is a concept that subsumes a number of aspects of time orientation including attitudes toward time, its utilization, attitudes toward its utilization, degree of planfulness directed toward the future, etc. Investigators have explored the development of the concept of time and its dimensions (e.g., Sturt, 1925), the development of proficiency in time duration estimation (e.g., Fraisse, 1963), and degree of future commitments and mental health (e.g., Schonfield, 1973). In spite of the large set of investigations about various aspects of time, two significant questions have received scant attention regarding temporality, namely:

1) how frequently do persons in their day-to-day endeavors mentally "dwell" in the past, present, and future, and
2) if persons are thinking either retrospectively or prospectively, what amount or degree of extension is ordinarily indulged in?

It would be of further interest to know how persons vary as a function of age, sex, social class, and culture along these two dimensions. This is a report of a large-scale, *in vivo* investigation of person's consciousness addressing these questions.

Method

A series of seven studies designed to explore various facets of the temporality question were conducted. In each, some variant of a technique called "consciousness sampling" was employed. Consciousness sampling proceeds from the assumption that if you want to know what people are thinking about, you ought to ask them what they were, in fact, thinking about. Such a technique further assumes, in harmony with the notions of most of mankind (but not necessarily in line with the theoretical stance of some scientists), that consciousness exists and that persons can assess and report the approximate contents of their minds for some short period of the past.

Study I

In 1966, an area sample of 320 Boulder, Colorado, residents was conducted controlling for time-of-day between the hours of 8:00 a.m. and 8:00 p.m. The first person answering the door of selected residences was asked, "What were you just thinking about?" and "What would you say was the central content or focus of your thinking over the past half hour?" The sample was confined to those between the ages 18 and 40 and over 59. Verbal responses were taken down longhand and later coded by 10 trained coders averaging 98% agreement on the temporality dimension *vis-a-vis* the category, "Does this response indicate that the subject was thinking mainly about the past, the present, or the future?" The rejection rate was less than 6%.

Study II

As Study I had confined itself to residences and adults, Study II took in younger people in varying situations including school, home, recreation settings, and church. Time-of-day was controlled for, while the proportion of the sample of younger people who were contacted in each setting was matched to what appeared to a panel of students to approximate the amount of time per day that children would spend in the given setting. Five hundred ten children were interviewed at school and 133 at home comprising the bulk of the sample of 769 persons aged 4 to 21 drawn in 1967 in Menomonie, Wisconsin; 49 were interviewed at church or Sunday School, 25 while engaged in lovers' lane activities, and 52 while attending football games, movie houses, and a teen center. The same questions posed in Study I were employed, and 14 trained coders performed the categorizations. Twenty categories were employed, including: (a) temporality, (b) instrumentality (was this person acting upon or preparing to act upon things or persons/or being acted upon, being passive?), (c) egocentricity (was this person concerned about his wants, wishes, desires, needs or another's?), (d) mood (subject indicated whether he was happy, neutral, or unhappy over the past half-hour), and (e) situation-tiedness (was subject thinking about the situation or its events he was found in/thinking about something unrelated to his situation). Rejection rate was less than 1%.

Study III

A class of 255 introductory psychology students was shown how to fill out a questionnaire about what they were thinking in the past instant, and then interrupted 21 times over the course of the semester of fall, 1968, to find out what they had been thinking about in the past instant. Dimensions included temporality (the past, the present, or the future), their transient mood at that instant (happy, neutral, or unhappy), and to what degree their thoughts were related to the situation at hand (completely tied to the situation/ about the class, or classmates, etc., remotely tied to the situation/ about school or schooling, completely unrelated to the situation/ unrelated to any consideration of the class, the topics of the class, etc.). Students also completed: (a) two separate administrations of the Barron Ego-Strength Scale, (b) the Eysenck Personality Inventory, and (c) the Cameron Religious Dimensions Scale. Reasonably complete results were obtained on 187 subjects.

Study IV

Over a two-year period starting in 1969, 4,420 persons ranging in age from 8 to 99 were interviewed by the author and student volunteers across all daylight hours (a third was interviewed between the hours of 8:00 a.m. and 12:00 p.m., a third between 12:00 p.m. and 4:00 p.m., and the remainder between 4:00 p.m. and 7:00 p.m. — of course, in certain situations, as in school, this was not possible, so the time-in-situation was divided into thirds and these thirds were equally-sampled-from). The interview was always unexpected, administered individually or, at times to two or three persons simultaneously, with the interviewer informing the subject that we wanted to know about his thoughts just before we interrupted him. Children and teenagers were usually interviewed in school or while recreating, while adults were usually interviewed at home or at work. The at-home sample was obtained via a strict area sample of areas of Los Angeles, Louisville, Detroit, and Evansville (762 males and 959 females, with a rejection rate of 28%); the at-work sample was obtained by college student volunteers from their co-workers in Detroit, Evansville, and Louisville (931 males and 507 females occupying 84 different job locations with a rejection rate of less than 1%); the at-school sample was drawn by a

classroom-time-grade selection process whereby certain proportions of the students in given classes had their work interrupted and
the questionnaire was filled out by the subjects (244 males, 233
females with a rejection rate of less than 1% at two different
schools, one in Kentucky and the other in New Jersey); the at-
church sample was obtained by the interruption of cooperating
Sunday School classes and the private approaching of designated
worshippers during services at four churches (12 males and 30
females, one rejection); the at-leisure sample was obtained by
"staking-out" certain areas in 11 different locations in Louisville,
Los Angeles, and Denver, and interviewing every k th person who
entered the area (six shopping areas, two beaches, two parks, and
one organized ball game provided 221 males and 521 females and a
rejection rate of less than 1%). While persons were not assessed in
all the kinds of situations and performing all the kinds of activities
that are common in our culture, the vast majority of persons in our
society spend the majority of their waking lives in the situations we
sampled, engaging in the kinds of activity we interrupted. We
interviewed 2,250 females and 2,170 males distributed over the
life-span and achieved an overall rejection rate of less than 11%.

Subjects were handed a questionnaire which inquired "What
were you thinking about in the last 5 minutes? Were you mainly
thinking about something that went on in the past, is or was
happening (now, in the present), or is going to or may happen in the
future?"

Study V

In the summer of 1972, 884 persons aged 8 to 97 residing in
Glenwood Springs, Colorado, three small towns around San Francisco and Los Angeles were interviewed by the author and paid
interviewers. An area-sample yielded 462 subjects at-home, 391
were interviewed (as above) at-leisure, while an additional 13 were
obtained at-work and 18 at-school. The same questionnaire utilized
in Study IV was employed. The overall rejection rate was less than
9%. Subjects were also classified as higher status if the head of the
household was a professional, or person of some authority (i.e.,
foreman, police chief), and classified as lower status if other (i.e.,
factory operative, clerk).

Study VI

In 1972, Dr. Desai supervised the drawing of a sample of 351 males and 183 females ranging in age from the late teens to old age in and about Ahmedabad, India, in the situations at-work and at-leisure. Interviewing was conducted by nationals, the rejection rate was less than 1%. The question posed in studies IV and V was translated into the Gujarat language by Dr. Desai. At about the same time, a student of the senior author, Mr. Lloyd McPherson, had his parents interview a sample of 80 males and 136 females aged 10 to 84 in and about Sekondi-Takoradi, Ghana in the situations at-school and at-leisure. The questionnaire was in English; subjects unable to read English had the questions presented in their native language *ad lib*. There were no rejections in Ghana. Paid nationals administered the Iranian translation of the questionnaire to 493 males and 398 females at-home, at-work and at-leisure in 18 locations, mainly urban; rejection rate was less than 10%. Because of the difficulties attendant to drawing cross-national samples, the methods used to generate a representative sample were more formally "correct" in the United States, less strictly met in India and Iran, and still less strictly met in Ghana.

Study VII

In the spring of 1973, 1,031 persons aged 9 to 91 residing in Louisville, Kentucky were interviewed via an area-sample yielding 433 persons at-home. Three hundred ninety-one were interviewed following the same procedures as in the fourth study, and 449 persons were interviewed at-work (following the same procedures as in the fourth study). Overall rejection rate was $< 12\%$. The questionnaire asked "What were you thinking about in the last 5 minutes?" (which was open-ended), then the same item as in the preceding study was followed by: (b) "If it was in the past or future, how far away in time was it? (a few minutes ago, or (from now); about a half hour; about an hour; within a few hours; within a day; within a few days; within a week; within a few weeks; within a few months; within a year or so; within a 5-year span; within about a 10-year span; within about a 20-year span; within about a 30-year span; over 30 years); (c) "Name something you think about that happened in the past" (open-ended); (d) "How long ago did this happen?" (open-ended); (e) "Name an event or thing you often think about that will or might happen in the future" (open-ended); (f) "When do you think this might happen?" (open-ended); (g) "How much have you planned or prepared for this? (please make an X on the line below)" (this item was superordinate to a line that was marked into 5 equal parts and anchored on one end by "I have not planned and/or prepared for it" and at the other by "I have planned and/or prepared for it as much as I possibly could"). Subject also provided his age, sex, and the occupation of head of the household.

Findings

Studies I, II, IV, V

We found no systematic sexual, situational, time-of-day, locational, racial or religious differences; therefore, the life-span results are presented by age-groups and generations after Cameron (1969) in Table 3.1. The older subjects characteristically evidenced the lowest frequency of future-orientation, whether indexed by consciousness of the "last instant," the "last 5 minutes," or the "last half-hour." (X^2 for old frequency of future-orientation in last 5 minutes vs. other frequency of future-orientation was greater than 37; $df = 1$; $p<.001$). The highest frequency of future-orientation was found in the 8-11-year-old group for each of the life-span studies in the United States. The only exception came in temporality over the past half-hour in which the 8-11-year olds registered the second-highest frequency of future-orientation (Table 3.1). For every age-group, the "last instant" of consciousness was more present-oriented and less past-and future-oriented than for consciousness over the "past half-hour."

In all but two of the 22 categorizations, present-orientation is most frequently present in consciousness, and past-orientation least frequently represented. The size and excellence of our samples enable us to estimate how persons in our culture apportion their consciousness along the temporality dimension. For the "past instant," if we consider children as those subjects aged 4 through 11, then the average frequency of their past-orientation was 11%, future-orientation was 31%, and present-orientation was

TABLE 3.1

Temporal Orientation Across the Life-Span

Age, Generation N Past-Present-Future	4-7 93 Pa-Pr-F	8-11 464 Pa-Pr-F	12, 13 433 Pa-Pr-F	14, 15 369 Pa-Pr-F	16, 17 429 Pa-Pr-F	Young Adult 1,484 Pa-Pr-F	26-39 1,136 Pa-Pr-F	Middle-aged 898 Pa-Pr-F	56-64 224 Pa-Pr-F	Old 210 Pa-Pr-F
In last instant	11-47-23	23-159-92	3-75-25	15-79-25	15-94-32	(10-135-44)*			(12-108-32)*	
% of responses	14-58-28	8-58-34	3-73-24	13-66-21	11-67-23	(5-71-23)			(8-71-21)	
In last 5 minutes	0-2-0	35-72-81	53-139-137	48-102-99	36-82-74	228-718-516	137-635-345	98-547-237	30-134-55	33-125-44
% of responses		19-38-43	16-42-42	19-41-40	19-43-39	16-49-35	12-57-31	11-62-27	14-61-25	16-62-22
During last half hour	18-33-25	26-128-104	13-48-28	26-32-33	16-53-52	(19-100-63)*			(17-96-36)*	
% of responses	24-43-33	10-50-40	15-54-32	29-35-36	13-44-43	(10-55-35)			(11-64-24)	

* The younger sample ($\underline{N}$ = 204) was aged 18 to 40, the older sample ($\underline{N}$ = 159) was aged 60 and over; their number is not included in the $\underline{N}$s listed under each age-group.

TABLE 3.2

Temporal Orientation as a Function of Social Class

Class		8-11 # (%)	12, 13 # (%)	14, 15 # (%)	16, 17 # (%)	Young Adult # (%)	26-39 # (%)	Middle- aged # (%)	56-64 # (%)	Old # (%)
Higher	Past	1 (13)	1 (8)	2 (20)	5 (20)	5 (8)	9 (12)	7 (9)	1 (13)	Ø
	Present	4 (50)	5 (38)	4 (40)	10 (40)	34 (52)	46 (61)	49 (65)	5 (63)	4 (67)
	Future	3 (38)	7 (54)	4 (40)	10 (40)	26 (40)	20 (27)	19 (25)	2 (25)	2 (33)
Lower	Past	9 (21)	4 (13)	4 (14)	10 (20)	27 (13)	11 (10)	8 (12)	3 (18)	10 (23)
	Present	14 (33)	8 (26)	11 (39)	15 (30)	106 (50)	64 (56)	43 (66)	11 (63)	27 (61)
	Future	20 (47)	19 (61)	13 (46)	25 (50)	80 (38)	39 (34)	14 (22)	3 (18)	7 (16)

58%. If we consider those subjects aged 12 through 17 as adolescents, their frequency of past-orientation was 9%, future was 23%, and present was 69%. If we then average the child, adolescent, early-adulthood, and late-adulthood frequencies, we arrive at an estimate of 8% past-, 25% future-, and 67% present-orientation for the members of our culture. Thus persons in our culture are 2½ times as apt to think about the present as about the future, and thrice as apt to think about the future as the past in any given 5-minute period. Applying the same analysis to the "last half-hour" of consciousness, we arrive at an overall estimate of 14% past-, 33% future-, and 52% present-orientation — thus matching the estimate derived from the "last 5 minute" analysis.

Subjects for whom social status was indexed are presented in Table 3.2. No clear evidence of either lower or higher status persons differing in their temporal orientation was uncovered.

Those dimensions of thought that were differentially related to temporality for children are displayed in Table 3.3. The characterizations of the "last instant" and "last half-hour" of consciousness are combined in the presentation. Instrumentality was related to temporality — ($X^2 = 6.96$; $df = 2$; $p < .03$) with thoughts of the past more apt to incorporate actions of the subject. Children were more likely to be thinking of their own desires when contemplating either the past or the future ($X^2 = 17.7$; $df = 2$; $p < .001$). The degree of situation-tiedness of consciousness was more apt to be remote or unrelated when either the past or future was contemplated ($X^2 = 19.9$; df 4; $p < .001$).

Study III

The interrelations between temporality and the psychological dimensions selected for study with college students in class are presented in Table 3.4. Frequency of thinking about the future (while in-class, at least) was related to frequency of thinking about the past, while frequency of present-thinking was negatively related to frequency of past-and future-thinking. Frequency of moods of happiness was positively related and frequency of moods of neutrality was negatively related to frequency of thinking about the past. Frequency of present-orientation was negatively related to frequency of moods of happiness and positively related to frequency of moods of neutrality. There was a tendency for frequency

TABLE 3.3

Children's and Adolescents' Time-Orientations Relative to Instrumentality, Egocentricity, and Situation-Tiedness ("last instant" and "last half hour" combined)

Time-Orientation	Instrumentality		Egocentricity		Situation - Tiedness		
	being acted upon	acting upon	concern with own desires	concern with others' desires	completely situation-tied	remotely tied to situation	unrelated to situation
Past	69	43	53	42	54	61	45
Present	363	136	266	118	507	147	106
Future	242	79	218	59	95	131	212

TABLE 3.4

Correlation Matrices for Time-Orientation vs. Mood, Situation-Tiedness, Neuroticism, and Ego-Strength for College Students

Time-Orientation	Intercorrelations		Mood			Situation - Tiedness			Eysenck Neuroticism (N = 157)	Barron Ego - Strength	
	present	future	happy	neutral	unhappy	completely	remotely	unrelated		first administration (N = 163)	second administration (N = 153)
Past	-.28**	.48***	.17*	-.27**	.05	-.36***	.05	.18*	-.14	-.25**	-.18*
Present		-.17*	-.22**	.32***	-.09	.40***	-.07	-.36***	-.12	-.12	-.03
Future			.10	-.33***	.11	-.30**	-.04	.22**	-.03	-.34***	-.32***

*$\underline{p}$ < .05, **$\underline{p}$ < .01, ***$\underline{p}$ < .001

of thinking about the future and past to be positively related to frequency of moods of happiness and unhappiness ($p < .10$), while frequency of future-thinking was negatively related to frequency of moods of neutrality. Frequencies of past and future-orientations were generally negatively related to frequency of consciousness being situation-tied, while present thinking's frequency was positively related to being completely situation-tied and negatively related to being unsituation-tied. Scores on the Barron Ego-Strength Scale were generally negatively related to frequency of thinking about either the past or future.

Study VI

The results for the Iranian, Indian and Ghanaese subjects are presented in Table 3.5. For both India and Ghana there were only hints of possible differences between persons along different points of the life-span. In Iran a difference between young adults and younger vs. those aged 26+ is evident, with the younger more frequently future-oriented, and the older more frequently past-oriented ($X^2 = 31.5$; df = 2; $p<.001$). The Indian, ($X^2 = 37.4$; df = 2; $p<.001$), Ghanaese ($X^2>100$; df = 2; $p<.001$), and Iranian ($X^2 = 18.4$; df = 2; $p<.01$) results differed from the United States results, and they also differed from each other ($X^2 = 32.6$; df = 3; $p<.001$).

Study VII

Temporal orientation of respondents in Louisville is reported in Table 3.6. The same general finding of increasing present- and declining future-orientation is apparent, while the absolute parameters associated with the 3 orientations is quite similar to those reported in Table 3.1. As with the previous studies (Table 3.2) there was no difference in temporal orientation as a function of social class.

Degree of extension into the future when thinking about the future when interviewed is summarized in Table 3.8 and degree of extension into the past when thinking about the past is summarized in Table 3.7. Degree of extension into the past did not vary (Md test for those aged 40 and older vs. those younger $X^2 = 2$; NS). There was a tendency for the median to indicate further extensions into the future as a function of age, while persons over 39-years old

TABLE 3.5

Temporal Orientation Over the Past 5 Minutes in India, Ghana, and Iran

Age	Less than 18 n	%	Young adult n	%	26-39 n	%	Middle-aged n	%	56-54 n	%	Old n	Total
India												
Past	16	22	38	21	39	17	23	21	1	20		117
Present	26	36	70	39	102	46	44	40	3	60		245
Future	30	42	72	40	91	41	43	39	1	20	2	239
Ghana												
Past	35	38	25	27	4	23						64
Present	16	17	22	24	6	35	2	40				46
Future	42	45	46	49	7	41	3	60			3	98
Iran												
Past	44	25	122	32	105	47	51	52	3	27	2	327
Present	49	28	89	23	46	20	21	21	3	27	0	208
Future	80	46	171	44	70	31	25	26	4	36	1	351

TABLE 3.6

Temporal Orientation in Louisville, Kentucky
(in per cent)

Age n	5-11 11	12,13 18	14,15 30	16,17 40	Young adult 289	26-39 299	Middle-aged 220	56-64 64	Old 45	Total
Past	9	11	13	10	15	16	14	9	22	14
Present	36	56	40	43	41	50	56	64	64	49
Future	55	33	46	48	45	34	30	27	13	36

TABLE 3.7

Extension Into the Past by Age Group
(Md underlined)

Age	5-11	12, 13	14, 15	16, 17	Young adult	26-39	Middle-aged	56-64	Old
A few minutes		1	1		8	5	5	2	1
Half an hour					2	1			2
An hour		—				1	2	1	
A few hours			1		3	2	3		1
A day			—	3	3	10	2		
A few days		1	1		4	3	2	—	
A week			1	1	2	2	2		
A few weeks					4	5	3		1
A few months					6	4	4	1	2
A year or so	1				3	4	5		1
5-year span					3	10	1	1	
About a 10-year span					2				
About a 20-year span					1				
About a 30-year span								1	1
Far into the past (hundreds of years)					1		2		1
% extending over 5 years	Ø	Ø	Ø	Ø	10	Ø	6	17	20

TABLE 3.8

Extension Into the Future by Age Group
(Md underlined)

Age	5-11	12, 13	14, 15	16, 17	Young adult	26-39	Middle-aged	56-64	Old
A few minutes	2				1		3	1	
Half an hour					1				
An hour					1		1		
A few hours	1			1	3	4	1		1
A day				2	6	4	4	2	
A few days					7	10	4	1	1
A week	1			1	8	10	2	5	
A few weeks		1	5	2	13	16	14	1	3
A few months	2	7	7	9	56	64	48	15	6
A year or so	1	1	2	10	37	26	28	5	4
5-year span		4	4	5	61	42	26	6	4
About a 10-year span			2	1	12	15	21	4	4
About a 20-year span				1	5	5	11	2	3
About a 30-year span			1	1	1	3			
Over 30 years				1	1	1		1	
Far into the future (hundreds of years)				1	1	5	1		
% extending over 5 years	0	0	19	14	9	14	18	16	27

more frequently contemplated the distal future (over 5-years away) than those younger did ($X^2 = 11.7$; df = 1; $p<.001$). Persons reported a greater extension of future orientation (Md = "a few months") than of past orientation (Md = "a few weeks") (Kolmogorov-Smirnov $X^2 - 9.20$; df = 2; $p< .03$).

The most frequent responses to the future event "often thought about" are summarized by age-group in Table 3.9 and past event in Table 3.13. Clearly life-task and life-activity contemplations vary as a function of age. Noteworthy is the relatively constant frequency of nomination of "vacation-trip" kind of event. The claimed planfulness regarding this event as indexed by the selection of a point on a line representing a continuum of no planfulness through maximal planfulness is summarized by age-group in Table 3.10. The 14-17-year olds too "claimed less planfulness" than the 18-25-year olds "claimed" (Kolmogorov-Smirnov $X^2 = 45.5$; df = 2; $p<.001$). The 18-39-year olds "claimed more planfulness" than the 56 and over year olds claimed (Median test $X^2 = 7.11$; df = 2; $p<.06$). The social class difference in "planfulness" as indexed by point-on-line selection is summarized in Table 3.11. Respondents from the higher social class more frequently chose a point on the line of "planfulness" closer to "maximal planfulness" than respondents from the lower social class (Median test $X^2 = 4.65$; df = 1; $p<.04$; Kolmogorov-Smirnov $X^2 = 25.7$; df = 2; $p<001$).

Estimates of extensions into the past and future for frequently thought about events are summarized by age group in Table 3.12 Persons in the last half of the life-span claimed to think further into the past about the "thing they often think about" (Md = 5 years) and those persons younger than 40-years of age claimed (Kolmogorov-Smirnov $X^2 = 41.6$; df = 2; $p<.001$). The same analysis yielded no difference between the pre- and post-40-year olds in claimed extension of futurity (Kolmogorov-Smirnov $X^2 = 3.39$; NS). It will be noted that the "typical retrospective thought" (Table 3.8) located but a "few weeks" into the past, compared with the "often thought about" event that located "5 years" into the past. Similarly, the "typical prospective thought" (Table 3.7) located "a few months" into the future, compared with the "often thought about" event that located "a year" into the future. "Typical thought" generally featured considerably less temporal extension than "often contemplated events."

TABLE 3.9

Most Frequently Reported Kind of Future Event "Often Thought About" Across the Life-Span

Age group N	<14 25	14-17 72	18-25 290	26-39 273	40-55 216	56-64 54	65+ 38
Event (% Reporting)	trip (24) vacation (33) sports (17)	marriage (17) vacation (10) schooling (7) sports (7)	work-job (12) marriage (12) schooling (11) vacation (7) parenthood (7)	work-job (15) vacation (11) world problems (7) sex-love life (6) parenthood (5)	vacation (13) retirement (8) world problems (7)	vacation (22) retirement (19) world problems (7) personal death (4)	personal death (8) retirement (8) vacation (8) world problems (5) enter nursing home (5)

TABLE 3.10

**Reported Planfulness as a Function of Age
(Md underlined)**

		Degree of Claimed Planfulness								
Age Group	N	No Planfulness (%)	*	*	*	Midpoint	*	*	*	Total Planfulness (%)
<14	25	4 (16)	3	Ø	1	<u>4</u>	2	Ø	2	9 (36)
14-17	72	25 (35)	4	<u>4</u>	2	7	4	2	4	20 (28)
18-25	290	62 (21)	9	18	<u>5</u>	36	36	26	15	83 (29)
26-39	273	82 (30)	7	10	<u>14</u>	29	21	13	5	92 (33)
40-55	216	81 (37)	5	14	2	<u>21</u>	14	13	5	61 (28)
56-64	54	25 (46)	1	<u>3</u>	2	3	3	3	1	13 (24)
64	38	15 (40)	2	<u>2</u>	Ø	6	1	2	1	9 (24)

TABLE 3.11

Reported "Planfulness" Regarding Future Event by Social Class (Louisville)
(Md underlined)

	No Planfulness	*	*	*	Midpoint	*	*	*	Total Planfulness
Higher (M = 240)	22	3	5	2	12	4	16	5	32
Lower (M = 652)	33	4	5	2	11	2	7	6	28

TABLE 3.12

Temporal Extension of "Often Contemplated" Past and Future Events by Age Group
(Md underlined)

Age Past	few min.	half hr.	one hr.	few hrs.	one day	few days	one week	few weeks	few months	one year	5 years	10 years	20 years	30 years	over 30 years
<14	1		1		6	2	1	5	3	5	1	2			
14-17	4	1			9	4	5	10	15	15	7	3	1		
18-25	1	2	3	8	25	15	20	16	53	45	60	8	3	3	2
26-39	3	2		7	11	13	20	25	37	28	63	32	14	17	2
40-55	1	1		2	12	5	14	18	23	18	32	24	20		8
56-64					4	2	1	4	6	7	13	5	2	3	6
65+		1		1			3	1	5	2	10	4			7
Future															
<14											5	2		2	
14-17	1			1	2		1	1	9	3	9	3	1	1	
18-25		1	1	3	6	7	8	7	16	12	57	12	5	3	1
26-39	3	1		4	4	10	9	13	57	32	43	14	6		
40-55	1		1	1	4	4	2	16	59	26	23	20	11	3	1
56-64					2	1	5	15	15	28	6	4	2		
65+		1		1		1		3	6	3	3	4	2		1

TABLE 3.13

Most Frequently Reported Kind of Past Event "Often Thought About" Across the Life-Span

	Age Group (% Reporting)						
N	**<14** **25**	**14-17** **72**	**18-25** **290**	**26-39** **273**	**40-55** **216**	**56-64** **54**	**65+** **38**
	vacation (17)	sports (17)	marriage (7)	vacation (8)	work (10)	vacation (30)	death of other (18)
	party (13)	vacation (15)	vacation (4)	work (6)	vacation (8)	trauma to other (9)	vacation (16)
	sports (8)	schooling (15)	love-life (4)	marriage (6)	death of other (3)	trauma to self (4)	work (11)
	pet(s) (8)	friend(s) (11)	good times (3)	accident (6)	retirement (3)	world events (4)	hospitalization (5)
		accident (7)	party (3)	love-life (4)	marriage (3)	marriage (4)	
		childhood (4)	work (2)	parenthood (3)	world events (3)	accident (4)	
		fight (4)	friend(s) (2)	bad times (3)	trauma to other (3)	retirement (4)	
		phone call (4)	hospitalization (2)	military service (3)	success of other (3)	religious event (4)	
		buying car (4)	bad times (2)	new home (3)		work (4)	
		work (4)	schooling (2)	schooling (3)		grandparenthood (4)	
		eating (3)	accident (2)	hospitalization (3)			
		death of other (3)	military service (2)				

Discussion

Time Orientation of the Old Aristotle commented on what he believed to be the relatively greater frequency of reminiscing on the part of the old. Contemporary psychologists have tended to echo his sentiments in this regard, and some have begun to erect theories concerning the mental health of those who reminisce less. Before proceeding to describe the advantages and/or disadvantages of reminiscence on the part of the old, it would appear reasonable to establish that, in fact, the old do reminisce more frequently. Were this confirmed, then we might profitably proceed to establish the parameters associated with the reminiscence phenomenon. It certainly appears to be "jumping the gun" to erect theories about the reasons, functions, and usefulness of a phenomenon before establishing that the phenomenon exists. We issued a caution in this regard in our first report of temporality in consciousness (Cameron, 1972), and in light of the additional evidence, the caution appears well taken. Even if our United States aged subjects (i.e., aged 80 or over after Cameron, 1969) are considered separately, of these 20 subjects, 20% reported thinking about the past, 20% about the future, and 60% about the present — offering little hope that a substantial change in conscious temporality occurs at the end of the life-span. While Aristotle may have observed the phenomenon in his day and culture, his notion appears inapplicable to the contemporary United States population. It is instructive that the Iranian data fall in an Aristotelian direction — particularly as the Iranian culture is, of our set of test cultures, the one most apt to be similar to the culture in which Aristotle resided. Initially (Cameron, 1972) we suggested that though the United States old did not appear to think more frequently about the past, they might ordinarily extend their retrospective thought further in the past than younger persons. The results garnered in the seventh study regarding typical thought (Table 3.7) fall against this possibility. Our United States findings suggest that frequency of retrospective thought traces a constant function across the life-span, and further, that the extension associated with retrospective thought is similarly invariant.

McMahon and Rhudick (1967) have offered some evidence that old people talk about events in their life-histories more frequently than young people do. Our seventh study (Table 3.12) provided evidence that older people extend further into the past when thinking about "often contemplated" events. Clearly persons are more apt to talk about that which they often contemplate than those things they infrequently think about. Thus the greater retrospective extension that various theorists note may well have been due not to age-differences in ordinary *consciousness*, but age-differences in ordinary *conversation*.

Butler (1963) has theorized and written about a "life-review" that is a " . . . naturally occurring, universal mental process." in old age. He has argued that this process is a necessary and psychologically beneficial one. On the one hand, in the seventh study, in which a person so engaged might well have "shown up" in the data, apparently no one was "caught" "life-reviewing." As this "life-review" might not occupy much "mental space," perhaps it is not surprising that we "caught" no one. However, the kinds of past events "often thought about" (Table 3.13) might reasonably be expected to provide some evidence of this "life-review." Study of Table 3.13 suggests that while old persons on the average may delve somewhat farther back into the past for their frequently contemplated past events (Table 3.12) — and given their years and greater opportunity for selection, such appears almost "necessary" — one must be struck with the *contemporaneity* of the responses to the life-stage of the persons involved. Those who have just been children report thinking about childhood and sports, those who are married but a few years think about marriage, those who have recently started on the cycle of lessened health think more frequently about health matters, those who are watching their cohorts expire think about death and dying. The "life-span mental process" suggested by these data offers nary a hint of a life-review While these data do not preclude the possibility of a universal "life-review," they do tend to place a strain on both the universality and "naturalness" of the presumed process. Perhaps if we had asked for biographies we would have gotten something "life-reviewish," but in our "fishing expedition" through consciousness, we found no evidence of a "life-review" in the pond.

Neugarten (1964), Kastenbaum and Durkee (1964) and Pollack and Kastenbaum (1964) have contended that the old (and young) repudiate the future for the present. To the degree that a higher frequency of contemplation of the present occurs at the "expense" of contemplation of the future in the old (Table 3.1), these theorists' contention would appear somewhat supported. However this support must be tempered by the finding that persons in the last half of the life-span generally thought more frequently about the *remote* future than persons in the first half, not what one would expect of those who had "repudiated" the future. Further, the highest frequency of "prospectivity" being found among the youngest members of our sample is also nonsupportive of the Neugarten-Kastenbaum notions. The "repudiation" argued for might better be related to the "planfulness" dimension of our investigation. Here (Table 3.10) a curvilinear relationship is in evidence, with the older and younger persons in our sample indicating less planfulness as indexed by point-chosen along a line representing the dimension. As the kinds of things about which one could plan differed along the life-span (Table 3.9), one would need to draw a much larger sample than we have to enable comparison of the degree of planfulness claimed by persons of various ages regarding the same kind of event (i.e., "vacation"). Even if it could be demonstrated that holding the kind of event "constant," a curvilinear relationship between age and claimed planfulness existed, a reduction of planning for the future is uncertainly related to "repudiation." Having mastered many skills and having done so many things correctly in the past may reduce the need for planning. If "repudiation" occurs, we might well expect that the extension claimed by the old regarding their frequently thought about future event (Table 3.12) would be less compared with the pre-old. But such is not the case, with the old's median of "a year" into the future congruent with the overall median for the entire sample.

It would appear that some rethinking and retheorizing about temporality in old age is in order. In 1973, the senior author presented an extended report on some of our research on temporality in which it was stated that ", . . the future is most mentally exciting to preadolescents, who have adolescence and its activities, young adulthood and its events, and, in the distant future, child-rearing, professional endeavors, and demise to contemplate. Each older generation has less future to look forward to or worry about and spends less time on it. The past is always with one, but never dominant. The *now,* the present, rich and full of reasons for mental attention, belongs to the adult. He has arrived — life is doing, performing, acting upon him and he upon it — no longer to wonder about, but to handle, to cope with, to master. While the preadolescent and the adolescent live for the day *when,* adults *are.*"

If youth mentally prepares correctly for the future, the correct habits are ingrained, and the suitable skills learned, then life can be more comfortably lived without "taking thought for the future." Now in light of our additional data, the above should be modified somewhat. It appears that while the old do not engage in prospective thinking as frequently, they rather "make up for it" by thinking with greater extension and perhaps on a somewhat broader stage (e.g., a greater frequency of contemplation of "world and social problems"). While the old apparently do contemplate death and dying more frequently (see Cameron, Stewart, and Biber, 1973), this topic does not or is not sufficient to eliminate prospective thought as Thompson and Strieb (1961) appear to believe "At this age, except for those who hold a strong religious conviction of an afterlife, there is really very little to look forward to as individuals." *Au contraire,* the old appear to differ but little from the middle-aged in degree of prospectivity within the limits of changing life-tasks. While theorists may possess the "broad picture" and expect the old to be "winding down" in anticipation of demise (e.g., the disengagement theory of aging by Cumming and Henry, 1961), it appears that real people in the real world may be unwilling to "kill it before it dies" and just continue to live until they don't.

Mental Health and Temporality. There appear to be four possible basic positions to be taken in regard to the relationship between temporal orientation and mental health. Generally, one could argue that past-, present-, or future-orientation or "atemporality" lends itself to mental health. Each position has its advocates.

Buhler (1968) has argued that the mentally healthy person lives predominantly in the present. Mental health, as she sees it, stems largely from accepting what one is and has rather than rethinking past mistakes or fleeing to future possibilities. This kind of emphasis on present-thinking appears as a dominant characteristic of the hedonists and existentialists. Jesus apparently promoted similar notions (". . . do not be anxious about tomorrow, tomorrow will look after itself. Each day has troubles enough of its own."

Matthew 6:34). If one can reasonably index temporal orientation through sampling consciousness, and the present attempt is seen as adequately doing such sampling, then our results suggest that old persons, as a class, ought to display better mental health and children poorer mental health for the generations.

No theorist to our knowledge has contended that persons ought generally to orient toward the past (though some writers of fiction have entertained the notion). However, a number of theorists have endorsed or have tended to endorse a higher degree of retrospectivity on the part of the old. Erikson (1950, 1959) advocates a position similar to that taken and elaborated by Butler (1963). In a "life-review" the old person is to find reasons for his existence and the events of his life and locate himself within the stream of humanity. As we found retrospectivity unrelated to age, no generation receives encouragement from this quarter.

"Atemporality" is a component of the meditative religions and the "theory" of the drug culture. While the method of arriving at atemporality may be as important as the state itself (Progoff (1963), Suzuki (1964) and Masters and Houston (1966)), atemporality is highly valued and eagerly sought by both orientations. The procedures we followed precluded indexing the incidence of atemporality.

The currently dominant position emphasizes the desirability of future-orientation. Adler (1925) provided one of the strongest endorsements of futurity when he contended that it was one of the best single indices of mental health. He has been followed by a host of psychologists including Allport (1950), May (1958), Fisk (1957), Neugarten and Garron (1959), Kastenbaum and Durkee (1964), and Spence (1968). To these theorists futurity includes components of goal-setting and planfulness. On the one hand, our results suggest that the sheer volume of futurity may decline as a function of age; thus arguing for reduction of "mental health" as a function of age (perhaps as society corrupts a la Rousseau). Yet we simultaneously uncovered some evidence that with age the more distant future may be more frequently contemplated — perhaps this "makes up" for the reduction in volume. To confound the issue are our results in regard to "planfulness." To the degree that choosing a point along a line representing "planfulness" indexes planfulness, the second quarter of the life-span features the most planfulness.

While we did not attempt to sample "goal-settingness" *per se* this would appear to be somewhat indexed by the "reasonableness" of what persons claimed to "often think about that was yet to occur." The tasks/things nominated by the respondents of the various generations here appeared "reasonable" for persons in their position on the life-course. If the "prospectivists" are correct, it would appear that the healthiest persons would locate in and about early adulthood.

Some of the results of Studies II and III bear upon the question of temporal orientation and mental health. Instrumentality, that is, the person acting as an agent and effector in his environment, is often considered an important component of mental health (Schonfield, 1973). In Study II, in which children's and teenager's reported conscious contents were coded (Table 3.3) it will be noted that instrumentality was most highly associated with prospective thought. To the degree that instrumentality, as we have used the term, relates to mental health, then those who indulge in the most retrospective thought might be expected to be the most "healthy." As the generations did not differ in frequency or extent of retrospectivity, it might then be argued that the generation that engaged in the least prospective and most present-oriented thought might well be the healthiest. Regarded in this light we have a "vote" for the mental health of older persons. In Study III, in which the thought patterns of college students were studied over a 10-week period, we had 2 indices of "mental health." The Eysenck Neuroticism Scale, which ostensibly indexes mental distress, was unrelated to frequency of mode of temporality. Score on the Barron Ego-Strength Scale, designed to index mental "robustness," was negatively related to frequency of retrospective and to prospective orientation. The negative association with retrospective thought falls against no generation, but the negative association with prospective thought, if it falls against any, falls against the youngest generations. While we would hardly contend that we have a clear test of Adler's contention that degree of futurity is one of the best indices of mental health, to the modest degree that we do have a test, our results fall in a direction contrary to his position.

Planfulness Across the Life-Span. To our knowledge no theorist has addressed himself directly to the question of planfulness across the life-span. Some have commented on parts of the life-span and the planfulness presumably present at a given age. Piaget has written voluminously on the growth of the adult mind from that of the child. It appears (Piaget, 1966; 1928; Flavell, 1963; Ginsburg and Opper, 1969) that Piaget believes that planfulness is acquired gradually in childhood, with the pre-adolescent characteristically concrete-present-unplanful in his thought while the adolescent is considered to be abstract-possibility-future-planful in his. Piaget appears to believe that this process continues, resulting in even more adult planfulness. At the other end of the life-span, the disengagement theory (Cumming and Henry, 1961) has promoted a view that the old withdraw from planning their future. Kastenbaum and Durkee (1964) suggested that the hospitalized old even more frequently withdraw from planning. Our evidence in this regard is summarized in Table 3.10. To the degree that planfulness is adequately indexed by a subject's locating a point along a line said to represent planfulness, and the claims of planfulness index actual planfulness, Piaget is supported in his belief that younger adults are more planful than adolescents. On the other hand, we found no evidence that adolescents are more planful than preadolescents. Au contraire, results tended in the opposite direction. At the other end of the life-span, the Cumming and Henry contention appears to fare well. Planfulness declines as a function of age after middle age is attained. The reason for this decline is not apparent from our data, but certainly disengagement notions do not provide the only explanation of the results. If during younger adulthood suitable skills and competencies had been acquired, it is conceivable that the degree and/or amount of planfulness could be reasonably re-duced. If a person has provided for his retirement financially, then he has at least one of the major components of retirement "taken care of." As so much of life is cyclical, many of the problems of the future are the same as the problems of the past, and one can reasonably expect that what has worked in the past might well work in the present. This appears related to what many inves-tigators have termed "rigidity," and various aspects of rigidity or conservatism may well be related to having formed satisfactory strategies of behavior in reaction to a number of specific situations. As Ossorio (1966) has noted, since success is so important to persons, a workable solution to a problem tends to push any person toward a "conservative" or status quo response to a similar situation. As old persons have lived longer, and have presumably solved or conquered more problems successfully, part of their "conservatism" or "rigidity" might be explained not as a function of age *per se*, but rather as due to experience.

Social Class Differences. Numerous thinkers (e.g., Hollingshead, 1949; Gans, 1962; Komarovsky, 1967) have agreed that the lower classes of society are not as foresighted or planful as the higher classes (a point on which even socialists (e.g., Bang, 1955) and their opponents agree). Banfield (1968) puts the case strongly when he argues that the lower-class person "lives from moment to moment. If he has any awareness of a future, it is of something fixed, fated, beyond his control. . . . Impulse governs his behavior, either because he cannot discipline himself to sacrifice a present for a future satisfaction or because he has no sense of the future." Buttressing this argument there have been a number of studies in which lower-class and middle-class children were given tokens redeemable immediately for some small reward or redeemable some days or weeks later for a larger reward. Generally, the lower-class children opted more frequently for the lesser reward. However, components of trust, both of the situation and of the giver, enter into these studies as confounding variables, making the case for the lack of planfulness as being the primary variable questionable. Further, such studies do not bear upon whether, as Banfield suggests, the lower-class persons have a different sense of future and/or are less frequently willing to plan for the future. The present series of studies appears to bear directly on these issues. On the one hand, we have reasonably clear evidence that temporality, as we indexed it, did not vary as a function of social class in either Study V or VII. In the seventh study (Table 3.11), it was found that claimed planfulness as we indexed it did vary as a function of social class, with the lower class on the average claiming a lower planfulness. Thus, while Banfield argues that the lower planfulness of the lower class may stem from a cognitive inadequacy ("no sense of the future") or a motivational difference ("cannot discipline himself to sacrifice"), our evidence suggests that the first explanation is probably not the case, while the latter may well be (although our data do *not* suggest that lower class persons "cannot," rather that they somewhat less frequently claim the amount of planfulness claimed by higher-class persons).

Temporality Across Cultures. Temporality may have such a different meaning within one culture as compared to others that one might consider temporality within each society as a unique event in the Boasian tradition (Boas, 1928). Another possibility, that cultures locate along an evolutionary continuum (Engles, 1942; Sahlins and Service, 1960), would have us "extract" the cultural distinctives from the evolutionary "stream" in regard to temporality. Depending on the point of view from which one proceeds, assessing temporality across the life-span across cultures introduces either one (the culture) or two (the distinctives of the culture and the stage on the evolutionary continuum) independent variables to the cohort-age-index trinity (Schaie, 1967) that one employs within a given culture.

From a cultural-distinctives standpoint, both Indian and Iranian cultures are often interpreted as being relatively "atemporal" (Nakamura, 1966, Vreeland et al. 1957). Indian history is notoriously indifferent to exactitude in regard to dates, and, for that matter, to the "fact" of events that might have transpired. Iranian history is considerably more reliable. To the degree that one can legitimately characterize the temporality of a people from general impressions of an anthropologic sort, it has been argued that each person in India comes to see himself as part of an ongoing cycle of life. The cycle existed in the past and will appear again and again. The Gujarati, relative to other Indians, are known for their planfulness and resourcefulness. Attempting to apply the anthropologic appraisals to data of our sort, it would appear reasonable to expect Indians to mentally "live" most frequently in the present and least frequently in the past.

One would expect Iranians to be very present-oriented from the ethnographic materials available (e.g., Frye, 1953). Vreeland et al. (1957) go so far as to opine that the past and future have little meaning except as they influence the present. In the older cohort, remembrances of past glory as compared with the present might also be likely. The present government is emphasizing the future to a great degree, and so one might find more frequent future orientation among the younger cohorts. Overall, we would expect the present to predominate, and the future to run last in frequency for older Iranians, and perhaps some elevation of the future at the expense of the past for younger Iranians.

The Ghanaese orientation toward time is often judged as rather similar to that of Indians and Iranians. Hoepli (1971) suggests that the Ghanaian's " . . . problems are the problems of life itself — food, shelter, birth, death — (he) seldom lifts his glance very far beyond his own horizon (p. 18)." Apter (1968) in harmony with the opinions of Kingsley (1899) and Sormani (1967), feels that " . . . there is a tendency among the Ghanaese to regard the present as embodying all time (p. 63)." Their predilection toward leisure is further noted by most students of the culture. While an emphasis upon leisure does not necessarily imply timelessness (one could seek leisure to prepare for some future extraterrestrial life), in the absence of information to the contrary, it implies it. The application of these anthropologic appraisals to the thrust of our study would suggest the primacy of present-orientation, with future-orientation appearing less frequently than retrospective contemplation, considering the religious and cultural emphasis upon one's ancestors (and, of course, we may be dealing with the time-bias of Western eyes).

Clearly if our results can be taken at face value, application of anthropologic appraisals and/or our application of them fared poorly from an empirical standpoint. The absolute order of the Indian results fall in expected direction, but the magnitude of the difference between the "present" and "future" is "out of line" with what we expected. The Ghanaese and Iranian results fall almost directly opposite to our expectation in both order and magnitude. While the meaning of the words "past," "present," and "future" might be somewhat different among Ghanaese, the official language is English and very few of the respondents required assistance from the interviewers. Our Iranian questionnaire was successfully back translated by two independent judges. As is so often the case with cross-national studies, we are left wondering at the interpretation of the responses.

From an evolutionary perspective, Marx (1961) contended that the philosophy of capitalism was the spirit " . . . of renunciation, of privation and of savings . . . of *asceticism*. Its true ideal is the *ascetic* but *usurious* miser and the *ascetic* but *productive* slave. Its moral ideal is the *worker* who takes a part of his wages to the savings bank. . . . (for the) . . . less you eat, drink, buy . . . etc., the more you will be able to save and the *greater* will become your treasure which neither moth nor rust will corrupt — your *capital.*" While others (e.g., Sahlins and Service, 1960; Collier, 1963; Cohen, 1966) may cast the notion differently, there seems to be general agreement among social evolutionists that precapitalist societies would be expected to evidence a higher incidence of present- and possibly past- and a lower incidence of future-orientation than capitalist societies. The United States results featured the lowest incidence of future- and highest incidence of present-orientation. Our only "hit" in regard to expectations was the United States lowest incidence of past-orientation. As evolutionists stress the "planfulness" component of futurity, perhaps indexing this aspect and/or sampling additional representatives of capitalist and precapitalist societies will end up buttressing their case. But in the limited test we were able to generate, social evolutionary theory received limited support and considerable disconfirmation.

Temporality Across the Life-Span. The emergence of a sense of time as a developmental process has received considerable attention from psychologists. Inquiry has included investigation of : (1) the order in which aspects of time are acquired. (2) whether this order is a function of training or the expression of some intrinsic phenomenon, (3) the development of "reasonable" estimation of the duration of some event, (4) the process of learning to "tell time," and (5) the psychological sense of the speed of the passage of time.

Sturt (1925) cites the work of Stern, Preyer, and Decroly and Degan which involved the observation and interpretation of "what concepts the 1 to 3-year-old child must be employing" and the linguistic development of the child *vis-a-vis* temporal word-use. She argued that the child probably develops a sense of the present first, then a sense of the past, and last a concept of the future. Piaget (1966; 1938), Flavell, 1963, Ginsburg and Opper, 1969 appear to argue that a sense of futurity is acquired much later in life, around adolescence. Piagetian "futurity" implies planfulness and not mere anticipation. He appears to contend that through preadolescence the child is concrete-present-unplanful, while at adolescence and beyond he becomes abstract-possibility-planful in his thinking. Piaget appears to argue that not only are preadolescents *ordinarily* not future-oriented, but that they are largely incapable of being so.

In our second study, involving the questioning what people were thinking about, when we interviewed children aged 4 through 7, we noted no particular difficulty in coding their responses as referring to the past, present, or future. In Studies II, IV, and V, we interviewed a substantial number of 8- through 11-year olds. Comparison of the parameters associated with the coded (Table 3.1, row 1) and respondent-chosen categories (Table 3.1, row 3) reveals the typical adult expansion of the past and future at the expense of the present when one moves from a "last instant" to a "last 5 minutes" segment of cognition. The distributions of temporal orientation for this aged respondent is similarly "reasonable." Thus as regards the ability of preadolescents to think about the future, it would appear that they can and do. In our limited test of planfulness (Table 3.10), preadolescents answered the item in a way consistent with the interpretation that they knew what we were asking, and could appraise their own thinking. If the set of responses on these two lines of questioning can be taken at something resembling "face value," then preadolescents not only *can* be planful and indulge in future thinking, but if differences between them and adolescents exist, they favor the Piagetian futurity of the former!

While incidence of future-thought traced a monotonic decline across the life-span, planfulness as we indexed it peaked in early adulthood (18 through 39). These years include the launching of careers, marriages, and families. Planfulness may well be socially and/or psychologically "required" of early adulthood. The middle-aged differed only slightly from the old in incidence of reporting thinking about the future (Table 3.1), and not at all in planfulness (Table 3.10), but the future things that the middle-aged reported as often thought about (Table 3.9) have a different cast to them than those reported by the old. The old certainly appear aware and anticipatory of their withdrawal from the social stage (e.g., nursing home, death). But the temporal "beat goes on." Things different than those nominated by the middle-aged occupy mental "center stage," but the temporality directed toward them is quite similar to the temporal orientation of the middle-aged. In the last half of the life-span, persons were busy devouring the present with but a seasoning of planfulness. Perhaps, as these are the persons who have lived life the most, some degree of wisdom attends their temporality. Those who escape death narrowly often report that the "now" becomes more precious to them — perhaps that is a major lesson of living.

As our research (with the exception of the third study) was cross-sectional, our interpretative remarks must await further testing to assure that we have not indexed some combination of age and cohort differences. As one of the major differences between older and younger cohorts in the United States is the greater education of the latter, the higher social class would include more highly educated persons, and we found only small social class differences in planfulness, it would appear that we are probably dealing with age rather than cohort effects, but only time will tell.

REFERENCES

Adler, A. *Individual psychology*. London: Routledge and Kegan Paul, 1925.

Allport, G. W. The individual and his religion. New York: MacMillan, 1950.

Apter, D. E. *Ghana in transition*. New York: Atheneum, 1968.

Aristotle, cited by Schuster, D. B. A psychological study of a 106-year-old man. *American Journal of Psychiatry*, 1952, *109*, 112-119.

Banfield, E. C. *The unheavenly city*. Boston: Little, Brown, 1968.

Bang, G. *Crises in European history*. New York: New York Labor News, 1955.

Boas, F. *Anthropology and modern life*. New York: Norton, 1928.

Botwinick, J. *Aging and behavior*. New York: Springer, 1973.

Buhler, C. The course of human life as a psychological problem. *Human Development*, 1968, *11*, 184-200.

Butler, R. N. The life review: an interpretation of reminiscence in the aged. *Psychiatry*, 1963, *26*, 76-76.

Cameron, P. Age parameters of young adult, middle-aged, old and aged. *Journal of Gerontology*, 1969, *24*,, 201-202.

Cameron, P. The generation gap: time orientation. *The Gerontologist*, 1972, *12*, 117-119.

Cameron, P. Temporality across the life-span. Extended report presented to the Southeastern Psychological Association, April 8, 1973, in New Orleans.

Cameron, P. and Biber, H. Sexual thought across the life-span. *The Gerontologist,* 1973, *13,* 144-147.

Cameron, P., Stewart, L., Craig, L. and Eppelman, L. J. Thing vs. self vs. other mental orientation across the life-span: a note. *British Journal of Psychology,* 1973, *64,* 283-286.

Cameron, P., Stewart, L. and Biber, H. Consciousness of death across the life-span. *Journal of Gerontology,* 1973, *28,* 92-95.

Cohen, J. Subjective time. In Fraser, J. T., ed., *The Voices of time.* New York Braziller, 1966.

Collier, R. M. A holistic-organismic theory of consciousness. *Journal of Individual Psychology,* 1963, *19,* 17-26.

Cumming, E. and Henry, W. H. *Growing old: the process of disengagement.* New York: Basic Books, 1961.

Efron, R. Temporal perception, aphasia, and *deja vu. Brain,* 1963, *86,* 401-416.

Engels, F. *The origin of the family, private property, and the state.* New York: International University Press, 1942.

Erikson, E. H. *Childhood and society.* New York: Norton, 1950.

Erikson, E. H. *Identity and the life cycle.* New York: International University Press, 1959.

Fink, H. H. The relationship of time perspective to age, institutionalization and activity. *Journal of Gerontology,* 1957, *12,* 414-417.

Flavel, J. H. *The developmental psychology of Jean Piaget.* New Jersey: Van Nostrand, 1963.

Frye, R. N. *Iran.* New York: Holt, Rinehart and Winston, 1953.

Gans, H. J. *The urban villagers.* New York: Free Press, 1962.

Ginsburg, H. and Opper, S. *Piaget's theory of intellectual development.* New Jersey: Prentice-Hall, 1969.

Hoepli, N. L. *West Africa today.* New York: Wilson, 1971.

Hollingshead, A. B. *Elmtown's youth.* New York: Wiley, 1949.

Kastenbaum, R. *New thoughts on old age.* New York: Springer, 1964.

Kastenbaum, R. and Durkee, N. Young people view old age. In R. Kastenbaum, ed., *New thoughts on old age.* New York: Springer, 1964.

Keniston, K. *The young radicals.* New York: Harcourt, Brace, and Jovanovch, 1968.

Kingsley, M. H. *West African studies.* New York: Barnes & Noble, 1899.

Komarovsky, M. *Blue-collar marriage.* New York: Vintage, 1967.

Lewis, C. N. Reminiscing and self-concept in old age. *Journal of Gerontology,* 1971, *26,* 240-243.

Marx, K. *Economic and philosophical manuscripts of 1846*. In Fromm, E. *Marx's concept of man*. New York: Ungar, 1961.

Masters, R. E. L. and Houston, J. *The varieties of psychedelic experience*. New York: Holt, Rinehart, and Winston, 1966.

May, R., Angel, E. and Ellenberger, H. F., ed., *Contributions of existential psychotherapy*. New York: Basic Boosk, 1958.

McMahon, W. W., Jr. and Rhudick, P. J. a3Psychodynamic studies on aging: creativity, reminiscing, and dying. New York: International University Press, 1968.

Nakamura, H. Time in Indian and Japanese thought. In Fraser, J. T., ed., *The voices of time*. New York: Braziller, 1966.

Neugarten, B. *Personality in middle and late life*. New York: Atherton, 1964.

Neugarten, B. L. and Garron, D. V. Attitudes of middle-aged persons towards growing older. *Geriatrics,* 1959, *14,* 21-24.

Ossorio, P. G. *Persons,* Los Angeles: Linguistic Research Institute, 1966.

Piaget, J. Time perception in children. In Fraser, J. T., ed., *The voices of time*. New York: Braziller, 1966.

Pollack, J. and Kastenbaum, R. Delay of gratification in later life: an experimental analogue. In R. Kastenbaum, ed., *New thoughts on old age*. New York: Springer, 1964.

Progoff, I. *The symbolic and the real*. New York: Julian, 1963.

Sahlins, M. D. and Service, E. R., eds., *Evolution and culture*. Ann Arbor; University of Michigan Press, 1960.

Schaie, K. W. Age changes and age differences. *The Gerontologist,* 1967, *7,* 128-132.

Schonfield, D. Future commitments and successful aging. The random sample. *Journal of Gerontology,* 1973, *28,* 189-196.

Spence, D. L. The role of futurity in aging adaptation. *The Gerontologist,* 1968, *8,* 180-183.

Suzuki, D. T. *An introduction to Zen Buddhism*. New York: Grove Press, 1964.

Thompson, W. E. and Streib, G. F. In R. W. Kleemier, ed., *Aging and leisure*. New York: Oxford University Press, 1961.

Vreeland, H. H. et al. *Iran*. New Haven: Human Relations Area Files, 1957.

4

CHILDREN'S CONCERNS/CONCERN ABOUT CHILDREN

Mankind always lives but 30 years from savagery. Unless the children are cared for, unless they are socialized properly, the civilized world ends. Everybody is in favor of "proper rearing" — but what is proper or correct? A "hot" and a "warm" issue from the readings in this section. Psychologists have made a lot of noise over television violence (it's almost our #1 issue in terms of publicity, research time and publications). The reading obviously casts the issue as more peripheral than central. Oh well, honorable men differ . . .

Secondhand tobacco smoke appears to loom rather large in the minds of children, yet is, at best, a warm issue within our society. So many things can be, and undoubtedly are, influential in the socializing of children, that these two issues comprise but a drop in the issues bucket.

THE EFFECTS OF VIEWING "VIOLENT" TELEVISION UPON CHILDREN'S AT-HOME AND IN-SCHOOL BEHAVIOR

What effect does the viewing of aggressively-hostile-violent television programming have upon the behavior of children? Although much has been said, both popularly and professionally about this issue, the two national commissions treating the topic have been unable to come to firm conclusions (Eisenhower, 1969; Steinfeld, 1972). We report the results of a study in which the effect upon in-home and in-school behavior of kindergarteners exposed to an in-home "diet" of either "violent" or "pacific" television programming for a three-week period was examined.

Method

We contacted the superintendent and the eight kindergarten teachers of the school district of River Rouge, Michigan (a suburb of Detroit, which, according to the 1960 census, almost exactly matched the United States average in income and size of households, while about a quarter of its population was Negro). We outlined our plans and they agreed to cooperate. It was determined that the district probably serviced 349 kindergarten children at that time, and a letter requesting the cooperation of all parents was mailed above the name of the superintendent of schools to the residence of each kindergartener. The letter was followed up by personal contact with the parent(s) explaining the nature of the project and their involvement in it. Of 292 parents that were contacted, 288 agreed to participate. Over the course of the seven-week study, 54 of the children either withdrew from school, were absent for an entire week, or moved and could not be relocated in time to assure guide-delivery; thus, our eventual number of kindergarteners was 254 in the experimental conditions and 43 who we considered controls.

After the initial parent-contact, the children within each room were divided by sex, and first the boys and then the girls were randomly placed into one of the four experimental conditions. The children of the four parents who refused to cooperate and all those children whose parents we could not contact were placed in the in-school control group. As this was an exploratory study, we felt that it was more important to have as many children as possible in the experimental groups than to have a classical control group. The initial number of children in each of the four experimental groups was: "straight violent" 74; "violent-pacific" 72; "pacific-violent" 71; and "straight pacific" 71. After the above-mentioned attrition, the number of children in each of the four experimental groups was 66, 64, 61, and 63, respectively. The "straight violent" group received three weeks of violent television programs; the "violent-pacific" group received two weeks of violent followed by a week of nonviolent television; the "pacific-violent" group received two weeks of nonviolent television followed by a week of violent television; and the "straight pacific" group received three weeks of nonviolent television.

Classification of TV programs. A panel of five students and the authors, through consultation with the Detroit television stations, their memories, and program descriptions, classified all television programs scheduled for the next week into two categories — "violent" or "pacific." The criterion was "Does this program show a person, or an animal or cartoon character representing a person, hit, strike, shove, throw or shoot objects at, or in any physical, nonverbal way demonstrate violent, hostile, aggression toward any other person or animal representing a person?" If a program had one or more such incidents, it was classified as "violent;" if none, it was classified as "pacific." Hockey and basketball were classified as "violent;" tennis as "pacific." Most situation comedies were classified as pacific and most dramatic shows as violent (all crime and western shows fell here). Most monster movies fell into the pacific category (monsters are not persons). All cartoons featuring nonhumans who buffeted each other about (such as Bugs Bunny) were classified as "pacific," while those cartoons that featured humanoids who assaulted each other (as Spiderman) were classified as "violent." We had to guess about the content of only a couple of programs, and, to our knowledge, only one guess was incorrect.

The panel met about a week before each television week started and did the classification. Then two television "guides" were constructed, one violent and the other pacific. The appropriate one was then mailed to the homes of the participating parents. During each of the three experimental weeks, an attempt was made to contact each home twice to encourage them to abide by the guide and to answer any questions that might have arisen (overall, we averaged about one and a half contacts per week). The first week's mailing went smoothly, but the second week's was partially lost in the post and we had to hand-deliver the appropriate guides. The next week's guides were all hand-delivered. All television guides were personally picked up when possible at the beginning of the next week's programs (which, for our purposes, started Saturday morning). As might be expected, a certain percentage was not retrieved from each group (perhaps the family was not at home, in which case the new television guide would be dropped off, but the old one could not be retrieved until Monday). There were many different reasons for loss of the marked, old television guide among which were "We lost it . . . it was just here a moment ago . . ." and "The dog ate it."

Responsibilities of cooperating parents. Cooperating parents were told that they were to control their child's television viewing as per the television guide we provided them. If a child wanted to watch television, he had to watch one of the listed program on his television guide for that time slot. If there was no listed program, he could watch what he pleased (without exception, there was always at least one pacific program on television at any time; however, there were many time periods when no violent program was available). The parent was to further indicate which programs the child watched on each day (it takes effort to look up the correct programs, and even more effort to locate a pencil and mark; and our parents were more apt to do the monitoring than they were to do the indicating).

Responsibilities of cooperating teachers. All eight kindergarten teachers in the district graciously agreed to cooperate with us. Teachers knew that the study was going on, but were asked to deliberately avoid finding out into which experimental condition their children were placed. For the first five weeks of the study, each teacher was provided a list of the children in her classroom and asked to note the number of physically-aggressive-hostile behaviors performed by each child against any other child, by child, by incident, per day. That is, any child whom she saw hit, push, strike, throw an object at, or in any other physical, nonverbal way, aggress against another child was to be located on the list, and a check placed by his or her name. If the same child performed another such behavior on the same day, he would receive another check, and so forth. As would be expected, the amount of recorded "violence" varied from classroom to classroom (one of the teachers was quite a disciplinarian; almost none of her children ever were recorded as having behaved "violently" — we subsequently checked on her informally "Could she really have *that* calm a class, maybe she's just not recording?" — she really did have that calm a class). It should be noted that this was taken into account in the design of the study, since an equal number of children from each room fell into each of the four experimental conditions. Further, as luck would have it, about the same proportion of controls came from each teacher's classroom(s) (some teachers had two).

Parental-report data. At the end of the three manipulation weeks, one of the parents was contacted and asked, "Have there been any changes in your child's behavior?"; (if so) "What were they?" At the end of the seventh week the interview was repeated and one of the parents was then asked, "Did you expect your child to change because of the television programs he was watching?"; (if so) "How did you expect him to change?" It should be noted that the parents were not forewarned that they would be making any of these appraisals and, by asking for their expectations *after* they had made their reports, we increased the possibility that what they claimed they had expected would jibe with what they had reported (it is a commonly-known person-maxim that persons in our culture like to be correct, and, given the chance, will tend to make their predictive prowess appear greater rather than smaller (Ossorio, 1966). In other words, knowing that the results might well be biased, we deliberately designed the reporting so that expectations would more likely jibe with the reports rather than vice versa.

Results

Television viewing. The universe of television programs accessible to children during the three-week manipulation period was mainly "passive." The majority of movies (72%) fell into our "violent" category, while the majority of the regularly-scheduled programs (84%) were placed in our "passive" group. Overall, giving each program equal weight irrespective of length, 30% of the television programming was violent and 70% passive. Groups subjected to "violent" television watched less television that was monitored and recorded by their parents.

In-school violent-hostile-aggressive behavior. It must be noted at the onset that we found no completely legitimate way to analyze the single-blind data from the teachers. Children were absent at varying times throughout the experiment. Only a handful of children in each experimental group were not absent at all. It would be quite illegitimate to perform any conventional parametric analysis upon only their data. Hence the following analysis, which permits a "feel" for the results, even though it is, admittedly, only a "better-than-nothing" solution.

First we took the number of times in the week the child had performed a violent-aggressive-hostile behavior and divided it by the number of days in attendance for the first base week, each of the three manipulation weeks, and the second base week which gave us a weekly index of in-class "violence." Each child's index for each of the succeeding weeks was compared with his initial index in Week 1. The number who changed in a more "violent" direction were marked with a plus (+); the number who changed in a more "passive" direction were marked with a minus (−). The "fluid" model reifies aggression-violence-hostility into a "natural" substance or force that must be regularly discharged by acting-out or through vicarious experience. The "copycat" model assumes that persons will tend to do the kinds of things that they see others doing (that is, if a person observes another person doing a violently, aggressively, hostile act, he will be more apt to commit a violently, aggressively, hostile act — either the same act that he witnesses or another act from the set of acts designated as violent, aggressive, and hostile. The exact parameters describing a particular act are never duplicated and usually not even approximated except in a highly controlled situation such as a laboratory. This circumstance has led some researchers to talk about "disinhibition" as a function of viewing certain kinds of acts (e.g., Bandura, Ross, and Ross, 1963). If more of the others in their experience do aggressively-hostile-violent things, then they will do more; while if the others in their experience do nonaggressively-hostile-violent things, they will "copy" them. Both theories assume that television provides psychologically-real-others.

Because the preponderance of pluses (+) or minuses (−) could be expected to vary randomly, nonrandomicity can be examined with the sign test. Thus, for the "straight violent" group, the second week should have found more children changing toward violence than toward nonviolence under the "copycat" theory; this occurred and was scored a *hit*. The same should have occurred for Week 3, but the changes did not fall in either direction which was scored a *miss*. Week 4 should have seen more violent changes and did, a *hit*. Week 5 should have seen a tapering off with more changes toward passivity; this occurred and was scored a *hit*. Further, when the violence level for each child for Week 4 is compared with the violence level for Week 5, there should be more nonviolent changes; there were (6+/11−), a *hit*. For the "violent-passive" group, Week 2 should have seen relatively more violent changes; there were more nonviolent changes, a *miss*. Similarly for Week 3, a *miss*. For Week 4, where passivity dominated the television screen, the prediction would be uncertain; however, comparing Weeks 3 and 4, the preponderance of changes should have been toward passivity; they were equivalent (7+/7−) and was scored, a *miss*. For the "passive-violent" group, Week 2 should have seen a preponderance of nonviolent changes; there were and this was scored a *hit*. the same was true of Week 3; also scored a *hit*. When the changes in Weeks 3 and 4 are compared, there should have been a preponderance of violence; there were (9+/7−) and was scored a *hit*. For the "straight passive" group, Week 2 should have been seen a greater number of nonviolent changes; there were and this was scored a *hit*. The same was true of Week 3, a *hit*. Week 4 was uncertain, neither a hit nor a miss. Week 5 should have seen more changes toward violence, and did, a *hit*. A comparison of the changes in Weeks 4 and 5 should reveal a greater number of changes toward violence; the numbers were equal (7+/7−) and was scored a *miss*. Thus we had 10 hits and 5 misses which would give us a p of .31 in favor of the "copycat" theory. As is so often the case with sex differences, of the 25 possible comparisons of mean violent-aggressive-hostile acts per week for boys and girls, the boys' mean was greater in 23 which is associated with a p of less than .001.

In the base week (Week 1), the average "level of violence" for the "violent" treatment boy groups was .1078 vs. .1107 for the "pacific" boy groups. If we consider the difference between these two groups' means as the base, then the difference between these two groups should increase during the next week relative to the base week if the "copycat" model were valid or decrease if the "fluid" model were valid. The same relationship should obtain for the next week's means relative to the base week's. For girls, the "copycat" model applied and this was scored as 2 *hits;* for boys the same analysis yielded a *hit* and a *miss.* During the fourth week, the change week for the two middle groups, the "copycat" model would predict an upward or level mean for the "straight violent" group compared with the previous week's mean. Boys were up, girls were up, 2 *hits.* For the "violent-pacific" group, the "copycat" model would predict a downward level compared with the previous week's mean. Boys were up, girls were down, *1 hit, 1 miss.* For the "pacific-violent" group, the "copycat" model would predict an upward swing compared with last week's mean. Boys were up, girls experienced no change, *1hit, 1 miss.* For the "straight pacific" group, the "copycat" model would predict a downward or level tendency compared with the previous week. Boys were down, girls were up, *1 hit, 1 miss.* For the fifth week, the "copycat" model would predict a downward swing for the "straight violent" group. Boys were down, girls were down, 2 *hits.* The intermediate groups would be simply questionable, but for the "straight pacific" group, the prediction would be upward relative to the previous week. Boys were up, girls were up, 2 *hits.* Of the 16 possible predictions, 12 were hits for the "copycat" model which is associated with a two-tail probability of less than .08.

In-home behavioral change. Parental report of changes in children's behavior included changes other than those along the violent-aggressive-hostile continuum. Many of the changes referred to activity level (e.g., "more active," "louder"), some referred to activity and/or pathological behavior (e.g., "more aggressive," "argumentative"), and others referred to parabehavior (e.g., "nightmares," "wets bed"). The classificatory scheme or weightings of behavior were *post hoc;* we were not sure just what kinds of parental report we would get beforehand. However the ratings appeared psychologically sensible and were evenly applied to all four experimental groups. It should be noted that only a small proportion of the changes reported by parents were pathological *per se*. Therefore we analyzed the data two ways. First, all changes suggestive of some pathology were weighted and the means taken and compared. Then only those kinds of behaviors suggestive of active, acting-out kinds of pathology or lack of such pathology were compared.

Parental report for the first three weeks was examined. If amount of change were directly related to the amount of "violent" television programming in harmony with the "copycat" model, we would have expected the means for the groups to run, highest for the "straight violent" group (#1), the next highest for the "violent-pacific" group (#2), next highest for the "pacific-violent" group (#3), and lowest for the "straight pacific" group (#4). We obtained an ordering of 1, 2, 4, 3 under both systems of scoring. The rank-order correlation associated with this relationship is .73 which is associated with a p of less than .25. Comparing groups 1 and 4 for all pathology with t, we derived a value of 1.37 which is associated with a p of less than .20 with a $df = 127$; for acting-out pathology the t was 2.02, $p < .04$.

The seventh-week interview of parents resulted in a total pathology mean of .364 for the "straight-violent" group (13 children were reported as having changed), .219 for the "violent-pacific" group (18 children reported as changed), .312 for the "pacific-violent" group (16 children reported as changed), and .0317 for the "straight-pacific" group (12 children reported as changed). For acting-out pathology, the respective means were .333, .296, .197, and .0635. Comparing the straight-violent and straight-pacific groups on all pathology, the t was 1.835 which, with 127 df, is associated with a p of less than .08. Comparing the same groups on acting-out pathology yielded a t of 1.76, $p < .09$.

The expectations and reported outcomes by the parents at the end of the seventh-week interview were examined. There was little or no relationship between professed expectations and reported outcomes. Of the 59 changes, 41 were associated with no expectations, four were "correct," four were "wrong," six were not specific enough to know whether the person had been right or wrong, and 16 or the expectations were associated with no change.

Comparison of in-home and in-school behavioral changes. There was little if any correspondence between in-home and in-school changes. For instance, during Week 2, the total number of home changes was 29 and school changes was 65. Only 10 of the children were reported as having the same kind of change at home and at school, and three had opposite changes. Of the 65 children who changed at school, if there had been a random mix into did-change-at-home and didn't-change-at-home categories, we would have expected about 12% to change in both places in similar ways; we got about 15%. The same relationship obtained for the two other weeks of manipulation, so we uncovered no evidence that behavioral changes similar to those reported at home would be more likely than chance to be found or reported at school.

Discussion

The meanings of the concepts "violent," "aggressive," and "hostile." Buss (1961) defines aggression as "a response that delivers noxious stimuli to another object." This is obviously not what most people mean by aggression because under it every doctor who administers a "hypo" is aggressing against his patient, or most teachers are aggressing against their students by teaching. Bandura and Walters (1965) suggest that aggressive acts are that class of behaviors that ". . . could injure or damage *if* aimed at a vulnerable object." This definition serves us no better, for then chopping down a cherry tree would be aggressive because the tree was vulnerable, and we definitely aimed to damage it.

What conditions must be met before we can correctly characterize an act as aggressive? The act: (a) must have the effect of crimping another's range of behavior; (b) must advance or plausibly appear to advance the interests or social position of the actor; (c) must have rather strong or powerful social or personal effects relative to other acts in that social situation; (d) the actor must be the initiator of the interaction; while (e) all of the above strictures can be tempered by the status of the actor.

An instance of hostile behavior is one that meets the following two criteria: (a) the person involved must have reason to believe that the other person or persons will be displeased by it; and (b) the person involved must *want* to displease the person annoyed.[1]

Hostile-aggressive acts can only be committed against persons. You cannot aggress against a tree or a car (you may get "mad" at them; that is, you may act against them in a way analogous to how you would act against a person you were angry with, but as you well know or others will inform you, it's "silly" to be really angry with the thing — after all, it's not to blame). If a person lets the air out of your tires, you have reason to be angry — but with him. If you drive over nails with the same result, no one in his right mind would be angry with the nails (though perhaps with the damn fool who put them there).

Violent acts always involve a considerable expenditure of energy. The consequences of violent acts almost always involve physical hurt or destruction and/or a considerable expenditure of energy. Thus storms which are violent are usually powerful and usually involve physical destruction. Acts that are violent such as a violent murder not only have severe consequences but also inform of severe physical damage.

Our linguistic system, then, allows for three levels or degrees of aggressive or hostile behavior. A person can commit an aggressive or hostile act, an aggressively hostile act, or a violently aggressive or hostile act. Although it is possible for behavior to be aggressive and violent yet not hostile (as a virulent interruption into a conversation) or hostile and aggressive but not violent (as squelching an underling at a party), it does not seem possible to commit an act that is hostile and violent without its being aggressive also.

One cannot "just by looking" confidently tell whether a given act or series of acts is aggressive or hostile or both. We must know more information about the social context before we can adequately and correctly characterize a person's behavior.

A comparison of naturalistic vs. laboratory findings. Bryan and Schwartz (1970), in the most recent review of the literature, conclude that it " . . . seems quite clear that models as presented in films are capable of evoking a wide range of responses . . . , from aggression to courage and self-sacrifice. . . . thus providing support for the assumption that laboratory findings pertaining to modeling phenomena will be generalizable to a variety of naturalistic

[1] L. Berkowitz, *Aggression: a social psychological analysis* (New York: McGraw Hill, 1962), p. IX. Berkowitz vacillates between considering hostility and aggression as synonymous and appearing to consider the combination of hostility and aggression as different from aggression *per se* which he terms "instrumental aggression."

settings." A most interesting appraisal, for the question immediately springs to mind, "Which findings?" In the Hicks' (1965) study, involving "aggression toward an inflated doll" (!), the children who were shown models "aggressing" against the doll, *aggressed* against the doll far more than the controls who *didn't aggress at all!* Are we to take this experiment as demonstrating that children who are not exposed to models will never "aggress" against inflated dolls? A "finding" that just about no one would treat seriously for we know that children often buffet dolls. If we generalize as Bryan and Schwartz have, then conceivably this study demonstrates that children who are never provided models for aggression will never aggress! The widely-known Bandura, Ross, and Ross (1963) effort does not indicate whether every single experimental child "aggressed against the Bobo doll," but it would be rather strange if children provided with the paucity of materials to play with *didn't* "aggress." Clearly these and similar experiments depend for their generalizability upon the misuse of the concept "aggression" (see above). Without this misuse, their experiments are rather trivial demonstrations that children will often do, or try to do, what they see others doing. The characteristic of "playing fast and loose" with our linguistic system is not confined to the misuse of the concept "aggression." In the Midlarsky and Bryan (1967) study, when children, who were encouraged by an experimenter that expressed joy and/or hugged them, did not pull a lever that would get them some candy, their behavior was characterized as "a self-sacrificing response." Since others have most capably assailed the intellectual sophistry and inherent triviality of such social psychological experiments (Champanis, 1967; Ossorio and Davis, 1969), we will refer the readers to their labors.

The most distressing aspect of such experiments is that many psychologists ask society to treat the results most seriously, and as applicable to situations-in-general ("[t]he results of the present study provide strong evidence that exposure to filmed aggression heightens aggressive reactions in children" [Bandura, Ross, and Ross, 1963]). It is questionable whether the results of a study performed upon 96 children's play with a Bobo doll constitutes "strong evidence." Had the children, after having watched the "assault" on the Bobo doll, *turned upon the experimenters* then "strong evidence" would have been presented. Perhaps the president of the Society for the Preservation of Bobo Dolls would consider such evidence "strong." But if children reacted to television drama by regularly assaulting their parents or guardians, society would hardly require the sophisticated subtleties of laboratory psychologists to outlaw their presentation. Obviously, in our culture, children learn quite early that "drama" is not "real life" (we and others utilized young children because we know they are less apt to have learned this principle well). An experimental situation is one situation. It is already known that what a person will do, or how he reacts in one situation, bears no necessary relationship to his behavior in other situations. Many behaviors are situation-specific. To find out how children will react to a given input "in general," we must sample their reactions in a variety of situations. The lab-situation simply does not constitute an adequate sample of situations-in-general. When we talk about aggressive-responses-in-general, we must sample not only situations but aggressive responses. Such comments are, or should be, truisms to professionals trained in the heritage of Brunswik's insistence on representative design.

In the experiment reported here we were not primarily interested in contributing evidence toward the argument of whether "violent-aggressive-hostile models generally tend to elicit similar behaviors from the viewers." Rather, we have provided information that bears on only one, albeit practical, situation, namely "Does the viewing of violent-aggressive-hostile models on home television tend to elicit a greater frequency of acts from the set of acts characterized as violently-aggressively-hostile and/or socially undesirable behaviors at home and/or at school?" It will be noted that we tested in the very situation we hoped to generalize to. Our investigation constitutes only one limited test of the first and more general proposition.

Relevance of our study to the social issues of television violence. The relevance of our study to the current social issue of the amount of hostile-aggressive-violence on the television screen is not certain. We must emphasize that this was one test of the possible effects. This test took place in one community, with one modest sample of kindergarteners, eight teachers, and all in one slice of time. Parents appear to have been reasonably diligent in monitoring what their children watched on television at home, but there was no control over the commercials, at least one of which featured a bloody brawl between two boxers, and ended with a knockout. We also had no control over the television programs children might have seen at their neighbor's or elsewhere. A judicious estimate of amount of control would suggest that about 75% of the television viewing of each child was "controlled." Thus each experimental group received about 75% "correct" television and 25% "?." Unlike the results obtained in the laboratory, in all experimental conditions, most children appear not to have changed. In all experimental conditions, almost as large a minority of children changed against the "copycat" model as changed toward it. However, in harmony with the way most investigators have construed the results of their laboratory experiments, there was a tendency for children to change toward the "copycat" rather than toward the "fluid" model. We sampled kindergarteners who are still learning to be persons. Whether the same effect would appear in a three-week study with significantly older children, although an empirical issue, is unlikely.

Examining our data as they pertain to the validity of the "copycat" and "fluid" models, if we regard all changes in individual children's behavior as due to the "influence" of one of these two models, at most, experimental groups experienced 120 changes per the $254 \times 3 + 129 = 891$ child-weeks in harmony with the "copycat" and 107 in harmony with the "fluid" model. Thus, 13.5% of the child-changes were toward the "copycat" vs. 12.0% toward the "fluid" model. During the same period, 39 changes were recorded for the control group's $29 \times 4 = 114$ child-weeks, or a "normal" rate of change of about 33.6%. As the experimental children as a whole had a rate of 25.5%, putting much emphasis on the slight difference in favor of the "copycat" model would appear strained.

If we sound uncertain, it is because we are. More work will have to be performed to arrive at a reasonably judicious decision. Since social policy is usually made in the absence of most relevant information, yet must be made, it should be noted that our results tend to weigh in the following directions: (a) most children's at-home and at-school behavior is not affected by exposure to violent-aggressive-hostile interpersonal relationships on television; and (b) it appears that the minority of children whose behavior is affected, more frequently tend to perform a slight surplus of aggressively, hostile, violent acts rather than performing such acts less frequently.

REFERENCES

Bandura, A., Ross, D., and Ross, S. Vicarious reinforcement and imitative learning. *Journal of Abnormal and Social Psychology*, 1963, *67*, 601-608.

Bandura, A. and Walters, R. H. *Social learning and personality development*. New York: Holt, Rinehart, and Winston, 1965.

Berkowitz, L. *Aggression: a social psychological analysis*. New York: McGraw-Hill, 1962.

Bryan, J. H. and Schwartz, L. Effects of film material upon children's behavior. *Psychological Bulletin*, 1971, *75*, 50-59.

Buss, A. R. *Psychology of aggression*. New York: Wiley, 1961.

Champanis, A. The relevance of laboratory studies to practical situations. *Ergonomics*, 1967, *10*, 557-577.

Eisenhower, M. S. *Commission statement on violence in television entertainment programs*. Washington, D. C.: Government Printing Office, 1969.

Hicks, C. Imitation and retention of film-mediated aggressive peer and adult models. *Journal of Personality and Social Psychology*, 1965, *2*, 97-100.

Midlarsky, D. and Bryan, J. H. Training charity in children. *Journal of Personality and Social Psychology*, 1967, *5*, 408-415.

Ossorio, P. G. *Persons*. Los Angeles: Linguistic Research Institute, 1966.

Ossorio, P. G. and Davis, K. E. *The self, intentionality, and reactions to evaluations*. Boulder: University of Colorado, 1966.

SECONDHAND TOBACCO SMOKE:
CHILDREN'S REACTIONS

Although a lot of research has focused on the effects of smoking on the smoker, relatively little research has been performed on the effects of smoking on the nonsmoker. While two-thirds of the nation's children reside with smokers, Speer is the only investigator to have reported the reactions of nonsmokers to secondhand tobacco smoke. In the present study, the psychological and symptom reactions of children to secondhand tobacco smoke were explored.

Method

Study I.

In the fall of 1969, 1,710 children aged 7 to 15 residing in Evansville, Indiana were approached in shopping centers, play-grounds, on-the-street, while playing in their yards, and, in a few cases, at school, by college student volunteers. The questions were read to them and their replies recorded verbatim for each subject. Each child was drawn away from any group that he happened to be with and his opinions solicited privately so that group pressure would be minimal. In all cases a total sample of all children present in a given situation was attempted so that selection-of-subject bias would be minimal. Twenty-five children refused us an interview (a rejection rate of less than 2%).

Interview. This interviewer introduced himself "Hi, I'm a student at the University. Would you answer a few questions for me? Thanks. (1) How do you feel about someone smoking around you? Do you like the smoke, dislike the smoke, or don't you care one way or the other?" (For every other interview the first two possible responses were reversed.) if the child either liked or disliked secondhand smoke, he was asked, "How much do you (like, dislike) the smoke? Do you (like, dislike) it: a whole lot, a lot, a little bit?" (For every other interview, the responses were read in reverse order.) (2) "Does your body react when someone smokes around you? Like do your eyes water, or your nose run, or something like that? (If yes.) Oh, what happens to you?" (All reactions were recorded.) (3) Do either of your parents smoke? (If yes.) Which one(s)? How do you feel about their smoking? I mean are you proud of them for smoking, or worried about their health, or their dying from it, or something like that?" (All reactions were recorded along with the age and sex of the child.)

Studies II and III.

The next two studies attempted to eliminate some of the possible methodological shortcomings of the first study, and expand upon both the meanings and generalizability of the results of Study I. Study II was conducted in the fall of 1970 in Louisville by the author, Theadore Johnson, and student volunteers. Four hundred sixty-four children were interviewed in shopping centers, on the street, and at play. Questions No. 2 and No. 3 were changed by utilizing only the first sentence of each. In Study III the author interviewed 216 Los Angeles children in winter, 1970. Besides the questions in Study II, when the questions applied, the following were asked: (4) "How do you feel about your parent(s) nonsmoking? (5) Would you love 00000 more if (s)he stopped smoking? (6) Would you respect 00000 more if (s)he stopped smoking? (7) Would you love 00000 less if (s)he started smoking?, and (8) Would you respect 00000 less if (s)he started smoking? The rejection rate for the last two studies was less than 1%.

Results

Children's psychological reactions to secondhand tobacco smoke in Study I are summarized in Table 4.1. For the 7-12-year olds, 76% disliked secondhand tobacco smoke, 21% reported indifference, and 3% said they enjoyed it. For those aged 13 to 15 proportionately fewer children reported disliking secondhand tobacco smoke (56%), 37% reported indifference to it, and 7% claimed to enjoy it (X^2 corrected for continuity comparing under- and over-13-year-olds = 102; df = 2; $p < .001$). The strength of positive affect toward secondhand smoke was weaker than the strength of negative affect toward it — while the modal indicant of degree of liking was characterized as "a little bit" by those who liked it, the modal degree of disliking was characterized as "a whole lot" by those who disliked it. Results of the three studies were virtually identical along this dimension.

A larger proportion of children who liked secondhand smoke and who were indifferent to secondhand smoke came from families in which at least one parent smoked ($X^2 = 17.6$; df = 2; $p < .001$), although, for all three groups, the majority of children came from families in which smoking was practiced.

TABLE 4.1

Children's Psychological Reactions to Second Hand Tobacco Smoke

		7-12-year olds		12-15-year olds		% of children from homes where tobacco smoking is practiced
		n	%	n	%	
	a whole lot	7	1	6	1	
like	a lot	8	1	11	2	
	a little bit	17	2	21	4	
						89
	a whole lot	497	44	166	30	
dislike	a lot	164	15	72	13	
	a little bit	187	17	78	14	**65**
indifferent		241	21	210	37	**71**
	totals	**1121**	**101**	**564**	**101**	

The data were first broken down into cells formed by cross-tabulating age, sex, psychological reaction, to secondhand smoke, degree of psychlogical reaction, and the presence or absence of symptoms to secondhand tobacco smoke, to explore the possibility that there might be systematic differences in family-exposure-history for these subject-groups. None were encountered. That is, no evidence suggested that the presence of reported symptoms was related to either the presence or absence or kind of tobacco smoking in the family of the child.

Table 4.2 summarizes the reported symptomatic reactions to secondhand smoke by psychological reaction for the three studies. Speer's results are included for comparison. While the 7-12-year olds were more frequently annoyed by secondhand smoke, dislikers reported the same frequency of each symptom irrespective of age. No differences between the sexes nor between levels of intensity of psychological reaction were uncovered. Speer's categories of symptoms were employed, however, "wheezing" and "hoarse-

TABLE 4.2

Children's Symptom Reportage

	eye irrita-tion	nasal irrita-tion	head-ache	cough	throat	nausea	dizzi-ness	other	none
Children's Responses: Study I									
Likers (n = 70)	20 (29%)	6 (9%)	5 (7%)	10 (14%)	3 (6%)	4 (6%)	5 (7%)	3 (4%)	28 (40%)
Dislikers (n = 1,174)	613 (53%)	164 (14%)	167 (14%)	509 (44%)	90 (8%)	144 (12%)	119 (10%)	71 (6%)	184 (16%)
Indifferent (n = 451)	175 (39%)	20 (4%)	28 (6%)	109 (24%)	11 (2%)	18 (4%)	22 (4%)	14 (3%)	220 (49%)
Total	**808 (47%)**	**190 (11%)**	**200 (12%)**	**628 (37%)**	**104 (6%)**	**166 (10%)**	**146 (9%)**	**88 (5%)**	**432 (25%)**
Speer's 250 nonallergic nonsmokers	(69%)	(29%)	(32%)	(25%)	(6%)	(9%)	(6%)	(8%)	(?)
Children's Responses: Studies II and III									
Likers (n = 17)	4 (24%)		1 (6%)	1 (6%)				3 (18%)	9 (53%)
Dislikers (n = 439)	163 (37%)	40 (9%)	19 (4%)	134 (30%)	13 (3%)	15 (3%)	10 (2%)	16 (4%)	143 (33%)
Indifferent (n = 220)	55 (25%)	3 (1%)	3 (1%)	22 (10%)		2 (1%)	3 (1%)	6 (2%)	140 (64%)
Total	**222 (33%)**	**43 (6%)**	**23 (3%)**	**157 (23%)**	**13 (2%)**	**17 (3%)**	**13 (2%)**	**25 (4%)**	**292 (43%)**

ness" were judged rather difficult and unusual concepts for children (no child used the term "wheezing" and only two mentioned "hoarseness"). "Nausea" was used by a handful of children, usually "makes me feel like throwing up" or "sick to my stomach" were employed. In almost all of the cases the coding of responses was extremely clear-cut — if the child complained of "eyes watering" it was classified as "eye irritation." "Headache," "cough", "sore throat," and "dizziness" were coded only when the child used the term. All other reactions were classified as "other."

An examination of Table 4.2 reveals that: (1) children who disliked secondhand tobacco smoke were more apt to report one or more symptomatic reactions. If we order the proportion of respondents in each study by frequency of reporting a given symptom, the highest frequency was reported by the "dislikers" in 14 of the 16 comparisons (sign test $p < .01$). (2) A majority of the members of all categories in Study I reported one or more symptomatic reactions to secondhand tobacco smoke. A majority of the "dislikers" in Studies II and III also reported one or more symptomatic reactions. For Study I, about 14% of the children who "disliked," 69% of the children who "liked," and 54% of the children "indifferent" to secondhand tobacco smoke reported one or more reactions ($X^2 = 87.1$; df $= 2$; $p < .001$). Almost without exception, reportage was lower in Studies II and III than in Study I. (3) At all ages, the most common reactions to secondhand tobacco smoke were coughing and eye irritation.

Children's reactions to their parents smoking were categorized into 8 categories: pride in their smoking, "glad they do," worry about parental health, worry about parental health with mention of possible death or dying, disliking of smell, on breath or clothing, concern about the cost of smoking, "I don't care," and "other." Interviewers recorded the reaction immediately, and if it did not fit a category it was taken down verbatim as "other."

Children's reactions to parental smoking is presented in Table 4.3. Two major differences between Studies I and II and III are apparent: (1) children generally reported less concern about their parents in the two latter studies, and (2) children more frequently indicated a desire that their parents quit smoking. Children's reactions to parental smoking varied somewhat with age of respondent. While for the samples as a whole about 4% of the children in Study I

TABLE 4.3 Children's Reactions to Parental Smoking

Psychological Reaction	Proud	Glad	Worry Health	Worry Death	Bad Smells	Worry Cost	Don't Care	Other	Wish they would quit
Study I									
7-12-year olds									
Like (n = 30)	7 (23%)	15 (50%)	7 (23%)	3 (10%)	2 (7%)	4 (13%)	3 (10%)	2 (7%)	
Dislike (n = 554)	2	3	318 (57%)	192 (35%)	155 (28%)	88 (16%)	48 (9%)	47 (8%)	
Indifferent (n = 164)	3 (2%)	3 (2%)	68 (40%)	35 (21%)	30 (18%)	16 (10%)	21 (13%)	9 (5%)	
13-15-year olds									
Like (n = 32)	2 (6%)	6 (19%)	13 (41%)	11 (34%)	7 (22%)	6 (19%)	6 (19%)	1 (3%)	
Dislike (n = 211)	1	1	120 (62%)	60 (31%)	54 (26%)	52 (25%)	8 (4%)	26 (12%)	
Indifferent (n = 155)		6 (4%)	73 (47%)	38 (25%)	31 (20%)	25 (16%)	20 (13%)	18 (12%)	
Studies II and III									
Children (7-12-year olds)									
Likers (n = 8)			1				4 (50%)		3 (38%)
Dislikers (n = 8)		1	84 (41%)	19 (9%)	20 (10%)		28 (14%)	36 (17%)	82 (40%)
Indifferent (n = 45)		1	6 (13%)	1	4 (9%)		22 (49%)	11 (24%)	11 (24%)
Teenagers (13-15-year olds)									
Likers (n = 5)			2 (40%)				2 (40%)	2 (40%)	
Dislikers (n = 80)			37 (46%)	12 (15%)	17 (21%)	2 (3%)	6 (8%)	9 (11%)	38 (48%)
Indifferent	1	1	17	11	2	1	36	22	21

expressed approval of their parents' smoking, about 13% were indifferent, and about 84% disapproving, the 7 to 8 year olds average 4%, 13%, and 73% as compared with 3%, 14%, and 83% for the teenagers.

Los Angeles children's reactions to parental nonsmoking are summarized in Table 4.4. No child indicated disappointment or disapproval with his parents' nonsmoking, while most were approving. That parental smoking is strongly disapproved by children is pointed-up in Table 4.5. Most children and many teenagers indicated that both the love and respect they directed toward their parents was dampened by parental smoking.

TABLE 4.4

Reactions of Los Angeles Children to Parental Nonsmoking

7-12-year olds ($\underline{n}$ = 95)		Reaction	13-15-year olds ($\underline{n}$ = 39)	
$\underline{n}$	%		$\underline{n}$	%
6	6	proud of	1	3
78	82	glad they don't	28	72
		glad — good for their health	2	5
10	11	okay — don't care	8	21
1	1	against our religion		

Discussion

Comparison of the results of Study I with Studies II and III suggests that the "true" values for symptomatic reactions to secondhand tobacco smoke and regard of parental smoking lie somewhere between the values reported. While Study I was possibly "contaminated" by suggestive examples in the questions, persons often cannot think of genuine reactions without "prompting." With prompting, some persons will "give you what you seem to want." The results of Studies II and III cannot be taken at face value because of their lack of prompting. Children are known to be both more suggestable and forgetful than adults.

Secondhand tobacco smoke is clearly an annoyance to most children. In this regard, they appear to differ little from adults. The most recent survey of what adults find most annoying in their daily lives found secondhand tobacco smoke the tenth most frequently nominated annoyance for the population as a whole.

Although the health effects, if any, of secondhand tobacco smoke are yet to be established (although the correlational research reported by Cameron et al. is suggestive), there seems little room to doubt that symptoms occur in most children as a result of exposure. While physiological irritation and disease are two different domains, with the possibility of complete independence always possible, it would seem very possible that physiological irritations would result in a higher incidence of disease.

Children's attitude toward their parents' smoking is generally one of worry and concern for their parents. Well it might be since both school and the mass media preach the harmful effects of smoking.

For children-in-general in our society, tobacco smoking appears to be both a psychological and and physiological irritation. Further, for most of the children who reside with a smoking parent, the habit is psychologically troubling and disruptive of the parent-child relationship to some degree.

It is more than casually interesting that we found relatively little overlap between physiologic irritation and psychological preferences. Of course our linguistic system treats persons as belonging to one linguistic subsystem and the bodies they inhabit as belonging to another, but for those who adhere to a monistic worldview, in which persons like or dislike things because of their effects upon their bodies, the finding must be somewhat troubling. Being physically irritated gives a person in our culture a possible reason to dislike the substance that caused the irritation; however, it is clearly not a sufficient reason. Many children who were physically irritated liked secondhand tobacco smoke (and possibly, for some, because of the irritation). Further, to have one's parent or parents like something gives one a reason to like it also; however, this too is

TABLE 4.5

LOS ANGELES CHILDREN'S CLAIMED LOVE AND RESPECT FOR
THEIR PARENTS AS A FUNCTION OF STARTING OR STOPPING
TOBACCO SMOKING

age group		Toward nonsmoking parents			Toward smoking parents		
		yes	no		yes	no
children	love less if start?	29 (33%)	59 (67%)	love more if stop?	58 (72%)	23 (28%)
(aged 7-12)	respect less?	29 (34%)	57 (65%)	respect more?	54 (67%)	21 (26%)
n = 158)						
teenagers	love less if start?	3 (8%)	36 (92%)	love more if stop?	8 (25%)	24 (75%)
aged 13-15)	respect less?	15 (39%)	24 (62%)	respect more?	15 (47%)	17 (53%)
n = 58)						

not a sufficient reason to like something. Many children who disliked secondhand smoke came from families where smoking was practiced and undoubtedly, some of these children disliked secondhand tobacco smoke precisely because their parents smoked. The consistency of the fraction of the sample that experienced physical irritation as a consequence of exposure for both sexes and for all ages (about 65%) suggests that secondhand tobacco smoke may be symptomatically distressing to most of the United States population.

Current social policy has proceeded as though only smokers are affected by the use of tobacco. Such is clearly not the case. Two-thirds of the children of the United States reside with a smoker or smokers, and if our findings can be generalized to the population-of-children, not only do most children find secondhand tobacco smoke annoying to some degree, but most smoker's children are distressed by this parental habit which children believe to be harmful.

REFERENCES

Cameron, P. The presence of pets and smoking as correlates of perceived disease. *Journal of Allergy,* 1967, *40,* 12-15.

Cameron, P., Kostin, J. S., Zaks, J. M., Wolfe, J. H., Tighe, G., Oselett, B., Stocker, R., and Winton, J. The health of smokers' and nonsmokers' children. *Journal of Allergy,* 1969, *43,* 336-341.

Cameron, P., Anderson, S., Weiss, R., and Devlin, J. Urban America's most common annoyances. Paper delivered at Rocky Mountain Psychological Association Convention, Denver, May 12, 1971.

Ossorio, P. G. *Persons,* Los Angeles: Linguistic Research Institute, 1966.

Speer, F. Tobacco and the nonsmoker. *Archives of Environmental Health,* 1968, *16,* 443-446.

5

INTELLIGENCE

We observe a 6-year-old accomplishing something that one might reasonably expect of a 10-year old in our culture. We make a mental note that the 6-year old is perhaps "bright" or has been privy to special information or training. If on subsequent occasions we observe the 6-year old accomplishing things that 8- or 9- and sometimes only 11-year olds ordinarily successfully do in our culture, we decide that the 6-year old is "intelligent" or "bright" or "smart" to describe this class of pleasantly unexpected performance. Clearly the "stuff" of intelligence or any other personality trait is performance. One does not assess "intelligence *per se*" directly because the concept intelligence is, like all other concepts, an invention of the linguistic community immeshed in the network of other invented concepts. At best we can sample the performance of a person over a number of situations, and if he does the "smart" thing rather frequently, we conclude that he is "bright" or intelligent. If he *always* or almost always does the brighter thing, we judge him very smart or quite intelligent. We may even devise various pencil and paper problems or test for a person to do, and if he does much better than his peers on this sort of puzzle or problem we might consider him smarter than one who does less well. We might even quantify the amount of or degree of "betterness" that this person displayed on our test and count him as being at an intelligence level of say, 165 or what have you. However, even if we had a 9-year old who performed most admirably on our test, perhaps achieving an "IQ" of 210, it would never cross our mind, and hopefully no one else's either, to make him the head of state or president of Harvard. The most intelligent 9-year old is necessarily far too ignorant for either position (that is, he is not smart enough to handle either job).

Obviously our linguistic system possesses a general concept of intelligent performance as opposed to less intelligent performance. This general concept is and has been invoked historically in the assessment of children's intelligence, and is and has been utilized to rank adults on intelligence. Before considering the literature and evidence regarding intelligence across the adult life-span, we will review the "meaning" or "hallmarks" of intelligent performance and intelligent persons in our linguistic community. We will then review: (1) the beliefs of various cultures regarding intelligence across the adult life-span, (2) the self-reported judgments of adults regarding their own intelligence, (3) the performance of adults of various ages in areas that our culture considers indicative of intelligence, and (4) the performance of adults of varying ages upon "IQ" and other "paper and pencil" tests.

"Intelligence" is not a "thing" in the same sense that a pencil is a "thing," but rather in the sense that "neuroticism" or "masculinity" is a thing. It would be surprising indeed if we were to find a structure or property of the brain that corresponded to "neuroticism," and one that corresponded to "egocentricity," and one that corresponded to "kindness," and one that corresponded to "intelligence," and so forth for the 3,000 or so personality characteristics bandied about in common parlance. While theoretically such a correspondence between "mental phenomena" and "brain phenomena" is possible, its truth would require a reification combined with a realistic reductionism to a well nigh incredible degree. This is not to say that the brain is not involved in intelligence, or neuroticism, or kindness, etc.; obviously it is. People who have suffered brain damage often are more or less kind, more or less intelligent, more or less feminine, than they were before the injury. But we must note our ignorance, for frequently after brain injury or surgery " . . . patients who acquit themselves adequately on psychometric examinations . . . none the less exhibit gross deficiencies in their everyday behavior (Zangwill, 1966)."

Obviously the concept "intelligence" existed long before psychologists and psychometricians invented IQ tests. The concept enabled members of our linguistic community to explain or account for "why," when "everything else was equal," persons performed better or worse than others on a variety of socially important tasks. The "everything elses" would include equal exposure to explanations of how to do these tasks, and other forms of equal opportunity, absence of debilitating distractions (we would consider inhabiting death row a rather adequate explanation of poorer performance on a variety of tasks), and essential equivalence of social status and the like. Any test of intelligence to be "worth its salt" would have to predict to real performance of a socially important kind in the real world. If a test purporting to test intelligence did not predict to a socially-valuable outcome, it would be, ipso facto, invalid. One of the most successful and well-known IQ test devisers, David Wechsler, noted that " . . . even our best tests of intelligence give only incomplete measures of the individual's capacity for intelligent behavior. This situation is reflected by various lines of evidence, the most familiar of which is the fact that individuals with identical test ratings (e.g., IQ's) may differ markedly from one another in regard to level of global functioning as judged by practical criteria, that is, criteria against which the tests were presumably validated to begin with. The main reason for this, however, does not lie, as is generally assumed, in the unreliability of our tests; nor does it lie in the fact that many of our tests are influenced to a considerable degree by such factors as education, constrictive environment, etc. More basic than any of these is the fact that our intelligence tests as now constituted measure effectively only a portion of and not all of the capacities entering into intelligent behavior (Wechsler, 1943, p. 101)." Wechsler here noted that intelligence tests must be validated against "real world" performance and takes the position that an intelligence test ought to tap into the several capacities (or "faculties") that lie behind the varieties of socially-valued performances.

Another approach argues that we should examine the kinds of performance that lead us to invoke the concept "intelligent," and then might try to build a test that samples the various performances to index intelligence. That is, instead of trying to sample from the capacities that "go into" the performances that "count," we ought to sample the performances that count *per se*. Cameron (1973) suggested that intelligent behavior is characterized by:

1) being performed with greater knowledge of possible and ac-

tual consequences; and/or,

2) being performed with greater speed; and/or
3) being performed with less expenditure of energy or substance of value (i.e., more efficiently).

Such a definition may be more appropriate within industrial nations, where heavy emphasis is placed upon time and energy saving. Societies exist in which the "beauty" or aesthetic composition of a behavior count for as much or more than sheer efficiency. From this perspective, intelligent persons are characterized by:

1) behaving intelligently more frequently, and/or
2) knowing more socially-valued or worthwhile things (in general or in particular); (counting the number of blades of grass in your lawn would be information. But since it would not be considered socially-valuable it would "make you dumber" rather than smarter to acquire such knowledge.), and/or,
3) being able to do more socially-valued or worthwhile things (in general or in particular), and/or
4) being able to innovate and/or create socially-valued things; (All new or novel things are not socially-valuable. Only a small set of new things are even innovative and an even smaller set of innovative things cause society to rise up and call you "creative."), and/or
5) being able to learn to do a harder or more difficult socially worthwhile task than their average peer, and/or
6) being able to learn to do a socially worthwhile task faster, and/or
7) being able to learn a larger volume of socially-valued material in a given unit of time.

Retrieval of memory is important in "2" and "3" — having known in the past but not knowing today doesn't "wash." Even knowing, yet needing hours to "dredge it up" counts far less than knowing and immediately producing. The first three characteristics favor the older members of our culture due to their store of knowledge, while the last two favor younger adults (or even teenagers) as their minds are not "filled" with information that interferes with the acquisition of new information. Children's minds are not structured (or "seasoned") enough to assimilate and reproduce material in a socially-valued manner except in the sense of being "good" for a child. The above "lists" are all understood as "relative to peers."

Children's peers are determined with a fine measure — an 8-year old is not to be compared with 10-year olds. but with 8-year olds. Adults are all peers. An adult may be judged relative to persons about his age (which is the kind of comparison an employer might make). However, one is often compared with all other adults — which is the "stuff" of Nobel prizes and beauty queens. While it is undoubtedly noteworthy that one may be terribly attractive for a 55-year old (*particularly* noteworthy for the 55-year old), one is simply not thereby "terribly attractive" *per se*. Similarly, while a person may be quite alert for a 95-year old, that does not make him "quite alert."

"Intelligence," as with most trait concepts, can be applied broadform (he's intelligent) or in a limited sense (he's an intelligent rider). Being generally intelligent counts for more than just being an intelligent performer of some sort. "Intelligence brownie points" are summed up as a combination of "points earned" via hallmarks 1 through 7 above. A well-rounded (scores in 5 or more hallmarks) intelligent person, "picks up additional points" for well-roundedness. Likewise a person who loads his points all in one area is not considered as bright ("he's a whiz in math, but out-to-lunch in dealing with people"). In the extreme, such a person is considered an "idiot savant."

Intelligence is not "fixed at birth," but can be and is modified. Self improvement is built-in to the concept, and so, conversely, is decline. Since the more a person knows of socially-valued information the more intelligent he is, you increase your intelligence by learning new things. If one wants to become more intelligent, one can — by application of the time necessary to know more about and/or how to do socially-valued things. Unfortunately, you can also *lower* your intelligence by "sitting it out." Persons who decide that they "have arrived" (perhaps they get married or decide they've reached their goal), become less knowledgeable, and thus less intelligent.

Beliefs About Intelligence Across the Adult Life-Span

Studies regarding beliefs about older and younger adults are few, and only one inquired relatively directly regarding beliefs about intelligence. Cameron (1973) had 317 Detroit adults, drawn via an area probability sample, and approximately evenly divided among the young adult, middle-aged, and old generations, answer the following:

"How do you believe the three age groups (young adults, middle-aged, and old) compare in

a) possession of general knowledge? (know the most/the least),

b) possession of problem-solving ability (have the most/least)? If we count "most" nominations as 2 and "next-most" as 1, then Table 5.1 is arrived at. The middle-aged are obviously believed to be the "intellectual heavyweights" in our society. It is unfortunate that intelligence *per se* was not sought after.

TABLE 5.1

BELIEFS ABOUT THE INTELLECTUAL ABILITIES OF THE GENERATIONS

	generation		
	young adults	middle-aged	old
possession of general knowledge	220	463	268
possession of problem-solving ability	201	507	243

There is not much to choose between the old and young adults in regard to their intellectual abilities. The small difference favors the old. As respondents were asked to rank order the generations and not to estimate how much more one generation possessed problem-solving ability relative to the others, we cannot determine how much more intelligent the middle-aged are considered to be relative to, say, young adults (e.g., we can't simply inspect the 463 vs. 220 scores and conclude that the middle-aged are to be judged about twice as intelligent).

In less technologically advanced societies, the old probably would fare better in opinions about generational intelligence. It is conceivable that the old would rank alongside or perhaps ahead of the middle-aged. After all, Cicero, 2,000 years ago, opined that ". . . intelligence, reflection, and judgment reside in the old." As industrail societies increase the technological component of social functioning at an ever-accelerating rate, we can expect the old to fare less well in the future. Probably the position of post-young adults pre-middle-aged will "pick up" the intellectual "credits" lost by the old. While the old suffer ignorance as the price of progress, young adults must endure ever greater amounts of training and certification and it is entirely possible that young adults also will lose "credits" on the issue.

A nationwide survey of about 10,000 tenth and twelfth graders conducted in 1962 sought opinions regarding IQ tests and intelligence via an in-school-administered questionnaire (Brim, Glass, Neulinger, Firestone, and Lerner, 1969). Responses to one of the hundreds of items concern us here. Students were asked to choose one of the following responses regarding "intelligence": "fixed at birth," "increases through part of life," or "continues to increase throughout life." These teenagers overwhelmingly (88%) selected the "continues to increase throughout life" response. (When we run questionnaires of this type, just because a respondent chooses one of our alternatives (and he rather appears a dolt if he doesn't take *one)*, it does not mean that this answer completely or even adequately reflects his opinions. It may just be the "closest" to his views — and all of the choices may be "poor" or even "awful" from his standpoint. Or it may even be "tied" with another alternative because his opinion is somewhere in-between or "sort-of" closer to this than that.) Anyway, if the responses to this item somewhat adequately tap respondent opinion, then we have these "near adults" agreeing to a considerable extent, that, all things being equal, the older a person is, the more intelligent he is.

The students' opinion does not necessarily clash with that of the adults' presented above. Persons can believe that a given individual continues to expand his intellectual competency as he ages and simultaneously believe that society is "changing under his feet" so fast that he becomes "dated" in spite of himself. It would be most interesting to see both surveys carried out in a preindustrial society. If our speculations are correct/valid then maximal intelligence would be thrown further back along the life-span.

Self-Reported Intelligence Across the Adult Life-Span

Brim, Neulinger, and Glass (1965) conducted a nationwide survey of 1,482 adults in which respondents were to compare their intelligence with that of other adults, real and hypothetical, as enumerated in Table 2. Clearly most adults consider themselves rather "average" in intelligence — which they ought to, if we are measuring "objective" appraisals of intelligence rather than some sort of "morale" or "self-confidence" factor.

TABLE 5.2

ADULTS' COMPARISON OF THEIR INTELLIGENCE
WITH THAT OF OTHER ADULTS

mine is	% higher	% same	% lower
"average person in the U. S. today"	21	71	8
"my father"	36	47	17
"my mother"	40	47	14
"my brother(s)"	21	64	15
"my sister(s)"	21	68	11
"my spouse"	19	56	25
"my children"	26	39	35

There appears to be a bit of a bias against females in Table 5.2, with fathers and brothers registering somewhat higher in intelligence than mothers and sisters. However, in the main, peers (e.g., "average person," "siblings") are judged equal in intelligence (it's interesting that about two-thirds of the responses are "same," which is about the same proportion that is included when one goes one standard deviation from the mean in either direction — the area within a normal curve that most scientists consider "average"). There is also a kind of "conquer the parents" phenomenon — ego "beats" his parents, but "loses" to his progeny.

There were age differences in Table 5.2, with older person less frequently selecting "higher" and more frequently choosing "lower." However, educational attainment was also differently related to how a person rated himself. The more highly educated person, was more apt to check "higher" and less likely to tic "lower." This is altogether reasonable. A person who has had more schooling presumably "knows more socially-valued things" (#2 on the list of intelligence hallmarks) than someone who has had less. If you go to school, you are being exposed to the things that society says "count." As older people have, as a group, significantly less education than the middle-aged or young, Brim et al. may not have observed an effect of age *per se,* but rather a difference in education that happened to be associated with age. (It would, of course, have been appropriate for the investigators to have cross-sorted their results by age and education).

This possibility is made more attractive by the results of the Cameron (1973) study of 317 adult Detroiters described above. His respondents were asked "how would you compare yourself with all other adults of your sex in:

a) possession of general knowledge, and
b) possession of problem-solving ability (above average/ average/below average)?"

An index of socioeconomic status that combined income and educational achievement was included in the analysis of the study. There were no differences in the response patterns of young adults, middle-aged, and old for these items. However, those of higher socioeconomic status more frequently checked "above average" in general knowledge and tended toward the same with problem-solving ability. Shades of the Brim et al. effort, females more frequently chose "below average" in regard to problem-solving ability and tended in the same direction for general knowledge.

Manifestations of Intelligence: Achievements and Power

One way in which postsavage societies display their opinions about intelligence in adulthood is in their selection of who will wield power. In the not too distant past, world shattering decisions were often made by those who happened to exit the correct genitals. But even kings and potentates had to choose advisors, and their choices were predicated in large part upon judged intelligence. In England, after 1720, nominal representatives of "the people" chose the prime minister. Again, intelligence (coupled with sundry political considerations) played a significant part. The ages of the 63 men whose careers span almost 600 years of British history are graphed in Figure 5.1. The same general pattern of ages tends to be followed in the case of United States presidents. The peak age-of-choice is displaced somewhat younger than it "would have been" if some of these ministers had not resigned/quit, become infirm, or died in office. Neither the populace of Great Britain nor of the United States has more than an indirect hand in selection of candidates.

FIGURE 5.1

Ages of the Chief Ministers of England, 920 to 1720, and of the British Prime Ministers, since 1721

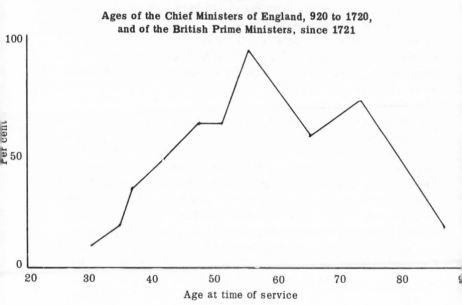

Age at time of service

Yet it is not altogether unfair to judge that when relatively rapid, world shattering decisions are to be made, those of about the age of 60 are chosen.

The debating-society, lawmaking end of constitutional government is more frequently handled by somewhat younger persons (see Table 5.3). But we are not talking about "spring chickens" but rather persons around 50-ish.

TABLE 5.3

AGES OF U.S. SENATORS AND REPRESENTATIVES, 1799 to 1925

year		representatives		senators	
	#	median whole age	#	median whole age	
1799	108	44	39	45	
1825	217	42	63	47	
1849	241	43	70	50	
1875	301	47	82	52	
1899	373	48	75	58	
1925	435	53	96	58	

SOURCE: Lehman, 1953, p. 269.

When weighty, long-term, social issues require less than instant responses and massive research is necessary, the old serve (see Figure 5.2). In this area of policy-making, we appear to be dealing with the "wisdom" component of intelligence. (Rapidity of response is more a consideration on the battlefield or in the courtroom — correctness of response, all things considered, is more valued in situations where one can "take all the time needed").

Plato's notion that a person ought not to assume important leadership roles until the age of 50 for lack of wisdom finds ready example throughout modern life. In the religious sphere, older persons are entrusted with the carrying on and interpretation of tradition (in the Christian church, "the elders" are specifically charged with maintenance of the faith). Generally the same is found in various voluntary organizations ranging from the Veterans of Foreign Wars to the Optimists.

Another area of endeavour that speaks to the intelligence of adults is that of scientific and professional activity. The various fields of human endeavous prize different exemplars of intelligence. While all emphasize innovations (which in a small number of instances are creative), the artistic community is relatively more

FIGURE 5.2

Ages of the Justices of the United States Supreme Court

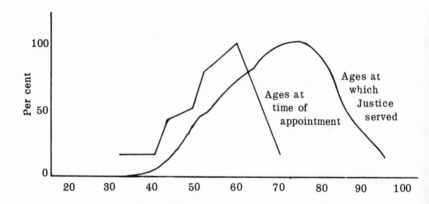

taken with innovation (i.e., #4 above), the scholarly pursuits emphasize the synthesis of socially-valued information (i.e., #1 and #2 above) into more intellectually assimilable structures, and the sciences fall somewhere in between. Table 5.4 summarizes the proportions of output produced in each decade of life for 738 persons who lived to age 79 or over.

It would be unfair to confine outselves solely to longevous innovators. Science does, after all, proceed with the assistance of all types. Table 5.5 presents an analysis similar to that in Table 5.4 for persons of varying life-spans, but only considering *notable* contributions. It will be noted that, unlike works-in-general, these notables occur more frequently in the 30's than in the 40's, 50's, or 60's as above. Further, this group of innovators is even more selective than the group included in Table 5.4. While not very many people live to age 79 and over, even fewer generate a notable contribution. (A good general rule is that fewer than 10% of professionals in a field produce over 90% of the output, and considerably less than 1% of the output is notable, and an even smaller fraction of this is baptized "creative"). The expectation that older persons will

TABLE 5.4

PROPORTIONS OF OUTPUT PRODUCED IN EACH DECADE OF LIFE
(Median Category Underlined)

Field	Number of men	Number of works	Age					
			20's	30's	40's	50's	60's	70's
Scholarship								
Historians	46	615	3	19	19	_22_	24	20
Philosophers	42	225	3	17	20	_18_	22	20
Scholars	43	326	6	17	21	_21_	16	19
Means			4	18	20	_20_	21	20
Sciences								
Biologists	32	3456	5	22	_24_	19	17	13
Botanists	49	1889	4	15	22	_22_	22	15
Chemists	24	2120	11	21	_24_	19	12	13
Geologists	40	2672	3	13	22	_28_	19	14
Inventors	44	646	2	10	17	10	_32_	21
Mathematicians	36	3104	8	20	20	_18_	19	15
Means			6	17	22	_21_	20	15
Arts								
Architects	44	1148	7	24	_29_	25	10	4
Chamber musicians	35	109	15	21	_17_	20	18	9
Dramatists	25	803	10	27	_29_	21	9	3
Librettists	38	164	8	21	_30_	22	15	4
Novelists	32	494	5	19	_18_	28	23	7
Opera composers	176	476	8	30	_31_	16	10	5
Poets	46	402	11	21	_25_	16	16	10
Means			9	23	26	21	14	6

Source: Dennis, 1966

generate the "notables" places the scientific community under
obligation to especially recognize such contributions from younger
sorts. Therefore if one is fortunate/smart enough to generate even
one of these "notables," he is placed in such a revered position and
showered with so many honors and duties that he is probably
rendered even less likely than before the "event" to uncork another.
Table 5.5 is a summary of 1,540 notable contributions by 980
individuals in 10 different fields of endeavors as compiled by
Lehman (1953), one of the pioneers in such research. Note that this

(Median category underlined)

Age at time of death	Per cent of output contributed during successive decades							
	Under 20	20-29	30-39	40-49	50-59	60-69	70-79	80-89
Prior to 50	5	32	<u>50</u>	14				
50-59		23	<u>39</u>	28	9			
60-64	1	17	32	<u>27</u>	20	4		
65-69		8	38	<u>28</u>	16	10		
70-74	2	15	<u>36</u>	28	13	6		
75-79		10	<u>28</u>	27	20	10	4	
80-84		12	32	<u>28</u>	15	9	3	1
85+		8	29	<u>26</u>	22	9	3	2

TABLE 5.5

PROPORTIONS OF NOTABLE CONTRIBUTIONS PRODUCED
IN EACH DECADE OF LIFE

comprises *less* than two such contributions per noteworthy chap.

The "over 50" pattern is also displayed in American Medical Association presidents, college and university presidents, and business leaders listed in *Who's Who in Commerce and Industry* (see Figure 5.3). Examination of the distribution in Figure 5.3 reveals many exceptions to the rule-of-50, but the rule holds rather well considering the diversity of field. There are at least 3 areas in which quite young persons often "shine." Mozart was composing music of worth before the age of 8, and there have been mathematicians who have flowered in their teens or even earlier. Poets too, often tend to be rather young — with many performing admirably in their late teens or early twenties. There is something "weird" about music, mathematics, and poetry. Freshness often wins the worm in these fields of endeavour. One *can* compose an attractive tune without any formal instruction in music — to be able to whistle is to be able to innovate. Other fields seem to demand rather large amounts of knowledge before one can even participate. There never has been and probably never will be a 5-year-old philosopher or psychologist who will achieve even a tiny fraction of what Mozart accomplished at the same age.

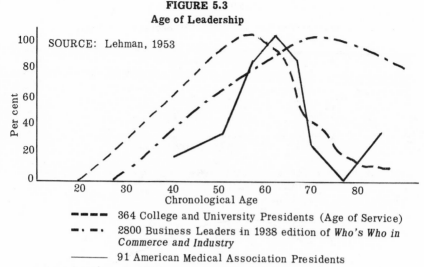

FIGURE 5.3
Age of Leadership

SOURCE: Lehman, 1953

Per cent

Chronological Age

▬ ▬ ▬ ▬ 364 College and University Presidents (Age of Service)
▬ ▪ ▬ ▪ 2800 Business Leaders in 1938 edition of *Who's Who in Commerce and Industry*
───── 91 American Medical Association Presidents

The Performance of Adults On Intelligence Tests

One of the "open" questions regarding intelligence concerns how we might test it and the content of the test. A ready answer is provided by one large set of investigators. Taking off from Binet's successful separation of children into those who ought to learn normally from those who might require some sort of special education, these psychologists have proceeded as though they believed that "intelligence is what IQ tests measure." If one administers IQ tests to adults of varying ages, then the peak of scoring occurs somewhere between the late teens and twenties and declines thereafter. This picture is "true" for just about all IQ tests, although those with subscales that are added in some fashion to generate the total IQ score typically yield different curves of success for each of the subscales. Also, the shape of the curve for the total score on IQ tests varies depending on whether one performs a cross-sectional or longitudinal study. The typical cross-sectional study, in which one "slices" across adults of all ages at one time, generates outcomes much like that in Figure 5.4. So if one wishes to talk about "how things are," after about age 30, the older the cohort the lower its score on such tests, and, according to the assumption that IQ score = intelligence, the lower the intelligence. As there is no "zero" point on the IQ scale, we cannot say "how much more intelligent" younger adults are than older adults. If we wish to explain whether this difference is due to aging *per se*, or to some set

FIGURE 5.4

Representative Cross-Sectional IQ Scores in Adulthood

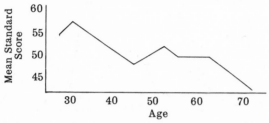

SOURCE: Schaie and Strother, 1968, utilizing the Primary Mental
Abilities IQ Test.

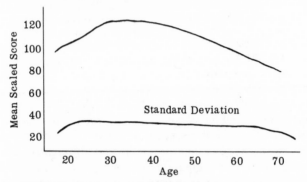

SOURCE: Matarazzo, 1972, summarizing the WAIS IQ Test
Standardization Sample.

of cohort factors, then a longitudinal study, in which the same
persons are tested at least twice with some intervening time between, is called for.

One of the major cohort-related factors that has a decided influence upon IQ score is degree of education. In 1890 about 7% of
those of secondary school age were enrolled in school, in 1950 the
figure was over 75% and in 1970 it was over 80%. The more educational experience a person has the better he tends to do on IQ tests,
therefore older persons, as a group, are at a decided disadvantage.
This phenomenon is pointed up by the scores earned on the Army
Alpha IQ test in World War I vs. the score obtained in World War
II. The World War II recruits averaged about three years more
formal schooling (plus, of course, the other advantages of radio and
more frequent testing). But, most importantly, those in World War
II scored much higher on the Alpha. In fact, 85% of the scores of

those in World War II were above the median of the World War I soldiers (Tuddenham, 1948)!

The general course of IQ scores indexed longitudinally is usually similar to that exhibited in Figure 5.5. Such studies have tended to produce IQ scores that "hold" through much of the life-span, declining only toward the end. However, the bane of longitudinal studies enters into the results. In the study from which Figure 5.5 is taken (Schaie and Strother, 1968), only 302 of the original 500 were retested seven years later. Baltes (1968) and others have noted that there is almost certainly an attrition of the least able from samples of this sort. Had these "missing" 39% been included, the picture would probably not be as kind regarding notions of stability or increase of IQ score in adulthood.

FIGURE 5.5

Longitudinal IQ Scores in Adulthood

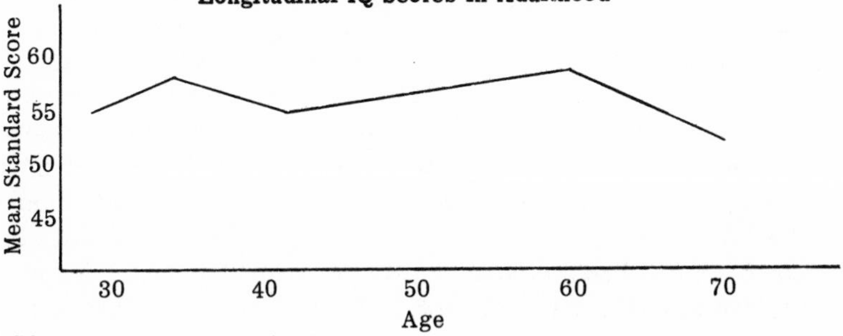

SOURCE: Matarazzo, 1972.

Figures 5.4 and 5.5 illustrate another general finding. Age differences (or decrements) tend to locate on "performance" subscales such as numerical computation, opposites, digit symbols, digit reversals, picture arrangements and series completions. Diminutive or no differences in IQ score are generated with subscales indexing vocabulary or general information.

But, and this is a LARGE "but," do IQ tests adequately index or tap adult intelligence? If they do not, much of the above can be viewed as "interesting," but not to be taken too seriously. Pressey and Kuhlen (1957) were quite critical of the utilization of "schoolbookish" tests to index adult intelligence. They argued that the "real" life-space of adults is far removed from the content of IQ tests. As such, they contended that an intelligence test ought to be made up of items culled from the daily experiences of adults. How can professional psychologists disagree on such a fundamental issue? An answer may be found in the assumptions underlying construction of IQ tests. If you will reexamine the quotation from Wechsler at the beginning of the chapter, you will note that he says that our IQ tests " . . . measure effectively only a portion of and not all of the capacities entering into intelligent behavior." Obviously he believes that intelligence is "made up of" capacities combined in some sort of multiplicative or additive fashion. Matarazzo (1972) in the same vein states that we " . . . do not know what the ultimate nature of the "stuff" is which constitutes functional intelligence (p. 80)." That "fundamental things" or "stuff" lie beneath intelligence is also assumed in the widely employed Thurstone Primary Mental Abilities Test — these five subtests are considered to index "primary" mental abilities. If intelligence is, in fact, made up of fundamental "stuffs," then it ought to make small difference whether one indexes these stuffs with school-related or job-related contents. If the basic, underlying stuff is tapped into, then it's tapped into . . . period. On the other hand, if intelligence is a linguistic invention, a convenience of the linguistic community, that does not correspond to some "general" factor, or any set of "specific" factors, then we are dealing with quite a different animal. Then our concept "intelligent" does not lie above or below any of the specific activities for which it is invoked for explanation. If we were to completely index "it," we would have to index it in all the situations in which we find it convenient to invoke it (and there is almost always a more and a less intelligent way to do anything). "It" would be non-content-specific (not contentless). "It" would be culture-specific (that is, one could not possibly utilize an intelligence test valid for one culture in another culture). "It" would also be subculture-specific to a considerable degree (the kinds of events which would lead us to invoke the concept on the farm would differ from the kinds of events that would suggest its employment in the slum, and both would differ from the kinds of outcomes that would suggest its use in the classroom). While the *concept* "intelligence" exists independently of any specific content or action, our invocation of the concept is appropriate only in the face of specific content. Since intelligence is content-tied, and since the contents of adult-life are quite different from the contents of child-life, any intelligence test generated from this point of view would necessarily be age-specific in our culture. Children in our culture do one set of things (and as most of them go to school, we find it useful to utilize the concept "intelligence" to explain their school-like performances) and school-related IQ tests do a decent job of indexing their intelligence. Adults do a myriad of things ranging from keeping house, to writing, to selling, to designing, to key punching IBM cards, etc., so that an effective "general" intelligence test would be most difficult to devise. From an intelligence-testor's standpoint, children in our culture have the "decency" to uniformly "spend" their intelligence in school while adults "invest" in so many areas as to make us despair of ever doing an adequate job of it.

From this point of view, because of the extreme specialization that occurs among adults in our society, a highly valid general test of intelligence cannot be devised. However, a "middling" test can be approximated by sampling from the content areas that fall largely in the domain that adults in our culture hold "in common." Such a test must fall considerably short of the ideal instrument, because a person's expertise in a limited area, particularly in our culture, can more than easily compensate for his lack of general "brights" (Einstein, for instance, could have been woefully deficient in writing skills, driving skills, marriage skills, literary knowledge, etc., and still qualify as a very intelligent person due to brilliance in his specialty). This circumstance of adults can be contrasted with the activities of children, who spend their time in a common pursuit — school. One can reasonably estimate children's intelligence with application of a "schoolbookish" test. The same test, applied to adults would, from this point of view, apply only to those pursuing careers within a field rather academic by nature. Even in such a field, innovation and creativity enter in (something pretty much absent from school) as well as many aspects of interpersonal "getting on" that are nonacademic, so that such a test would, at best, render a very rough approximation of intelligence.

Two studies have been performed within this "ordinary discourse" orientation. Both are more in the way of demonstration studies, however, the results generated by the efforts are rather similar. In 1957, Demming and Pressey constructed an intelligence test of items locating in three content domains: use of the yellow pages of the phone directory; knowledge of common legal terms, and knowledge of professionals and the services they provide. Sample items were: "Where in the yellow pages of the telephone directory would you look if you wanted to buy an airedale? Under heating equipment, kennels, shoe stores, real estate, dairy equipment? A document controlling disposition of one's property at death is called a bond, title, contract, will, equity? The person to baptize a baby is a naturalist, notary public, nurseryman, magistrate, clergyman? The test was administered to: (1) a sample of 762 high school/college students, and members of Golden Age clubs (603 of the sample were under age 25), and (2) 147 inmates of the Ohio State Penitentiary, who were automatically given the test upon entry to the grey halls. While the usual decline in conventional IQ test scores and lower educational attainment with age was found, the results of the practical intelligence test ran counter (see Figure 5.6).

More recently, Cameron and Smith (1973) construct⌐ ⹁ an intelligence test concerning general knowledge that was verbally administered to a convenience sample of 100 Caucasians aged 12 to 80. Items included: "Is California closer to Mississippi or to Pennsylvania? What does "ts" mean in a recipe? The seventeenth century comprised the years from _____ to _____. How many justices are there on the Supreme Court of the United States?" The results of this study are also summarized in Figure 6. It will be noted that both studies suggest that intelligence increases from young adulthood to middle age and then "holds" or declines slightly.

Demming and Pressey noted that educational attainment appeared to be either unrelated or negatively related to success on their examination. Cameron and Smith tested specifically for influence of educational attainment upon the score on their test, and found none. While the results of these studies hardly constitute solid evidence that "book learning" is of small value in the real world (far from it, as we shall shortly discuss), they certainly suggest that it counts for precious little in matters practical.

We arrive at a choice-point. Are the older adults more intelligent than the younger as suggest by Figure 5.6, or less intelligent as indicated by Figure 4? Insofar as elegance of sampling and sheer bulk of studies are concerned, the latter contention is the choice. But science often drops mountains of time and effort on blind

FIGURE 5.6

Outcomes of "Practical Intelligence" Tests
Demming and Pressey's College and Golden Age Club Respondents
(% above the median)

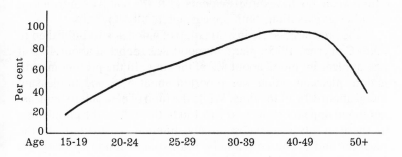

Demming and Pressey's Penitentiary Respondents

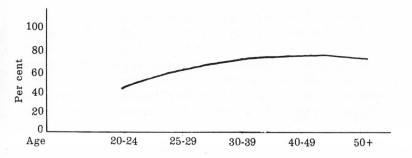

Cameron and Smith's Convenience Sample (mean and S.D.)

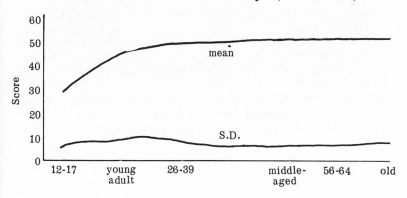

FIGURE 5.7

Distribution of IQ Scores, and Occupation
(mean ± one standard deviation)

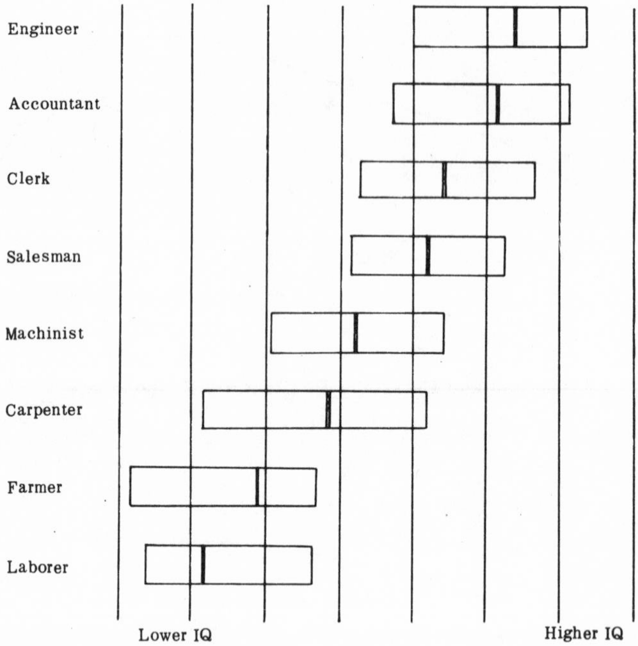

SOURCE: Yerkes, 1942.

alleys. Could the application of "schoolbookish" intelligence tests be one of these? In the opinion of the author, while conventional IQ tests have taught us some things, they have not proven their worth for the scientific study of adult intelligence. Further, they have raised a potential "smoke screen" regarding the contribution of intelligence as opposed to educational attainment/social status in successful job performance.

Why have professional psychologists clung so tenaciously to the IQ test? There are a number of possible reasons. First, there is a tremendous literature with many intriguing problems yet unresolved concerning IQ scores. Secondly, there is an inertia to the whole enterprise — "it worked in school research, by damn, and, besides we know a lot about them." Further, psychologists may well be caught up in the societal use of IQ scores to legitimize the differences between the social classes in wealth and influence.

Just about every informed person has seen a presentation of IQ vs. social status of occupation (Figure 5.7), or the relationship between IQ and socioeconomic success (Table 5.6). The inference that one is encouraged to draw is clear — the higher the IQ the better suited a person is to pursue the choice occupations. Further, those in the higher occupations are more intelligent. The "cream rises to the top"; "them that has, deserves." Some have even proposed that our social system is evolving into a "meritocracy" based on IQ (e.g., Bereiter, 1969; Herrnstein, 1971). While the discussion that follows has to do only with the producers in our social system (we know very little about the psychology of the wealthy property holders), the implication of the "meritocracy" is clear: as the wealthy lie above the highest professional in wealth and influence, they must be more intelligent (and of course, they may be).

ADULT IQ BY DECILES

An analysis of the relative contributions of IQ scores as an index of intelligence, social class of father, and educational attainment to socioeconomic success has been performed by Bowles and Gintis (1973). Utilizing pools of data collected by others and some standard statistical manipulations, they constructed some relatively understandable "success tables" holding the several variables constant. Table 5.7 summarizes their efforts regarding the differential probabilities of attaining economic success for persons of equal levels of education and social class background, but differing levels of adult IQ (as indexed by the Armed Forces Qualification Test). Adult IQ is not inconsequential — intelligence is displayed in IQ test performance (although Bowles and Gintis are more "generous" with this assumption than I would be). Yet IQ is not of overwhelming significance in socioeconomic success as a comparison of Tables 5.6, 5.7, 5.8, and 5.9 makes clear. Bowles and Gintis feel that as currently utilized, the IQ test *appears* to separate the members of our society into various educational tracks, and these determine the chances at the various occupations, but, in actuality, the IQ scores serve largely to divert attention from the maintenance of priviledged position on the part of the advantaged.

For "legitimization" based on IQ to be effective, the members of our social system would have to believe in the validity of IQ tests. Further, they would have to believe that it made sense and/or was fair to sort out persons for advancement on the basis of IQ scores. As the lower classes in any social system usually bear the brunt of whatever inequities the system generates, it would be especially desirable that they believe in legitimization via IQ tests. The Brim et al. (1969) interviews with adult and teenage Americans bear on these points. First, as to essential validity, when asked "do you think the kind of intelligence measured by intelligence, IQ, or aptitude tests matters much in life?" For adults, of the four responses available, 11% chose "matters more than anything else," 58% took "matters a great deal but is no more important than other things," 19% selected "does not matter as much as other things,"

TABLE 5.6

PROBABILITY OF ATTAINMENT OF DIFFERENT LEVELS OF ECONOMIC
SUCCESS FOR INDIVIDUALS OF DIFFERING LEVELS OF IQ BY DECILES

Adult IQ by Deciles

		10	9	8	7	6	5	4	3	2	1
	10	30.9	19.8	14.4	10.9	8.2	6.1	4.4	3.0	1.7	0.6
	9	19.2	16.9	14.5	12.4	10.5	8.7	7.0	5.4	3.6	1.7
Economic Success by Deciles	8	13.8	14.5	13.7	12.6	11.4	10.1	8.7	7.1	5.3	2.8
	7	10.3	12.4	12.6	12.3	11.7	11.0	10.0	8.7	7.0	4.1
	6	7.7	10.4	11.4	11.7	11.8	11.5	11.0	10.1	8.7	5.7
	5	5.7	8.7	10.1	11.0	11.5	11.8	11.7	11.4	10.4	7.7
	4	4.1	7.0	8.7	10.0	11.0	11.7	12.3	12.6	12.4	10.3
	3	2.8	5.3	7.1	8.7	10.1	11.4	12.6	13.7	14.5	13.8
	2	1.7	3.6	5.4	7.0	8.7	10.5	12.4	14.5	16.9	19.7
	1	0.6	1.7	3.0	4.4	6.1	8.2	10.9	14.4	19.8	30.9

corresponds to a correlations coefficient r = .52

For instance: For an individual in the 85th percentile in Adult IQ(x=9), the probability of attaining between the 20th and 30th percentile in Economic Success in 5.3% (the entry in column 9, row 3).

TABLE 5.7

DIFFERENTIAL PROBABILITIES OF ATTAINING ECONOMIC SUCCESS FOR PERSONS
OF EQUAL LEVELS OF EDUCATION AND SOCIAL CLASS BACKGROUND BUT
DIFFERING LEVELS OF ADULT IQ

Adult IQ by Deciles

	10	9	8	7	6	5	4	3	2	1
10	14.1	12.3	11.4	10.7	10.1	9.6	9.0	8.5	7.8	6.6
9	12.4	11.4	10.9	10.5	10.2	9.8	9.5	9.1	8.6	7.7
8	11.4	10.9	10.6	10.4	10.2	9.9	9.7	9.4	9.1	8.4
7	10.7	10.5	10.4	10.3	10.1	10.0	9.9	9.7	9.5	9.0
6	10.1	10.2	10.2	10.1	10.1	10.1	10.0	9.9	9.8	9.5
5	9.5	9.8	9.9	10.0	10.1	10.1	10.1	10.2	10.2	10.1
4	9.0	9.5	9.7	9.9	10.0	10.1	10.3	10.4	10.5	10.7
3	8.4	9.1	9.4	9.7	9.9	10.2	10.4	10.6	10.9	11.4
2	7.7	8.6	9.1	9.5	9.8	10.2	10.5	10.9	11.4	12.4
1	6.6	7.8	8.5	9.0	9.6	10.1	10.7	11.4	12.3	14.1

Economic Success by Deciles

corresponds to a standardized regression coefficient   = .13

For instance: Suppose two individuals have the same levels of Education and
Social Class Background, but one is in the 85th percentile in Adult IQ ($x = 9$),
while the other is in the 15th decile in Adult IQ ($x = 2$). Then the first individual is 10.9/9.1 = 1.2 times as likely as the second to attain the 8th decile in Economic Success (column 9, row 8, divided by column 2, row 8).

SOURCE: Bowles and Gintis, 1973.

and 13% opted for "does not matter at all." It is difficult to decide
from this pattern of response just how valid IQ tests are believed to
be. However, the responses to the item "given tests as they are now,
do you think it is fair to use intelligence, IQ, or aptitude tests to help
make the following decisions?

	adults	teenagers
	% yes	% yes
to decide who should be hired for a job?	58	33
to decide who should be promoted on a job?	46	24

suggests that adults are more "sold" on the validity and fairness of the utilization of IQ tests than are teenagers. Of even greater significance for the Bowles-Gintis argument, adults of lower socioeconomic status *more* frequently answered "yes" to the "promotion" item!

TABLE 5.8

DIFFERENTIAL PROBABILITIES OF ATTAINING ECONOMIC SUCCESS FOR PERSONS OF EQUAL ADULT IQ BUT DIFFERING LEVELS OF EDUCATION

Years of Schooling by Deciles

x	10	9	8	7	6	5	4	3	2	1
y 10	33.2	20.6	14.6	10.6	7.7	5.5	3.8	2.4	1.3	0.4
9	19.9	17.8	15.1	12.7	10.5	8.5	6.6	4.8	3.1	1.2
8	13.8	15.0	14.2	13.0	11.6	10.1	8.5	6.8	4.8	2.3
7	9.9	12.6	13.0	12.7	12.1	11.2	10.0	8.5	6.6	3.5
6	7.2	10.4	11.6	12.1	12.1	11.8	11.2	10.1	8.4	5.1
5	5.1	8.4	10.1	11.2	11.8	12.1	12.1	11.6	10.4	7.2
4	3.5	6.6	8.5	10.0	11.2	12.1	12.7	13.0	12.6	9.9
3	2.3	4.8	6.8	8.5	10.1	11.6	13.0	14.2	15.0	13.8
2	1.2	3.1	4.8	6.6	8.5	10.5	12.7	15.1	17.8	19.9
1	0.4	1.3	2.4	3.8	5.5	7.7	10.6	14.6	20.6	33.2

Economic Success by Deciles (row label, y-axis)

corresponds to a standardized regression coefficient   = .56

For instance: Suppose two individuals have the same Adult IQ, but one is in the 9th decile in Level of Education (x = 9), while the other is in the 2nd decile (x = 2). Then the first individual is 15.0/4.8 = 3.12 times as likely as the second to attain the 8th decile in Economic Success (column 9, row 8, divided by column 2, row 8).

SOURCE: Bowles and Gintis, 1973.

Table 5.9

DIFFERENTIAL PROBABILITIES OF ATTAINING ECONOMIC SUCCESS FOR PERSONS OF
EQUAL EARLY IQ BUT DIFFERING LEVELS OF SOCIAL CLASS BACKGROUND

Social Class Background by Deciles

y\x	10	9	8	7	6	5	4	3	2	1
10	27.7	18.5	14.1	11.1	8.8	6.9	5.3	3.9	2.5	1.1
9	18.2	15.8	13.8	12.1	10.5	9.0	7.6	6.1	4.5	2.4
8	13.7	13.8	13.0	12.1	11.1	10.1	8.9	7.6	6.1	3.7
7	10.7	12.0	12.1	11.8	11.3	10.7	9.9	8.9	7.5	5.0
6	8.4	10.5	11.1	11.3	11.3	11.1	10.7	10.0	9.0	6.6
5	6.6	9.0	10.0	10.7	11.1	11.3	11.3	11.1	10.5	8.4
4	5.0	7.5	8.9	9.9	10.7	11.3	11.8	12.1	12.0	10.7
3	3.7	6.1	7.6	8.9	10.1	11.1	12.1	13.0	13.8	13.7
2	2.4	4.5	6.1	7.6	9.0	10.5	12.1	13.8	15.8	18.2
1	1.1	2.5	3.9	5.3	6.9	8.8	11.1	14.1	18.5	27.7

Economic Success by Deciles

corresponds to a standardized regression coefficient $\beta = .46$

For instance: Suppose two individuals have the same Childhood
IQ but one is in the 9th decile in Social Background, while the
other is in the 2nd decile. Then the first is 18.5/2.5 = 7.4 times
as likely as the second to attain the top decile in Economic Success (column 9, row 10, divided by column 2, row 10).

Source: Bowles and Gintis, 1973

REFERENCES

Batles, P. Longitudinal and cross-sectional sequences in the study of age and generation effects. *Human Development,* 1968, *11,* 145-171.

Bereiter, C. The future of individual differences. *Harvard Educational Review,* 1969, Reprint series number *2,* 162-160.

Bowles, S. and Gintis, H. I.Q. in the U.S. class structure. *Social Policy,* 1973, *3,* 1-27.

Brim, O. G., Glass, D. C., Neulinger, D., and Firestone, I. J. *American beliefs about intelligence.* New York: Russell Sage, 1969.

Cameron, P. Which generation is believed to be intellectually superior and which generation believes itself intellectually superior? *International Journal of Aging and Human Development,* 1973, *3,* 257-270.

Cameron, P. and Smith, A. An ordinary discourse definition of intelli- gence. Paper presented to the American Psychological Association Convention, Montreal, August 27, 1973.

Demming, J. A. and Pressey, S. L. Tests "indigenous" to the adult and older years. *Journal of Counseling Psychology,* 1957, *4,* 144-148.

Dennis, W. Age and achievement: a critique. *Journal of Gerontology,* 1956, *11,* 331-337.

Dennis, W. Creative productivity between the ages of 20 and 80 years. *Journal of Gerontology,* 1966, *21,* 1-8.

Herrnstein, R. I.Q. *Atlantic Monthly,* 1971, *51,* 43-64.

Lehman, H. C. *Age and achievement.* Princeton: Princeton University Press, 1953.

Matarazzo, J. D. *Wechsler's measurement and appraisal of adult intelligence.* Baltimore: Williams and Wilkins, 1972.

Pressey, S. L. and Kuhlen, R. G. *Psychological Development Through the Life Span.* New York: Harper & Rowe, 1957.

Schaie, K. W. and Strother, C. R. A cross-sequential study of age changes in cognitive behavior. Psychological Bulletin, 1968, *70,* 671-680.

Tuddenham, R. D. Soldier intelligence in World Wars I and II. *American Psychologist,* 1948, *3,* 54-56.

Wechsler, D. Nonintellective factors in general intelligence. *Journal of Abnormal and Social Psychology,* 1943, *38,* 101-103.

Yerkes, R. M. *Psychological examination in the U.S. Army.* Memoirs of the National Academy of Science, 1921, *15.*

Zangwill, O. L. Psychological deficits associated with frontal lobe lesions. *International Journal of Neurology,* 1966, *5,* 395-402.

6

SEXUALITY

Human sexuality is totally learned. Those who would house human sexuality in a physiologic or phylogentic tent quickly find the bindings strained and limbs popping out of every crevice. The outrageous sexual diversity of humankind mocks any attempt to physiologize so outlandish a domain. Outside of needing organs for coupling purposes, physiology is incidental to the human sexual process. While this notion may run afoul of those steeped in the reductionistic-realistic mode of thought, there are a number of lines of evidence that fit the "exclusive learning" model rather well.

First, there is the tremendous cultural diversity in "onset of age of sexing." In a number of primitive cultures, humans as young as five participate in the sexual game. Lest this strike the reader as "horrible" it should be remembered that old English law sets the age of consent at seven — and the state of Delaware followed suit. There are cultures, such as Ireland, in which full-fledged "sexing" does not generally commence until the 20's. Physiologically-based events display no such variability. Irrespective of culture, the average age of breast-budding takes place within approximately a three-year span. The same appears to be the case with "testicular drop." While there is a fairly wide within-culture diversity of, say, the appearance of luxuriant pubic hair (which is certainly linked to hormonal balance and control) on the average, none of the quasi-sex-related activities that are known to be tied to biology displays anything like the 20-year variability associated with "onset of age of sexing."

The diversity of object of sexual desire is another problem to those who would case human sexuality in a biologic jacket. There are humans who prefer car mufflers, other that prefer animals, humans who prefer their own sex, and those who prefer the opposite sex. No one has demonstrated *any* biological difference between homosexuals and heterosexuals although numerous attempts have been floated. Certainly it would be awkward to argue that a person who "lusted after horses" had a physiological quirk. There are those who are disgusted by the notion of being urinated on, and others who celebrate it as a "golden shower." When three-spined sticklebacks perceive an appropriately shaped reddish-spotted outline, into a mating dance they do go. The poor beasties can be fooled into making exhausted fools of themselves. Not so with mankind. We might make fools of ourselves over sex, and even become exhausted, but the objects of our desires are as diverse as the "wee fish's is predictable."

Then there's the problem of frequency. While the norm for females is to menstruate once, and only once, every 28 days, the norm for "frequency of sexing" for humankind is as diverse as those who have tried it and given it up for lent vs. those who can't wait for their organ to heal so they can get it sore again. Similarly there is the problem with age of cessation. While the age of the menopause is rather nicely "fixed" biologically, the age of cessation for human sexuality is incredibly diverse. Hot dripping sex, is, to some considerable degree, the province of the young, but there are some, like Ben Franklin (the *real* father of our country with at least 72 children to his credit) who bid faire to "die in the saddle" and yet others who have pretty well "packed it in" by age 30. Both within and between cultures, sexual diversity is so great as to exhaust the patience of all but the most dedicated "physiologilists."

Within the Western culture, sex has taken a turn to the "high" side lately. Females, especially, are being wooed by the mass media. If words can melt, femalekind ought soon to be turning the rape rate back upon their brethren. At this point, it appears that females just don't like sex as much as males do (sorry Charlie). Those males that hunger after sex-starved females may just have to pull a "Rip Van Winkle."

There are a number of considerations that suggest that it would be difficult to induce females to "like sex as much as men do." From the male end of things the penis is both an organ of convenience and a pleasure center. With rare exception, it neither gets diseased nor is it associated with other than joy. Not so for females. While it is probably arguable as to whether the organs are equally convenient, there is no doubt that the female organ is easily infected (my medical friends estimate an infection from one of about a dozen parasites per adult female each year). Further, every month it is associated with an inconvenient "time," questionable odors, and, last but from far least, pregnancy — she bears and delivers the issue of love-making. One would speculate that a great deal of pleasure would have to ensue from such an organ to compensate for what she has to "put up with." Adding insult in injury, ofttimes the female's pleasure is contingent upon the love-making skills of her partner. Since not every male is "up to snuff" in such regards, "compensation" takes a holiday.

THE GENERATION GAP: BELIEFS ABOUT SEXUALITY AND SELF-REPORTED SEXUALITY

Which generation believes itself the sexiest and which is believed the sexiest by the other generations? Although numerous investigators have measured various indices of sexuality for varying samples of adults to date, samples of the generations are lacking. The present study was performed to partially rectify this situation.

Method

Subjects. In order to determine which ages should be included in the generations "young adult," "middle-aged," and "old," a pilot study was conducted which empirically established that, linguistically speaking, persons are young adults aged 18 to 25 inclusive, middle-aged from 40 to 55, and old from 65 to 79 (Cameron, 1969). Desiring to represent these age-groups as adequately as possible, and realizing that there might be sex differences in the results, six strict area samples of the city of Detroit (excluding the inner city), for Caucasians only, were performed. Three hundred and seventeen Ss were approached at home at least twice to assure a low rejection rate, and were paid $2 for the interview. Through a system of almost unlimited call-backs we ended up with 19 rejections (i.e., a rejection rate of <6%). Interviewers were 12 trained, paid college students. Slightly over 50% of the data were recalled and verified both to clarify ambiguities, or correct mistakes, and to assure that no "dry labbing" had occurred.

Interview. S was approached by asking him to fill out a questionnaire concerning his beliefs about adults. He was assured anonymity, asked to fill out the interview in another part of the residence, and then, when finished, to seal the interview in an envelope provided for the purpose. The interviewer: (1) induced the S to cooperate, (2) delivered the materials, and (3) answered any questions that the S might have (there were relatively few). Whenever asked questions about the questionnaire, the interviewer read the question aloud for the respondent, and in a few cases provided minor definitional clarification. When leaving, the interviewer induced the S to record his phone number on the envelope, and when outside, recorded the address. Whenever an S had neglected to answer any question(s), a person other than the interviewer reinterviewed the S by phone or in person and requested completion. The data were thus made over 99% complete. Each interviewer interviewed an equal number of males and females evenly distributed over the three age-groups to control for any idiosyncratic interviewer effects. Half of the subjects in each sample were administered the "opinions" part of the questionnaire first, and the other half the "self-report" part first.

Questionnaire. Ossorio's (1966) analysis of our linguistic system suggests that a person's behavior is the resultant of six independent variables. For a person to perform a behavior he must: (1) *know about* the behavior, (its consequences and effects), (2) *want* to do it, (3) *know how* to do it, (4) have the *capacity* to do it, (5) must make the *attempt,* and (6) must have the *opportunity* to do it. Further, the incidence of any given behavior will vary as a function of all these variables (for instance, a person with limited social access to a behavior may engage in it more than once with greater success due to a greater number of attempts). If Ossorio's common-language-related analysis is correct, then we would expect a questionnaire based upon it to approximate maximal intelligibility to Ss, as well as maximal intelligibility of results whether to professional or laymen. Accordingly, the following 14 items were constructed in as close conformity to Ossorio's analysis as the author could achieve. All responsibility for adequate representation is, of course, the author's. The "opinions" part of the questionnaire was introduced: "How do you believe the three age-groups (young adults, middle-aged, and old) compare in:

1) Knowledge about sexual techniques? Know the most (*fill in*)? Know the least (*fill in*)?

2) Sexual desire? Want sex the most (*fill in*)? Want sex the least (*fill in*)?

3) Skill in performing sexual activities (aside from any physical differences)? The most skilled (*fill in*)? The least skilled (*fill in*)?

4) Frequency of attempts to have sexual relations? Try the most (*fill in*)? Try the least (*fill in*)?

5) Physical capacity for sexual activity (aside from any differences in skill)? The most able (*fill in*)? The least able (*fill in*)?

6) Frequency of physical activity? Do the most (*fill in*)? Do the least (*fill in*)?

7) Access to sexual partners? Have the most opportunities (*fill in*)? Have the fewest opportunities (*fill in*)?

The "self-appraisal" part of the questionnaire was a mirror of the above, consisting of a Lickert Scale (above average, average, below average). It asked: "How would you compare yourself with *All Other Adults of Your Sex* in:

1) Knowledge about sexual techniques?
2) Sexual desire?
3) Skill in performing sexual activities (aside from any physical differences)?
4) Frequency of attempts to have sexual relations?
5) Physical capacity-ability for sexual activity (aside from any differences in skill)?
6) Frequency of physical sexual activity?
7) Access to sexual partners?

S was also asked his age, sex, his income to the nearest $500 for the past year, and the highest grade he completed in formal schooling. SES was computed by multiplying the number associated with income (e.g., 1 = under $5,000; 2 = $5,000-$7,999; 3 = $8,000-

$11,999; 4 = $12,000+) by 2 and adding it to the number associated with education (1 = completed less than 8th grade; 2 = 8th-11th; 3 = H.S. diploma; 4 = some college; 5 = B.A.; 6 = M.A.; 7 = Ph.D.). All analyses broke SES into two levels, those scoring 9 or higher and those scoring 8 or less.

The mean ages of the samples were 21.0 for the young adults, 48.2 for the middle-aged, and 70.2 for the old. SES levels were 8.89, 9.39, and 6.02 respectively (educational levels were 3.52, 3.25, and 2.49 with the young and middle-aged, thus falling between the "H.S. diploma" and "some college" categories, while the old fell between the "8th-11th" and "H.S. diploma" categories; for income, the groups averaged 2.68, 3.10 and 1.79, with the young thus averaging under $8,000 a year, the middle-aged over $8,000 and the old under $5,000).

Results

Knowledge about sex: All generations agreed that the middle-aged know the most and the old the least about sex. A three-way fixed-effects analysis of variance (3 generations x set x 2 levels of SES) revealed no generational, sexual or SES main effects — this belief appears societywide.

Sexual desire: The generations, sexes, and SES levels agreed — the young have the greatest and the old the lowest sexual desire.

Sexual skill: The middle-aged were universally considered the most sexually skillful and the old the least skillful.

Sexual attempts: Again, essential unanimity that young adults make the most and the old adults the fewest sexual advances.

Physical sexual capacity: The young were generally regarded as possessing the most sexual capacity and the old possessing the least.

Social opportunity: The generations agreed that the young have the most and the old the least access to sex partners.

Sexual frequency: There was general agreement that the young achieve the highest and the old the lowest frequency of sexual activity.

Self-Reported Sexuality Since S report of "above average" was scored a 3, "average" a 2, and "below average" a 1, means scores could range from 1 (low) to 3 (high). This range can be divided into three equal segments, from 1.0 to 1.67, 1.67 to 2.33, and 2.33 to 3.0, with the lowest subrange considered below average and the highest as above average. Similarly, the "average" range can be divided into 3 equal segments, with points of division at 1.88 and 2.11 for low and high average.

Knowledge about sex: Young adults considered themselves more knowledgeable about sex than the old considered themselves, and tended toward greater confidence in their knowledge than the middle-aged. While the young considered themselves high average and the middle-aged average in knowledge, the old considered themselves low average. Though there are no SES differences, at every age level men felt themselves more knowledgeable than women, even though each sex was asked to rate itself relative to their own sex.

Sexual desire: The young considered themselves high average in sexual desire, the middle-aged exactly average, and the old below average. Males generally claimed greater desire than females.

Sexual skill: The Young and middle-aged considered themselves average in sexual skill, while the old felt themselves below average. Females considered themselves less skillful, while greater feelings of skill were associated with SES.

Physical capacity: The young and middle-aged considered themselves average and the old below average in felt physical capacity. SES was associated with self-appraised sexual capacity.

Sexual attempts: The young adults and the middle-aged felt their number of attempts at sex were average, while the old felt themselves below average in this respect.

Social opportunity: The young felt they had more social opportunity than the middle-aged (average vs. low average), who felt they had more than the old.

Sexual frequency: The young and middle-aged judged themselves average in sexual frequency, while the old considered themselves quite below average.

Discussion

Our population's opinions about the sexuality of the generations appear stereotypic, with no variation by age, SES, or sex. The middle-aged are believe to be cognitively superior sex-wise, knowing more about sex and being more sexually skilled. The young are believed more virile, desiring, attempting, more physically capable, and achieving more sex. Further, the young are provided the greatest access to sex partners. The old are seen as well-nigh sexless — desiring little, knowing little, attempting little, and getting less.

"Common sense" psychology appears rather robust in this instance. These stereotypes seem to have considerable basis in fact. Though the self-reported rank-order of means always ran from young adult down to old, if we consider the stereotypes predictions, our sample "hit" on 38 of 42 tries.

Since the old have lived longer, and presumably have therefore sexed more, their below-average appraisal of their sexual knowledge and skill is puzzling. Have the old, who after all *produced* via sexing, forgotten what they once knew, or do they feel they were culturally deprived in their fertile years? Has their lack of sexual desire and/or opportunity caused what they presumably once knew to "leak" from their minds, or are we dealing with a cultural-gap in sexual knowledge?

When newsmen or evangelists want to get older people annoyed with the young, tales of youthful sexuality seem "sure fire." Why? Possibly the "sex-gap" between the young and the old is not mainly developmental as has been generally supposed (e.g., Kuhlen, 1964; Christensen and Gagnon, 1965), but cultural. Perhaps the old feel "gypped" relative to what "they could have done at your age." If the old didn't claim so much sexual ignorance, we might more readily suspect they had adjusted their desires and attempts to the "way things are." But their claimed ignorance makes the "cultural-gap" interpretation attractive.

Women of all ages claimed less sexual desire, knowledge, skill, and physical capacity than men. This generalized lower female "sexiness" has been found in just about all previous studies (Anderson, 1959). Though much has been said of the recent liberation of women's sexuality, nary a hint of such turned up in the results.

Higher SES Ss rated their sexual skill and physical capacity higher. Their feelings of greater physical capacity seem consonant with the generally better health of the financially better off members of our social system. That they should feel more sexually skillful would seem appropriate in light of their supposedly more varied sexual experience (Kinsey, Pomeroy, and Martin, 1948).

It is common knowledge that people forget *skills* that fall into disuse, but many theories of learning posit eternal retention of abstract knowledge. Though it might possibly cost him his academic career, it would be interesting for a researcher to find out to what degree, if any, the old are really less sexually knowledgeable.

REFERENCES

Anderson, J. E. The use of time and energy. In J. E. Birren, ed., Handbook of aging and the individual. Chicago: University of Chicago Press, 1959. Pp. 769-796.

Cameron, P. Age parameters of young adult, middle-aged, old, and aged. *Journal of Gerontology,* 1969, *24,* 199-200.

Christenson, V. and Gagnon, J. H. Sexual behavior in a group of older women. *Journal of Gerontology,* 1965, *20,* 351-356.

Kinsey, A. C., Pomeroy, W. B., and Martin, C. E. *Sexual behavior in the human male.* Philadelphia: Saunders, 1948.

Kuhlen, R. G. Developmental changes in motivation during the adult years. In J. E. Birren, ed., *Relations of development and aging.* Springfield, Illinois: Charles C. Thomas, 1964, Pp. 209-246.

Ossorio, P. G. *Persons.* Los Angeles: Linguistic Research Institute, 1966.

SEXUAL THOUGHT THROUGHOUT THE LIFE-SPAN

with Henry Biber

Sex has been and continues to be a topic of active psychological investigation. Investigators have explored the techniques of sexual behavior (Masters and Johnson, 1966), varieties of sexual behavior (Kinsey, Pomeroy, and Martin, 1948), numerous studies of sexual attitudes ranging from premarital sexual encounters to sex in senescence, amounts of sexual conversation (Cameron 1970a), and physiological and pharmacological correlates of sexual maturation (Reynolds and Wines, 1948, 1951). With the exception of the rather limited reports of Cameron (1967, 1970b), no normative data concerning the kind and frequency of human sexual thought are available.

It seems reasonable to proceed with the investigation of thought as a topic of legitimate scientific concern in its own right (Ginnane, 1960). It is known that much of human behavior is engaged in without thinking (Ossorio, 1966). Most of the motor skills that persons exhibit are so routinized that they are unaccompanied by thought, while the same circumstances obtains with the various emotional states (Gosling, 1962). As persons are almost always thinking, some species of human endeavor must be thought about much more than they are exhibited in observable behavior. Is sex one of these species? Does sexual thought trace the same developmental pattern as interest in sex, or observable sexual behavior? Some theorists (e.g., Linden and Courtney, 1953) have contended that a resurgence of sexuality occurs in senescence. While it appears that a resurgence of observable sexual behavior does not generally occur (Kinsey et al., 1948), is this resurgence possibly expressed in greater mental investment?

Thought can be considered as occurring at two levels of activity. At one level, many kinds of thought seem to flit through the mind; often, seemingly independently of these snatches of thought, the mind is focusing in on a topic of some concern to the person. While no sharp mental "line" separates these two kinds of thought, the distinction is at least as old as William James (Boring, 1933). The present report presents normative data regarding the frequency of both ephemeral and focal sexual thought throughout the life-span.

How We Sampled Thoughts

As the contents of thought might vary as a function of time-of-day, situation, and activity, 4,420 persons ranging in age from 8 to 99 were interviewed or asked to fill out a questionnaire equally-frequently across all daylight hours in the most frequent situations of daily life — in school, while engaging in recreation, at home, or at work. The at-home sample was obatined via a strict area sample of areas of Los Angeles, Louisville, Detroit, and Evansville (762 males and 959 females, with a rejection rate of 28%); the at-work sample was obatined by college student volunteers from their co-workers in Detroit, Evansville, and Louisville (931 males and 507 females, occupying 84 different job locations with a rejection rate of less than 1%); the at-school sample was drawn by a classroom-time=grade selection process whereby certain proportions of the students in given classes had their work interrupted and the questionnaire was filled out by the subjects (244 males and 233 females, with a rejection rate of less than 1% at two difference schools, one in Kentucky and the other in New Jersey); the at-church sample was obtained by the interruption of cooperating Sunday School classes and the private approaching of designated worshippers during services at four churches (12 males and 30 females, 1 rejection); the at-leisure sample was obtained by staking out certain areas in 11 different locations in Louisville, Los Angeles, and Denver, and randomly interviewing one of every so many people who entered the area (6 shopping areas, 2 beaches, 2 parks, and one organized ball game provided 221 males, and 521 females and a rejection rate of less than 1%). While persons were not assessed in all the kinds of situations and performing all the kinds of activities that are common in our culture, the vast majority of persons in our society spend the majority of their waking lives in the situations we sampled, engaging in the kinds of activity we interrupted. We interviewed 2,250 females and 2,170 males distributed over the life-span and achieved an overall rejection rate of less than 11%.

The questionnaire was introduced "What were you thinking about over the past 5 minutes?" Did you think about sex or were your thoughts sexually-colored — even for a moment (perhaps it crossed your mind)?" "What was the central focus of your thoughts over the past 5 minutes?" (among the 14 possible responses was "about a personal problem-topic concerning sex").

What Was Found

Before reporting the results, we should like to explain the massing of the findings instead of their presentation by situation or by mode of assessment. Two hundred of the at-home sample were administered the questionnaire without interviewer assistance. No differences between self- or interviewer-administration nor between the samples drawn from the various cities were uncovered. Further, no difference in frequency of possible replies as a function of time-of-day nor situation for most variables (including frequency of thoughts of sex) was discovered (the only differences found concerned mood and situation-specific thoughts, i.e., children at-school thought more frequently about school than did children at-leisure, adults at-church thought more frequently about religion than adults at-home, etc.). The trends we uncovered evidenced themselves in each situation we sampled, hence both the combina tion of results and reason to regard our results with considerably more confidence than the probabilities associated with the particular outcomes.

There were no systematic variations in sexual thought as a function of marital status or race. Sexual thought varied by age and sex. Our sample consisted of 119 males and 116 females aged 8 to 11, 146 males and 177 females aged 12 and 13, 130 males and 137 females aged 14 and 15, 104 males and 207 females aged 16 and 17, 541 males and 629 females aged 18 to 25, 472 males and 443 females aged 26 to 39, 379 males and 366 females aged 40 to 55, 97 males and 95 females aged 56 to 64, and 82 old males and 80 old females. For males, the percentage of respondents in each age-grouping who reported that sex had "crossed their mind in the last 5 minutes," was, starting at the youngest, 25, 50, 57, 51, 48, 33, 20, 19, and 9 for the old. For females the corresponding percentages were 27, 39, 42, 33, 19, 9, 12, and 6. For males, the percentage of respondents in the corresponding age-groups who reported that sex had been the focus of their thought in the last 5 minutes was 4, 16, 10, 14, 10, 8, 4, 3, and 0. For females, the percentages ran 4, 11, 11, 6, 6, 2, 2, 0, and 0. Clearly the frequency of both in-passing and focal sexual thought was curvilinearly related to the life-span, reaching a high point in the teenage and young adult years. With but three exceptions, of the 18 comparisons, males reported more sexual thought than females (the sign test places the probability of such an outcome at less than .004).

Where Has All the Sex Gone

Human thought broaches sex much more frequently than sexual behavior is engaged in. While investigators in both the United States of America and Japan (Asayama, 1957) have found relatively low amounts of sexual behavior among boys before the age of 15, the frequency of thinking about sex is essentially constant for the males of our sample from the age of 12 through 25. While American girls seldom experience coitus before the age of 16 and only by 16 have approximately half of them ever kissed or petted, the 16-year olds in our sample are essentially indistinguishable from our 12- and 13-year olds in amount of mental "space" devoted to sex. The co-relation between sexual behavior and sexual thought appears far from coincident, both in absolute incidence and in ages of highest frequency.

Both the Japanese and United States of America reports of sexual behavior concluded that on the average males engaged in sexual behavior earlier in life than females, and achieved and maintained a higher incidence of the various kinds of sexual behavior. Clearly our results evidence no indication that males start thinking about sex more frequently at a younger age than females, but do provide evidence that males think about sex more frequently at all ages than do females.

What people talk about has been theorized to follow closely what people think about (Jesus opined that what people thought generated what they talked about and said). In the only large-scale study reported to date, college students were found to talk about sex about 17% of their conversational time (Cameron, 1970[b]). In the present study the average amount of time spent thinking about sex in-passing averaged about 40% for young adults while focal sexual thought averaged about 8%. The rules of conversation include a demand that usually some sort of logical progression be followed, so probably most of what we have termed in-passing thought would not be mentioned, as it is so often alogical. We would expect the frequency of a subject's being the topic of conversation to fall below the in-passing rate, and somewhere close to the focal rate (possibly a little lower or higher). Our present data thus generates a reasonable match between the incidence of sex and sex as a conversational and mental topic for young adults.

When asked to estimate what percentage of the time they thought about sex, 188 Boulder, Colorado, adults estimated a median of 20% for 18- to 22-year olds, 8% for 28- 35-year olds, and 1% for those over 60 (Cameron, 1967). The average adult (about 45 years of age) reported an estimate of about 8%. In the present investigation, -aged averaged about 15% in-passing sexual thought and 3% focal sexual thought. As with conversation, the absolute percentage of time spent thinking about sex is probably closer cognitively to the focal than the in-passing estimate. Thus estimates of percentage of time spent in thought about sex approximate the frequency of what appears to be the actual time spent thinking about the topic.

Verwoerdt, Pfeiffer, and Wang (1969) have reported results of interviewing a convenience sample of older persons about certain aspects of their sexual lives four times during a 10-year longitudinal study. While the initial sample consisted of 260 persons 60-years of age or older, various kinds of attrition sharply reduced the number of subjects providing complete data over the decade (one of the last studies was concerned with 39 subjects). The questions of primary interest for the purposes of this paper were (a) "How would you describe your sexual feelings at the present time?" (a psychiatrist rated the subject's response as indicating "strong"/ "moderate"/"weak"/or "no" interest in heterosexual coitus), and (b) "How often, on the average, do you have sexual intercourse at the present time?" (the psychiatrist rated the response as indicating heterosexual sexual intercourse of "more than once per week"/ "once per week"/"once every 2 weeks"/"once per month"/ or "none"). Verwoerdt et al. (1969) construed the first question as indexing sexual interest (why subjects were not asked directly about their interest in sex or heterosexual sexual intercourse instead of inferring interests from feelings is not made clear).

While Verwoerdt et al. allow that sexual outlets other tnan heterosexual coitus exist and were not indexed, they report that the degree of sexual interest inferred by the psychiatrists from the responses of the subjects declined for both males and females with age. They also report that the percentage of their sample whose responses the psychiatrist judged as expressing some interest in heterosexual coitus remained at 56% over the decade. Verwoerdt et al. construed their findings as indicating that sexual interest declines with age (but, by only indexing feelings about heterosexual coitus, they ignored the possibility of increasing sexual interest in masturbation, bestiality, homosexuality, etc.). While it may correspond with the reality of sexual interest in old age, the conclusion does not necessarily follow from their results. They also reported that interest in heterosexual coitus was judged as more frequently expressed by males and to a stronger degree. The percentage of the sample who reported some heterosexual coitus declined from 44% at the beginning to 20% at the end of the decade. Verwoerdt et al. construed this as evidencing "declining sexual activity." Again, the concept sexual activity subsumes activities other than heterosexual coitus, so that the conclusion does not necessarily follow from their results. Generally males were found to report more frequently some heterosexual coitus, and more frequent coitus if sexually active in this way. Our findings of declining frequency of contemplation of sex with age and the greater mental sexiness of males at all points along the adult life-span are similar to the Verwoerdt et al. results. However, if our subjects could have reported thinking about sex when contemplating: (a) a member of their sex, (b) an attractive dog, (c) a *Playboy* centerfold, or (d) any of the varieties of non coital heterosexual sexual behavior, there is no conceptual necessity for similarity between the two sets of findings.

We unearthed no evidence that sexuality as manifested in thought increased markedly in old age. Linden and Courtney's (1953) notion of a spurt in sexuality in old age thus finds no support in the cognitive domain.

REFERENCES

Asayama, S. Comparison of sexual development of American and Japanese adolescents. *Psychologia*, 1957, *1*, 129-131.

Boring, E. G. *The physical dimensions of consciousness*. New York: Century, 1933.

Cameron, P. Note on time spent thinking about sex. *Psychological Reports*, 1967, *20*, 741-742.

Cameron, P. The words college students use and what they talked about. *Journal of Communication Disorders*, 1970, 336-46. (a)

Cameron, P., Biber, H., Brown, N., Siro, M., and Colden, C. Consciousness: Thoughts about world and social problems, death, and sex by the generations. Paper read at Kentucky Psychological Association, Sept. 25, 1970. (b)

Ginnane, W. Thought. *Mind*, 1960, *69* 372-390.

Gosling, J. Mental causes and fear. *Mind*. 1962, *71*, 289-306

Kinsey, A. C., Pomeroy, W. B., and Martin, E. E. *Sexual behavior in the human male*. Philadelphia: Saunders, 1948.

Linden, M. E. and Courtney, D. The human life cycle and its interruptions. *American Journal of Psychiatry*, 1953, *109*, 906-915

Masters, W. H. and Johnson, V. E. *Human sexual response*. Boston: Little, Brown, 1966.

Ossorio, P. G. *Persons*. Los Angeles: Linguistic Research Institute, 1966.

Reynolds, E. L. and Wines, J. V. Individual difference in physical changes associated with adolescence in girls. *American Journal of Diseases of Children*, 1948, *75*, 329-350.

Reynolds, E. L. and Wines, J. V. Physical changes associated with adolescence in boys. *American Journal of Diseases of Children*, 1951, *82*, 529-547.

Verwoerdt, A., Pfeiffer, E., and Wang, H. S. Sexual behavior in senescence. II. Patterns of change in sexual activity and interest. *Geriatrics*, 1969, *24*, 137-154

HOW SEXY AND DEATHY ARE AMERICANS?

with

Darius Bahador, Jundi Shapur University

K.G. Desai, University of Gujarat

Lloyd McPherson, University of Jamaica

Some have accused Americans of running the sexiest culture on earth. Our females often appear "topless," we have widespread "softcore and hardcore" pornography and many have noted United States "preoccupation with sex." In Iran, women dress far more "modestly," pornography of any stripe is difficult to obtain, and sexuality appears far more "suppressed." Ghana and India, for differing reasons, appear to locate somewhere between the United States — Iran extremes.

Americans also appear increasingly concerned with death (Cameron, 1977). The United States has been called the world's most violent culture. Critics of television suggest that nowhere else do people ordinarily see the depiction of so much death and gore. The United States is the leading arms merchant and therefore the leading death merchant of the world. Of our set of peoples, Indians are probably the least well-off economically. Indians probably see more actual death and dying than the other peoples. Are these factors reflected in each general populace's frequency of thinking about death?

One way of indexing Americans' sexiness or "deathiness" is to sample what they think about and then compare the frequency with which they think about sex or death with the frequencies exhibited in other cultures.

Method

Subjects. We attempted to representatively sample the contents of consciousness in each of the four countries chosen for investigation. Within the limitations of cross-national research we sought to sample persons of both sexes across the life-span, evenly distributed across the daylight hours, and within the various typical situations in which persons might find themselves in that society. Our approximations fell considerably short of this ideal. In India, the sampling took place at-work, and at-leisure; in Ghana, at-school and at-leisure; in Iran, at-home, at-work, and at-leisure; and in the United States, at-home, at-leisure, at-work, and at-school. The median age of those interviewed in each society fell within the "young adult" generational category (i.e., aged 18 through 25 — after Cameron, 1969). In the United States, 2,530 males and 2,679 females were interviewed, in Iran the corresponding figures were 493 and 398, in India 351 and 183, in Ghana 80 and 136. Subjects were always to be approached unawares and then interviewed on-the-spot regarding their consciousness. Sampling was conducted in and about Ahmedabad, India; Sekondi-Takoradi, Ghana; Detroit, Evansville, Louisville, Los Angeles, and a number of small towns in the United States; and in 18 different cities/locations, mainly urban, in Iran.

Interviewers were paid nationals in India and Iran, a mixture of paid and volunteer nationals in the United States, and a native husband-wife team in Ghana. The interview included the following items (translated into the Gujarati language in India and Persian in Iran): What were you thinking about in the last five minutes? (a) Did you think about death or dying — even for a moment (perhaps it crossed your mind)? (b) same as (a) for sex, (c) What has been the central focus of your thought? (1) about personal problems — topics concerning sex, (2) about personal problems — topics concerning death.

TABLE 6.1

FREQUENCY OF CONTEMPLATION OF DEATH ACROSS THE LIFE-SPAN IN IRAN, INDIA, GHANA, AND THE UNITED STATES

Age-Generation		<18	young adult	26-39	middle-aged	56-64	old	average %
U. S. Male	n	480	576	488	398	102	86	20
	peripheral (%)	24	13	17	21	15	29	3
	focal (%)	4	1	3	2	1	6	
Female	n	579	652	443	336	95	86	26
	peripheral (%)	29	18	21	21	27	38	4
	focal (%)	3	3	3	2	3	9	
India Male	n	44	93	152	58			9
	peripheral (%)	7	11	7	12			3
	focal (%)	2	5	2	3			
Female	n	24	71	53	33			10
	peripheral (%)	∅	25	9	6			2
	focal (%)	∅	4	∅	3			
Ghana Male	n	30	38	8				24
	peripheral (%)	30	29	13				4
	focal (%)	3	8	∅				
Female	n	62	57	11				40
	peripheral (%)	39	35	45				11
	focal (%)	10	4	18				
Iran Male	n	53	204	148	79			48
	peripheral (%)	43	48	49	52			22
	focal (%)	17	15	21	33			
Female	n	121	182	77	18			49
	peripheral (%)	60	45	40	50			14
	focal (%)	11	6	12	28			

TABLE 6.2

FREQUENCY OF CONTEMPLATION OF SEX ACROSS THE LIFE-SPAN IN IRAN, INDIA, GHANA AND THE UNITED STATES

Age-Generation		<18	young adult	26-39	middle-aged	56-64	old	average %
U. S. Male								
	peripheral (%)	46	48	33	20	19	9	37
	focal (%)	11	10	8	4	3	∅	8
Female								
	peripheral (%)	39	33	19	9	12	6	23
	focal (%)	8	6	2	2	∅	∅	5
India Male								
	peripheral (%)	5	16	4	9			9
	focal (%)	∅	3	2	7			3
Female								
	peripheral (%)	29	10	9	3			13
	focal (%)	∅	3	9	∅			3
Ghana Male								
	peripheral (%)	47	61	75				61
	focal (%)	37	26	38				34
Female								
	peripheral (%)	32	33	45				37
	focal (%)	11	11	18				13
Iran Male								
	peripheral (%)	42	62	53	42			40
	focal (%)	4	10	10	14			10
Female								
	peripheral (%)	31	45	43	44			41
	focal (%)	16	4	14	∅			9

Results

For our modest sample of cultures it appear that United States nationals are about middling in sexiness and deathiness as indexed by their reported contents of consciousness (see Tables 6.1 and 6.2). Generally, it appears that males are cognitively sexier than females across cultures (comparing male vs. female rates of contemplation for each age group, in 14 of 17 comparisons the male frequency was higher — sign test $p < .02$). No systematic cross-cultural sex difference in "deathiness" was evident.

Discussion

Both the sex and death merchants appear to be wrong. In spite of all, Americans appear "just middling" sexers and/or deathers. Of course we sampled only in four societies — a larger sample of cultures would be required to "nail it down." But our results appear unlikely to differ dramatically from that added from other cultures.

One of our most impressive findings is the comparability of the frequencies of lethal and sexual contemplation by the populations of the societies we studied. When one considers the differences in language and culture, rejection rates and adequacy of sample, the overall similarities are far more striking than the differences. Sex and death are "hot" sensitive topics the world over. That we were able to carry this study out and arrive at similar findings suggests that the similarities across cultures may be greater than the differences in these humanly important domains.

REFERENCES

Cameron, P. Age parameters of young adult, middle-aged, old and aged. *Journal of Gerontology,* 1969, *24,* No.2.

Cameron, P. Immolations to the juggernaut. *Linacre Quarterly,* 1977, *44,*; no. 1.

SELF-REPORTED DEGREE OF PLEASURE ASSOCIATED
WITH SEXUAL AND OTHER ACTIVITIES
ACROSS THE LIFE-SPAN

What is the degree of pleasure associated with sexual activity as compared with the other entries in the domain of pleasure? Various indicies of pleasure have been reported, ranging from checklists of activities ordinarily performed, to inferences from kinds of sexual behaviors engaged in. To date, the degree of pleasure that adults claim to derive from sexual activity has apparently not been indexed directly. As the degree of pleasure associated with a particular activity must be judged relative to other kinds of pleasure rather than just "read off" from the responses to an item or series of items regarding sexuality, we sought to practically "exhaust" the domain and locate sexual activity within it.

Method

The questionnaire was first designed by culling the literature for perspectives on what "must" or ought to provide pleasure to persons of our culture. Then a questionnaire with the Likert-like format of the final version was prepared and administered to 132 Ss ranging in age from 11 to 70 in New Albany, Indiana. Those categories that "caught" relatively few nominations were deleted, and those categories frequently nominated by the respondents on the open-ended part of the questionnaire were included on the second-generation version. The same procedure was followed for a sample of 76 respondents from Louisville, Kentucky.

The following resulting items were to be responded to as "this activity gives me (the most pleasure/more than an average amount of pleasure/an average amount of pleasure/less than an average amount of pleasure): church-religious activity/housework (sewing, cooking, etc.)/drinking alcoholic beverages/daydreaming–just thinking/eating/hobbies/listening to music/parties/reading/being with pet(s)/shopping/sexual activity/sleeping/smoking tobacco/participating in sports/watching sports/traveling/watching television/visiting-socializing/doing my job-work-occupation/being with my family/being out in nature.

Area cluster samples were drawn from Los Angeles, Louisville, and Hollywood, Maryland ($n = 370$) (rejection rate <14%), supplemented with convenience samples from along the South Atlantic seaboard ($n = 104$), and 344 parochial school children aged eight through 18 from a Maryland school.

Respondents were told that we were interested in determining what gave people in our society pleasure and were asked to fill out anonymously the questionnaire. Interviewers were both paid and volunteer. Respondents also answered other questions regarding their educational status, income for the past year, and whether they smoked, drank, or owned a pet.

age	n	Male % "most"	$\overline{x}$	% "no"	rank order
<12	93	17	3.0	20	14
12,13	41	23	2.3	7	10
14,15	10	40	1.9	--	6.5
16,17	17	53	1.8	--	2
young adult	88	55	1.7	1	1.5
26-39	70	50	1.7	--	1
middle-aged	48	39	2.0	2	2.5
56-64	9	1	2.7	--	9.5
old	17	6	3.8	38	17.5
		Female			
<12	109	6	3.9	40	20
12,13	54	14	2.6	9	14.5
14,15	11	--	3.2	18	17.5
16,17	32	22	2.7	3	14.5
young adult	78	46	2.0	4	5
26-39	61	26	2.3	5	5.5
middle-aged	55	16	2.9	16	15
56-64	15	14	3.6	29	17
old	30	3	4.1	48	19

TABLE 6.3

CLAIMED PLEASURE ASSOCIATED WITH SEXUAL
ACTIVITY ACROSS THE LIFE SPAN

Results

Claimed pleasure associated with sexual activity across the adult portion of the life-span is summarized by sex and age in Table 6.3. "The most pleasure" was scored as "1" and "no pleasure" was scored as "5." Both sexes evidenced a decline in the pleasure claimed to be derived from sexual activity as a function of age/cohort (both X^2s with 4 df were greater than 25; $p < .001$). Females more frequently than males selected "the most pleasure" and "more than an average amount of pleasure" responses for the questionnaire as a whole.

Intercorrelations between education, income, SES (a composite score) are summarized by sex in Table 6.4. Clearly, for both males and females, higher educational attainment was associated with claiming a greater degree of pleasure from sexual activity. Income, on the other hand, was not associated with claimed degree of pleasure derived from sexual activity.

Age changes/differences for the various kinds of pleasure are reported in Table 6.5. Both sexual and occupational activity were curvilinearly related to age for both males and females and all correlations associated with a probability of more than .001 and/or obviously nonlinear were "bumped" from the Table.

	Male			Female		
	sex pleasure	age		sex pleasure	age
education	-.22***	-.03		-.21***	.24***
income	-.09	.34***		-.10	.03
SES	-.12	-.29***		-.19***	.23***

*** = P less than .001

TABLE 6.4

CORRELATIONS BETWEEN VARIOUS PLEASURABLE
ACTIVITIES AND AGE BY SEX

Males		Females
-.28	hobbies	-.30
	listening to music	-.24
-.32	parties	-.48
-.41	being with pet(s)	-.36
	shopping	-.30
-.38	participating in sports	-.50
-.37	watching TV	-.27

TABLE 6.5

CORRELATIONS BETWEEN VARIOUS PLEASURABLE
ACTIVITIES AND AGE BY SEX

The relative ratings of each pleasure for the sexes by age is displayed in Table 6.6.

Discussion

The importance of locating claimed pleasure associated with "sexual activity" (or any other pleasure for that matter) within the domain of pleasurable pursuits is indicated by the rank order of "sexual activity" for each sex's array (see Table 6.6). If the investigator had selected X^2 statistic he might well have concluded "no difference" between young adult males and females in claimed pleasure associated with sex and scored a "victory" for the "sexual liberation of women." But the relatively small numeric difference (which is further reduced by female selections of the "higher" categories) is belied by the number of pursuits ranked higher by females.

Mark Twain (1942) argued " . . . the human being, like the immortals, naturally places sexual intercourse far and away above all other joys . . . . The very thought of it excites him, opportunity sets him wild; in this state he will risk life, reputation, everything — even . . . heaven itself — to make good that opportunity and ride it to the overwhelming climax. From youth to middle age all men and all women prize copulation above all other pleasures combined

TABLE 6.6

RELATIVE RANKINGS OF PLEASURABLE ACTIVITIES BY AGE AND SEX

Males

≤12-years old	16/17-years old	young adults	middle-aged	old
sports	parties	music/sex	family	family/watch spts/reading
travel/TV	sex	nature	nature/sex	TV
hobbies	music	traveling	music/job	nature/eating
pets/watching sports	eating	hobbies/sports	eating	sleeping
parties/music	nature	eating/parties/family	watching spts/traveling	church
family	sleeping	job/visiting	hobbies/sleeping/TV	traveling
eating	traveling	sleeping	visiting/sports	music
sleeping	visiting/TV/daydream	reading	pets/church	visiting
visiting	hobbies/job	watch spts/pets/daydream	parties/tobacco	hobbies
nature	alcohol	TV/alcohol	reading	shopping
sex	sports/family	church	daydreaming	daydreaming
reading/church	pets	shopping	alcohol	tobacco/job
shopping	watching spts/reading	tobacco	shopping	sex/sports
job	church	housework	housework	pets
daydreaming	shopping			housework/parties
alcohol	tobacco/housework			alcohol
tobacco/housework				

Females

≤12-years old	16/17-years old	young adults	middle-aged	old
music	music	music	family	nature
parties	traveling	nature	music	family
family/travel/hobbies	nature/parties	family	nature	music
nature	hobbies/sports	traveling	traveling	church/traveling
TV/sports/pets	visiting/eating	sex	visiting/job/reading	reading
shopping	shopping/job	parties	hobbies	visiting
visiting	family/shopping	shopping/visiting	church	hobbies
sleeping	TV/sleep/sex/pets	hobbies/eating	parties/eating/sleeping/	job
read/daydreaming/	watch spts/church/read	sleeping	housework/TV	sleeping/housework
eating/watch spts	housework	reading/job	sex	eating/shopping/pets
job/housework	alcohol	TV	shopping	parties
church	tobacco	sports/housework	pets/sports/daydreaming	daydream/watch sports
sex		church/pets	watching sports	sex
alcohol		daydreaming	tobacco	sports
tobacco		watching sports	alcohol	alcohol
		alcohol		tobacco
		tobacco		

. . . . (p.17)." He also opined that women enjoy sex more than men because of their ability to volley climax (shades of Masters and Johnson). But alas, though the "sexual revolution" is upon us, and female sex magazines enjoy healthy sales, and the tube is moist with daytime sex, and commentators assure that the female's appetite is being loosed from a dark age of its imprisonment, our results suggest that females just don't like sex as much as males. And while, as Twain put it, the male "wick" may be feeble in the face of the potentially ravenous demands of the female cavern, it would appear that males generally have little to fear currently from the gentle race. Or perhaps, as we are indexing "things as they are" rather than how they might be, males are somehow responsible for the female position on the matter (perhaps if males put up a better show . . .).

Our most consistent finding was the declining valuation of a host of activities as a function of age. Essentially nothing was ranked higher, and many activities declined with age. In a rather grab-bag study (710 subjects were to rate both frequencies and pleasure associated with 320 activities including "shoplifting," "shaving," "being stubborn") Lewinsohn and MacPhillany (1974) reported declining frequencies and satisfaction as a function of age. In the present, more-superordinate-categories study, age decline was associated with some active (parties, shopping, sports), social (parties), and solitary (hobbies, television) pursuits. Since life-satisfaction stays constant through the life-cycle, satisfaction must be wrest from a declining pool of satisfiers.

REFERENCES

Lewinsohn, P. M. and MacPhillany, D. J. The relationship between age and engagement in pleasant activities. *Journal of Gerontology,* 1974, *29,* 290-294.

Twain, M. *Letters from the earth*. Greenwich, Connecticut: Fawcett, 1942.

7

MASCULINITY/FEMININITY

Even as "good mental health" is to a considerable degree culture/ specific, so it is with "masculinity" or "femininity." "Masculine" is what is practiced and/or is characteristic of males within a given culture. Since the functions and consequent personalities of males vary from culture to culture it is not useful to regard "masculinity" as an attribute of human males *per se*. The sexes do differ in almost every culture — in roles and personality. "What might systematically separate the sexes irrespective of culture?" is a question that can be asked. But just because it is askable provides no guarantee that it is a good question. The only reliable-appearing answer seems to be "in infancy and somewhat beyond, males are somewhat more excitable/exploratory than females." But how much cultural influence might affect even week-old humans is unknown, perhaps enough to account for even the small differences that have been found to date.

Because such a question is unprofitable does not mean that we should abandon the use of the concept "feminine." It is quite a useful descriptive summary of an aspect of a person's activities and/or personality. Usefulness determines veracity. A male who acts in a feminine manner is different from one who acts in a masculine manner. How good or bad such actions are or are thought to be is determined by society. Certainly there is little merit in tossing out these valuable concepts in a fit of misguided "women's lib."

MASCULINITY-FEMININITY IN THE AGED

Are the aged more similar to the feminine or masculine personality style? Are the sex differences in personality more divergent or convergent with age? Further, are the aged more interested in feminine activities, and, if so, why? Studies seeking to answer these questions have found equivocal results. The present research was undertaken to assist in answering these questions.

Materials and Methods

Subjects. An aged (over 59-years old) and a younger) (aged 18 to 40) sample were compared along the masculine-feminine continuum. The young and 69 of the aged were drawn by a random area sampling technique encompassing Boulder, Colorado. Another 38 aged were obtained by a random selection of tenants residing in a cooperative "golden years" apartment. The young females had a mean age of 31.5, S.D. = 7.67; the aged females a mean age of 70.65, S.D. = 8.71; young males = 26.09, S.D. = 6.67; aged males = 70.46, S.D. = 8.43. The socioeconomic status (SES) of the young as measured by a weighted average ranging from 5 (high) to 1 (low) and incorporating educational level, occupational status, and last year's income was 3.26 while that of the aged was 2.38; $t = 7.27$; $p < .0.01$. All Ss were Caucasian.

Tests. As differing results have been obtained by investigators utilizing interest and more broad range personality tests, we used both. The Symonds (1936) Areas of Human Concern Ranking Scale, which asks S to rank 15 broad areas of concern in terms of personal appeal, was used to tap the interest patterns of the samples. The Berdie (1959) Femininity Adjective Check List, which has been standardized on about 1,200 college students with males scoring at about 8 on the scale and females at about 16, was used as a measure of global personality.

Approximately half of Ss were randomly selected to take the Symonds and/or Berdie scale(s). The above tests were administered as follows: (1) equally often within hour intervals from 8:00 A.M. to 8:00 P.M. to control for time-of-day bias; (2) equally often by male and female interviewers to control for sex-of-interviewer bias; (3) by each administrator to Ss in each of the four subsamples to control for idiosyncratic influences of interviewers; and (4) by interviewers ignorant of the aims of the study to guard against experimenter-hypotheses-formation bias (Rosenthal, 1963).

The interviewers were paid college students, ten of each sex. The S refusal rate was 5%. Females constituted about 75% of respondents in each of the four subsamples. All sampling took place on April 4 and 5, 1966.

Results

Masculine-feminine personality style. Table 7.1 summarizes the mean femininity scores of the aged and the young grouped by sex. Since the one-way analysis of variance was significant at the .05 level, a series of *post hoc t* tests was performed to clarify the relationships. Clearly the aged females were equivalent to the male young while the male aged were even more masculine than the young males. Although the data might have been analyzed with a two-way analysis, the unequal Ns in the cells suggested a multiple regression analysis. The regression analysis indicated that age accounted for about 5% and SES about 2% of the variance associated with this relationship. As SES was positively and age negatively associated with femininity while the SES of the young surpassed that of the old, the differences in femininity were apparently exaggerated. Nonetheless, the aged were probably more masculine.

Masculine or feminine interests style. Table 7.2 presents the empirical differences between males and females for our total sample along those dimensions of the Symonds Scale significant at or beyond the .10 level. Since there are 15 dimensions in the Symonds array, one or two of these findings may be artifactual. Using the relationships in Table 7.2 to define masculine-feminine interest patterns we examined the same dimensions for the young and aged samples in Table 7.3 On the face of it, the aged males tended toward more feminine interests (five of the six differences between the young male means were in a feminine direction; p <0.11) and aged females toward masculine interests (four of the six differences between the young female means and the aged female means were in a masculine direction). But the multiple regression analysis indicates that only one of the relationships, that of "sexual adjustment," was associated with age in the main. SES seems to be the prime determinant of interest patterns in our samples. Thus, although our data definitely support the concept that the aged have convergent interests (five of the six differences between the young males' and females' and the aged males' and females' means show the aged subsamples' means closer together; p <0.11), they suggest that this tendency is associated with SES rather than age *per se*.

Turning to our second question of whether the sex differences in personality are convergent or divergent with age, a tendency in the data favors the former. Combining the differences between the male and female means for the aged and the young for the Berdie and Symonds Scales, we find six of the seven differences smaller for the aged than for the young sample (p <0.07).

Discussion

In 1936 both Terman and Miles and Strong reported extensive normative research on their respective instruments aimed at measuring masculinity-femininity in the first case and vocational interests in the latter. Both studies reached the same conclusion — the old are more feminine than the young. Both studies involved administering questionnaires to about 3,000 unsystematically selected Ss varying in age and socioeconomic status. Analysis of data collected on Strong's Vocational Interest Blank by sex instead of by occupation led to the finding that feminine interests increase with age. In the Terman and Miles study an interests test and a series of word-association tests were employed. Again it was found that interests are more feminine in the aged.

Kelly (1955) performed the only longitudinal study of masculinity-femininity and his results contradicted those of Terman and Miles and Strong. Using 500 of his students he readministered the Allport-Vernon and the Strong Vocational Interest Blank 20 years later (mean age at first testing, 25; at second, 45). The Allport-Vernon revealed changes in both sexes, but usually they were in the same direction and not consistently toward either the masculine or feminine direction. The SVIB definitely indicated

Table 7.1. Means of the Aged and Young Samples
on the Berdie Femininity Scales.

Subsample	N	Mean	S.D.	ts
1. Young females	55	14.82	4.21	1,2=5.22; $P<0.01$
2. Aged females	45	9.02	6.34	1,3=4.06; $P<0.01$
3. Young males	19	8.74	5.89	1,4=7.13; $P<0.01$
4. Aged males	13	5.00	4.30	2,3= .19; NS
	—	—	—	2,4=2.56; $P<0.02$
$F = 5.510$, df $= 3/128$; $P<0.01$				3,4=2.01; $P<0.06$

Variable	r	R	R^2
Age	−.22	.22	.047
SES	.16	.26	.068

Table 7.2. Empirical Differences in Interests
Between the Sexes on the Symonds Scale.

	Sex Adjustment		Recreation		Moral Qualities	
	Mean	S.D.	Mean	S.D.	Mean	S.D.
Females (N=72)	11.70	3.96	8.06	4.47	4.81	3.31
Males (N=35)	8.57	4.56	5.89	5.29	6.48	3.02
	$t = 10.8$;		$t = 2.06$;		$t = 2.53$;	
	$P<0.001$		$P<0.05$		$P<0.02$	

	Home & Family		Attractiveness		Philosophy of Life	
	Mean	S.D.	Mean	S.D.	Mean	S.D.
Females	4.08	3.29	7.58	3.78	4.16	3.36
Males	5.44	3.68	9.19	4.05	5.78	4.86
	$t = 1.84$;		$t = 1.71$;		$t = 1.74$;	
	$P<0.10$		$P<0.10$		$P<0.10$	

Note.—The Symonds scale is negatively scaled, i.e., the larger the value the
less the expressed interest.

Table 7.3. Age-Sex Differences on the Symonds Scale
Along Interests Differentiating the Sexes.

	Sex Adjustment		Recreation		Morality	
Subsample	Mean	S.D.	Mean	S.D.	Mean	S.D.
Young females (N=48)	9.21	4.44	8.10	4.44	4.83	3.39
Aged Females (N=34)	12.62	3.74	8.01	4.50	4.77	3.15
Young males (N=24)	8.33	4.44	5.54	6.16	6.62	3.25
Aged males (N=11)	9.10	4.73	6.63	4.40	5.90	2.87
	MRE:		MRE:		MRE:	
	age $= 14\%$;		NS		SES $= 8\%$	
	SES $= 2\%$					

	Home & Family		Attractiveness		Philosophy of Life	
	Mean	S.D.	Mean	S.D.	Mean	S.D.
Young females	4.06	3.39	7.45	3.72	3.98	3.27
Aged females	4.11	3.15	7.91	3.82	4.40	3.56
Young males	5.44	4.12	9.54	3.41	6.68	5.19
Aged males	5.45	3.16	8.40	5.03	3.82	3.72
	MRE:		MRE:		MRE:	
	SES $= 5\%$		SES $= 9\%$		SES $= 8\%$;	
					age $= 3\%$	

Note.—MRE = Multiple Regression Estimate of variance of dependent
variable accounted for utilizing age and SES as independent variables.

that the interest pattern of both sexes had become more masculine!
Recently Aaronson (1964) administered the MMPI to 98 hospitalized Ss between the aged of 15 and 65 and concluded that the
response pattern offered no evidence of increasing femininity of
masculinity with age.

The present study offers some resolution of the contradictions.
Both Strong and Terman and Miles assumed that interests were
reflectants of personality, and correctly so, but interests are not
solely personality determined; accessibility to and success in various kinds of endeavors also determine interests. The lower SES
and general physical weakening of the aged often precludes participation in the relatively expensive and vigorous masculine activities. One often has to be content with what one can do, and
what one does is generally what one professes to desire (i.e., to be
interested in). As both the Terman and Miles and Strong data were
collected during the depression it is unlikely that their aged were
financially "better off" than ours. Kelly's study is the only one that
holds SES constant and no feminine trend evidences itself. Of
course, his sample could hardly be considered "aged" or, for that
matter, typical. The lack of a representative sample also largely
obviates the value of Aaronson's work.

Our own research (Cameron, 1967) makes the value of research
on the hospitalized questionable in the formulation of normative
theory. The word-association similarities of the Terman and Miles
research may have been a reflectant of personality or knowledge
changes (early research on children usually found males considerably less verbally proficient), the unrepresentative drawing of their
sample, or differences in SES. In any case empirical research offers
little support for Neugarten's (1964) contention that the "sexes
become increasingly divergent with age." On the contrary, they
apparently become convergent with regard to interests and personality.

Jung's (1939) concept that femininity becomes dominant with
age also appears rather unlikely. Feminine *interests* perhaps, but
the masculinity evidenced by our data based on a representative
sample seems clear cut as does Kelly's. Certainly even Aaronson's
study offers no encouragement to Jungian theory. If one were to
make an intelligent guess based upon the empirical data available,
it would seem a view that personality becomes more structured and

less pliable (masculine) while applying itself to largely feminine endeavors due to physical deterioration and economic necessity would be the most supportable.

Summary

A representative sample of young adults (aged 18 to 40, N = 162) and aged (over 59, N = 117) were administered the Berdie Femininity Check List and Symonds Areas of Human Concern Interests resented which indicates that while the *interests* of the aged may be more feminine their basic personality style is more masculine than the young.

REFERENCES

Aaronson, B. S. Aging, personality change and psychiatric diagnosis. *Journal of Gerontology,* 1964, *19,* 144-148.

Berdie, R. R. A femininity adjective check list. *Journal of Applied Psychology,* 1959, *43,* 327-333.

Cameron, P. Ego-strength and happiness of the aged. *Journal of Gerontology,* 1967, *22,* 199-202.

Jung, C. G. *The integration of the personality.* New York: Farrar & Rinehart, 1939.

Kelly, E. L. Consistency of the adult personality. *American Psychologist,* 1955, *10,* 659-681.

Neugarten, B. L. A developmental view of adult personality. Chapter 7 in: Birren, J. E., ed., *Relations of Development and Aging.* Springfield, Illinois: Charles C. Thomas, 1964, pp. 176-208.

Rosenthal, R. On the social psychology of the psychological experiment; the experimenter's hypothesis as unintended determinant of experimental results. *American Scientist,* 1963, *51,* 268-283.

Strong, E. K. Jr. Interests of men and women. *Journal of Social Psychology,* 1936, *1,* 49-67.

Symonds, P.M. Changes in problems and interests with increasing age. *Psychological Bulletin,* 1936, *33,* 789.

Terman, L. M. and Miles, C. C. *Sex and personality.* New York: McGraw-Hill, 1936.

MASCULINITY/FEMININITY OF THE GENERATIONS: AS SELF-REPORTED AND AS STEREOTYPICALLY APPRAISED

Of the 3,000 or so personality traits in common parlance, masculinity and femininity are of succifient psychological import to warrant inclusion in many of the personality inventories that claim breadth of coverage (e.g., the MMPI, the CPI). Inclusion occurs without resolution of two areas of controversy regarding the nature of masculinity and femininity. One of these areas concerns whether masculinity and femininity form a single continuum, locating on opposite ends, or constitute two continua. Personality scales typically assume that masculinity and femininity are a continuum [1] Yet major personality theorists appear to regard masculinity and femininity as two continua [2,3]. No one appears to have asked the populace directly whether masculinity and femininity are taken to be one or two traits, but some investigators have had numbers of persons select descriptions of "typical" masculinity and femininity from lists of adjectives [4] or true-false items [1] and have inferred either single of multiple continua from their results.

The other areas of controversy concerns the course of masculinity and femininity across the life-span. Jung appears to have contended that the feminine component of personality becomes more dominant late in the life-span [3], while Neugarten has argued that the personalities of the "sexes" becomes increasingly divergent with age" [5]. Most of the empirical research on the issue has focused on either the beginning [6,7] or the end of the life-span [8,9].

In economically advanced societies the roles of the sexes are converging. If personality structure follows role performance, the personalities of the sexes ought to be converging also. At some future date, the roles of males and females may be so similar as to obviate the distinctions "masculine" and "feminine." Such is not the case today. Gender concepts enjoy both popular and professional currency. For one reason or another, professional psychologists (including the present author) have shied from asking persons about their masculinity or femininity directly. Rather, scales ostensibly indexing "genderness" have been devised, administered, and analyzed with varying results. In the present investigation, subjects from the young adult, middle-aged, and old generations were asked to rate themselves on masculinity and femininity and to report their judgments of the "genderness" of the same three generations [10].

Method

An area sample of 317 while Detroiters, half of them female and divided among young (aged 18 to 25 years) middle-aged (40 to 55 years), and old (65 to 79 years) adults was administered a questionnaire that included the assessment of the respondent's beliefs about his own masculinity/femininity and how the generations compared in their masculinity and femininity. After an introduction, the respondents were asked, "How do you believe the three age-groups (young adults, middle-aged, and old) compare in

1) femininity of personality-style;
2) possession of feminine sorts of interests;
3) masculinity of personality-style;
4) possession of masculine sorts of interests;
5) possession of feminine sorts of skills (ability to do things usually done by women in our society — as cooking, ironing, etc.);
6) social pressure for them to do feminine sorts of things.
7) possession of masculine sorts of skills (ability to do things usually done by men in our society — as hold a job, know how to fix a car);
8) social pressure for them to do masculine sorts of things?"

Respondents indicated which generation they believed had the most and least of each.

Respondents were then asked to rate themselves as "above average," "average," or "below average" to the questions, "How would you compare yourself with all other adults of your sex in:

1) femininity of personality-style;
2) possession of feminine sorts of interests;
3) masculinity of personality-style;
4) possession of masculine sorts of interests;
5) possession of feminine sorts of skills (ability to do things

usually done by women in our society — cooking, ironing, etc.);

6) social pressure on you to do feminine sorts of things;

7) possession of masculine sorts of skills (ability to do things usually done by men in our society — as hold a job, know how to fix a car);

8) social pressure *on you* to do masculine sorts of things?"

The two administrations were counterbalanced.

The respondent was also asked his age, sex, income to the nearest $500 for the past year, and the highest grade completed in formal schooling. Socioeconomic status was computed by multiplying the number associated with income (e.g., 1 = under $5,000; 2 = $5,000–$7,999; 3 = $8,000–$11,999; 4 = $12,000+) by two and adding it to the number associated with education (1 = completed less than eighth grade; 2 = 8th–11th; 3 = high school diploma; 4 = some college; 5 = B.A.; 6 = M.A.; 7 = Ph.D.). All analyses broke socioeconomic status into two levels — those scoring nine or higher and those scoring eight or less.

The mean ages in years of the samples were 21.0 for the young adults, 48.2 for the middle-aged, and 70.2 for the old. Socioeconomic status levels were 8.89, 9.39, and 6.02, respectively (educational levels were 3.52, 5.25, and 2.49, with the young and middle-aged thus falling between the "high school diploma" and "some college" categories, while the old fell between the "8th–11th" and "high school diploma" categories; for income, the groups averaged 2.68, 3.10, and 1.79 with the young thus averaging under $8,000 per year, the middle-aged over $8,000, and the old under $5,000).

Results

Beliefs about Generational Masculinity and Femininity As each dimension (e.g., 1 through 8 above) investigated is conceptually independent of the others, both the "most" and "least" response for each dimension were treated with a 2 (sex) x 3 (generation) x 2 (socioeconomic status level) fixed-effects analysis of variance. The reported beliefs of the generations about the generations did not vary by generation and six (of a possible 48) main effects reached conventional significance levels. The results are grouped in Table 7.4. Females less frequently than males reported believing that the old (a) are least feminine (F $(1,303) = 8.76$; $p < .01$); (b) are least feminine in interests (F $(1,303) = 4.83$; $p < .05$); (c) are most masculine (F $(1,303) = 4.34$; $p < .05$); and (d) possess the fewest feminine skills (F $(1,303) = 8.99$; $p < .01$). Higher socioeconomic status persons more frequently reported believing that the old possessed the most (F $(1,303) = 8.98$; $p < .01$) and fewest (F $(1,303) = 9.07$; $p < .01$) feminine skills.

Generally, the respondents reported believing that (a) the middle-aged are the most and the old the least masculine; (b) the middle-aged possess the most and the old the least masculine interests; (c) young adults and middle-aged possess the most and the old the fewest masculine skills; (d) the most social pressure to do masculine things falls on the middle-aged and the least such social pressure is applied to the old; (e) young adults and middle-aged are the most and the old are the least feminine; (f) the middle-aged possess the most and the old the least feminine interests; (g) the middle-aged possess the most and young adults the fewest feminine skills; and (h) the most social pressure to do feminine things falls on young adults and the middle-aged.

Self-reported Masculinity and Femininity The same three-way fixed-effects analyses of variance for self-report items yielded no statistically significant generational or social class main effects or interactions. The sexes differed in reported "genderness" as can be seen in Table 7.5. All of the *F* values comparing the responses of the sexes were larger than 50 and the probabilities associated with such *F* values $<.0001$. Both sexes strongly affirmed their "genderness" and denied "opposite-genderness". Both sexes reported themselves much above average on possession of appropriate-gender skills, interests, and "genderness," average in "social pressure to do appropriate-gender things," "quite below average on opposite-gender skills, interests, and "opposite-genderness," and lowest on "social pressure to do opposite-gender things."

Discussion

Popular belief holds that there are considerable differences be-

Table 7.4. Stereotypic Beliefs About Masculinity-Feminity Along the Adult Life-Span

	Young Adults	Middle-Aged	Old
Masculinity			
the most masculine are	105	180	25
the least masculine are	113	27	171
most masculine in interests	134	162	18
least masculine in interests	89	22	204
most possessed of masculine skills	177	132	8
least possessed of masculine skills	61	36	220
most social pressure to do masculine things on	104	188	24
least social pressures to do masculine things on	133	27	156
Femininity			
the most feminine are	166	111	38
the least feminine are	97	49	170
most feminine in interests	139	132	43
least feminine in interests	96	41	178
most possessed of feminine skills	43	174	99
least possessed of feminine skills	222	32	63
most social pressure to do feminine things on	151	117	49
least social pressure to do feminine things on	110	54	153

Table 7.5. Mean Self-Appraisal Masculinity-Femininity
(1 = below average, 2 = average, 3 = above average)

	Males	Females
Own gender skills	2.40	2.42
Own gender interests	2.29	2.23
Overall "genderness"	2.15	2.20
Judged social pressure to do own gender things	2.03	1.98
Opposite gender skills	1.72	1.47
Opposite gender interests	1.48	1.53
Overall "opposite genderness"	1.46	1.43
Judged social pressure to do opposite gender things	1.36	1.30

tween the generations along the gender dimension. Middle age is the generation with the strongest claim to both masculinity *and* femininity. The middle— aged apparently, all things taken into consideration, are believed somewhat more masculine than feminine. While they are believed to be somewhat more feminine than masculine in skills, they are also believed to be somewhat more masculine than feminine in interests. Young adults are believed to be somewhat more feminine, overall, than masculine even though they are considered rather strong in possession of masculine skills and weak in feminine skills and about equally masculine and feminine in interests. The old are seen as almost neuter — *sans* hair, teeth, and "genderness." The old are judged reasonably possessed of feminine skills, and overall, judged rather more feminine than masculine.

Masculinity is associated with virility and power in our culture. There is evidence that the members of our society believe the middle-aged is the wealthiest and most powerful, the young adult generation the next most powerful and wealthy, and the old least along both dimensions [11]. General opinion also seems to have it that the middle-aged are the most sexually skilled, the young most sexually desirous, and the old lowest on both sexual counts [12]. Our present results suggest that common opinion credits males from both the young adult and middle-aged generations with pronounced "genderness," while withholding "genderness" from old males. Not so with the old female. Even with her low overall femininity, she is still credited with considerable feminine skill. While some social commentators (e.g., Atcheley, 1972) [13] have waved eloquent over the plight of the male in retirement (he has left the economic center stage, the place of status conferment) as compared to that of the female (who continues pretty much with life-as-usual) popular opinion not only shares but probably antedates this view. If we accept that "genderness" is a valued attribute, then with this dimension, as with so many others 14, 15, consensually-speaking, the middle-aged is the "generation of choice." Contrarywise, the old is lackluster.

Self-reports by the members of the generations stand in sharp contrast to consensual beliefs. While the members of the various generations agreed that the old were the least masculine, this belief did not lower the self-ratings along the dimension by old persons. It would appear that two psychological domains were being tapped — the one consisting of beliefs about abstract-generations, the other judgments about the rather concrete self.

Common opinion holds that masculinity and femininity trace somewhat different courses across the life-span. While both peak in middle age and reach their nadir in old age, after middle age masculinity plummets. Femininity appears to rise more slowly and descends more gradually (see Table 7.4). If common opinion validates psychological theory, then Jung's contention that femininity comes to predominate in old age receives slight support. Naugarten's notion of gender divergence with old age receives no such support — in fact, the relative "genderlessness" of the old by such a standard weighs against her view. The self-report data offer encouragement to neither theorist. Nothing about our results suggests that the respondents had particular difficulty with the gender concepts. On the contrary, the amount of agreement and "sprayed" responses across the generations is of about the order one would expect in handling a moderately difficult concept on which stereotypes exist.

The use of masculinity-femininity scales to index the course of genderness across the life-span is subject to serious reservations on a number of counts. Most are nothing more than empirically-discovered response-differences between the sexes in answering a set of true-false yes-no items which bear no necessary conceptual relationship to the gender concepts. Psychologists have enough difficulty interpreting the answers to direct questioning to expect much of substantive value to emerge from such intellectual scrapple. Though some could justifiably claim that with age persons display a response pattern on various interests scales that is more similar to the feminine than the masculine pattern, interests are but a subset of attitudes [9, 16, 17]. Many more subsets of attitude (e.g., values, beliefs, opinions) would have to be indexed before even attitude could be reasonably characterized by genderlikeness across the life-span. Cameron had persons across the adult life-span choose their traits from an adjectival checklist and could claim evidence that with age, persons' appraisals of their trait structure were more similar to the pattern typically chosen by males than that typically chosen by females [9]. But the concept of genderness subsumes components of interests, values, traits, behavior and role patterns, etc. Indexing any one or even several of these personality components for "genderlikeness" cannot establish gender-differences-in-general across the life-span. As each component comprises a "distinctive descriptive system", each "speaks only for itself" [18]. A component (as interest-in-general) may trace a "feminine -like" while another component assumes a "masculine-like" direction, while still other components with age veer toward neither gender. Whether genderness is, so to speak, the product of various personality components in unknown, but if it is, we are far from being able to specify which components and even further from knowing what "weights" each component is to be given in the calculation. As such, it is undoubtedly not only intellectually safer but more informative to address questions of genderness-across-the-life-span directly (as in the present investigation) rather than assessing various personality components whilly-nilly for gender-ness and then passing the various outcomes together (as with the MMPI).

There is evidence, obtained from both direct questions ("Have you sometimes wished you were of the opposite sex?" "Have you ever wished that you belonged to the opposite sex?" [19, 20] and indirect means (picture preferences [6], sexual symbol preferences [21] that females in our society more frequently than males claim a desire to switch their gender. But there is no evidence in the present study to suggest that female adults consider their gender identification any weaker than males consider their gender identification. The present investigation suggests that if genderness is established in early childhood it is maintained — for adulthood at least — at constant "strength" until demise. Direct answers to direct questions are about as close to truth as psychologists can generally come. Thus while it may not be the case, it will take a rather impressive array of evidence to demonstrate that felt masculinity and femininity are other than constant across the adult portion of the life-span.

The linguistic community appears to regard masculinity and femininity as two separate concepts rather than as opposite poles of a continuum. Our subjects were not asked directly about whether they were dealing wtih one or two separate concepts, but the stereotypic responses that case both maximal masculinity and femininity into the middle-aged generation makes such an interpretation attractive. It is conceivable that both could be opposite ends of a continuum and still be granted to the middle-aged, but such a usage would appear strained.

Recently Oeschger and Cameron read and evaluated all of the magazine articles on homosexuality that were indexed in *Reader's Guide to Periodical Literature* over the past half-century [22]. It was found that the frequency of articles about homosexuality had increased considerably of late. Further, that the "tone" of the articles had, on the average, changed from one of disgust and abhorrence during the 1920s and 1930s to one of neutrality in the last decade.

This "mass media pressure" encouraging toward homosexuality appears to be occurring in more than just the magazine literature. As the mass media are currently "warp and woof" of our social system, and in their own right constitute a part of social pressure, it is more than interesting that our subjects should judge the "social pressure on you to do the opposite gender things" (Table 2) as furthest below average of any of the variables studied. Perhaps the media message is not "getting through". If the media continues its homosexually inclined pressure, it will be interesting to see whether the mean for this item swings upward with the passage of time. If the proportion of women in the work force remains relatively constant, a replication of this study a decade hence ought to provide an index of the media's efficacy to effect attitudinal change.

The present data appear to document "the way things are" vis-a-vis beliefs and self-reports regarding genderness circa 1970 in the spirit of the descriptive psychology argued for by Ossorio [18]. Even young children manifest gender interests and develop some semblance of gender appropriate skills in their play. Adults maintain gender interests and skills far into decline. Why do adults impute lower femininity and masculinity to the old? How is this imputation maintained in the face of constant self-reported genderness? Research into the antecedents of gender identification and/or imputation will be required to answer such questions and explicate how "the way things are" came to be.

REFERENCES

Aaronson, B. S. Aging, Personality Change and Psychiatric Diagnosis, *Journal of Gerontology*, 1964, *19*, 144-148.   [8]

Atchley, R. C. *The Social Forces in Later Life: An Introduction to Social Gerontology.* Belmont, California: Wadsworth, 1972.   [13]

Brown, D. G. Masculinity-Femininity Development. *Journal of Consulting Psychology*, 1957, *21*, 197-202.   [6]

Cameron, P. Age Parameters of Young Adults, Middle-Aged, Old and Aged. *Journal of Gerontology*, 1969, *24*, 201-202.   [10]

Cameron, P. Confirmation of the Freudian Psychosexual Stages Utilizing Sexual Symbolism. *Psychological Reports*, 1967, *21*, 33-39.   [21]

Cameron, P. The Generation Gap: Which Generation is Believed Powerful versus Generational Members' Self-Appraisals of Power. *Developmental Psychology*, 1970, *3*, 403-404.   [11]

Cameron, P. The Generation Gap: Beliefs About Sexuality and Self-Reported Sexuality. Developmental Psychology, 1970, *3*, 272.   [12]

Cameron, P. Masculinity-Femininity of the Aged. *Journal of Gerontology*, 1968, *23*, 63-65.   [9]

Cameron, P. Premedicare Beliefs About the Generations Regarding Medicine and Health. *Journal of Gerontology*, 1972, *27*, 536-539. [15]

Cameron, P. Suicide and the Generation Gap. *Life-Threatening Behavior*, 1972, *2*, 194-208.   [14]

Erikson, E. Inner and Outer Space: Reflections on Womanhood. Daedalus, 1964, *93*, 582-606.   [2]

Gallup, G. *Gallup Poll.* Princeton: Audience Research, Inc.   [19]

Jenkin, N. and Vroegh, K. Contemporary Concepts of Masculinity and Femininity. *Psychological Reports*, 1969, *25*, 679-697.   [4]

Jung, C. G. *The Integration of the Personality.* New York: Farrar & Rinehart, 1939.   [3]

Lunnebork, P. W. and Lunneborg, C. E. Factor Structure of MF Scales and Items, *Journal of Clinical Psychology*, 1970, *26,*, 360-366. [1]

Neugarten, B. L. A Developmental View of Adult Personality; *in* Birren, J. E., ed., *Relations of Development and Aging.* Springfield, Illinois: Thomas, 1964.   [5]

Oeschger, D. E. and Cameron, P. Homosexuality as Depicted in the Popular Literature: 1921-1971. Paper presented at the Kentucky-Indiana Psychilogical Associations Convention, April 27, 1973. [22]

Ossorio, P. *Persons.* Los Angeles: Linguistic Research Institute, 1966. [18]

Strong, E. K. Jr. Interests of Men and Women. *Journal of Social Psychology*, 1936, *1*, 49-67.   [16]

Terman, L. M. *Psychological Factors in Marital Happiness*. New York: McGraw-Hill, 1938.   [20]

Terman, L. M. and Miles, C. C. *Sex and Personality*. New York: McGraw-Hill, 1936.   [17]

Vroegh, K. Masculinity and Femininity in the Elementary and Junior High School Years. *Developmental Psychology,* 1971, *4,* 254-261.   [7]

8

PARENTHOOD/
SELF-CENTEREDNESS

Children freshen the race. They replace the departing and de-lethalize and socialize their keepers. Before parenthood the self is largely housed within the skin. Time is measured in distance from demise. Satisfaction is judged more in personal terms ("what's in it for me?"). Childhood launches us upon a lethal path. The lone walker ventures nearest the precipice. Heights of pleasure are less, and despair more readily attained.

The young are the executioners of our kind. Young males serve in our armies and their female counterparts slay their issue. If, on their deathbed, a button existed which, if pushed, would incinerate the world, many singletons would fail to neglect it. That others should endure — eating, sexing, having fun — while ego "checked out" would be intolerable. Given the opportunity to realize "when I die, the world dies," the solitary traveler would be quite apt. Religions attempt to decenter the ego and redirect or at least mute the fury attending the solitary orientation. But parenthood is *the* event that wrenches the ego from the skin and glues it to humanities' fortunes and betterment. In children, part of the self transcends death, and pleasure is measured not just in terms of "mine" but also "theirs." Existence is shared in a way that provides more opportunities for satisfaction (and sorrow). Amusement is gained from living not only one's, but one's childrens' lives. The adventure of life is no longer a distance to travel, but a cycle.

Children "glue" our society together in innumerable ways. Many is the marriage that endures "because of the children" — not only for the good of the children, which is a consideration, but also for both parents to be around their progeny. Since part of the ego gets absorbed by one's children, and that part will be affected by society, a new motivation to better the world comes into being. The following readings evidence some of these phenomena.

It will be noted that mothers generally claim to prefer their first-born. Much of this preference is undoubtedly a consequence of the effort it takes to reorient oneself from singlehood and do a new thing. *Love follows voluntary effort.* The first child is the hardest to rear, and generally the most beloved. In human interaction reciprocity is the general rule, and it appears that the oldest children claim greater love and admiration for their parents (Rankin and Bahnson, 1976, had 373 males rate love and admiration for their parents and found firstborns claiming more of both — on the average parents "get what they paid for," and society "gets more than it paid for.")

REFERENCES

Rankin, E. and Bahnson, M. B. Relation of birth order and sibling constellation to attitudes toward parents. Paper presented at Eastern Psychological Association Convention, New York, N.Y., 1976.

HOW MUCH DO MOTHERS LOVE THEIR CHILDREN?
with Steven Blumberg and Bill Sherman

"There is nothing worse than an unwanted child" is a common motto of the pro-liberalized-abortion campaign. Presumably the motto is not to be taken literally (*some* things must be worse), but is to be construed as "unwanted children are destined to have a less satisfying life than children who are wanted." An important factor bearing on the life-satisfaction of a child is the affection he enjoys from his mother. If initially-unwanted children are held in lower regard by their mothers than initially-wanted children, this circumstance would constitute a reason for their lives to be less enjoyable. But do mothers of initially-unwanted children love their children less, and, if so, to what degree? How many children are born unwanted, and to what degree are children loved by mothers in our society? While the issue is of importance, and the questions of the sort often asked in ordinary and professional discourse, only this study by Sears, Maccoby, and Levin (1957) was found to bear directly on these topics.

Method

We can determine the degree of affection or love that a person holds for another in basically two ways: (1) we can ask the person how he feels about the other, or (2) we can observe how the person treats the other person or the interests of the other person. Neither way is certain to generate the "truth." If we ask a person how he feels about another, he may simply lie; or perhaps be mistaken about how he feels. If we observe how a person treats another or the interests of another, we may find ourselves deceived by actions, or we may incorrectly construe the meaning of many of the acts we observe. While both methods have their advantages and pitfalls, the first is certainly the least expensive and most direct and we employed it.

Two studies were performed. Both utilized the same questionnaire, however some of the data of the first study was destroyed by an errant janitor before it could be completely analyzed. In the first study, 132 women were interviewed in shopping centers in and around Louisville and in urban parts of New Jersey. As it was hoped to generate normative results, strict area-probability samples in Louisville were first attempted. In spite of initially good rapport (potential respondents accepted the questionnaire in about two-thirds of the attempted interviews) and what appeared to be reasonable ways to assure anonymity, the highly personal nature of the questionnaire generated a refusal rate of over 95% under these circumstances. After 20 interview-hours of defeat we tried administering the questionnaire in shopping centers to every kth mother who passed by. Our success was considerably better in this situation, with a rejection rate of less than 10%. The second study was performed in shopping centers and generated 93 respondents ranging in age from 19 to 64 with a rejection rate of less than 10%.

Respondents were informed of the status of the interviewer, the general purpose of the investigation "to find out how women feel about their children," and were told to fill out the questionnaire away from the interviewer and any other person, to seal the completed questionnaire in the envelope provided, and to return it to the interviewer. They were further assured that the interviewer would not open the envelope personally and that only the senior investigator would record her answers and then would destroy the questionnaire. Before being given the questionnaire, the woman was asked how many children she had; if she had only one, she filled out a questionnaire on the one, if she had three or more, a table of random numbers was used to select the child about whom she would answer the questionnaire. After she had completed the questionnaire, an additional child was randomly selected and she answered regarding this child.

The questionnaire asked for the: (1) age of the mother; (2) age of the child; (3) religious preference; (4) when the subject felt life began; (5) if she had ever had an abortion; (6) how she felt when she learned she was pregnant (I regretted it more than anything else/I felt rather indifferent about it/I was glad/I wanted this child more than anything else); (7) how she felt at the point during pregnancy when life is felt by the mother (I felt deeper regret than I felt at the time of learning of my pregnancy/I felt no difference in feelings/My love for the child grew as my pregnancy evolved); (8) whether she had attempted to terminate the pregnancy; (9) if she would have had an abortion if it had been possible; (10) if she would have given the child up for adoption if she knew the child would be well cared for; and (11) would she go through this pregnancy again if she had it to do over. She was then to pick the statement that best described her regard for her child at birth, and at present ("upon the birth of my child, my overall feelings were: I loved him more than anyone else/I loved him next-most to the one I love the very most/I loved him more than most people I love/I loved him about as much as most of those I love/I loved him a little/I liked him/I felt rather indifferent toward him, but would help him in time of trouble/I felt rather indifferent toward him/I disliked him a little/I disliked him/I hated him a little/I hated him/I hated him more than most people I hate/I hated him next-most to the one I hate the most/I hated him more than anyone else" while the same response choices were available, suitably modified for tense for "my overall feeling today toward my child is" . . . .)

Results

We interviewed 225 women concerning 309 of their children, and were able to analyze complete data from 93. The median age of the sample was 42.5 and ranged from 19 to 64 in age. Four of the 225 women claimed that they had had an abortion.

Data on regard toward wanted and unwanted children was provided by 93 women on 128 children. Twenty-nine of the mothers had one child, 27 had 2 children, 35 had 3, 17 had 4, 10 had 5, 3 had 8, and 3 had 9. Attitudes toward the child from discovery of pregnancy to present regard is presented in Table 8.1. Apparently, at least in retrospect, most women were pleased with pregnancy. While no mother reported that she felt less kindly toward the child at the quickening, most indicated that their love for the child grew at this event. By birth, the mothers that initially regretted the child claimed to love their child more than most people they loved ("I loved him more than anyone else" was scored 1, while "I hated him more . . . " was scored 15), but differed significantly from the initially ecstatic mothers in claimed affection for the child (t - 2.159; df = 43; p <.05). At the time of interview no difference in claimed affection for the child between these two initially divergent groups of mothers existed (t = 1.32; df = 43; NS). The "indifferent" and "glad" mothers fell in between the two extreme groups along all dimensions.

The reactions of mothers who said that they would have had an abortion or actually tried to abort the child are presented in Table 8.2. Clearly, at the time of the interview these children were held in the same regard as the "average" child, while there is a suggestion that children about whom such a decision might have been made or was unsuccessfully carried out were regarded somewhat less favorably than the average child at birth.

Three mothers said that they "possibly" would have given out their child for adoption if it entailed no expense to themselves. All the rest said they would not have given it out. All of the mothers who said that they would have had an abortion or actually attempted an abortion said they would not have given out the child for

TABLE 8.1

Initial Reaction To Pregnancy and Affect Toward Child Through Present

Felt about pregnancy	Affect at birth	Affect at time of interview	Affect at quickening, stayed love		Affective changes between birth and present	Have this child again?	
			same	grew		yes	no
Regret (n = 10; 8%)	$\bar{X}$ = 3.50 S.D. = 2.23 range 1-7 Md 3	2.80 1.05 1-4 3	5	5	+ = 3 - = 2	6	3
Indifferent (n = 20; 16%)	$\bar{X}$ = 2.75 S.D. = 1.97 range 1-7 Md 2	2.45 1.36 1-5 2	3	17	- = 5 + = 6	15	5
Glad (n = 61; 48%)	$\bar{X}$ = 2.15 S.D. = 1.20 range 1-6 Md 2	2.47 .86 1-4 2	16	42	- = 23 + = 10	51	10
Ecstatic (n = 35; 28%)	$\bar{X}$ = 1.94 S.D. = 1.19 range 1-5 Md 1	2.26 1.27 1-4 2	1	30	+ = 3 - = 30	29	2

TABLE 8.2

Maternal Affection For Children

They Would Have Aborted If It Had Been Possible

Mother's age	Number of Siblings	Child's age	Affection at birth	Affection at time of interview	Would she have child again?	Sibling number
?	4	6 to 10	1	3	yes	1*
27	3	?	6	3	no	3
55	3	adult	7	2	yes	3
They Tried Unsuccessfully To Abort						
?	4	6 to 10	1	3	yes	1*
38	3	10 to 16	1	4	yes	2

*same child.

adoption.

Birth order was related to reported regard at birth and at time of interview, as is evident in Table 8.3. For both studies, the mean regard for children decreased as a direct function of birth order. As the first two categories corresponding to a score of "1" or "2" are exclusive (either the most loved or next-most loved person) some reduction with the addition of loved persons to one's phenomenal social space would appear almost inevitable. However, in one-child families, while a mean affect of 1.93 existed toward the child at birth, at the time of interview the mothers reported a mean affect of 1.62. In families with two, three, or more children, the mean estimate of love toward the first child declined from birth to the time of interview.

About half of all mothers changed their affective appraisals of their children (Table 8.1), and most of these appraisals (44 as compared with 22) were downward. Ten of our mothers provided data on two of their children. For these 10 mothers, the first child, at birth, was reported as loved more than a later child in 5 instances, and lower in one instance; the second child was rated lower in one instance; third children were rated higher in 2 and lower in 4; and

TABLE 8.3

Love of Mothers as a Function of Ordinal Position of Child

Child number	n	Affect at birth	Present affect	Change
1	175	1.87	2.18	−.31
2	57	2.38	3.01	−.63
3	47	2.84	3.15	−.31
4 or more	29	2.93	3.24	−.31

fourth children lower in 2 instances. it the time of interview, the first child was rated higher in 3 instances and lower in 1; second and third children were each rated higher in one and lower in one; while fourth children were rated lower in 2 comparisons.

Another indication of greater maternal love for the first child is revealed by comparing the frequency of rating the first child as the "most loved" with the frequency of rating other children as the "most loved." In families with two or more children, the first child was designated the "most loved" in 11 of 49 instances as compared with 1 second child being so defined out of a possible 12 second children. In families with three or more children, the first child was designated "most loved" in 7 of 24 instances as compared with 1 of 24 for the third child.

Age-of-mother was related to maternal child-regard. Middle-aged women (those aged 40 to 55 inclusive, after Cameron, 1969) reported that love for their child had increased since birth in 6 instances and declined in 21. Non-middle-aged women reported an increase in 14 instances and a decrease in 9 ($X^2 = 8.5$; df = 1; $p < .01$).

The mother's religion was related only to when she felt that life began. Eighty-five percent of the Catholics felt that life began at conception, as compared with slightly less than half of the Protestants and a third of the Jews. However, almost all of the women who did not believe that the child was alive at conception, believed that life began at the quickening. Only 6% felt that the child's life began at birth. Four of the women claimed to have had an abortion; of these; 3 were Protestant, one gave no religion. Of the four women who claimed they would have had an abortion if it were possible or claimed they had tried to abort, 3 were Protestant and the other provided no religion.

Mothers reported that they felt a lower affection than love for 15 of the 309 children at birth (5%) and for 19 (6%) of the children at the time of interview. Only two children were "hated," two were "disliked," two were "disliked a little," six were regarded with indifference "but would help him in time of trouble," and the rest were liked to some degree.

Discussion

How do women usually feel when they discover they are pregnant Sears, Maccoby and Levin (1957) reported interviews with 329 selected New England mothers who were asked how they felt when they found they were pregnant with their child who was now in kindergarten. Coders who later listened to their recorded remarks judged that about 78% had been pleased, about 15% had been uncertain, and about 10% had been displeased. Our results, based upon the mother's own choice of characterization of how she felt about her newly-discovered pregnancy, correspond closely with the Sears et al. findings. Seventy-six percent of our mothers indicated pleasure at discovery, 16% said they were indifferent, and 8% were quite displeased. As these studies were done at different times, in different locations, and with different methodology, yet arrived at similar results, it seems likely that the "true" parameters of self-professed feelings United States population lie close to those reported in the two studies.

Do women change their feelings about their children from pregnancy to the present, and, if so, how? The only test of how mother's affect toward the child might have changed since the initial discovery of pregnancy in the Sears et al. (1957) study consisted in the responses to the question "whether it would have been better to wait longer before having this child?" Four per cent of the mothers responded affirmatively and Sears et al. construed this as evidence that most of the mothers who were initially displeased came to accept their children by the time they were in kindergarten. There are reasons besides actively disliking the child to think it "would have been better to wait for this birth," and the question itself presumes that the child would have been born in any case, so the conclusions of Sears et al. are not necessarily warranted by the answers of the mothers. In our study, it is clear that mothers who initially believed their pregnancy to be "the worst thing that ever happened to them" came to feel about the same degree of affection for their children as the mothers who were initially estatic' about the pregnancy. For each of the four groups of mothers in our study ("regretters," "indifferent," "pleased," "ecstatic"), the course of love or affection for the child traced a common path. The quickening found most mothers starting to love their child-to-be more than they had initially, and birth found only a handful (5%) reporting less than love for the child. By the time they were interviewed — most of their children were teenagers or adults — only 6% of the women reported less than love for their children. *No matter what the initial attitude toward pregnancy, mothers currently claim to love their children to about the same degree as other mothers claim to love their children.*

Do mothers favor the firstborn? The Sears et al. (1957) study reported that there was a tendency for mothers to be more pleased with being pregnant with the first child than with later children. In the present study, clear evidence of maternal favoritism for the first child occurred in feelings at birth and feelings at time of interview. On the other hand, Lesko (1954) in a study of 40 two-child families, reported that professionals rated parental behavior toward the older child as being somewhat "less warm" than that evidenced toward the second child. We do not necessarily have an instance of a discrepancy between what people profess and what they do. Lesko's study of the impressions of professionals of the child rearing patterns of 40 families seems at variance with the interviews with over 400 women in the Sears et al. and present study. Lesko's report summates the impressions of both maternal and paternal behavior toward their children while an outside observer was present; while our study concerned itself with maternal attitudes. Possibly both studies validly reflect the current state of family life in the United States. Perhaps mothers ordinarily favor the first child more than other children, but change their behavior to present a "fair" image when an outsider is present. Perhaps it indicates greater love when a mother is "less warm" to her child. Lesko admitted of considerable uncertainty in the interpretation of her findings — many dimensions were explored but only a few differences were found to be statistically significant. Neither set of data can be regarded as definitive — more representative samples will have to be questioned and observed to settle the apparent discrepancy. Yet interviews with over 400 women in three locations would seem more likely to generate representative results than the observation of 40 mothers in one location.

Implications for the "liberalized abortion" debate. We feel that the implications of this study on the question of the adoption of more permissive abortion laws are direct and obvious. If the belief that "there is nothing worse than an unwanted child" lies behind a decision to make abortion more readily available, let it be noted that our results indicate that initially-unwanted children end up no worse off with regards to how mothers claim to feel about them than initially-wanted children. Our study does not "settle the issue" of what happens to initially-wanted vs. initially-unwanted children. We only assessed what mothers claimed, not what they do, nor what the fathers do, nor how the children claim to feel, nor how the children claim to be treated. However, our study is an empirical beginning in a veritable sea of opinion and should not be taken lightly. Generally psychiatric opinion about the psychological effects of being a "wanted" or "unwanted" child holds that there is a much more unfavorable prognosis for the unwanted child. But the abortion decision is made before the child is, in fact, wanted or unwanted. The abortion decision must be made while the mother knows her child only in her imagination. The same kinds of considerations that have led psychiatric opinion to question the possible mental health of the "unwanted" child have led psychiatrists to deplore parent-child separation. Yet the empirical findings regarding the effects of parent-child separation are equivocal at best (Munro, 1969), and this circumstance enhances the possibility that psychiatric opinion may be errant or unsubstantiated in this case.

Women contemplating abortion must make the decision at the least favorable time insofar as the possible child's interests are concerned. Women who were most regretful of the pregnancy now claim they would have the child again given the opportunity. While the sample of "attempted"/"wishful" aborters is small, most of these women now feel they would have the child again. On the other side of the ledger, about one of every six mothers who were initially pleased with pregnancy would chose not to have the child again. Initial feelings about pregnancy predict to only a very limited degree how a mother will eventually feel about her child. Most children are loved no matter how the mother felt initially, but the aborter-to-be must make her decision in the absence of such perspective. Her decision must be made quickly, and the chances of later regret loom large. Persons undergoing serious physical disturbance are less apt to make judicious choices, and placing the burden of such a final and irreversible decision on a pregnant woman in distress would appear less than kind. Our study would indicate that, at the least, a woman who has an abortion will have lost someone she would have loved. At the worst, she must live with the knowledge that she has participated in killing a potential human being.

REFERENCES

Cameron, P. Age parameters of young adult, middle-aged, old, and aged. *Journal of Gerontology,* 1969, *24,* 201-202.

Lasko, J. K. Parent behavior toward first and second children. *Genetic Psychology Monographs,* 1954, *49,* 96-137.

Munro, A. Parent-child separation: is it really a cause of psychiatric illness in adult life? *Archieves of General Psychiatry,* 1969, *20,* 598-604.

Sears, R. R., Maccoby, E. E., and Levin, H. *Patterns of child rearing.* Evanston, Illinois: Row, Peterson, 1957.

DO UNWANTED PREGNANCIES
PRODUCE UNWANTED CHILDREN?

While both professional and lay opinion rather easily generate the notion that "unwanted pregnancies result in unwanted children," *empirical* as opposed to intuitive or plausible evidence to buttress this claim is largely absent. How good a predictor of eventual regard of child is one's reaction to the pregnancy which is to result in that child? In a time of liberalized abortion, the question is more than academic. Further, since the United States Supreme Court has not settled the father's rights regarding a pregnancy, differences between the sexes might prove informative. Only four studies have been reported on the general issue of parental regard and these provided evidence to suggest that parental regard of pregnancy does not predict eventual regard of child. No study "settles the issue" but it appeared worthwhile to add to the literature, since having children is among the more important life decisions for adults, and the area cries for empiricism. For instance, Borosage (1973) claimed ". . .unavailability of legal abortion becomes a problem when unwanted children are allowed to be born. The literature in the behavioral sciences offers abundant evidence of the tragic consequences of being unwanted. Such persons become "battered" children; they fill the welfare rolls; they become inadequate parents themselves, thus perpetuating a vicious circle from generation to generation."

Method

An area sample in Louisville, Kentucky, in which both parents were asked to participate yielded 121 fathers and 131 mothers who answered questionnaires regarding 144 children, of these, 105 had both parents reporting (rejection rate was less than 23%).

Parents simultaneously and independently answered a questionnaire regarding one of their progeny chosen at random by the experimenters. A lengthy questionnaire (taking about 45 minutes) centered about retrospective appraisals of reaction to the pregnancy, reaction to the quickening, whether the child was wanted, whether an abortion was desired, love of the child at birth, love of the child today, and whether, if given the opportunity, the parent would have the child again.

Results

Father's claimed present regard of a child was related to : (1) his reaction to the pregnancy ($r = .18$; $p < .06$); (2) whether the child was wanted or not ($r = .21$; $p < .03$); and (3) whether the father wanted an abortion at the time ($r = .30$; $p < .002$). Mother's reported feelings about all three were unrelated to her current claimed regard of child (*r's* in order were .11, .14, and .02, all NS). As this was a retrospective study, mental "smoothing" and "face saving" ought, if anything, to have elevated the correlations. Eighteen children were reported as being in the category "just as soon not have had" by one or both parents (agreement was reached on only one child). *Seventeen of these children were female* (23% of the female progeny in the sample), yet sex of child was generally unrelated to claimed love of child.

Discussion

While the notion that an "unwanted pregnancy produced an unwanted child." is plausible, even compelling to some (Borosage, 1973; Forssman and Thuwe, 1966), subjected to direct *empirical* scrutiny, it appears of little merit. The correlations between fathers' reports bearing on the proposition are very modest and, at best account for perhaps 9% of the variance. Correlations between mothers' reports bearing on the notion are "zilch." Our results jibe with those of: (1) Cameron and Cury (1974) who claimed "reactions to a child in hand are entirely different from those to a 'bun' in the oven'," and (2) Dytrych, Matejcek, Schuller, David, and Friedman (1975), in their findings of almost no psychological differences between children born to Czechslovakian women twice denied an abortion and a control group of normally delivered children. If the Supreme Court of the United States was seeking, in part, to reduce the numbers of "unwanted children" by legitimizing abortion in the first six months, it appears to have made a sexual mistake. The modest gem of truth contained in the notion appears to apply only to *fathers*. By leaving the decision to abort exclusively to the pregnant woman, the court bypassed the sex to which the proposition somewhat applies!

Our results, obtained retrospectively, suggest that legalizing abortion probably has no effect on reducing the proportion of unwanted children. A prospective, longitudinal study in which a random sample of pregnant females desiring an abortion but who are denied an abortion is compared with a random sample of controls, would be of interest as confirming or disconfirming our findings regarding "wantedness." Forssman and Thuwe's (1966) quasi-prospective study of the *social* outcomes of children born to women denied an abortion (when appropriate controls are taken into consideration, Cameron and Tichenor, 1976), which suggested that there is no social difference between children born to women denied abortion and children born otherwise, coupled with the results of the Dytrych et al. (1975) effort, suggests that there also may be no *psychological* difference along the dimension of "wantedness."

Our results suggest that the United States Supreme Court ought to weigh very carefully the merits of the father's claims regarding progeny. Certainly more research is called for in this area. Only one child of 105 was agreed upon by both parents as "wished not born." The same general lack of agreement regarding abortion was evident in our results. It thus appears that if both prospective parents "voted" regarding an abortion, far fewer abortions would occur.

Female progeny, far less frequently than male progeny, were apt to be "wished for again." Female self-acceptance (or lack of it) might plausibly hinge somewhat upon parental regard. To the degree that parents communicate not "wishing for again" attitudes to their female children, they ought to feel less wanted. Our results suggest that when abortions occur as a result of an amniotic tap to determine the sex of child, female fetuses ought to feel more frequently the sting of the salt or knife. Further, that the United States Supreme Court should currently lay the abortion decision solely in the lap of the female poses some interesting questions. Is the sex most apt to be "not wished for again" the one most suitable to make the abortion decision? Will those members of a sexual class who are more apt to be lightly regarded choose to abort more ot less frequently?

REFERENCES

Borosage, V. Abortion in America. In *human sexuality: contemporary perspectives*. Morrison, E. S. and Borosage, V., eds. Palo Alto: National Press Book, 1973, pp. 253-269.

Cameron, P. and Cury, D. Parental regard of child as a function of initial reaction to pregnancy. Paper presented to Southern Society of Philosophical Psychology, Tampa, Florida, April 12, 1974.

Cameron, P. and Tichenor, J. C. The Swedish "children born to women denied abortion" study: a radical criticism. *Psychological Reports,* 1976, *39,* 391-394.

Dytrych, Z., Matejcek, Z., Schuller, V., David, H. P. and Friedman, H. L. Children born to women denied abortion. *Perspectives,* 1975, *7,* 165-171.

Forssman, H. and Thuwe, I. One hundred and twenty children born after application for therapeutic abortion refused. *Acta Psychiatrica Scandinavia,* 1966, *42,* 71-88.

THE EFFECTS OF PROGENY UPON LETHALITY
with Cynthia Carr and Kathy Scott

The effects of parents upon children provide a living for clinicians and grist for theoreticians. But the effects of children upon parents has been largely neglected. While the major religions of the world have touted the supposedly beneficial effects of children upon both their parents and society, only a handful of psychologists, most notably Erikson, have followed their lead. Progeny are supposed to lead to reduced egocentricity with consequently reduced lethality and increased altruism. If children have this salutary effect upon either personal and/or collective life the trend toward childlessness may bode ill. In the present investigation, a practical expression of lethality, driving habits, and an improbable manifestation of altruism, giving one's life for another, were examined for progeny-effect.

Method

An area sample of selected enclaves in rural St. Mary's County, Maryland, was utilized to draw a sample of 325 persons, 79 of whom were male, aged 18 and over. Males ranged in age from 18 to 70 with a median age of 40, females ranged from 18 to 72 and also registered a median age of 40. The questionnaire was self-administered by respondents. Questionnaires were delivered by trained student volunteers. The questionnaire ran: (1) are you licensed to drive a car? (Y/N); (2) do you drive now? (Y/N); (3) generally, how many times a week do you drive? (once or more a day/4-5 times a week/2-3 times a week/once a week/less than once a week/almost never/never); (4) how often do you drive carelessly? (once or more a day/4-5 times a week/2-3 times a week/once a week/less than once a week/almost never/never); (5) how many times a week do you exceed the speed limit? (once or more a day/4-5 times a week/2-3 times a week once a week/less than once a week/almost never/never); (6) how many traffic tickets have you received in the past 5 years? (7) while you were the driver, how many accidents have you been in, in the past 5 years? (8) what events in your life have influenced you to drive more safely? (9) did being married (or do you think that getting married would) influence you to drive more safely? (Y/N) (10) did having a child influence you to drive more safely (or do you think that having a child would influence you to drive more safely)? (Y/N) (11) did having a pet (or do you think that having a pet) influence you to drive more safely? (Y/N) (12) did having an accident (or do you think that having an accident would) influence you to drive more safely? (Y/N); (13) if there were a fire, and both your spouse and your oldest child were unconscious, and you knew that you could rescue only one before the flames engulfed them, and assuming you could carry one to safety, which one would you take? (spouse/ child); (14) same fire, same situation, but an unknown 5-year-old child and your spouse lie unconscious on the floor, which one would you take? (15) same fire, same situation, but your family pet and your spouse lie unconscious on the floor, which one would you take? (16) same fire, same situation, but an unknown child and your family pet lie unconscious on the floor, which one would you take? (17) same fire, however, you and your child are trapped, your child is unconscious. Assuming your spouse could rescue one of you, which of you would you tell your spouse to take? (age, sex, marital status, number of children, age of oldest child, and number of children living with were also determined.) Rejection rate was less than 15%

LETHALITY. With 95% of males and 89% of females licensed and 96% males vs. 92% females driving now, males claimed to drive more frequently (once/day) than females (4-5 times/week).

While there were no sex or age differences, progenied persons differed from the nonprogenied in claimed careless driving (Kolmogorov-Smirnov: (X^2 = 16.54<.001) with 82% of the progenied vs. 56% of the nonprogenied claiming "almost never or never" responses. Males claimed to exceed the speed limit more frequently than females (2-3 times a week vs. almost never; K-S: X^2 = 31.7 <.001) but there were no progenied/nonprogenied differences. While there was a difference between the sexes in getting traffic tickets favoring the females (84% vs. 64% of females reported no tickets)there was only a tendency for nonprogenied males to report fewer tickets (the progenied averaged .47 vs. the nonprogenied's .87; X^2 = 2.94 <.20). The same sex difference appeared in frequency of accidents but here the progenied males averaged .27 and the nonprogenied .87 with X^2 = 6.06 <.01. While married males more frequently than married females claimed that marriage had influenced them to drive more safely (X^2 = 4.0 <.05), overall 48% of the respondents "voted" for marriage as a delethalizing event.

The progenied differed dramatically from the nonprogenied in claimed influence of a child toward delethalizing driving with 75% of the progenied making such a claim vs. 32% of the nonprogenied supposing that such would occur (X^2 = 38.7 < .001). Twenty-nine per cent of the nonprogenied claimed a pet influenced them toward delethality vs. 17% of the progenied (X^2 = 4.41 <.04). Thirty-seven percent of the respondents claimed that having an accident led to better driving.

Quite clearly, of the open-ended and close-ended questions, the most claimed influence toward delethalizing driving came as a result of being progenied (75%) followed by getting married (48%), having had an accident (37%) and owning a pet (18%).

ALTRUISM. "crispy critters"

Spouse vs. oldest child: 62% of males vs. 30% of females would opt for the spouse (X^2 = 23.3 <.001); for females, those with progeny would more frequently opt for the child (76% vs. 53%; X^2 = 10.7 <.01); the effect was more pronounced (80% vs. 50%; X^2 = 7.04 <.01); for females with children under the age of 20; the same effect appeared with males with children under the age of 20 (X^2 = 7.28 <.01)

Unknown child vs. spouse: While 40% of the progenied vs. 35% of the nonprogenied opted for the unknown child the difference was statistically nil.

Spouse vs. family pet: 97% of respondents would take the spouse.

Oldest child vs. family pet: 99% of respondents would take the child.

Unknown child vs. family pet: 99% of the progenied vs. 97% of the nonprogenied would opt for the child ($X^2 = 4.1 < .05$).

Child vs. You: 97% of the progenied would opt for the child vs. 90% of the nonprogenied ($X^2 = 6.6 < .02$).

Discussion

An extensive review of the accident proneness and accident literature failed to reveal that any other investigator has ever come upon progeny status as an important variable in the etiology of accidents. Let it be noted that we appear to have a "live one" here and now. We already know that the nonprogenied are more apt to suicide and murder — now our results suggest that there is a generalized heightened lethality associated with childlessness. Whether the relationship runs "child reduces lethality" or "the less lethal opt to have children" cannot be settled from our results. BUT, and its a big but, the retrospective accounts of our sample, which jibe well with general clinical impression, fall toward the notion that *children have a salutary influence in reducing lethality.* In a sea of psychological findings of dubious practical import, this shimmers with meaning. While in the past most members of society had little opportunity to vent their lethality upon large numbers, today the opposite obtains. We now man missiles that can do a job on the world, and everybody drives machines that can do their bit on more than a few of us. It would be interesting and ironic indeed if, as man rushes to master nature, he also bought a childlessness that aided in his undoing.

The pet threat is well and hearty in our culture. As we have noted elsewhere (Cameron, 1969), the pet is a projection of the idealized self, as is, to some degree, a child. That some of our sample would choose to save the pet over a human testifies to the potential and actual dehumanizing effects of pet ownership. Numerous investigators have, with reason, championed the psychological utility of pet-ownership for distressed persons. But there is another, seamier side of the coin. The same projected self-love that can bring the distressed "out of their shell" can also provide a cocoon that insulates the self against other-concern. Pet love can lead to misanthropy, and I believe we have caught a glimpse of it here.

Altruism as a function of progeny-status scored a general "hit." While the spouse-unknown child item failed to elicit differences, the spouse-oldest child, unknown child-family pet, and child-you items all evidenced a progeny effect. Children are associated with greater altruism on the part of their parents. Besides being fetching, the little humans may well be enriching the well being of the race beyond their weight. While contemporary psychologists hate with a passion to endorse ancient aphorisms, it does rather appear that *childlessness is associated with the selfishness-selfcenteredness-selfservingness complex*. As out society is starting to choose childlessness more frequently, perhaps it is in order to pause and weigh the apparent advantages against the possible negative effects of such a choice.

REFERENCES

Cameron, P. Don't give your child a pet. Coronet, 1969, 7, 52-58.

SELF-CENTEREDNESS DURING ADULTHOOD

Questions of the selfishness, self-centeredness, and/or egocentricity of the sexes and generations often wend their way into professional and lay discourse. One issue concerns the motives of actors of various ages. Plato argued that persons had to be at least age 50 before they could be entrusted with the reins of society, in part due to a more altruistic or noble perspective lacking in youth. Erickson (1959) supported this general line of argument, contending that the higher level concerns for the preservation of a culture as an expression of generativity largely resides in the old. In contrast to "classical" opinion, Reich (1970) has made a case for the "better intent" or possession of a "higher set of motives" of the younger members of society with his *The Greening of America: How the Youth Revolution is Trying to Make America Livable*.

Another issue revolves about the contention of Darwin (1872), echoed by Montagu (1957), that man is innately disposed toward altruism and/or altruistic motives or feelings. While Darwin's (or perhaps Rousseau's) notion clashed with the dominant belief in original sin, it also contrasts sharply with the bulk of psychological opinion in which motives are acquired via learning.

Finally, both in the past when the franchise was under discussion, and currently, when the assumption of leadership roles is being considered, it has frequently been argued that females in our culture have a more self-sacrificing orientation than males. As such, it has been argued, they ought especially to vote/govern since such motivation is a valuable contribution to the political process.

While questions of generational and sexual self-centeredness is of some interest, scholars have not devoted an inordinate amount of effort toward them. Schaw and Henry (1956) and Cameron (1967) appear to have published the only empirical research on the issue to date. Additional data and suggestions for clarifying research will be presented in the present paper.

Method

Study I

From a large sample of 5,304 persons aged 8 to 99 from the western half of the United States the responses of young adults (aged 18 through 25), middle-aged (40 through 55), and old (over 64) (after Cameron, 1969), to the eighth item: "[f]or the last five minutes, were your thoughts mainly centered on yourself, your wants and wishes, or on someone else, their wants and wishes?") are considered here. The subsample consisted of 2,441 adults of which 1,274 were female. We interviewed persons in three situations, at-home, at-work, and at-leisure. The at-home sample was obtained by means of a strict area sample of areas of Los Angeles, Detroit, Louisville, and Evansville with a rejection rate of 28%. College student volunteers obtained the at-work sample from their co-workers in Detroit, Evansville, and Louisville in 84 different job sites with a rejection rate of less than 1%. Eleven different locations in Louisville, Los Angeles, and Denver including shopping areas, beaches, and parks were "staked out," and every kth person who entered the area was approached for an interview with a rejection rate of less than 1%. Slightly more females were interviewed at-home, about two-thirds of the at-work sample was male, about two-thirds of the at-leisure sample was female. Responses to the item did not vary by situation.

Study II

Six strict area samples of the city of Detroit (excluding the inner city and non-Caucasians) were performed for young adult males, young adult females, middle-aged males, middle-aged females, old male, and old females utilizing 1960 Census tract information to determine the proportions of each of the six samples that should come from each tract. Paid interviewers, subjects, and almost unlimited callbacks resulted in a rejection rate of less than 6%. Three hundred and seventeen subjects, almost equally apportioned between the 6 samples, self-administered a multi-item questionnaire of which two items have relevance: [h]ow do you believe the three age-groups (young adult, middle-aged, old) compare in self-centeredness _____ are the most selfish _____ are the least selfish?" and "compare yourself *with all other adults of your sex* in self-centeredness (selfishness) (below average/average/above average)."

Results

The distribution of responses in Study I is presented by generation and sex in Table 8.4. There are 690 young adult males, 294 middle-aged males, and 93 old males; 742 young adult females, 427 middle-aged females, and 105 old females in the sample. Both male ($X^2 = 35.3$; df = 2; $p < .001$) and female ($X^2 = 6.9$; df = 2; $p < .05$) responses were less frequently self-serving as a function of age. Young adult ($X^2 = 5.0$; df = 1; $p < .001$) and middle-aged ($X^2 = 5.7$; df = 1; $p < .02$) males more frequently indicated self-servingness than their female counterparts.

Three-way, fixed-effects analyses of variance (generation by sex by social status) uncovered no differences in opinions about the generations on the dimension of self-centeredness/selfishness in Study II. Nominations regarding the most and least self-centered/selfish generations are summarized in Table 8.5. Young adults were believed to be the most and the old the least self-centered/selfish generation. Self-reported appraisals of self-centeredness did not

TABLE 8.4

**Relative Frequency of Thinking About the Wants-Needs-Desires of Self
or Other Over the Last Five Minutes by Generation and Sex
(in per cent)**

	Young adult		Middle-aged		Old	
	about self	about other	about self	about other	about self	about other
Males	56	44	37	63	34	66
Females	37	63	29	71	32	68

TABLE 8.5

**Stereotypic Beliefs About the Self-Centeredness/Selfishness
of the Generations**

	Young adult	Middle-aged	Old
Considered most selfish by	62%	19%	19%
Considered least selfish by	18%	29%	53%

vary by generation, sex, or social status — respondents generally reported themselves as being low average on the dimension (mean of 1.66 on a scale ranging from 1 for "below average" to 3 for "above average").

Discussion

One of the difficulties in conducting and evaluating research in the area is the lack of standardization and attention to the linguistic use of relevant concepts. "Selfishness," "egocentricity," and "self-centeredness" are linguistic neighbors. Egocentricity defines an outlook, an attitude in which a person regards himself as the center of things. Solipsism epitomizes egocentricity. Selfishness and altruism both refer to motives underlying behavior when another person's interests are involved. One is selfish when he opts for self in face of the social "rights" of an other and altruistic when one voluntarily submerges his substantive interests to advance those of the other. A person who is self-centered is generally oblivious to the interests of others. While the egocentric person may tend to be unaware that the interests of others exist, the self-centered person is inattentive to other's interests. A person who is self-centered will generally generate self-serving behaviors, but he is not necessarily selfish. He could simply be so "wrapped up" in himself that he neglects to notice that another's interests are involved. Since both selfish and self-centered persons would more frequently evidence self-serving behavior, separating the two would require assessing persons' motives when conflicting interests were involved.

The two studies reported above fail to accomplish the kind of separation that would be most desirable. The first study permits examination of the relative frequency of self-servingness for the sexes and generations. We do not know whether males' more frequent self-servingness stemmed from more frequent selfishness and/or self-centeredness. Neither do we know whether females' more frequent other-servingness followed from more frequent altruism. Certainly there is a large segment of both self-serving and other-serving activities that are neither praise — nor blameworthy (there exists a veritable raft of studies in which any non-self-serving behavior is considered "altruistic" e.g., Midlarsky and Bryan,

1967). Unfortunately, the second study confounded selfishness and self-centeredness in the items employed. However, even with their limitations, the studies provide useful information.

The "classical" stance argues that the motivation of the old includes components of greater altruism, less selfishness, and less self-centeredness. The lessened self-servingness of the old exhibited in the first study could have been the outcome of any or all of these more noble motives. It is also conceivable, though rather unlikely, that it came about through the old's less frequent selection of that segment of self-servingness which falls outside moral opprobrium. It appears even less likely that Reichian youth have more frequently "happened" to select just that self-servingness which falls without disapproval. Specification of the motives that underlie the differential self-servingness of the generations is yet lacking. However, it seems reasonable to tentatively believe that the old are less self-serving out of a combination of more frequently noble and/or less frequently base motives. To accept this interpretation, one would have to discount the validity of self-appraised self-centeredness/selfishness of the second study. To characterize oneself as being either self-centered or selfish is to admit to *being* evil or base (not just to having done evil). Reporting one's motivational state of the last five minutes as being self-serving says almost nothing about one's overall personality (if the question were repeated to the same subject a number of times across situations it might well show a great deal about one's personality). Regarding the old generations' motives as more noble than those of young adults would jibe with the Kastenbaum and Cameron (1969) study of 15 three generational families in which each member was asked to nominate those family members to whom he gave and from whom he received affection. The grandparent generation gave more affection than it received, the middle generation "broke even," and the young adult generation received more affection than it gave.

As both studies were cross-sectional, their results may be due to age changes and/or cohort differences. The stereotypes about the course of self-centeredness/selfishness across adulthood (Study II) suggest an age-change interpretation. Were we indexing a cohort-related difference, it would appear unlikely that the relatively firm stereotypes about generational self-centeredness would exist in the populace. But age-related differences would presumably have been noted (or presumed) some number of eons ago, and this kind of knowledge/belief transmitted culturally (young adults did not differ from the old in the degree of stereotypy of their beliefs (Table 8.5), a phenomenon one would expect to hallmark a cultural "truth").

Persons may generally regard their own set of motives as being less selfish than that possessed by others. When adults were asked about what they were thinking, their responses taken down as close to verbatim as could be achieved, and later coded by raters according to whether the person appeared to be self- or other-serving, the majority of responses were classified as "self-serving" (Cameron, 1967). Both the earlier and the present study agreed in finding females generally less frequently self-serving than males were, but it appears that coders opt to regard the motives of a given person as being self-serving rather than not.

Females perform more of the serving/servant functions in our culture. It might appear that this aspect of their social role would account for their more frequent attitude of other-servingness in Study I, especially in light of the lack of a difference between the sexes in old age when there is also a diminution of role differences along this dimension. There are problems with such an interpretation, however. The difference between the sexes was considerably more pronounced in young adulthood than it was in middle age, and while we are unaware of an adequate role-count for the sexes across the life-span to point to, no role related difference appears to account for this phenomenon. Further, there is evidence that females think more frequently about serving others in our culture after the age of 13 (Cameron, Stewart, Craig, and Eppelman, 1973). Teenage girls do not appear to have more of a serving role than teenage boys in our culture. To make the task of adopting this interpretation more difficult, K. G. Desai of Gujart University in India (personal communication) has administered the "last five minutes of motivation" questionnaire to 466 adult natives, finding the sex difference reversed. Indian females would appear even more apt to perform serving functions than those in the United States.

Which sex is the more noble and consequently the best choice to vote or govern? On the surface, the results fall in a female-endorsing direction. Yet the dominant female role may render their other-servingness of small moment (the personal sacrifice of a slave is inconsequential compared to that of a master; the slave role prescribes sacrifice). One of the main-line arguments against political participation by females concerns their supposed "servile mentality." Specification of the motives underlying the more frequent other-servingness of females might prove a worthwhile endeavor for the feminist cause.

Darwin's suggestion that altruism is innate to man receives disconfirmation from our results. One expects an hereditable trait to express itself early in the life-span, or at least before the reproductive age. To the degree that altruism is indexed by frequency of other-servingness, its primary expression late into and after the childbearing age suggests that it is learned.

In the age of Watergate, noble intentions are not to be taken lightly. Old persons in our society may constitute a valuable moral resource. As indexed by beliefs about self-centeredness, "everybody" believes the old more noble than young adults. Consonant with this belief we found older persons less self-serving. Girded with such *armamentum,* the old would appear to have a solid base from which to argue for social treatment at least equal and perhaps superior to that accorded young adults.

HOW HUMAN ORIENTED IS THE MIND ACROSS THE LIFE-SPAN?
with

Darius Bahador, Department of Psychology, Jundi Shapur University, Ahwaz, Iran

K.G. Desai, Department of Education and Psychology, University of Gujarat, Ahmedabad, India

Lloyd McPherson, Medical School, University of Jamaica

How human oriented is the mind of man? Some British associationists argued that mental life was isomorphic with the contents of the sensorium — outside stimulation provided the "raison d'etre" for thinking. An extreme form of this notion was held by some of the Russian behaviorists (e.g., Sheckenov) who contended that in the absence of outside stimulation the mind would "wind down" to a virtual blank. As humanity constitutes but a tiny fraction of the "world stuff," were "mental isomorphism" the rule, people would think about people rather infrequently relative to other phenomena.

Taking a different tack, Whitehead (1926) suggested that the world is so incredibly dull that man has to energetically grace it with his creative efforts to make it interesting. From such a perspective man might well spend the majority of his mental energies upon his own kind — humans are considerably more animate than the bulk of nonhuman stuff, and additionally possess the capacity for good, evil, and a host of interesting attributes denied other creatures.

There are scattered hints that thinking about humans may constitute the bulk of the "stuff" of mental life. In infancy, Gibson (1970) found that the human or humanoid face was the object most frequently attended to when placed in competition with various nonhuman objects. Cameron (1972), in eavesdropping on the conversations of college students, found most sentence topics revolving about human interactions. Kalish (1969), registered surprise that the most commonly mentioned "first thought" of 323 persons who found themselves in a perilous situation was of concern for the effect upon others as a result of their demise. If persons ordinarily occupy themselves with thoughts of other humans, the surprise lies in maintaining ordinary patterns of cognition in the face of duress.

How does consciousness vary as a function of age? Freud and Jung contended that humans begin life rather inner-oriented, with high investment in self and self-generated events. Jung felt that as persons aged they returned to this "interiority" of early childhood. At least one investigator (Neugarten, 1964) has produced evidence which she construed as supporting his position. Does concern with self trace a "U-shaped" surve across the life-span? How large do interpersonal relationships figure in the thinking of older adults as compared with younger adults? Do these patterns hold up cross-culturally?

In apparent response to the women's movement, sex difference research is occupying a growing share of the psychological literature. A continuing question concerns which, if any, of the various sex differences are innate/hereditary and which are learned. In our culture boys are more frequently mathematically/mechanically inclined, while girls tend toward the verbal/social end of things. When infants were presented with photographs of faces and geometric figures, males spent more time gazing at the geometric and females more time staring at the face stimuli. Borosage (1973) has suggested that the face-geometric phenomenon and the male thing-orientation in our society might reflect innate predispositions on the part of the sexes, with females presumably more human-oriented. If such are manifestations of an innate disposition, then there might well be a tendency for males to think more frequently about things than females do and vice versa for contemplation of persons across cultures.

To what degree is consciousness invariant across cultures? How frequently does the mind trace certain patterns of content irrespective of cultural context and what are these patterns? If the mind is generally formed via either the "isomorphic" or "man centered" mechanism, evidence of it ought to turn up cross-nationally. Many psychologists including Freud, Jung, and Piaget have claimed that the mind is largely "set" and follows certain predilections regardless of culture. But the set of which these and other psychologists speak is cast in highly superordinate concepts (i.e., "formal operations," "ego," "shadow") which are not readily subject to empirical scrutiny. Is it necessary to theorize at such a superordinate level to capture the "cross-cultural action"? Perhaps man's cognitions are similar across cultures at a considerably lower level of conceptualization. Cantril (1965) demonstrated that most of the members of various nations could "handle" the notion of a "ladder of well-being" at both a personal and national level. While superordination can be profound, it can also hide the absence of specific content. Dropping down some levels to more subordinate concrete concepts permits empirical tests, albeit imperfect tests, of some of the more high-blown theory. In the present study, a set of "middle level" subordinate concepts concerning the mental "space" devoted to humans were indexed in five countries to explore such questions.

Method

We attempted to sample representatively the contents of consciousness in each of the five countries chosen for investigation. Within the limitations of cross-national research we sought to sample persons of both sexes across the life-span, evenly distributed across the daylight hours, and within the various typical situations in which persons might find themselves in that society. Our approximations fell considerably short of this ideal. In India, the sampling took place in the situations at-work, and at-leisure; in Ghana, at-school and at-leisure; in Spain, at-leisure; in Iran, at-home, at-work, and at-leisure; and in the United States, at-home, at-leisure, at-work, and at-school. The median age of those interviewed in each society fell within the "young adult" generational category (i.e., aged 18 through 25 [after Cameron, 1969]). In the United States, 2,530 males and 2,679 females were interviewed, in Iran the corresponding figures were 493 and 398, in India 351 and 183, in Ghana 80 and 136, and in Spain 65 and 45. Subjects were always to be approached unawares and then interviewed on-the-spot regarding their consciousness. Sampling was conducted in and around Madrid, Spain; Ahmedabad, India; Sekondi-Takoradi, Ghana; Detroit, Evansville, Louisville, Los Angeles, and a number of small towns in the United States; and in 18 different cities/locations, mainly urban, in Iran. Interviewers were paid nationals of India and Iran, a mixture of paid and volunteer American and Spanish students in Spain, and a native husband-wife team in Ghana. The interview included the following items (translated into the national language): What were you thinking about in the last five minutes? (a) who were you mainly thinking about? (wasn't thinking about people/myself/somebody else /a group or groups of people); (b) were your thoughts mainly centered on yourself, your wants and wishes, or on someone else, their wants and wishes? (mainly on myself/mainly on somebody else) (this item was not utilized in Spain); and (c) for the last 5 minutes, what has been the central focus of your thought? (19 items followed including "about personal problems — topics concerning interpersonal relationships with somebody else"). In the United States and Ghana, where people are rather used to being asked such questions by strangers, the interview was accomplished with a minimal introduction. In Iran, India, and Spain, each interview was typically preceded by fairly elaborate explanations of why the interview was requested and what use might be made of the results (in Iran, great resistance was encountered lest the interview be a front for the CIA and most of the introductory remarks were directed to assurances that in fact this was a scientific enterprise and not a covert operation). As the interview aimed at spontaneity, this probably contaminated the results in some unknown way. In each location, an attempt was made to choose respondents according to some random procedure (stratified area sampling was employed to generate the at-home sample in the United States; all at-leisure samples were generated by taking every *k*th person who entered the designated interview area; all at-work samples were obtained *ad lib* rather than through a random procedure, however, to the degree possible, everyone in each work situation was interviewed to reduce bias; and at-school samples consisted of all the students in classrooms provided by the respective authorities. Rejection rates were 39% in Spain, 11% in the United States, 10% in Iran, 1% in India, and none in Ghana. It appears that our efforts toward randomicity were somewhat successful in that no systematic differences as a function of location for these items of the questionnaire were uncovered. The limited number of subjects and high rejection rate in Spain render the results there little more than suggestive.

Results

Frequency of reporting in thinking about things, self, or other(s) is summarized by sex, generation, and society in Table 8.6. Testing for possible systematic cross-national differences by applying Jonckheere's (1954) ordering test to the corresponding "cells" in which four or more subjects fall in the Table, it can be seen that United States nationals reported "out-thinking" the other nationals in contemplation of others and things at the expense of contemplation of self (combinatorial $p < .0001$) in 25 of 30 possible comparisons, United States nationals reported a higher frequency of contemplation of other(s); in 27 of 30 comparisons a lower frequency on contemplation of self; and in 24 of 28 comparisons, a higher frequency of contemplation of things). From a man *qua* man perspective, contemplation of others was more frequently reported than either contemplation of things or self in 36 of 41 comparisons (sign test $p < .001$); for the non-United States sample, in 23 of 28 comparisons "self" was more frequently reported than "things" (sign test $p < .001$), but the United States results ran 12 of 12 "things" more frequently reported than "self" (sign test $p < .001$). Taking the non-United States data as a whole, American nationals were about thrice as apt to report thinking about things and half as apt to report thinking about the self as these non-United States subjects.

The transitory motivational state indexed by the self-interests-serving vs. others-interest-serving item's outcomes are presented by sex, generation, and society in Table 8.7. As the life-span was considerably underrepresented in Ghana and underrepresented in India and Iran, comparisons were made between Ghana and the other three nations by combining subjects through the age category 26-39 for each society. In these comparisons, neither Ghanian males (X^2 <2; NS) nor females (X^2 <2; NS) differed from their American counterparts. However, Ghanian females more frequently reported other-serving motives than Indian (X^2 = 3.85; df = 1; p <.05) and Iranian (X^2 = 12.1; df = 1; p <.001) females did. Comparisons between the Indian and United States data were made with the subject-reports through middle age, with males of the societies not evidencing a difference in frequency in reported other-servingness, and American females more frequently reporting other-servingness than Indian females did (X^2 = 19.5; df = 1; p <.001). Iranian males (X^2 >50; df = 3; p < .001) and females (X^2 >35; df = 3; p < .001) reported more frequent self-servingness than their American counterparts did. From a life-span perspective, both American males (X^2 >50; df = 5; p <.001) and females (X^2 >50; df = 5; p < .001) evidenced declines in frequency of reporting self-serving motives with advancing age, but the results from India, Iran, and Ghana neglected to follow suit. American males more frequently reported self-servingness than American females did (X^2 = 16.4; df 1; p < .001). A similar pattern was not found in the non-United States data.

Both the American (X^2 > 50; df = 1; p < .001) and Iranian (X^2 = 8.68; df = 1; p < .01) females more frequently reported thinking about interpersonal relationships than their respective male cohorts did. The information from Spain is most limited, and attenuation of results from the last half of the life-span is present in all but the United States sample. Further, with the exception of the Ghanian and United States samples there is a "bunching" of teenage respondents in the ages 15, 16, and 17. However, inspection of Table 8.8 suggests that the peak frequency of reporting contemplation of interpersonal relationships for both sexes in the five societies falls within approximately a ten-year span, from about

TABLE 8.6

Thing vs. Self vs. Other Thought: Five Societies

Age, generation		8-17 $\underline{n}$ (%)	Young adult $\underline{n}$ (%)	26-39 $\underline{n}$ (%)	Middle age $\underline{n}$ (%)	55-64 $\underline{n}$ (%)	Old $\underline{n}$ (%)
India male	thing			1(1)			
	self	13(31)	36(36)	58(36)	21(33)	1	2
	other	29(69)	64(64)	104(64)	42(67)	1	1
female	thing			2(3)			
	self	12(50)	42(49)	24(38)	25(61)	1	
	other	12(50)	43(51)	38(59)	15(39)	1	
Ghana male	thing	9(31)	11(31)	1(13)			1
	self	5(17)	3(8)	4(50)			
	other	15(52)	22(66)	3(38)			1
female	thing	7(12)	6(11)				1(25)
	self	21(36)	11(20)	4(36)			3(75)
	other	30(52)	38(69)	7(64)	3		
U.S. male	thing	130(21)	121(18)	115(15)	103(22)	30(25)	20(17)
	self	99(16)	92(13)	77(10)	62(13)	12(10)	12(14)
	other	395(63)	473(69)	564(74)	302(65)	76(64)	81(69)
female	thing	108(15)	129(16)	82(16)	80(19)	22(21)	26(25)
	self	92(12)	102(13)	60(11)	40(9)	10(10)	12(12)
	other	537(73)	553(71)	387(71)	311(72)	71(69)	64(63)
Spain male	thing		3(9)	1(5)	1(20)	1(25)	
	self		8(25)	5(26)		1(25)	
	other		21(66)	13(62)	4(80)	2(50)	1
female	thing		1(3)	2(50)	1		
	self		8(24)	2(50)			
	other		24(73)		2		
Iran male	thing	9(17)	22(11)	28(19)	6(8)	3(33)	
	self	13(25)	59(29)	57(39)	41(53)	2(22)	
	other	30(58)	121(60)	63(43)	31(40)	4(44)	1
female	thing	6(5)	16(11)	8(11)	2(11)		
	self	34(29)	49(28)	35(46)	6(33)	1	
	other	78(66)	113(63)	33(43)	10(56)	1	

TABLE 8.7

Self-Serving vs. Other-Serving Interests: Four Societies

Age, generation		Under 18 n (%)	Young adult n (%)	26-39 n (%)	Middle age n (%)	56-64 n (%)	Old n (%)
India male	self	23(54)	49(53)	73(48)	27(47)	1	
	other	20	44	78	30	1	2
female	self	17(71)	45(63)	29(57)	19(58)	1	
	other	7	26	23	14	1	
Ghana male	self	17(59)	21(57)	4(50)	1		1
	other	12	16	4	1		1
female	self	28(47)	27(51)	5(45)	1		2(50)
	other	31	26	6	2		2
U.S. male	self	322(52)	388(56)	232(39)	146(35)	46(39)	32(34)
	other	303	302	356	277	72	61
female	self	344(46)	274(37)	243(46)	124(29)	37(36)	34(32)
	other	397	468	283	303	67	71
Iran male	self	28(54)	118(61)	83(60)	47(60)	3(43)	1
	other	24	76	55	31	4	
female	self	82(70)	117(68)	43(59)	12(67)	2	
	other	36	55	30	6		

TABLE 8.8

Frequency of Thinking About Interpersonal Relationships: Five Societies

Age, generation	8-11		12, 13		14, 15		16, 17		Young adult		26-39		Middle age		56-64		Old	
Sex	m	f	m	f	m	f	m	f	m	f	m	f	m	f	m	f	m	f
Ghana n	4	8	3	6	12	18	11	29	38	57	8	11	2	3			2	4
Ghana f				1		6	1	5	7	15		1		2			1	
Ghana %				17		33	9	17	18	26		9		67			50	
India n			44	24					93	71	152	53	58	33	2	2	2	
India f			8	9					34	19	38	9	15	`		1		
India %			·18	38					38	27	25	17	26	18		50		
U.S. n	141	157	185	205	156	162	126	205	739	809	581	578	467	465	113	119	91	124
U.S. f	19	27	26	72	43	63	42	89	206	271	102	135	72	98	10	17	11	13
U.S. %	13	17	14	35	28	39	33	44	28	34	18 ·	24	15	21	9	14	12	10
Spain n									32	35	21	4	6	5	5	1	1	∅
Spain f									10	16	4	∅	1	∅	∅	∅	∅	
Spain %									·31	46	19		17					
Iran n			53	121					204	182	148	77	79	18	9	2	1	
Iran f			13	36					46	64	27	16	12	∅	1	∅		
Iran %			25	30					23	35	18	21	15	∅	11	∅	100	

(under 18) — note under India, 12, 13 column

TABLE 8.9

FREQUENCY OF THINKING ABOUT INTERPERSONAL RELATIONSHIPS: FIVE SOCIETIES

	sex	highest % (age group)	Md %	mean % for total sample
Ghana	M	18 (YA)	4.5	11
	F	26 (YA)	17	22
India	M	38 (YA)	22.5	27
	F	38 (18)	22.5	24
Iran	M	25 (18)	18	20
	F	35 (YA)	25.5	29
U. S.	M	33 (16, 17)	15	21
	F	44 (16, 17)	24	29
Spain	M	31 (YA)	18	23
	F	46 (YA)	∅	36

age 16 through age 25. Table 8.9 makes this relationship more clear. The frequency of reported frequency of contemplation of interpersonal relationships appears to rise and fall from this point in a fairly regular manner in each culture. In each of the five societies, thinking about an other was about twice as frequently reported as was thinking about a group of others.

Discussion

It would be presumptuous on the basis of such limited evidence to generalize to humankind. However, some of the uniformities in our results suggest that from a man *qua* man standpoint, the following propositions may well be worth entertaining as valid:

1) For all but perhaps the very beginnings of the life-span, humans think more frequently about other humans than one-self or things.

2) The late teens and early adulthood feature the highest frequencies of thinking about interpersonal relationships.

It may also be worth noting that in these five societies, the sex that thought most frequently about interpersonal relationships also thought more frequently from an other-serving orientation.

What, if anything, does dominate the mind of man? Our findings appear crisp enough to answer "not things" and most assuredly "humans." The meaning of "not thinking about persons" is not identical with the concept "things." In English, "things" also subsumes "persons," but within the context of the question, it appears reasonable to consider that we were, in fact, tapping the thing-self-other dimension of thought. In each culture, of the nineteen possible responses to "what was the focus of your thought" (and choices such as money-finances/my family/my work were included here), *the* highest frequency of choice for the life-span as a whole was the category "interpersonal relationships." People are the "stuff" of mental life. So to speak, man creates not only his society but also his mind. Across these societies at least, the mind is humancentric, the center of the mental world is man. Our techniques have yet to be applied to the study of individual differences. It could well be that persons who are more "into" rats and "brass instrument" psychology exhibit a higher frequency of "thing thought" while those psychologists who gravitate toward the "softer" end of the field are considerably more "human oriented." It is striking that social science, which is essentially concerned with human activity, has received the highest support in man's history within the United States and that our sample generally exhibited the highest frequency of contemplation of persons and other-servingness. Along almost any sort of ranking, whether per capita income or per capita energy consumption, the United States would emerge at the top of our set of societies. Could it be that relative "freedom from want" permits people to spend even more mental energies on people? Following the changes in either Iran or India in material prosperity ought to allow a test of the notion that "mental humanism follows prosperity" (as, of this date, we have not found social class differences along this dimension, the phenomenon may only turn up societywide). And, of course, as there are so very many variables acting simultaneously in cross-national research, these speculations may be terribly wide of the mark.

Riesman (Reisman, Glazer, and Denny, 1953) has suggested that the United States has become, over time, a society that is "other directed" in a search for group approval, or the approval of the generalized other. If the United States population was, at one time, more like the populations of Iran or India, then our results would suggest that as societies industrialize they move toward greater concern for the *welfare* of others. This is quite a different dimension of other-orientedness. Perhaps his speculations are largely valid and in some way our United States sample reported concern with the welfare of others out of concern for how these others would regard them. But such an interpretation appears strained. So where Reisman notes the other-orientedness of Americans and construes this as concern with judgment-of-self-by-others, we find the American orientation considerably more benign. Unless our American subjects were considerably more interested in some form of "social desirability" or lying than the subjects from our other cultures (and the rejection rate would argue against this), taken at anything approximating face value, Americans may just be more concerned about the welfare of others. While "policing the world" is undoubtedly more related to hegemonic reasons, other-serving motives may also play some part.

The contents of dreams would appear related to the contents of consciousness (they are, after all, housed in the same structure). In Hall and Van de Castle's (1966) report of "norms" for American college student dreams (taken from a thousand dreams), another person was about twice as apt to appear in a dream as a group of other persons. We found the same 2:1 ratio in our "other" vs. "group of others" categories in each of the five societies. But while our American females reported contemplating others more frequently even as Hall and Castle's females somewhat more frequently reported the presence of others in their dreams, the same sex difference did not appear cross-nationally. Other persons appeared in about 90% of American college students' dreams compared to the approximately 70% of American subjects who chose our "mainly thinking about [an]other[s]" in the present report. As Hall and Castle did not have a "self" category, this may well account for the discrepancy.

Jung (1933, p. 17) contended that in old age "an inexorable inner process enforces the contraction of life. For a young person it is almost a sin, or at least a danger, to be too preoccupied with himself; but for the aging it is a duty . . . " Neugarten and Gutmann (1958) had 131 adults aged 40 to 70 to tell a story about the feelings of two older and two younger persons in a picture. Older more

frequently than younger respondents, described the older characters' feelings in a way Neugarten and Gutmann construed as related to internal interests and inner dynamics. From such evidence
Neugarten has argued that there is an " . . . increased interiority of
the personality with age (1968)." Characteristics of this "interiority" include "[p]reoccupation with the inner life; . . . emotional
cathexes toward persons and objects in the outer world; . . . decrease; . . . a movement away from outer-world to inner-world
orientations . . .; . . . a lessened sense of relatedness to others
. . .; . . . self-preoccup[ation] . . . [attending] increasingly . . . to
the satisfaction of personal needs (1964).'

The present results, while lacking the elegance and sophistication of inferring typical personal motivational states from a particular sample of adults' descriptions of old characters in a picture,
appear to bear directly on a number of these Jungian-Neugartian
notions. Within the limitations of cross-sectional, cross-national
sampling and self-report, two psychological phenomena appear:

1) The frequency of contemplation of interpersonal relationships declines after young adulthood.
2) Evidence of a differential ratio of thing-self-other contemplation across the life-span is absent.

While the decline in frequency of contemplation of interpersonal
relationships (Table 3) might be construed as offering some limited
support to the theory, the lack of a decline in contemplation of
"other" coupled with an absence of an increase in contemplation
of "self" (Table 8.6) would appear discrepant. The at least
equally-frequent concern about (an)other's interests with age (Table 8.7) lays heavily against "interiority." These cross-national data
thus provide limited support and more substantial disconfirmation
for the notion of increasing self-centeredness as a function of age.

Speculations that males might be innately disposed toward
thing-orientation and females toward people-orientation were not
validated by the best single test in our data, the thing-self-other
item. While we would not go as far as Maccoby and Jacklin (1974)
and call the supposedly greater social-orientation of females a
"myth" (the females of Iran and the United States did report
thinking about interpersonal relationships more frequently than

the males), we uncovered no general sex differences along our three dimensions of thought. Had we found females more "social" along all three dimensions in all five cultures, the "innate sex difference" hypothesis might have appeared more attractive. But the results fell as they might from a strictly cultural-learning-of-expectations standpoint.

Laudably, Singer (1975) has decried the lack of systematic exploration of consciousness. He, Antrobus (1964) and Klinger (1971) have vigorously pursued the study of fantasy. An even larger number of psychologists are exploring altered states of consciousness, and the study of dreams has a long history. We would, however, point out that the neglect of the study of *ordinary* consciousness constitutes a serious deficit for the field. Daydreaming is a subspecies of consciousness, and concern with "altered states" brings "altered from what" immediately to mind. Research such as that which we have presented in this paper holds promise toward establishing a psychology of ordinary consciousness.

It appears worthwhile to note the *communalities* across these rather diverse societies in the reported contents of consciousness. In spite of linguistic and administrative difficulties, one must be impressed with the fact that questions about the contents of thought generated rather similar parameters. While each culture appears to provide the subordinate content of thought (as "what I'm going to do tomorrow"), these contents do not "swing" concepts at only a somewhat higher level of ordination much out of line. Perhaps those who have failed to find human cultures sufficiently similar have aimed either too high or too low. Conceivably at this middle level . . . a sample of thinking from a more primitive society is awaited eagerly.

REFERENCES

Antrobus, J. S., Antrobus, J. S., and Singer, J. L. Eye movements accompanying daydreaming, visual imagery, and thought suppression. *Journal of Abnormal and Social Psychology,* 1964, *69,* 244-252.

Borosage, V. Abortion in America. In E. S. Morrison and V. Borosage, eds., *Human sexuality: contemporary perspectives.* Palo Alto: National Press, 1973.

Cameron, P. Age parameters of young adult, middle-aged, old and aged. *Journal of Gerontology*, 1969, *24*, 201-202.

Cameron, P., Stewart, L., Craig, L., and Eppelman, L. J. Thing versus self versus other mental orientation across the life-span: a note. *British Journal of Psychology*, 1973, *64*, 283-286.

Gibson, E. J. The development of perception as an adaptive process. *American Scientist*, 1970, *58*, 95-107.

Hall, C. S. and Van de Castle, R. L. *The content analysis of dreams*. New York: Appleton-Century-Crofts, 1966.

Jonckheere, A. R. A test of significance for the relation between m rankings and k ranked categories. *British Journal of Statistical Psychology*, 1954, *7*, 93-100.

Jung, C. G. The stages of life. (Translated by R.F.C. Hull) In J. Campbell, ed., *The portable Jung*. New York: Viking, 1971.

Kalish, R. Experiences of persons reprieved from death. In A. H. Kutscher, ed., *Death and bereavement*. New York: Thomas, 1969.

Klinger, E. *Structure and functions of fantasy*. New York: Wiley, 1971.

Maccoby, E. and Jacklin, L. What we know and don't know about sex differences. *Psychology Today*, 1974, *8*, 109-112.

Neugarten, B. L. Summary and implications. In B. L. Neugarten and Associates, ed., Personality in middle and late life. New York: Atherton, 1964.

Neugarten, B. L. and Gutmann, D. L. Age-sex roles and personality in middle age: a thematic apperception study. *Psychological Monographs*, 1958, *72* (17, Whole No. 470).

Singer, J. L. Navigating the stream of consciousness: research in daydreaming and related inner experience. *American Psychologist*, 1975, *30*, 727-738.

Whitehead, A. *Science and the modern world*. New York: MacMillan, 1926.

9

ASSOCIATIONAL PATTERNS

Friends, lovers, spouses, children, parents, and relatives are the role stuff of social glue. While friendship probably never achieves the degree of "glue power" that family relationships do (see the Values, Needs, Wants reading), friendship is important. For some time the level of investigation of intimacy stayed where neighbors were automatically counted as friends, and no real distinction was made between most intimates and friends. The last two articles profitably address themselves to these kinds of distinctions.

How intimate *should* spouses be, how many intimate friends *ought* a person have, how often *ought* intimates communicate? These are the kinds of questions that cry for good descriptive studies with which to compare. Being an intimate takes time. Only so much time is allotted each of us no matter how high or low our station. How that time *should* be spent is, in part, dependent on how time is spent. A person can be too busy for intimacy — perhaps that's bad. But one can have so much time available that he is too bored (and boring) to maintain an intimate relationship. While there is currently an emphasis on intimacy and brightness of affect within our culture, it is by no means certain that either is the better or good. It would appear quite possible to argue that "what is" is close to "what should be" or even that "there's too much as it is." Since the domain of values is orthogonal to the factual realm. . .

GENERATIONAL HOMOPHYLY

with Arthur Cromer

Adults of all ages tend to make most of their friendships from among the members of their generation (Batten, Barton, Durstine, and Osborn, 1966). Whether this is the result of choice of happenstance is unknown. Members of a given generation may wish to associate more with members of other generations but be denied acceptance and settle for intergenerational relationships. Older persons' expressed desire for more friends (Hunter and Maurice, 1953; Roscow, 1967) may be the end result òf such a circumstance. On the other hand, the high incidence of intragenerational friendships may be the result of conscious homophyly.

Ours is often considered a pro-youth, anti-old culture (Clark, 1969). If this is true of our culture we might expect most people to prefer to associate with the young and few to want to associate with the old. Some ambiguous questionnaire results have been construed as indicating that a pro-youth, anti-old bias in association preferences exists (Kogan and Shelton, 1962; Tuckman and Lorge, 1953).

Disengagement theory posits that the old gradually withdraw from both voluntary and formal associations (Cumming and Henry, 1961). Under this rubric, the old should want to associate with others less than the generalized adult does. If, in fact, persons in our culture regard association with the old with antipathy, this could be their reaction to the disinterest of the old. If the old desire to associate with others as much as any of the other generations, we would have to abandon the disengagement theory explanation of the phenomenon.

To date, direct inquiry of representative samples of the generations regarding either their associational desires regarding each other or what the generations believe about each other's associational desires has not been reported. The present survey was designed to aid in providing evidence on each of the following hypotheses:

1) If our culture is pro-youth, all generations should prefer to associate relatively more with young adults than with other generations.

2) If our culture is anti-old, all generations should prefer to associate relatively less with the old than with other generations.

3) If disengagement theory validly applies to associational preferences, the old generation should desire to associate less with others than other generations do.

4) If conscious homophyly exists, each generation should desire to associate with itself more than with any other generation.

Method

In order to determine which ages should be included in the generational categories "young adult," "middle-aged," and "old" a preliminary study was conducted which indicated that persons are considered young adults when aged 18 to 25, middle-aged from 40 to 55, and old from 65 to 79 (Cameron, 1969). Desiring to represent these generations as adequately as possible, and realizing that there might be sex differences in the results, six two-stage area samples of the city of Detroit (excluding the inner city) — one for young males, one for young females, one for middle-aged males, etc. — were performed.

Twenty census tracts were systematically drawn after a random start from those lying within the city. The probable number of each generation within each tract was estimated utilizing the 1960 census, and each tract was weighted for each of the six kinds of subjects. Although we originally aimed at 50 of each kind of subject we ended up with 317 subjects due to a slight surplus of funds and a mix-up in two of the schedules. Subjects were approached at home at least twice to assure a low rejection rate and paid $2 for the interview. Through a system of almost unlimited call-backs we ended up with 19 rejections (rejection rate of less than 6%). Interviewers were 12 trained, paid college students. Slightly over 50% of the data were verified to assure that no falsification of data had occurred and to clarify ambiguities or correct mistakes.

The subject was approached by asking him to fill out a questionnaire concerning his beliefs and opinions about adults. He was assured anonymity, asked to complete the questionnaire in another

[1]This investigation was supported by PHS Research Grant No. MH1666-01 from NIH.

part of the residence, then, when finished, to seal the interview in an envelope provided for the purpose. The interviewer acted only to induce the subject to cooperate, deliver the materials, and answer any questions that the subject might have. When asked questions about the questionnaire the interviewer read the question aloud for the respondent, and, in a few cases, provided minor definitional clarification.

The interviewer asked the subject to record his phone number on the envelope, and after leaving the residence recorded the address. Whenever a subject had neglected to answer any question(s), a person other than the interviewer contacted the subject by phone or in person and requested completion. The data were thus made over 99% complete. Each interviewer contacted and interviewed an equal number of males and females evenly distributed over the three generations to control for any idiosyncratic interviewer-effects. Half of the subjects in each sample were administered the "opinions" part of the questionnaire first, the other half the "self-report" part first.

The "opinions" part of the questionnaire was introduced: "How do you believe the three age-groups (young adults, middle-aged, and old) compare in:

1) desire to associate with the old?
    ____have the most   ____ have the least
2) desire to associate with the middle-aged?
    ____ have the most   ____ have the least
3) desire to associate with young adults?
    ____ have the most   ____ have the least"

The "self-appraisal part" of the questionnaire was a mirror of the above, consisting of a Likert scale (above average, average, below average) introduced: "How would you compare yourself with *all other adults of your sex in:* (1) desire to associate with the old? (2) desire to associate with the middle-aged? (3) desire to associate with young adults?"

The subject was also asked his age, sex, his income to the nearest $500 for the past year, and the highest grade he completed in formal schooling. Socioeconomic status was computed by multiplying the number we associated with income (e.g., 1 = under $5,000, 2 = $5,000–$7,999, 3 = $8,000–$11,999, 4 = $12,000+) by 2 and adding it to the number we associated with education (1 = completed less than 8th grade, 2 = 8th to 11th, 3 = high school diploma, 4 = some college, 5 = B.A., 6 = M.A., 7 = Ph.D.). All analyses broke socioeconomic status into two levels, those scoring 9 or higher and those scoring 8 or less as this procedure divided socioeconomic status into two approximately equal parts for the sample.

The mean ages of the samples were 21.0 for young adults, 48.2 for the middle-aged, and 70.2 for the old. Socioeconomic status levels were 8.89, 9.39, and 6.02, respectively (educational levels were 3.52, 3.25, and 2.49 with the young and middle-aged thus falling between the "high school diploma" and "some college" categories, while the old fell between the "8th-11th" and "high school diploma" categories. For income, the generations averaged 2.68, 3.10, and 1.79 for the young thus averaging under $8,000 a year, the middle-aged over $8,000 a year, and the old under $5,000). Obviously younger and the older persons average lower income for varying reasons, including retirement by the old and schooling by the young.

Beliefs About the Generations' Affiliational Desires. It should be noted that the same 3-way, fixed-effects analysis of variance (age, sex, and SES) was employed for both parts of each of the "opinions" questions. However, since only one of the main effects (sex) for one of the 6 analyses reached conventional significance levels, and none of the interactions was statistically significant, the 6 analyses are not reported. Instead the frequencies of the various opinions are summarized in Table 9.1. The three generations agreed in believing that: (a) the old have the greatest and the young the least desire to associate with the old; (b) the middle-aged have the greatest and the young the least desire to associate with the middle-aged; and (c) the young have the greatest and the old the least desire to associate with the young. Clearly all three generations believed that: (a) the old and middle-aged have more desire for mutual interaction than either has for association with young adults; and (b) all generations are homophyllous in their associational desires.

Self-Appraised Generational Affiliational Desire. A 4-way fixed-effects analysis of variance (generation of judge × sex of judge ×

Table 9.1. Frequencies of Beliefs of the Generations about Preferred Generational Associations.

Believed to Desire to Associate	Young Adults	Middle-Aged	Old
Most with the old	28	132	156
Least with the old[a]	261	39	16
Most with the middle-aged	37	195	80
Least with the middle-aged	238	12	61
Most with young adults	182	114	18
Least with young adults	19	57	238

[a]For each generation a greater proportion of males than females believed that the young have the least desire to associate with the old; ($F = 3.2$; $df = 2$; $p < .05$).

Table 9.2. Four Way ANOVA: How the Generations Appraised Their Desire to Associate with the Generations.

Source	df	SS	MS	F
Between subjects	316			
Sex	1	84.0545	84.0545	184.43*
Judging	2	2.5120	1.2559	2.76
SES	1	.5358	.5358	1.18
Sex X judge	2	1.9957	.9978	2.19
Sex X SES	1	.0852	.0852	.19
Judge X SES	2	10.6918	5.3459	11.73*
Sex X judge X SES	2	1.9635	.9818	2.15
Subjects within group	305	139.0051	.4558	
Within subjects	634			
Judged	2	208.2118	104.1059	372.79*
Sex X judged	2	47.1931	23.5965	8.45*
Judging X judged	4	324.4269	81.1067	290.25*
SES X judged	2	24.1843	12.0922	43.30*
Sex X judge X judged	4	2.9196	.7299	2.61
Sex X SES X judged	2	26.7597	13.3798	47.91*
Judge X SES X judged	4	15.8624	3.9656	14.20*
Sex X judge X SES X judged	4	22.2776	5.5694	19.94*
Judged X subjects within groups	610	170.3499	.2793	
Total	950			

* = $p < .01$.

Table 9.3. Generations' Mean Judgments of Desire to Associate With Other Generations.

Generation Judging	Generation Judged			$\bar{x}_2$
	Old	Middle-Aged	Young Adult	
Old	2.10	2.14	1.94	2.06
Middle-aged	1.88	2.13	2.20	2.07
Young adult	1.77	1.93	2.42	2.04
$\bar{x}_1$	1.91	2.06	2.18	

socioeconomic status of judge × ratings across the generations) was performed and the results summarized in Table 9.2. Of the main effects in the "between subjects" portion of the analysis, females registered a greater overall associational desire than males (with "above average" scored a 3, "average" a 2, and "below average" a 1); females' mean was 2.13 vs. males' 1.99. The generations and socioeconomic levels did not differ in registered associational desire. The statistically significant socioeconomic level interactions lacked a discernable pattern and so proved elusive of conceptual explanation. The means associated with the judgments of the generations regarding their desire to associate with each of the other generations are displayed in Table 9.3.

Turning to the "within subjects" portion of the analysis, the generations were differentially desired as associates. The old was the least, middle-aged the next least, and young adult the most desired generation. The "judging × judged" interaction was examined with 2 *post hoc* analysis. Homoplyly was tested by comparing the sum of the diagonal means (2.10, 2.13, 2.42) with the nondiagonals ($t = 155.8$; $df = 308$; $p < .001$). The apparent next-youngest-generation effect was tested by comparing $2.14 + 2.20$ vs. $1.94 + 1.88$ ($t = 4.47$; $df = 103$; $p < .01$).

Discussion

"Desire to associate" is a concept that subsumes many motives. A person may desire to associate with a class of persons because he wants to influence, exploit, harm, or aid them, learn from or about them, be amused or entertained by them, or some combination of these. The present investigation suggests that the homophyllous associational patterns of our culture are to some degree a matter of choice rather than mere happenstance. Further, a next-youngest-generation preference and evidence of either a pro-young adult (t 2.18 - $(2.06 + 1.91)/2 = 2.62$; $df = 314$; $p - .01$) and/or anti-old (t 1.91 - $(2.06 + 2.18)/2 = 2.82$; $df = 314$; $p < .01$) sentiment were uncovered. Motives underlying associational preference were not determined.

Many plausible reasons can be advanced for homophyllous associational preferences. A person of one's own sex, generation, status, religion, etc. can reasonably be expected to share many of the same life-tasks as oneself. The more similar a person to oneself, the more predictable his attitudes and opinions are likely to be, and, additionally, the more interesting (as opposed to obnoxious or irritating) his deviations from expectations are apt to prove. Marriage, as well as a host of other human relationships, is more likely to be successful the more shared social attributes the members bring to the relationship. If a generational member seeks association for friendship, his peers appear a reasonable first choice. The next-youngest-generation preference might well be partially accounted for by the fact that one's progeny locate there. As such it might be expected that the motives underlying associational desire with this generation would include aiding, learning about, loving, and being amused by them. Other, less noble motives, enter in also. Here we might include "dirty old men" and others of a more exploitive bent.

Whether the members of our culture are anti-old and/or pro-young adult in their associational preferences cannot be determined from the results at hand. Their closer proximity to the reaper may make friendship-love associations with the old less desirable. If is takes about the same amount of effort to establish a loving relationship with a member of any generation, such expenditure on an old person is more apt to generate short-lived fruit. On the other hand, adults often regard young adults as delicious bodies harboring vacuous minds. Young adults are so inexperienced in living that they are often regarded with a large measure of the same amused light in which children bask. Persons do desire to associate with delicious bodies for entertainment purposes and with empty minds to have a hand in their filling, but the knowledge-gap would seem to counterbalance this effect. Though it is purely speculative, the "anti-old" appears more robust than the "pro-young adult" orientation.

The old clearly chose more than they were chosen (the overall mean of the generation's choices was 2.06, while on the average they were chosen 1.91). The middle-aged "broke even" (they chose 2.07 and were chosen 2.06), while the young adults came out "ahead" (2.04 vs. 2.18). Kastenbaum and Cameron (1969), in a study of the familial intergenerational giving and receiving of affect, uncovered evidence that within families the grandparent generation gives more affection than it receives while the grandchildren get more affection than they give. The present data suggest that, generationally speaking, this is also the case outside the family. Thus while direct evidence that the old are more lonely than the young or middle-aged is absent (Riley and Foner, 1968), the present study has uncovered evidence that suggests that the old ought to be more lonely.

The third hypothesis, that as part of the disengagement process, the old should desire to associate with others less than the middle-aged or young would desire, must be rejected as unsubstantiated. The overall old generation's mean associational desire was 2.06 compared to the middle-aged's 2.07 and the young adult's 2.04. Our results would suggest that desire to associate with other persons remains constant over the adult life-span.

While we did uncover evidence of conscious homophyly, each generation did not desire to associate with itself more than it desired to associate with any other generation. For the middle-aged, and old, desire to associate with the next-younger generation appeared stronger than desire to associate with their own genera-tion. The young adults were the most homophyllous generation, the old next-most homophyllous, and the middle-aged least. The "common sense" or "common opinion" part of our results suggests that most people regard homophylly as a powerful psychological force in associational preferences. According to this "common sense" the old should want to associate with the old the most of the generations, and the young should want to associate with the old the least. The self-report data fell in the predicted order. Common opinion judged that the middle-aged would most want to associate with themselves and the young would be the least interested. While the self-report data indicated that the young were the least inter-ested in associating with the middle-aged, the old turned up as the most interested in associating with the middle-aged. Finally, com-mon sense judged that the young would most like to associate with the young while the old would least like to, and the results were in the predicted order. If we apply Jonckheere's (1954) test for or-dered data to the predictions of common sense *vis-a-vis* the empiri-cal outcomes of the data, we arrive at a probability of $7/216$ ($p < .04$) favoring the "validity" of common opinion.

Of our hypotheses, the first and second, regarding "anti-old" and/or "pro-young adult" orientation in our culture cannot be answered with certainty. While we can expect social benefits to be conferred on actual and potential producers (young adults) and denied to nonproducers (the old), there is no necessity for associational preferences to trace the same pattern. Further research will be required to disentangle and weigh these two possible biases. Homophyly not only exists, but appears to exert a powerful influence on associational preferences. Disengagement theory did not predict preferences. The "surprise" in the investigation was the appearance of what appears to be a "next-youngest generation" associational sentiment. While we are some distance removed from being able to write a functional statement of associational preferences, the present results suggest that homophyly, anti-old, pro-young adult, and pro-next-youngest generation attitudes are some of the major terms to fit into the equation.

REFERENCES

Batten, Barton, Durstine, and Osborn, Inc., Ten/1966. *Report: An investigation of people's feelings on age*. Cited in Riley and Foner, 1969, as an unpublished report (1966).

Cameron, P. Age parameters of young adult, middle-aged, old, and aged. *Journal of Gerontology,* 1969, *24,* 201-202.

Clark, M. Cultural values and dependency in later life. In R. Kalish, *The dependencies of old people*. Ann Arbor: Institute of Gerontology, 1969.

Cumming, E., and Henry, W. E. *Growing old*. New York: Basic Books, 1961.

Hunter, W. W., and Maurice, H. *Older people tell their story*. Ann Arbor: Institute for Human Adjustment, 1953.

Jonckheere, A. R. A test of significance for the relation between m ranked and k ranked categories. *British Journal of Statistical Psychology,* 1954, *7,* 93-100.

Kastenbaum, R. D., and Cameron, P. Cognitive and emotional dependency in later life. In R. Kalish, ed., *The dependencies of old people*. Ann Arbor: Institute of Gerontology, 1969.

Kogan, N. and Shelton, F. C. Images of "old people" and "people in general" in an older sample. *Journal of Genetic Psychology,* 1962, *100,* 3-21.

Riley, M. W., and Foner, A. *Aging and society, Vol. I*. New York: Russell Sage Foundation, 1968.

Rosow, I. *Social integration of the aged*. New York: Free Press, 1967.
Tuckman, J., and Lorge, I. Attitudes toward old people. *Journal of Social Psychology*, 1953, *37*, 249-260.

HOMOPHYLY OF INTIMACY ACROSS THE LIFE-SPAN
with Timothy Weber, John Klopsch, John Gangi, and Scott Naramore

To what degree do "birds of a feather flock" when it comes to intimacy? How often are grandparents among the intimates in the life-space of a teenager, a factory worker included among the friends of a professional, a single person included as an intimate of one who is married? Research on this intriguing area is in its infancy and a study that sought to parcel the relative importance of family vs. friends in peoples' pool of intimates was overdue, hence the current effort.

Method

The respondents for our study were garnered via an area cluster sample technique in rural St. Mary's County, Maryland 1975-1976 (*n* = 355, aged 11 to 88, rejection rate < 22%); La Jolla and Claremont, California 1976-1977, (*n* = 104, aged 10 to 91, rejection rate < 8%); and Pasadena, California 1977 (n = 164, aged 13 to 82, rejection rate < 31%). Respondents were introduced to the questionnaire with the instructions, "we are interested in people's 'friendships.' " "Friends" could include spouses, parents, children, neighbors, lovers, etc. — in short, anyone who is a friend to you. People we know range from acquaintances to friends, etc. Below we have sketched this range as 1 (acquaintances) . . . 3 (friends), 4 (close friends), and 5 (intimate friends). We are interested in all the people in your life who are at level 5, that is, who are your intimates." The respondent then reported age, sex, educational attainment (pre-high school graduate/high school graduate/some college/college graduate/masters or doctorate), marital status (never married/married once/married once and now separated/divorced/widowed/married more than once and now divorced/separated/widowed/married more than once and now remarried/married more than twice and now remarried), social class (lower/working/skilled working/professional/higher student/of each level 5 intimates and himself. Further, respondents provided information on how long they had known the intimate, how often they communicated with the person, the mode of usual communication (phone/face to face/letter), how far apart they resided from the intimate, estimates of the level of reciprocal knowledge and caring, the relationship of the intimate, how many level 4 or 5 intimates had been dropped from the circle of intimates over the past year, how many more level 4 and how many level 5 friends the respondent would like to add, how many years respondent had been married, and how many children respondent had. (To preclude the disproportionate influence of a few persons on our results, respondents were limited to reporting on 10 intimates.)

Results

It should first be noted that the pattern of results was almost identical in all three waves of the study. Since we indexed intimacy patterns in quite disparate settings and came up with the same results, it appears that we are dealing wtih a reasonably representative "slice" of the populace of the United States, circa 1977.

Respondents' intimates are indexed by generation in Table 9.4. There was a close correspondence between the representation of a generation in our sample and the generations' representation in the sample of intimates (i.e., old persons comprised 7% of the sample of respondents and represented 8% of the intimates). Homophyly was indexed 2 ways. First, the fraction of the total pool of intimates aged within or one generation removed from the respondent's generation yielded the figures reported in the last column of Table 9.4. If one indexes age homophyly by both respondent and intimate falling within the same generation, then overall homophyly was 58%. Friends/neighbors' age homophyly was 68% while kin/sex-object age homophyly was 49%.

Degree and kind of sexual homophyly is tabulated by age and sex in Table 9.5. Considering only the sex-of-intimate irrespective of relationship, for males the degree of sexual homophyly ran, from those under age 18 to those old, 48%, 50%, 52%, 55%, 62%, and 44%; for females the corresponding figures were 63%, 58%, 62%, 63%, 66%, and 75%.

TABLE 9.4

AGE HOMOPHYLY

Respondent's Generation	% of Respondents	N	Intimate's Generation						Average # Intimates for those Reporting Intimates	# Respondents Reporting No Intimates	% of Homophyly
			18	Young Adults 18-25	26-39	Middle-Aged 40-55	56-64	Old			
<18 Male	12%	29	58(60%)	21(23%)	8	8	2	–	3.6	1 (1%)	84
Female		44	85(54%)	49(31%)	5	18	–	2		–	
YA Male	27%	67	18(7%)	191(76%)	22(14%)	15	4	1	3.8	2 (2%)	91
Female		95	24(7%)	206(58%)	68(19%)	45	9	3		2	
26-39 Male	34%	69	12	61(21%)	174(59%)	25(8%)	19	6	4.5	5 (8%)	82
Female		130	40	38(4%)	339(63%)	91(9%)	21	6		10	
MA Male	16%	39	14	11	41(24%)	85(49%)	10(6%)	13	5.4	5 (10%)	73
Female		57	30	35	55(18%)	120(40%)	26(9%)	32		5	
56-64 Male	4%	10	2	10	7	15(32%)	12(26%)	1(2%)	6.1	1 (5%)	70
Female		12	–	3	14	21(26%)	23(28%)	21(26%)		–	
Old Male	7%	15	–	2	18	10	18(20%)	40(45%)	6.2	2 (5%)	66
Female		25	10	6	9	24	17(12%)	80(55%)		–	
% of Pool of Intimates			12%	25%	30%	19%	6%	8%			

TABLE 9.5

SEXUAL HOMOPHYLY

Age	N	Male Respondent's			Sex of Intimate	N	Female Respondent's		
		Relatives	Spouse/Lover	Friend/Neighbor			Relatives	Spouse/Lover	Friend/Neighbor
<18	34	16		30	Male	37	16	15	27
		13	20	28	Female		25		74
YA	68	23		90	Male	87	43	65	42
		28	55	41	Female		73		120
26-39	71	34		118	Male	118	54	87	60
		42	61	50	Female		101		234
MA	36	34		53	Male	54	42	29	42
		25	23	38	Female		78		100
56-64	12	10		20	Male	12	19	7	17
		7	6	7	Female		22		24
Old	15	18		20	Male	21	17	7	12
		27	6	17	Female		28		76

TABLE 9.6

SOCIAL CLASS HOMOPHYLY

Respondent	% of Total Sample	N	Lower	Working	Skilled	Prof.	Higher	Student	Retired	Total	Average # Friends
Lower	1	5	3(43%)	1	2	-	-	1	-	7	1.4
Working	11	63	10	124(51%)	49	33	3	19	2	243	3.9
Skilled	21	123	12	69	248(48%)	109	14	55	-	513	4.2
Prof.	45	264	11	124	203	755(62%)	34	96	2	1225	4.6
Higher	3	16	-	7	3	15	21(46%)	-	-	46	2.9
Student	19	108	10	52	37	48	1	273(65%)	-	421	3.9
(Retired)		2	-	-	1	-	-	1	-	2	
		581	46	377	594	959	73	445		2496	
% of Intimates			2	15	24	38	3	18			

TABLE 9.7

MARITAL STATUS HOMOPHYLY

Status of Respondent	n	% of sample	(1)	(2)	(3)	(4)	Total # Intimates	# Reporting No Intimates	Average # Intimates
					status of intimates				
(1) Never married	179	30	449 73%	126 19%	49 7%	15 2%	679	6 3%	3.9
(2) Married once	328	55	285 18%	1101 70%	103 7%	84 5%	1575	13 4%	5.0
(3) Separated, widowed, divorced	63	11	63 26%	102 42%	65 27%	14 6%	244	0	3.9
(4) Remarried	23	4	14 14%	63 61%	10 10%	16 16%	103	3 13%	5.2
Total	593								
% of inmates in total sample			33%	54%	8%	5%			

Respondent's claimed social status is cross-tabulated with his judged social status of intimate in Table 9.6. Social status homophyly was 57% overall. Professionals claimed the highest average number of intimates, but they were "underchosen" as intimates relative to their representation in the respondent-pool. Marital status homophyly was 63% overall, with respondents clearly nominating like-status others as intimates (Table 9.7). Those separated, widowed or divorced were "underchosen" as intimates relative to their share of the respondent-pool.

Irrespective of age or sex, about a third of respondents included no friends/neighbors as intimates. Overall, 48% of the pool of intimates were friends/neighbors while 52% were relatives/sex objects.

Discussion

As with so many efforts in the field of "intimacy," we "sliced the pie" a somewhat different way. Consequently many other investigators' results cannot be directly compared with our own. The major advance that the current investigation presents over its predecessors is its requirement that respondents consider only those with whom they have an intimate relationship, and to report on all of these irrespective of whether they were friends, relatives, or lovers. Powers and Bultena (1976) interviewed 234 persons aged 60 or over regarding "is there any person you feel particularly close to? . . . someone you can really depend on; . . . someone who is closer to you than 'just' a friend?" (respondents were not permitted to nominate spouse or child). Powers and Bultena's question appears to demand a degree of reciprocity not called for in our study (e.g. "depend"), but a number of their findings jibe with our own. Forty-one per cent of their males and 59% of their females reported having an intimate friend compared with 56% and 78% of our 56+ year olds who reported having a nonrelated intimate. But, and this illustrates the problems attending the "old only" sample of Powers and Bultena, 71% of all our males compared with 66% of our females reported at least one intimate who was a nonrelative. Neither of our older samples statistically differs from the younger members of our samples! Powers and Bultena noted that about a third of those nominated as "close" were relatives. This was about the case in our study; however, it should be noted that at every age level the numbers of relatives of the opposite sex approximated the numbers of friends of the opposite sex. Powers and Bultena also reported that men were less sexually homophyllous than women in their nominations of intimates (over 90% of their females' friends vs. over 67% of their males' friends were of the same sex), just as we found (our figures for our 56+ year olds were 76% vs. 63%).

In their review article on friendship across the life-span, Gamer, Thomas, and Kendall (1975) note that both sexual and age homophyly have appeared to be very important in the formation of "friendships" between children (as with much of the sociological investigation of intimacy, degree of intimacy is imputed to subjects rather than being directly assessed). Proximity was concluded to be the major factor in friendship formation 'and probably in friendship maintenance by Gamer et al. The present study lacks young children as respondents, but for the portion of the life-span it covered, friendships and intimacies in general appeared to trace a common path. Early in the life-span intimacies were "hot." Intimates were somewhat less numerous, but seen most frequently face-to-face and almost daily. By middle-aged intimacy had "cooled," with more phoning and letter writing, and consequent "spacing" of interaction. Where younger persons generally claimed to be interested in acquiring more level 5 intimates, older persons usually claimed disinterest in such a prospect. Younger persons reported much more "changing of the intimate guard" than older persons. So to speak, younger people were willing to "flush" fair numbers of others through their intimacy grid while the old were inclined to "keep those that they had found." Proximity thus assumed a major role early in the life-span and a minor role late in the life-span.

Cameron and Cromer (1974) presented evidence which they suggested indicated that in adulthood, young adults were the most homophyllous and the middle-aged the least. As the last column of Table 9.4 indicates, while young adults were the most homophyllous, the old were the least. The discrepancy between what "ought to have turned up" extrapolating from a tangentially-related scale and direct questioning points up the intellectual danger of such speculations. Cameron and Cromer also suggested that as the old were underselected utilizing their index, the old might well have reason to be lonely. Again direct assessment bearing on the issue yielded contrary findings. Each generation was "chosen" in about the same proportion as it "chose," and no generation appeared to have any more reason than any other to "be lonely."

Each index of homophyly attests to the attraction of the same. With the continuum that runs from homophyly to indifference to xenophobia, our culture appears "loaded" toward the homophyly-tic end. As "pro" or positive affective energies are expended on those like oneself, less remains to extend toward those who are different. Sheer "balancing" of affect almost demands a large component of xenophobia.

We would be remiss not to mention the apparent "power of heterosexuality." Males in our culture appear to enjoy sex more than females (see the article on sexual pleasure in this volume) and males exhibited the least sexual homophyly. Further, the degree of sexual homophyly declined coincident with the peak of their sexual proclivities for both sexes (except for our old men, whom we choose to regard as a "sampling sport"). Each sex "leaned" toward the other in nominating intimates as it passed through the "hot breath" period in life. If we consider the "fallout" of heterosexing to be children, and relatives to be the fallout of heterosexing past, the the major "glue" that keeps the race one rather than twain (i.e., male and female) appears to be heterosexuality. In the relatively "free choice" situation of friends, only about 15% of the total pool of intimates was chosen from the opposite sex. Even within families, there were clear tendencies for males to nominate fathers and brothers as intimates more frequently than they nominated mothers or sisters (females did just the opposite). Similarly, when we consider the pattern of intimacies across the life-span, and subtract friends from this pool of intimates, we find that each generation is much more tied to humanity across the life-span as a function of their relatives than they are as a function of their friends. Once again the power of heterosexuality; not only does it join two sexes that appear rather disinterested in each other, but it also affectively links generations that are similarly disinclined. Heterosexuality thus not only creates our race, but replenishes and sustains it.

REFERENCES

Gamer, E., Thomas, J. and Kendall, D. Determinants of friendship across the life span. In *Life The Continuous Process,* F. Rebelsky, ed., New York: Knopf, 1975.

Powers, E. A. and Bultena, G. L. Sex differences in intimate friendships in old age. *Journal of Marriage and The Family,* 1976, *38,* 739-747.

10

STABILITY/POWER
AND INFLUENCE

Two "smaller" issues arise along the life-span. Yet both are of considerably more than passing importance — particularly the questions of generational control of the lives of other generations. Religion has been termed the domain of the gerontocracy, but politics might also be included but for some robust middle-aged. How much of the power of society resides with a particular age group is, of course, questionable. After all, those on top of the pyramidal power structure in our society do often happen to be old, but most of the old exercise as little power as teenagers. Yet the old proportionately "outvote" the young, and Plato argued that a person had to be at least 50 to be a guardian . . . .

THE GENERATION GAP:
BELIEFS ABOUT ADULT STABILITY-OF-LIFE

Which generation enjoys the most stability in life? Which wants stability the most? Which generation is believed to have the greatest opportunity to achieve stability in life?

Method

To assist in answering such questions, an area sample of 317

Detroit Ss divided between young adults, middle-aged, and old was drawn. Ss were asked to rate the three generations on (a) desire for stability, (b) possession of the requisite skills for achieving stability, (c) social provision for obtaining stability, and (d) actual possession of constancy and stability of life. S further rated himself as "above average," "average," or "below average" along each of the four dimensions, and provided socioeconomic status information.

Results

Three-way fixed-effects analyses of variance (generation × sex × socioeconomic status) were performed for each of the eight items. As no generational, sexual, or socioeconomic status differences or significant interactions were uncovered in beliefs-about-the-generations, the opinions of the Ss about the generations are summarized in Table 10.1. Clearly, it is believed that: (a) young adults desire constancy least, (b) the middle-aged possess the most skills requisite to achieving stability, (c) young adults experience the least stability, while (d) the old are provided the least social opportunity for stability-of-life.

Responses to the self-appraisal portion of the questionnaire are summarized in Table 10.2. Clearly, the generations do not differ in: (a) how skillful at achieving stability they see themselves, (b) how adequate they judge society's provisions toward stability for them, or, considering the fact that with socioeconomic status held constant the generations do not differ, (c) in claimed desire for stability in life. Young adults do seem to consider their lives less stable than the old consider theirs, and higher socioeconomic status appears associated with a belief that society provides one with more potent potential stability.

THE GENERATION GAP: WHICH GENERATION IS BELIEVED POWERFUL VS. GENERATIONAL MEMBERS' SELF-APPRAISAL OF POWER

Which generation is believed to be the most powerful and wealthy? How do the members of the generations on the average judge their relative wealth and power? Though much has been said about

TABLE 10.1

Consensual Beliefs About Which Generations:

	Young Adults	Middle-Aged	Old
Desires constancy most	53	139	122
Desires constancy least	229	33	52
Possesses most skills to achieve stability	73	186	52
Possesses fewest skills for achieving stability	168	26	117
Experiences most constancy	25	182	105
Experiences least constancy	223	20	59
Is provided the most social opportunity for stability	145	140	27
Is provided the least social opportunity for stability	78	32	203

TABLE 10.2

Mean Self-Ratings of the Generations as to How They Compared With Others-of-Their-Sex-in-General on:
(3 = above average; 2 = average; 1 = below average)

		N	mean	Statistically Significant 3-way Analysis of Variance F Ratios
a) desire for constancy and stability in life	young	100	$2.22 \pm .59$	
	middle-aged	107	$2.20 \pm .46$	age 6.4; $p < 0.05$
	old	102	$2.27 \pm .47$	SES 9.69; $p < 0.01$
b) possession of necessary skills	young	106	$2.29 \pm .57$	
	middle-aged	107	$2.27 \pm .48$	
	old	102	$2.19 \pm .55$	
c) degree of stability in life	young	106	$2.00 \pm .58$	age 5.36; $p < 0.05$
	middle-aged	107	$2.18 \pm .47$	
	old	102	$2.31 \pm .54$	
d) social provision for constancy in life	young	106	$2.13 \pm .52$	SES 5.68; $p < 0.05$
	middle-aged	107	$2.18 \pm .56$	
	old	102	$2.03 \pm .59$	

such questions of late, almost no empirical evidence buttresses any of the varying opinions. In the present study some answers were sought.

Method

An area sample of 317 white Detroiters, half of them female and evenly divided among young (aged 18 to 25), middled-aged (40 to 55), and old (65 to 79) adults (as empirically, linguistically defined; Cameron, 1969) was administered a questionnaire that included the assessment of the subject's beliefs about his own wealth and power and how the generations compared in their wealth and power. After an introduction, the subjects were asked, "How do you believe the three age-groups (young adults, middle-aged, and old) compare in: (a) possession of money and wealth? and (b) possession of power and influence?" Subjects indicated which generation they believed had the most and the least of each. Then subjects further rated themselves as "above average," "average," or "below average" to the questions "how would you compare yourself with all other adults of your sex in: (a) possession of money and wealth? and (b) possession of power and influence?" The two administrations were counterbalanced.

Results

A 3-way fixed-effects analysis of variance (3 levels of generation × sex × 2 levels of socioeconomic status) upon the "beliefs" part of the questionnaire revealed no statistically significant main effects of interactions for any of the 4 items and the responses of the three generations are separately presented without regard to sex or socioeconomic status. Clearly, all generations believed the middle-aged to be the most powerful and economically advantaged (Table 10.3) and young adults the least.

The same 3-way fixed-effects analysis of variance was performed upon the self-appraisal items. Although it is unknown whether the psychological units "above average," "average," and "below average" are equal, analysis of variance is known to be quite robust, and, at the worst, we are confronting differences in mean ranks. Clearly, those higher in SES believed themselves more

TABLE 10.3

GENERATIONAL BELIEFS ABOUT WEALTH AND POWER

		Young Adults	Middle-Aged	Old
Young Adults believed	wealthiest	9	70	27
	poorest	65	3	38
	most powerful	10	65	31
	least powerful	61	4	40
Middle-Aged believed	wealthiest	4	66	39
	poorest	72	8	29
	most powerful	10	65	24
	least powerful	67	8	34
Old believed	wealthiest	8	66	25
	poorest	67	2	33
	most powerful	12	73	17
	least powerful	56	3	43

wealthy (Table 10.4), while males considered themselves more powerful (Table 10.5).

Discussion

There is no doubt that the generations agree that the middle-aged are the most powerful, influential, and wealthy of the generations and young adults the least. The Census Bureau has published estimates that indicate that the middle-aged do, in fact, possess the greatest wealth, with the old next most wealthy and the young the least. (Statistical Abstract of the United States, 1968, p. 333). Of course, no comparable "objective" assessment of power has been published, but the young definitively seem the least powerful given our social structure. Overall, the opinions of the generations about the generations appear quite veridical.

Turning to felt power and influence, the same sort of veridicality appears. Since our sample was drawn from the city of Detroit, it seems safe to assume that it was mainly proletarian with a smatter-

TABLE 10.4

HOW MEMBERS OF THE GENERATIONS RATE THEMSELVES ON POSSESSION OF WEALTH
(3=above average, 2=average, 1=below average)

		Lower SES		Higher SES		Source	MS	F	P
		Males	Females	Males	Females				
young	N	21	24	32	29	Sex	1.27	3.75	$P < .07$
	$\bar{x}$	2.05	1.88	2.13	1.90	Age	.349	–	
	SD	.50	.45	.71	.56	SES	6.58	19.4	$P < .001$
middle	N	15	20	36	36	A x S	.141	–	
	$\bar{x}$	1.89	1.75	2.11	2.06	A x SES	1.92	5.63	$P < .03$
	SD	.56	.44	.85	.47	S x SES	.156	–	
old	N	37	46	15	4	A x S x SES	.083		
	$\bar{x}$	1.76	1.67	2.60	2.25	within	.339		
	SD	.55	.52	.51	.50				

TABLE 10.5

		Lower SES		Higher SES		Source	MS	F	P
		Males	Females	Males	Females				
young	N	21	24	32	29	Sex	1.26	3.35	$P < .10$
	$\bar{x}$	1.81	1.67	1.97	1.76	Age	.022	–	
	SD	.68	.48	.78	.51	SES	.446	–	
middle	N	15	20	36	36	A x S	.122	–	
	$\bar{x}$	1.93	1.70	1.86	1.64	A x SES	.368	–	
	SD	.59	.66	.64	.59	S x SES	.266	–	
old	N	37	46	15	4	A x S x SES	.178		
	$\bar{x}$	1.59	1.71	2.00	1.75	within	.375		
	SD	.55	.62	.53	.59				

ing of bourgeoisie and professional, none of whom have much to say about how our society functions. That those of higher SES did not feel themselves more powerful than those of lower SES should, it seems, be judged more a reasoned appraisal than some sort of "bad mouthing" — after all, the same subjects *were* aware of their relatively favored standing in terms of wealth (Table 10.4). It is interesting that those relatively favored by the "establishment" (the middle-aged, and those of higher SES) were not thereby persuaded that they had any greater control over society.

REFERENCE

Cameron, P. Age parameters of young adult, middle-aged, old, and aged. *Journal of Gerontology,* 1969, *24,* 201-202.

11

DEATH

The end — perhaps. . . . So vast a topic, yet as it has currently been played by psychologists, a scrambled bag at best. Philosophic slight of hand reigns supreme. Some (as Kubler-Ross, 1969) have organized "patterns of dying" and/or summarized their experiences with the dying and, *voila*, arrived at the "correct" way to die. Professional "religions" (other than Kubler-Ross') vie with religious professionals in providing pat answers to death and dying.

There are a profusion of "death scales" measuring every-which-thing. Typically, answers to questions about feelings, beliefs, and knowledge regarding death are all lumped together adding up to meanings that only a god could interpret.

REFERENCE

Kubler-Ross, E. *On death and dying.* New York: Macmillan, 1969.

THE IMMINENCY OF DEATH

While the New Testament claims men live their lives in fear of death (Hebrews 2: 14-15), Wahl (1959) has theorized that, ". . . a persistent feeling of personal invulnerability is puissant enough to enable the majority of mankind to remain relatively untroubled in the face of the vast array of facts which should convince them that death is the inevitable end of all men, even themselves [p. 16]." How imminent does death appear to members of our society? If they live in fear of death they must subjectively sense its press, while if a persistent feeling of invulnerability pervades death must appear rather remote. As our knowledge of the psychology of death is so limited (Feifel, 1959), the answer would appear useful.

Method and Results

This exploratory study utilized four samples. In the spring of 1966, 1,000 numbers were randomly called from the Denver metropolitan area phone book, and the S who answered was asked his age, sex, and estimate of his chances of dying within the next year. As might be expected of a highly personal and potentially disturbing issue broached by phone, only 431 of our sample gave a complete interview (a 39% response rate). Estimates were converted into chances/thousand to facilitate comparison with life tables.

Table 11.1 summarizes the results and compares the estimates with life table probabilities for the region. Clearly, Ss (a) overestimate their probability of dying within the next year relative to their actuarial probability, and (b) more closely approximate their actuarial probability with age.

Inspection of Table 11.2 reveals that at every age for which a sample greater than five exists, males approximate their actuarial probability of dying with a higher degree of accuracy than females. The probability of seven out of seven mean estimates favoring male accuracy $<.01$ ($df = 1/28$). As the refusal rate was so high in the initial sample, the first day of the spring 1967 semester all the students in five psychology classes at Stout State University were asked to estimate their probability of dying within the next year and to express this probability as some number from 0 to 1,000. There was one refusal. The Ss' ages ranged 18-25. The mean estimate for females $=387$; $SD=333$ ($N=56$), while for males the mean estimate $=323$; $SD =352$ ($N =46$) yielding a $t = .9280$; $p <.20$, one-tailed. The distributions of estimates for both sexes approximated a leptokurtic normal curve with sharp upturns at 999-1,000 and 1-2, and with the mode at 500.

With considerably more confidence in the normative nature of death overestimation, we thought it would be useful to explore: (a)

TABLE 11.1

MEAN ESTIMATES OF THE PROBABILITY OF DYING
WITHIN THE NEXT YEAR BY
SEX AND AGE RANGE

Subjects	Age range	Mean estimate	Actuarial[a]	Estimate/actuarial
Males				
1	1– 9	0	.74	—
36	10–19	91	.91	100
42	20–29	92	1.60	75
32	30–39	62	2.17	28.6
35	40–49	118	5.61	21
15	50–59	99	15.18	6.5
15	60–69	189	34.96	5.4
6	70–79	144	63.13	2.3
2	80–89	625	147.91	4.3
Females				
2	1– 9	80	.54	108.1
31	10–19	112	.42	266.7
62	20–29	118	.67	176.1
61	30–39	150	1.28	117.2
40	40–49	98	3.08	31.8
27	50–59	151	7.01	21.5
13	60–69	236	17.16	13.8
8	70–79	290	40.01	7.3
3	80–89	264	122.19	2.2

[a] Extrapolated from life tables for the Rocky Mountain region, United States Department of Health, Education and Welfare, 1962.

TABLE 11.2

RELATIVE PROBABILITY OF
DEATH ESTIMATE/
ACTUARIAL PROBABILITY FOR MALES
AND FEMALES COMPARED

Age range	Female degree of over-estimate/male degree of overestimate
10–19	2.7
20–29	2.3
30–39	4.1
40–49	1.5
50–59	3.3
60–69	2.6
70–79	3.2

TABLE 11.3

MEDIAN TEST BETWEEN THE DEATH ESTIMATES OF
THOSE SUBJECTS WHO HAD THOUGHT OF THEIR
DEMISE IN THE LAST 2 DAYS AND
THOSE WHO HAD NOT

Group	Had not thought of demise in last 2 days	Had thought of demise in last 2 days
Above median	28	45
Below median	55	23

$X^2 = 14.2$; $p < .001$.

how frequently people thought about their demise; (b) what brought their personal death to consciousness; and (c) in what regard they thought of their death. Ten psychology classes were polled annonymously to determine how many had thought about their "own personal death (demise) today or yesterday." One-hundred and eighteen said they had thought of their demise and 79 hadn't. Fifty-five of those who had thought of their demise were asked (a) "What happened or what were you thinking about that prompted you to think of your death?" and (b) "When you thought of your death, how did you picture yourself (dying in pain, lying in state, others grieving, et cetera)?" Reflecting on the death of a family member ($N=10$), of an auto accident ($N=5$), war ($N=4$), and the state of one's health ($N=4$) were the most common precipitant cognitions. The Ss thought of themselves in eternity facing judgment or wandering through darkness ($N=25$), at the end itself (from a violent death to passing away in sleep), ($N=16$), the grieving of others ($N=9$), and lying in a coffin ($N=5$).

Lastly, in the summer of 1967, we quota sampled 151 students under the age of 25 to determine if an association between death estimates and the frequency of thinking of one's demise existed. If the death estimate was to have psychological significance, it seems reasonable that those who gave higher death estimates would think more frequently of their demise. The interviewers were not informed of our hypothesis to guard against biasing the results. There were no refusals.

Thirty-three males said they had thought of their demise over the past 2 days and gave an average estimate of 414/1000 of dying within the next year. The 36 males who had not thought of their demise averaged a 273/1000 estimate. The 35 females who had thought of their demise averaged 530/1000 while those who had not averaged 285/1000. As the distributions of estimates were far from approximating a normal curve we performed a median test on the data. Table 11.3 summarizes the median test between the death estimates of those who had and had not thought of their demise over the last 2 days ($Md=400$). The contingency coefficient $(C)=.42$ indicates a fair degree of association between those two measures of death concern.

Discussion

A number of explanations for the obvious differences between the mean death estimates of the first and second samples present themselves. As our young sample indicated a fair degree of association between the frequency of thinking of one's demise and the death estimate, it is quite possible that Ss in the first sample who refused to advance an estimate were the more concerned with death (a phone interviewer of this nature would probably pose a greater threat to such a person). Perhaps the season had something to do with the results — Wisconsin winters would stimulate anyone's death wish. The intelligence, status, and locations of the samples were also different. But the continued replication of the main finding of gross overestimation of one's death imminency makes it appear normative while the correlation between the frequency of thinking about death and the death estimate suggests both are measures of death concern.

Although the probability of all 10 psychology class samples yielding higher death estimate means for females as compared to males is small (1/1024), and this tendency evidenced itself in most of the other subsamples, there does not appear to be any basal psychological significance to the fact. At least there is no indication in our data that females think more frequently of their demise (although Feifel, 1959, found otherwise). Perhaps death is more frightening to females than to males.

Axelrod, Freedman, Goldberg, and Slesinger (1959) found that a probability sample could estimate the number of births that would occur within the next 5 years with a high degree of accuracy. It is apparent that the same cannot be said of death probabilities. This overestimation is reminiscent of Jersild, Woodyard, and del Solar's (1949) report that parents grossly overestimate the chances of their children having an accident. Perhaps both Jersild et al.'s findings and ours reflect the helplessness experienced in the face of uncertain tragedy.

As a majority of college Ss (184 vs. 162) had thought of their own demise in the last 2 days, it appears fair to estimate that it is normative for college students to think of their own demise at least once every 3 or 4 days. It seems rather certain that individuals in our society do not generally feel "invulnerable" — apprehensive would appear a better characterization. Perhaps Wahl (1959) has been deceived by a defense mechanism (that is, feigned indifference). The New Testament appears more psychologically perceptive on this count.

REFERENCES

Axelrod, M., Freedman, R., Goldberg, D., and Slesinger, D. Fertility expectations of the U.S. population: A time series. *Population Index,* 1963, *29,* 25-30.

Feifel, H. Attitudes toward death in some normal and mentally ill populations. In H. Feifel, ed., *The meaning of death.* New York: McGraw-Hill, 1959.

Jersild, A. T., Woodyard, E. E., and del Solar, C.F. *Joys and problems of child rearing.* New York: Columbia Teachers College, 1949.

Wahl, C. W. The fear of death. In H. Feifel, ed., *The meaning of death.* New York: McGraw-Hill, 1959.

United States Department of Health, Education and Welfare, *Life tables for the geographic divisions of the U.S.: 1959-60.* Washington, D. C.: Government Printing Office, 1962.

CONSCIOUSNESS OF DEATH ACROSS THE LIFE-SPAN

with Lillian Stewart and Henry Biber

How often do persons think about death and dying? It is a tenet of clinical lore that too frequent contemplation of death is a symptom of pathology (Feifel, 1959). Yet the parameters associated with the "too" have not been delineated. Cameron (1968) reported the judgments of a convenience sample of college students regarding how frequently they thought about their own demise. Jeffers and Verwoerdt (1966) reported the appraisals of a sample of "elderly community volunteers" as to how often they "thought about death." This study attempted to determine how often the sexes and people in various age groups think about death and dying.

Method

As the contents of thought might vary as a function of time-of-day, situation, and activity, 4,420 persons ranging in age from 8 to 99 were interviewed or asked to fill out a questionnaire equally-frequently across all daylight hours in the most frequent situations of daily life — in school, while engaging in recreation, at-home, or at-work. The at-home sample was obtained via a strict area sample of areas of Los Angeles. Louisville, Detroit, and Evansville (762 males and 959 females with a rejection rate of 28%); the at-work sample was obtained by college student volunteers from their co-workers in Detroit, Evansville, and Louisville (931 males and 507 females occupying 84 different job locations with a rejection rate of less than 1%); the at-school sample was drawn by a classroom-time-grade selection process whereby certain proportions of the students in given classes had their work interrupted and the questionnaire was filled out by the subjects (244 males, 233 females with a rejection rate of less than 1% at two different schools, one in Kentucky and the other in New Jersey); the at-church sample was obtained by the interruption of cooperating Sunday School classes and the private approaching of designated worshippers during services at four churches (12 males and 30 females, 1 rejection); the at-leisure sample was obtained by "staking out" certain areas in 11 different locations in Louisville, Los Angeles, and Denver, and interviewing every eighth person who entered the area (6 shopping areas, 2 beaches, 2 parks, and 1 organized ball game provided 221 males and 521 females and a rejection rate of less than 1%). While persons were not assessed in all the kinds of situations and performing all the kinds of activities that are common in our culture, the vast majority of persons in our society spend the majority of their waking lives in the situations we sampled, engaging in the kinds of activity we interrupted. We interviewed 2,250 females and 2,170 males distributed over the life-span and achieved an over-all rejection rate of less than 11%.

The questionnaire was introduced

"What were you thinking about over the past five minutes? . . . (a) Did you think about death or dying — even for a moment (perphaps it crossed your mind)? (b) How would you characterize your mood over the past half hour? (happy, neutral, sad), and (c) For the last five minutes, what has been the central focus of your thought?"

(Among the 14 possible responses were "school or school problems-topics," "work or work problems-topics," and "personal problems-topics concerning interpersonal relationships with someone else." "A personal problem-topic concerning death and dying" was the fifth item on the list). Only the "in-passing" death question was asked of the New Jersey school sample.

Results

Before reporting the results, we should like to explain the massing of the findings instead of their presentation by situation or by mode of assessment. Two hundred of the at-home sample were administered the questionnaire orally while the rest of the at-home sample read and responded to the questionnaire without interviewer assistance. No difference between self-or interviewer-administration nor between the samples drawn from the various cities was uncovered. Further, no difference in frequency of possible replies as a function of time-of-day nor situation for most variables (including frequency of thoughts of death and dying) was discovered (the only differences found concerned mood and situation-specific thoughts, i.e., children at-school thought more frequently about school than children at-leisure did, adults at-church thought more frequently about religion than adults at-home, etc.) The trends in Table 11.4 evidenced themselves in each situation we sampled, hence both the combination of results and reason to regard our results with considerably more confidence than is expressed in the probabilities associated with the particular statistical tests employed.

Generational (after Cameron, 1969) differences for in-passing thought were significant for both males ($X^2 = 36.1$; $df = 8$; $p < .001$), with the highest frequency occurring in the early adolescent, young adult, and old groups for both sexes (Table 1). Male focal thought showed significant age differences ($X^2 = 8.1$; NS). Overall, males thought less frequently of death and dying in-passing ($X^2 = 21.3$; $df = 1$; $p < .001$) while there was no significant tendency for females to focus more upon death and dying ($X^2 = 1.0$; *NS*). For the males of our sample, in-passing thought averaged 17% while focal frequency averaged 3% (last column of Table 11.4). For the females, in-passing thought averaged 23% and focal thought averaged 4%. In-passing thought concerning death and dying bore a 6:1 ratio to focal thought about death and dying for both sexes. Thinking about death and dying in-passing or focally was not associated with mood.

Discussion

Apparently the young adults (i.e., those aged 18 to 25 inclusive) of both sexes think the least frequently about death and dying. Why should this be the case? For both sexes, the nadir of the mortality rate is reached between the eighth through eleventh years of life in our society. Perhaps young adults are too "busy" with love and marriage to contemplate death. Perhaps they have too many other problems to dwell upon.

The sex difference that suggests that women think more about death and dying has cross-cultural parallels. Colby (1963) found evidence that women dreamt of death about five times more frequently than men in a sample of 1,853 dreams from 75 different societies. Lee (1958) compared 114 Zulu women's dreams with 114 Zulu men's and found that the women were twice as apt to dream of the dead as men. If dream-content is largely coincident with the events experienced by persons in their daily life (Foulkes, 1964), then our finding of more frequent contemplation of death among females would jibe with their more frequent dreams about death and the dead. Interviews regarding attitudes toward death with a convenience sample of 260 adults, led Feifel (1959) to feel that ". . . women tend to think more frequently about death than do men." While the manner in which he arrived at this speculation is unclear (obviously the study of attitudes about death bears no necessary relationship to how frequently one thinks about death), he appears to have been correct.

When asked to "estimate your chance of dying within the next year" as some number from 0 (no chance of dying) to 1,000 (absolute certainty of dying), within a sample of 431 persons distributed across the life-span, women overestimated their chance relative to

TABLE 11.4. Percentages Reporting In-Passing and Focal Consciousness About Death and Dying.

Age-Generation		8-11	12-13	14-15	16-17	18-25 Young Adults	26-39	40-55 Middle-aged	56-64	65+ Old	Total
In-passing thought											
males	n	108	159	127	86	576	488	398	102	86	2170
	% engaged-in	19	26	30	17	13	17	21	15	29	17
females	n	120	165	136	158	652	443	336	95	80	2250
	% engaged-in	24	34	28	27	18	21	21	27	38	23
Focal thought											
males	n	68	61	88	86	576	488	398	102	86	1953
	% engaged-in	6	0	3	5	1	3	2	1	6	3
females	n	68	73	109	158	652	443	366	95	80	2044
	% engaged-in	6	5	4	1	3	3	2	3	9	4

their actuarial chance more than men did. In the present investigation, reports of thinking about death were more frequent among females than males. While thinking about one's own death constitutes a different conceptual domain than thinking about death and dying, it is not unreasonable to suppose that those who think more frequently about death and dying think more frequently about their own demise. Males think less about death, but they have reason to think more about death. At all ages, and for most causes of death, females are less apt to die than males. It might be argued that the "tough" image that males sport in our society would facilitate male repression of contempulation of death. But it could as plausibly be argued that part of the "tough" image would feature greater expression of "death-bravado" so that males would, to the degree that expression of death utterances influences admitting to thoughts of death, report a greater incidence of death-thought. Perhaps the higher incidence of death-thought among females is a contributor toward or a symptom of women's more frequent episodic instability in our culture (e.g., women typically score higher on the Eysenck Neuroticism Scale than men [Cameron, Frank, Lifter, and Morrisey, 1971]). Conventional (and professional) wisdom holds it "mentally healthy" to largely ignore inevitable occurrences ("Sure the button may be pushed today, but I don't think about it"; "We're all going to die, so why bother to worry about it?") If women do not, as frequently as men, "control" their thoughts, they may indulge in more frequent contemplation of inevitabilities with consequently heightened anxiety. Perhaps menstruation and other "female problems" remind women of their mortal nature more frequently than men are reminded by their day-to-day existence.

The sex difference may relate to the lower social status of women. There is some evidence that Negroes think more frequently about death than whites (Cameron, 1972). But Negroes and women similarly claim to value religion more than whites and men (Cameron, 1969) and appear to *contemplate* religion more frequently than whites and men (Cameron, 1972). Thoughts of religion and thoughts of death and dying have been found to occur together in adults of both sexes at considerably above chance levels and with a mutual frequency exceeding the mutuality discovered between either of these dimensions and any of the other dimensions of consciousness sampling (Cameron, 1970). It is possible that the sex difference in death-thought stems substantially from the sex difference in religious-thought (or vice versa). Unfortunately no above-chance mutuality between thoughts of death and religion for the pre-adults of our sample was uncovered, so this explanation falls to account for the more frequent contemplation of death and dying by females before adulthood. Further, this lack of mutuality may suggest that greater female religiosity might result in some substantial part from more frequent contemplation of death, or perhaps that pre-adults have not learned to associate death and religion. Clearly more representative samples of pre-adults will have to be drawn to certify the generality of this finding and the consequent plausibility of any of these speculations.

Jeffers and Verwoerdt (1966) reported the judgments of 140 elderly community volunteers regarding how frequently "they thought about death." The median estimate of these volunteers from six possibilities ranging from "never" to "always in mind" was "occasionally (once a week)." Clearly such a judgement involves reflecting upon one's customary thought-patterns and relating this judgment to the investigator's scale and is far less direct and compelling than the request of the present study to appraise one's thoughts over the past 5 minutes for the presence or absence of thoughts of death. Further, how representative these 140 volunteers were of "elderly persons in general" is open to greater question than our larger, more carefully-drawn sample.

When asked "[d]o death thoughts affect enjoyment of life?" a plurality of the Jeffers and Verwoerdt subjects, 47%, said, "no" while 40% said "yes". It might be argued that if thinking about death affects enjoyment of life, such thoughts ought to depress one's mood. We found no correlation between our subjects' reports of their mood over the past half hour and reports of having contemplated death or dying either in-passing or focally. Perhaps expecting the state of a person's mood over a half hour to be influenced by a thought is unreasonable, and a finer index of mood, perhaps covering only the past few minutes would uncover such a dampening effect.

Death appears a frequent visitor to consciousness. Sex has been found to cross the mind with only somewhat greater frequency than death and dying for the life-span as-a-whole, and sex brushes consciousness less frequently than death and dying after middle age (Cameron and Biber, 1973). The old persons in the Jeffers-Verwoerdt study estimated that they thought about death about once a week while the college students in the Cameron (1968) project estimated that they thought about their own demise about once every two days. If these two samples can be considered even approximately representative of the general population (and there are good reasons to judge them quite deficient in representativeness), people apparently think about death far more frequently than they estimate that they think about it. This is not the case with sex — people's estimates of how frequently they think about sex correspond rather closely with results derived from actual consciousness sampling (Cameron, 1973). Sex and death are both "taboo" topics — why then should frequency of death-thought be so dramatically underestimated while frequency of sex-thought is estimated accurately? Perhaps the difference in veracity of estimates indexes the degree of social and psychological "tabooness" of the two topics. If so, death must be many more times "taboo" and psychologically disruptive than sex for most people in our society.

REFERENCES

Cameron, P. The imminency of death. *Journal of Consulting & Clinical Psychology,* 1968, *32,* 479-481.

Cameron P. Valued aspects of religion to Negroes and whites. *Proceedings, Seventy-Seventh Annual Convention, (APA),* 1969.

Cameron, P. Religion as a component of consciousness. Paper presented at the Society for the Scientific Study of Religion, New York, Oct. 23, 1970.

Cameron P. Frank, F.D., Lifter, M. L., and Morrisey P. Personality differences between typical urban Negroes and whites. *Journal of Negro Education,* 1971, *40,* 66-75.

Cameron, P. Racial differences in contents of consciousness. In preparation, 1973.

Cameron, P. and Biber, H. Sexual thought throughout the life-span. *Gerontologist,* in press, 1973.

Cobly, K. M. Sex differences in dreams of primitive tribes, *American Anthropologist,* 1963, *65,* 1116-1121.

Feifel, H. Attitudes toward death in some normal and mentally ill populations. In H. Feifel, *The meaning of death*. New York: McGraw-Hill, 1959.

Foulkes, D. Theories of dream formation and recent studies of sleep consciousness. *Psychological Bulletin,* 1964, *2,* 236-247.

Jeffers, F. C. and Verwoerdt, A. Factors associated with frequency of death thoughts in elderly community volunteers. In *Proceedings of the Seventh International Congress of Gerontology,* Vol. 6 Vienna: Medical Academy, 1966.

Lee, S. G. Social influences in Zulu dreaming. *Journal of Social Psychology,* 1958, *47,* 265-283.

Suicide and the Generation Gap

Freud, and more recently Menninger (1938), has contended that the "death wish" increases with age. Certainly, the suicide rate increases with age, since for every 10,000 of their number, approximately 1 young, 2 middle-aged, and 3 old adults commit suicide each year (Maris, 1969). Yet, how do the generations compare in self-reported desire to die? Men are about three times as likely to commit suicide at any age, but are there generational and/or sex differences in self-reported suicide contemplations, attempts, or knowledge of ways to commit suicide? These and related questions were addressed in the following three-generation sample of adults.

Method

Subjects. In order to determine which ages should be included in the age categories "young adult," "middle-aged," and "old," a pilot study was conducted that empirically established that people are probably young adults when aged 18 to 25 inclusive, middle-aged from 40 to 55, and old from 65 to 79 (Cameron, 1969). Desiring to represent these age groups as adequately as possible, and realizing that there might be sex differences in the results, six samples of the city of Detroit (excluding the inner city) were procured — one for young males, one for young females, one for middle-aged males, and so on.

Subjects were approached at home at least twice to assure a low rejection rate, and were paid two dollars for the interview. Through a system of almost unlimited call-backs we ended up with 19 rejections, that is, a rejection rate of <6%. Interviewers were 12 trained, paid college students. Slightly over 50% of the data were recalled and verified both to clarify ambiguities or correct mistakes and to assure that no "dry labbing" had occurred.

Interview. The subject was approached by asking him to fill out a questionnaire concerning his beliefs about adults. He was assured anonymity, asked to fill out the questionnaire in another part of the residence, then, when finished, to seal the interview in an envelope provided for the purpose. The interviewer acted only to induce the subject to cooperate, deliver the materials, and answer any questions that he might have (there were relatively few). When asked questions about a particular item on the questionnaire, the interviewer read the question aloud for the respondent and, in a few cases, provided minor definitional clarification. When leaving the interviewer induced the subject to record his phone number on the envelope, and when outside recorded the address. Whenever a respondent had neglected to answer any question(s), a person other than the interviewer recontacted him by phone or in person and requested completion. The data were thus made over 99% complete. Each interviewer contacted and interviewed an equal number of males and females evenly distributed over the three age groups to control for any idiosyncratic interviewer-effects. Half of the subjects in each sample were administered the "opinions" part of the questionnaire first, the other half the "self-report" part first.

Questionnaire. On the "opinions" part of the questionnaire, the respondent was asked to fill in the blanks:

How do you believe the three age groups (young adults, middle-aged, and old) compare in:

1) desire to die? _____ are the most apt to want to die; _____ are least apt to want to die
2) Average number of suicide attempts per year? _____ have the hightest attempted suicide rate; _____ have the lowest attempted suicide rate
3) average number of successful suicides per year? _____ have the hightest suicide rate; _____ have the lowest suicide rate
4) social "understanding" of suicide attempts? _____ society

excuses the easiest; _____ society condemns the most
5) knowledge of ways to commit suicide? _____ know the most
   and best ways; _____ have the least knowledge.

The "self-appraisal" part of the questionnaire was a mirror of the above, consisting of a Likert scale (above average, average, below average):
How would you compare yourself with *All Other Adults of Your Sex* in:
1) desire to die?
2) knowledge of ways to commit suicide?
3) number of times you've seriously considered suicide?

Further, each subject was asked: "How many times have you tried to commit suicide in the past 5 years? _____." He was also asked his age, sex, income to the nearest $500 for the past year, and the highest grade he completed in formal schooling. Socioeconomic status (SES) was computed by multiplying the number associated with income (1 = under $5,000; 2 = $5,000-7,999; 3 = $8,000-11,999; 4 = $12,000+) by 2 and adding it to the number associated with education (1 = completed less than 8th grade; 2 = 8th-11th; 3 = H.S. diploma; 4 = some college; 5 = B.A.; 6 = M.A.; 7 = Ph.D.). Socioeconomic status consisted of two levels; those scoring 9 or higher and those scoring 8 or less.

The mean ages of the samples were 21.0 for the young adults, 48.2 for the middle-aged, and 70.2 for the old. SES levels were 8.89, 9.39, and 6.02, respectively. (Educational levels were 3.52, 3.25, and 2.49, with the young and middle-aged thus falling between the "H.S. diploma" and "some college" categories, while the old fell between the "8th-11th" and "H.S. diploma" categories; for income the groups averaged 2.68, 3.10, and 1.79, with the young averaging under $8,000 per year, the middle-aged over $8,000, and the old under $5,000.)

Results

Beliefs about the Generations. Before reporting the results, it should be noted that a 3-way, fixed-effects analysis of variance was employed in Tables 1 through 4 instead of a "simple" 3-by-3 array coupled with an X^2 statistic. It was felt that since sex and SES of respondents are so frequently found to be important independent variables, often, in fact, associated with more of the variance than age, their inclusion in the same analyses would make the contribution of age more certain and also provide the possibility of revealing suggestive interactions. We employed harmonic means to adjust for the unequal numbers in the cells formed by the 3 X 2 X 2 design.

Desire to die. The 3-way fixed-effects analysis of variance revealed no generational, sexual, or socioeconomic status differences or significant interactions (*Fs* for the main effects were all less than 1; one interaction's *F* was 1.2), and the results are combined in Table 11.5. Clearly the generations, sexes, and social classes believed that the old have the greatest and young adults the least desire to die.

TABLE 11.5: Which Generation the Generations
Believed Has the Greatest and Least Desire to Die

	Young Adults	Middle-aged	Old	Total
Have greatest desire	55	24	232	311
Have least desire	182	82	47	311

Suicide Knowledge. The 3-way analysis of variance disclosed a sex difference, and the sexes' beliefs are presented separately in Table 11.6 While both sexes agreed that the old are the least knowledgeable about suicide, males believed the middle-aged to be the most knowledgeable and the young the next most knowledgeable. Females believed the young and middle-aged to be about

TABLE 11.6: Generational Beliefs about Which Generation Has the Greatest and Least Knowledge about Ways to Commit Suicide

	Know Most			Know Least		
	Men	Women	Total	Men	Women	Total
Young adults	61	88	149	76	39	115
Middle-aged	67	52	119	14	8	22
Old	30	16	46	66	111	177

equal in their knowledge.

Suicide attempts. The analysis of variance indicated a significant sex difference, and the sexes' beliefs are presented separately in Table 11.7. While both sexes believed that the old make the fewest suicide attempts, females were more apt to believe that the young make the most attempts whereas males more frequently nominated the middle aged.

Suicide rate. The analysis of variance indicated significant age and sex differences. As Table 11.8 reveals, although both sexes generally agreed that the old have the lowest suicide rate, males attributed a higher rate to the old than did females. The young adults and old generally judged the middle-aged as the most frequent suiciders and the old as the least frequent. The middle-aged believed the young to be the most frequent suiciders and the old the least frequent.

TABLE 11.7: Which Generation Is Believed to Make
the Most and Fewest Suicide Attempts

	Young Adults	Middle-aged	Old
Make Most Attempts			
Females believed	89	58	11
Males believed	63	69	25
Make Fewest Attempts			
Females believed	22	26	110
Males believed	56	30	72

Social "understanding" of suicide. While all the generations agreed that the young are the most condemned and the old the easiest excused for committing suicide (Table 11.8), each generation generally overcondemned and underexcused itself relative to the other generations' appraisals. As with the preceding analyses, only the age effect was statistically significant.

Self-Appraisals

"Death Wish". Only socioeconomic status had a significant effect upon death desire. All groups claimed a below-average desire, while lower socioeconomic status persons claimed a higher desire than higher socioeconomic status persons did (on a scale of 3 for above average to 1 for below average, means ranged from 1.20 to 1.63 for the lower SES and 1.19 to 1.40 for higher SES).

Considerations of suicide. There were no statistically significant differences between the generations, sexes, or SES levels in re-

TABLE 11.8: Generational Beliefs about Successful Suicides

| | Suicide Most | | | | | | Suicide Least | | | | | |
| | Males Believed | | | Females Believed | | | Males Believed | | | Females Believed | | |
	Young	Middle	Old	Young	Middle	Old	Young	Middle	Old	Young	Middle	Old
The young adults believed	22	27	6	22	30	1	16	7	30	8	10	35
The middle-aged believed	25	20	6	33	20	2	19	11	23	11	17	28
The old believed	18	25	7	21	22	7	22	8	21	14	4	31

TABLE 11.9: Believed Social "Understanding" of Generational Suicide

| | Society Condemns the Most | | | Society Excuses the Easiest | | |
	Young Adults	Middle-aged	Old	Young Adults	Middle-aged	Old
The young adults believed	72	20	12	15	34	54
The middle-aged believed	53	38	16	31	26	50
The old believed	41	37	23	35	25	41
Total	166	95	51	81	86	145

ported considerations of suicide (on a scale of 1 to 3, means ranged from 1.00 to 1.41).

Suicide attempts. No statistically significant differences in suicide attempts were uncovered, as is evident in Table 8. Overall, the young reported at .132, the middle-aged a .00935, and the old a .050 rate, for an overall rate of .0639 for the past five years.

Knowledge of ways to commit suicide. Young adults claimed to know more about ways to commit suicide than the middle-aged, who in turn claimed more knowledge than the old. At all ages males claimed more knowledge than females.

Discussion

Psychoanalytic theory's claim of an increasing desire to die as adults age is apparently an opinion held by most adults in our society (Table 11.5), and, in the light of no generational differences in claimed desire to die (Table 6), quite possibly untrue. Of course, if psychoanalysts are referring to an unconscious "death wish", the data presented in Table 6 have no necessary bearing as they register conscious judgments. It is more than merely interesting, however, that a "depth" theory supposedly concerning itself with unconscious goings-on seconds the "common man's" theory about conscious material.

Since the suicide rate in adulthood is generally directly related to age, male beliefs about relatively more suicide attempts and successes (Tables 11.7 and 11.8) tend to make the male view slightly more "realistic." Nevertheless, both males and females generally agreed that the old have the lowest attempt and success rates. "Common sense" thus runs directly counter to demographic facts in this instance. A possible explanation is provided by noting that about 7% of the deaths of young adults are suicides while for old adults the figure is about .5% (Maris, 1969). Thus, relative to the number that die, young people are about 15 times more likely to commit suicide.

To perform an act intentionally, a person must know about it, want to do it, know how to do it, make the attempt, and succeed (Ossorio, 1966). The "common man" in our sample believed that the old have the greatest desire to die but the lowest level of knowledge of ways to commit suicide, which results in the old having the lowest suicide attempt and success rates. Thus if we can assume equivalent skill at committing suicide — and how one would acquire skill in such an act without terminating his existence is obscure — our "common man" obviously weights knowledge much greater than desire in the commission of this act, and, perhaps, of acts in general. If the weighting had been equivalent, then presumably the greater social "understanding" of old people's suicide would have tipped the common belief toward greater suicide among the old. That the belief runs directly counter to this, with the young seen as having the highest rate, suggests that our society places a great deal of stock in knowledge as opposed to desire. Possibly in Eskimo society, where, interpersonally at least, to desire is to get, the weightings would be just the opposite.

All the generations agreed that suicide among young adults is the most condemned, while among the old it is the easiest excused. Each generation seems to have displaced social condemnation toward and social excuse away from itself (Table 11.9). By making or believing suicide more socially condemned than it is, each generation is provided or provides itself with more of a reason not to do it.

That those of lower social status should generally rate their desire to die as greater provides yet another commentary upon our social system. To believe that those of lower socioeconomic status have less to live for and, now, to know that they believe it also would seem to place defenders of the status quo in double moral jeopardy. Menninger's (1938) contention that the old and males have a greater desire to die is not supported by the present data. Of course, his method of inferring desire to die from clinical interviews was methodologically quite different from our frontal attack on the question. Yet there is no compelling reason to believe that inferences from indirect material are more valid either in general or in this case. On the contrary, we are much more likely to take some sort of action if a person says, right out, that he wants to die or to commit suicide than if we have to infer it from some of his productions. Further, we sampled a population of normals while Menninger's sample consisted of the mentally disturbed — generally we would seem on safer ground in extrapolating from a population of normals to normals rather than from the distressed to normals.

Farberow and Shneidman (1957) classified 619 suicide notes into one of four categories: those ostensibly, in-the-main, reflecting the "wish to kill," "the wish to be killed," "the wish to die," or "unclassifiable. " Generally they found that those suicide notes from older subjects were placed more frequently into the "wish to die" category. Since only the productions of persons in a clear state of pathology were studied, the relevance of the data to statements about "people in general" is uncertain, but, insofar as attitudes toward one's personal demise of people-about-to-suicide are representative of the general population, the data are consonant with Menninger's notion.

While Durkheim and Henry and Short (1954) have argued that those of higher socioeconomic status have a higher suicide rate, Maris (1969) has argued for the opposite relationship. Our data have no clear bearing on the question of whether those of higher or those of lower SES commit suicide more often, but, by suggesting that those of lower SES have a greater professed desire to die, our results would appear to lend a small weight to Maris' contention.

If a person is to seriously contemplate suicide, he must not only desire his demise to a certain degree but must also consider the skills he possesses to accomplish the task. That is to say, it takes more effort to seriously consider suicide than it takes to register a desire to terminate one's existence. We would expect therefore that, generally, any given person's rating of his desire to die should be of greater intensity than a comparable rating of his actual suicidal contemplations. A comparison of Tables 6 and 7 reveals that in 8 of the 10 untied comparisons between the same cells for the two variables, desire to die captures a higher value than serious contemplations of suicide (sign test $p < .06$). It is also noteworthy that all of the means fall into the lower third of the possible range of 1 to 3 — on the average, generally people express a very low desire to die.

Though one might at first assume that the rate of serious contemplation of suicide would be congruent with the actual suicide rate, there is no logical necessity for such to be the case. Instead of the old having the highest and the young the lowest mean estimates, the generations reported essential equivalency (Table 7). Only a small minority of adults commit suicide each year, while many people report that they contemplate suicide a number of times in their lives (Cameron, 1968, found evidence that college students think about their demise on an average of once a week).

It appears generally accepted that there are about eight suicide attempts for every successful suicide (Stengel, 1964). Since there are about 15 suicides per 100,000 per year in the United States, there would be about 600 attempts per 100,000 over a five-year period. The present sample claimed a rate of .0639 for the last five years or almost exactly 10 times the expected figure of .0062 (generationally, the young reported a rate of .132, the middle-aged a rate of .00935, and the old a rate of .050; their corresponding "expecteds" would be .0036, .008, and .012). At least two possible interpretations of this estimate exist: (a) the reported rate is "true," which would mean that there are about 2 million suicide attempts in the United States every year, or (b) it is an overestimate, perhaps tied in some fashion to the psychological importance of such an act. Our knowledge of actual suicide attempts is so meager that quite possibly the extrapolated estimate of 2 million is " in the ball park" and the officially believed ¼ million is an underestimate. On the other hand, we know that when it comes to death, people grossly overestimate their actuarial probability of dying. (Cameron, 1968). Possibly this overestimate has a "psychological reality" quite out of proportion to its "demographic reality."

Students of suicide have agreed that males have a higher suicide rate than females. Part of the explanation of this phenomenon may be the male's greater knowledge of ways to commit suicide (Table 9). As Ossorio (1966) has noted, to act — in this case to commit suicide — a person must first know about suicide, must want to suicide, know how to suicide, and then, given the appropriate physical context, make the attempt. Clearly, a person who knows more about how to commit suicide will succeed more frequently than one who knows less, all other things being equal. In this case, although we don't know, in fact, whether males do know more, at least they think that they do. If further research finds that they do know more, part of the male-female suicide rate difference would be explained.

REFERENCES

Cameron, P. The Imminency of Death, *Journal of Consulting and Clinical Psychology,* 1968, *32,* 479-81.

Cameron, P. Age Parameters of Young Adult, Middle-Aged, Old and Aged. *Journal of Gerontology,* 1969, *24,* 201-2.

Farberow, N.C. and Shneidman, E.S. Suicide and Age, In E.S. Shneidman and N.L. Farberow, eds., *Clues to Suicide,* New York: McGraw-Hill, 1957.

Henry, A. F., and Short, J. F., Jr. *Suicide and Homicide,* New York: Free Press, 1954.

Maris, R.W. *Social Forces in Urban Suicide.* Homewood, Illinois: Dorsey Press, 1969.

Menninger, K. *Man against Himself.* New York: Harcourt, Brace & Jovanovich, 1938.

Ossorio, P. G. *Persons.* Los Angeles; Linguistic Research Institute, 1966.

Stengel, E. *Suicide and Attempted Suicide.* Baltimore: Penguin Books, 1964.

IMMOLATIONS TO THE JUGGERNAUT

Any sensitive observer of the contemporary American scene must be impressed with the death emphasis of our culture. From almost out of nowhere dramatic, lethal trends are flourishing within our society. Twenty years ago it was rare to find a course on death listed in a college catalog. Today, rare is the university without such course listings.

In 1973 the Supreme Court of the United States legalized abortion up to six months of age. In 1976 the state of California passed a "death with dignity" law. In between these two points, infanticide, which had been covertly practiced, became publicized. Prior to the Supreme Court decision, organ transplantation had stimulated thinking toward a "death with dignity" direction. Organ transplantation put an effective rest to the unsettled questions of the relationship between the human brain, personhood and consciousness. Prior to transplantation, particularly heart transplantation, the questionable assumption that all that is uniquely and distinctively human is contained in the cerebral cortex was unsettled. Bernard challenged medical ethics to come to a decision. The decision was made by default or perhaps in the overwhelming glare of public approval of the skilled surgeon's hand. In 1976, in the face of a popular press demand for her demise, the legal system of the United States consented to Karen Quinlan's death. Aside from the monkey wrench placed by her obstinate refusal to die, we might have had a national "death with dignity" law.

Over the past few years, the homosexual movement has emerged from the closet. Parades and appeals to various governmental bodies are the order of the day. Today it is academically *de rigueur* to regard homosexuality as being either as legitimate an expression of sexuality as heterosexuality, or at worst, a minor aberration. Twenty years ago the pill became widely disseminated. About fifteen years ago, pets became such a powerful influence in American life that every national general magazine and newspaper felt constrained to contain a pet column. In 1975 and 1976, the Supreme Court reinstated capital punishment.

Why now? Why at this point in our nation's history have these phenomena come upon us? Our nation is not operating in a vacuum. Given the strategic importance of the United States in world intercourse, what a given nation does not have in the way of deathward laws as compared to the United States, it is almost certainly destined to obtain. Again the question "why"? I would like to present the major reason for the existence of these phenomena and for even more lethal shifts in social policy . . . introducing the Juggernaut and kin.

The Juggernaut is the prime mover behind the plethora of human-life-crimping social policies. The Juggernaut is most starkly revealed in its basic character in Table 11.10.

"Producers" refers to all the workers in manufacturing, minting, utilities, transportation, communications, and farming. These persons comprise the heart and soul of a social system. All other kinds of services hinge upon them. Other persons in the system are not necessarily non-productive. About a third of the populace is children and teenagers who have small productive but clear replacement functions. Further, there are some ancilary workers who contribute in tangential ways to production (teachers and medical personnel, for instance, and to some degree government workers). But no matter how considered, the proportion of productive workers in the population has been steadily declining. Over the past 126

TABLE 11.10

Producers as a Proportion of the Population

Year	No. of Productive Workers in Millions			Total Population in Millions	Productive % of Population
	Agriculture	Goods	Total		
1850	4.9	2.7	7.6	23	33
1900	10.7	11.0	21.7	76	29
1920	11.1	16.5	27.6	106	26
1930	10.3	15.6	25.8	123	20
1940	9.5	15.9	25.4	132	19
1950	7.2	18.5	25.7	151	17
1960	5.5	20.4	25.9	178	15
1970	3.5	22.5	26.0	203	13

years the diminution in the proportion of producers in the population has been dramatic. In 1975 the United States reached a point where only 12% of the United States population as a whole, fell into the productive category, essentially a reduction of two-thirds in the proportion of those who are *necessary* for social functioning. This is the Juggernaut. In a social system such as ours in which profit is the impetus to production, in a system in which goods and services are provided basically to those who can pay and pay enough for a profit, the Juggernaut must eventually turn social policies against mankind. The intellectual noises of our day are cries of scarcity, of too many people. The sounds largely stem from the Juggernaut.

Forces at Work

Many forces are at work in every modern social system. To avoid gross oversimplification of a complex situation let's admit that there are a number of equally useful ways to analyze the components of society. From my perspective, the activities of a given society are influenced by eight forces. At times each is working independently relative to some or all of the others. Usually each is working against the aims and interests of one or more of the others, and, rarely do they all coalesce. These forces are:

1) the basic "ethics of a social system; the "real" way it functions, its working principles, including its aims and the means generally employed to attain these aims (the Juggernaut lives here);

2) the system-maintenance ethic. Preservation of the system at any and all costs is the general Machiavellian rule. Each bureaucracy also seeks to maintain and expand its power within the system;

3) the propaganda of the social system; the sugar coating and the various sacred principles that are sometimes related to the basic ethic, but more often than not, are unrelated in any meaningfully functional way to the basic ethic. These principles are espoused and proclaimed, frequently being identical in societies supposedly at war with each other (soul of the son of Juggernaut);

4) extra-system ethical systems; most of which, like Topsy, "just grew." Sometimes they emerged to meet possible needs of the past, but have hung around fighting for peoples' loyalties. Christianity, vegetarianism and most "isms" locate here;

5) within-system private interest groups, as, for instance, the Chamber of Commerce, Gulf Oil Corporation, Gay Liberation, etc;

6) fashions and fads that apprear to just "spring up"; often these have beginnings in and affinities with one or more of the other six, but they also often come and go as historic curiosities;

7) idiosyncratic, personal notions of prominent/influential people; no matter how bizarre, the personal beliefs of a head of state or of a famous singer have some influence;

8) the mass media's need for "news" or content. Often this modern phenomenon creates "something out of nothing" and bequeaths as a residue a new private interest group, a fad, or additional idiosyncracies.

Each of these forces is influencing modern society at all times. While official, main-line social policy is the outcome of the struggle between these forces, each influences social functioning to some degree. Only a part of official social policy achieves perfect or nearly-perfect expression. Most official policies merely set the stage on which real policy plays. There is no clean, one-to-one relationship between official social policy and what is actually done. Official social policy provides the setting for society's morality plays. Generally, real actions cannot deviate too far from the official rules. Therefore, all who seek to direct morality fight to control official social policy.

Each of these forces varies in the strength of its expression depending upon a multitude of factors. The "basic ethic" of a system typically exerts a strong, fairly constant pressure on social policy. It, after all, determines what most of the members of a social system actually do most of the time, and the Juggernaut is having a decided influence on what people do.

What a person does, and how he goes about doing it, has a powerful influence on how and what he believes. The propaganda of a social system also has considerable and relatively constant influence. While some ebb and flow of allegiance to the "verbal edifice" that a society erects will occur, usually societies "push" it enough that many, if not most, members of the society will bear the edifice in mind in many of their decisions and attitudes. As, in the long run, what people do has more influence upon what they believe than what they believe has influence on what they do, the basic ethic exerts an unremitting pressure upon official propaganda to bring it into line. Presumably, in a perfectly mature social system, there would be no difference between the ethic and the propaganda. But no known system has achieved anything approximating this perfection.

Extra-system interest groups exert highly variable pressure on social policy. Very few persons genuinely dedicate their existence to any of these systems. Most of the adherents are rather mildly endorsing the philosophy. Revivals and falling-aways are the norm, so that at times Christianity or environmentalism will have considerable impact upon society, but generally they will pipe minor notes.

Idiosyncratic influences and, more rarely, fads, may prove almost overwhelming. From an "ethic" standpoint, Hitler's dispatching of retardates made system-sense. But his treatment of the Jews was, from a system-maintenance standpoint, incredible.

Ethics and Pressure

The ethic of a system exerts about as much pressure on all the other influences as they exert upon social policy. Churches, for instance, constantly have difficulty reconciling the ethics their members actually practice with those that the church proclaims. As man is inherently casuistical, the church's teachings are pressed toward endorsement of the ethic. Often churches and other such special interest groups' members have three official, and ofttimes contradictory ideal systems inhabiting their minds: the "ancient" truths, the propaganda truths, and the ethical truths, all seen as emanating from official church dogma. Many of the intellectual endeavors of such bodies are directed toward apologies for such reconciliations. Thus many churches appear almost as "patriotic" as they are Christian, and often, the membership can only squarely agree on the patriotic/ethic-serving component, otherwise being scattered-every-which-way on the theological field.

As the ethic is the most important constant in the social policy equation, examination of it and the success of its expression in the United States is a good bet to provide explanation as to the content and the "now" of misanthropy. Capitalism, as a system, is dedicated to the production and sale of commodities. It is not concerned with getting men into heaven, or assuring a bountiful life for all. It is, in large measure, just because of capitalism's indifference to conflicting value systems, that it has swept before it any and all other kinds of social systems. Capitalism produces commodities cheaper than any other system. *How* it does this is of no concern to the buyer. He gets the price-break. Within the capitalist system, the less socially necessary labor-time expended per individual commodity, the cheaper it can be sold, and the more certain the profit. As the capitalist enterprise is dedicated to producing the cheapest product, no matter how that is accomplished, other kinds of values are, whenever possible, ignored. The surest way for a given capitalist concern to "make it" is to produce more with the same work-force, or produce as much with a smaller work-force. As demand is constantly changing, the safest course is toward the latter. Removal of men from production to the greatest degree possible is a clear goal. Similarly, the fewer the frills accorded the worker and the workplace, the cheaper the product can be produced and consequently sold. Cutting costs, no matter where they might be found is an important consideration. From a systems standpoint, it is indeed unfortunate that workers eat, require clothing, vacations, etc. The perfect worker would be one who worked and nothing more. Consumers if perfect, would consume and spend without limit. Each manufacturer earnestly searches for more customers even as he whittles away at his own workforce. The capitalist is encouraged to save lest he run shy of capital; he encourages saving and abstemiousness on the part of his workforce. This encouragement comes not just from example and admonition ("tuck a buck a day away"), but also under the fear of being unemployed for some period of time (a fate that regularly falls to a sixth of the United States work force in any given year). The basic ethic of capitalism ranges between the abstemious and niggardly.

This basic ethic shrieks in the face of the Juggernaut. From a systems standpoint the Juggernaut was destined to occur. Machines must necessarily disenfranchise man from production. But the niggardly-abstemious ethic of capitalism does not fawn upon such a circumstance. Since the basic substratum of society, the producers, consists of only 12% of the population (plus necessary ancillary workers) the rest of the work force is ancillary and/or boondoggling. While genuine human interests may or may not be served by many of the others who happen to be employed, from a systems standpoint, most of them are superfluous. The niggardliness of the capitalist ethic exerts a pressure toward the application of any and all persons to some semblance of productive effort. So all able bodied men, women and children are encouraged to do something reminiscent of producing. Even the not-so-ablebodied are stroked to expend effort to produce ("Hire the handicapped"). Additional pressures toward "providing jobs" come from the propaganda component of the social influences (the "liberals" derive the greater part of their sustenance from this quarter). The "conservatives" rightly recognize that the liberals are "throwing money to the wind." The liberals have generally been unable to more than cosmetize the situation, while the conservatives seek to make life so miserable for the nonproductive that they will voluntarily "check out." *Fundamentally* the system is working toward the elimination of all but the genuinely productive and those needed to replace them upon demise. The Juggernaut renders the greater portion of the remaining population unadulterated chaff.

The Juggernaut reduces the need for people but people continue to be produced. What is to be done with these people? The propaganda system's ethic is invoked to employ many of these superfluous people to meet the human needs of other superfluous people in the brittle, plastic socialism of the welfare state. The boondoggling son of Juggernaut is born. Today the son bids fair to eclipse his father. Because the young are kept in school to keep them out of the labor force, teachers are required, health professionals are required, etc. If there were no young, if there were far fewer young, the numbers of such service providers could be correspondingly reduced. The forces tending to efficiency have pushed the older from productivity to retirement. In retirement the old require an ever growing array of services. Many of the surplus of the labor force spawned by the Juggernaut are diverted to meet the needs of the elderly. If there were no old persons or if there were far fewer old, the numbers of such service providers . . . Since the monies, activities and policies have to be monitored, the bureaucracy grows apace. The keepers of bureaucratic records, the form makers, the form checkers, all of these grow. But if the numbers of people — particularly this surplus population — could be reduced, the son of Juggernaut could be reduced. And with his diminution would come the elimination of a veritable horde of service providers, suppliers, accountants, legalizers and the like.

Juggernaut's Daughter

While Juggernaut's son is past his teen years and threatens to impoverish the system, Juggernaut has spawned a daughter. Even as the son of Juggernaut is involved with increasing the number of government workers from the 3.5 million in 1935 to the 15 million in 1975, so the daughter of Juggernaut, social service spending, has burgeoned. In 1900 approximately 3% of the gross national product was expended by the various levels of government on social welfare. By 1975 this had grown to 19% of the gross national product. While much of the social welfare expenditure has been in public education, considerable growth has been affected in "freebie" sorts of programs such as "aid to dependent children," and other forms of welfare. Some of the people Juggernaut displaced are consuming the fruits of Juggernaut, albeit in a niggardly fashion. For something to do to or with the surplus population, programs are created for those marginally benefited by the system, and go a way towards providing for the many bureaucrats and professionals who husband the programs. Yet all these programs are added on. They are not truly part of the system except as a systems-saving effort. The plasticity of this chintzy "socialism" is evident to all.

Juggernaut and his son have existed long enough that the son has brought forth an issue, the grandson of Juggernaut. Kreps, (1962), noted that after the great depression and a war that pulled the United States social system from the depression, the United States economy started in another interesting cycle. As she pointed out, "With every wave of prosperity the unemployment rate in the United States falls. But the unemployment rate does not fall sufficiently to recoup the losses sustained in the previous depression. There is a stepwise function occurring in the unemployment rate. Generally each succeeding recession leaves an additional 1% residue of unemployed in the trough." In 1962 Kreps made a straight line prediction. She noted that if the system continued to operate as it had in the past she would have predicted an unemployment rate of 10% in 1975. The official rate was 9%. At this writing the federal government is hoping for a 7% rate for 1977, and the same or slightly lower for 1978. The grandson of Juggernaut has added yet another dimension to the press for the elimination of people.

As if the Juggernaut family were not large enough, the wife of Juggernaut has appeared on the scene. Tired of their quasi-productive status and 1½ class citizenship, the females of our social system are entering the labor force in ever-increasing numbers and exacerbating an already explosive situation.

The situation is obviously getting more dire. From every quarter the Juggernaut family presses upon the social system. Experience has shown that men are far more willing to offer themselves than their social system to destruction. A change in social system is, at most points in man's history, unthinkable. Some have argued, and their case has merit, that the ultimate of servitude, the ultimate endorsement of institutions over mankind is war. In the Juggernaut we face an even more formidable misanthropic foe.

As we look across our social system we see that every possible way of reducing the value of man, every possible way of reducing the number of men, is being implemented or social policy is being honed for such implementation.

So we see in our lifetimes the following transpiring: (1) First and perhaps foremost, abstinence from reproduction is encouraged in a multitude of ways: (a) More schooling is required which makes early entry into marriage less feasible. (b) Education/propaganda about the virtues of contraception and greater assurance that if *nothing* else is learned in school, contraceptive techniques and practice will be. (c) Late marriage is encouraged. This takes at least two forms. In the first, one is encouraged to play the field for various reasons and then after having "sowed oats," settle down. The other pole is represented by, "get your financial career house in order, then children." Recent studies have indicated that the housing pressure is inducing couples to lower fertility. (d) Childless marriage is being encouraged and as more people see themselves as professionals and as more professionals see themselves as duty-bound to remain childless or to have a minimum number of children, childlessness grows. (e) Delayed childbearing is encouraged, both from a selfishness standpoint as well as "getting to know one another and then having children." (f) Small families are encouraged. *Psychology Today* and other journals abound in articles extolling the virtues of the single child or two child family and all the concomitant benefits that supposedly accrue to such children. (g) Voluntary sterilization is encouraged. (i) All forms of nonreproductive sex are now being encouraged. This ranges not only from legitimizing masturbation but also involves the establishment of masturbation parlors throughout the United States, a phenomenon of relatively recent vintage. Straight line homosexuality creates no more problems for the Juggernaut. (j) All quasi-substandard forms of nonreproductive sex are being tolerated, ranging from bestiality to necrophilia to fetishism and cries for the legitimization of prostitution. All of these forms are singularly unapt to result in children. (2) Abortion has been legalized and is being encouraged, even mandated. This year, for the first time, a major United States city features a higher rate of abortions than of live births. The city? Our nation's capital. (3) Pets are being legitimized as adequate alternatives to childbearing. (4) Abortion is being encouraged for all and mandated for certain classes of persons, particularly those who are nonproductive or subsisting at the expense of the daughter of Juggernaut. Recall again the situation of abortion in Washington, D.C. (5) Amniocentesis is being encouraged as a national policy. Amniocentesis results in a fraction of involuntary abortions and opens up the posibility of further mandated abortions. (6) Infanticide (to be legalized) is even now being encouraged in an indirect way for infants born with deformities. (7) Suicide (to be legalized) is being encouraged. Particular emphasis is being directed toward the suiciding of young adults and teenagers. (8) Brain death is being accepted as death and beyond this, even the approximation of brain damage will be accepted as death indeed. (9) Defective and disabled persons may well be put to death. (10) An age set, probably 65, beyond which a person without means will not be provided extensive medical service. (11) An age set, probably 80, beyond which a person without means will not be provided medical service. (12) An age set, probably 85, beyond which a person will not be permitted to exist. These social policies flow naturally from the Juggernaut and his family.

The Juggernaut lives among us. He influences the literature of our time, the scope of our scientific reporting, the kinds of things upon which scientists will agree.

Society's Decision

Part of the magnificence of society's decision is its breadth of onset. In the past a "social decision" has often been made by the ruling class or group and then attributed to society as a whole. Today we are, in-the-main, dealing with a phenomenon of sufficient breadth to warrant characterizing it as "social." There is no plot. Garden variety thought processes have just been applied to the human surplus in much the same way it is applied to a surplus of workers within a given capitalist concern. When the work runs down, then people get laid off or fired. While those in power in our society are somewhat more behind the effort to rid society of its surplus (Nelson Rockefeller comes to mind), the general public is in step also. All across the nation, various groups and individuals are just deciding to "fire" some people permanently. Some groups are so situated in society that they naturally turn to firing the ill (such as M.D.'s). Others happen to sell drugs to reduce the quantity of human life (as drug corporations), still others tend to advance the charms of suicide or infanticide (some suicideologists, historians, etc.). Those with the means to immolate to the Juggernaut, are. Extra-system philosophic systems are being altered to conform to this new thrust (churches are falling all over themselves to be the first to approve the newest life-crimping technique). From a system's survival perspective this is as it should be. Voluntarism is far preferable to forced reduction. The most desirable voluntarism would feature the dying pleading to be killed (Gilmore is a Juggernaut immolant here), the unemployed contraceptizing/aborting/infanticiding their offspring and/or suiciding, large segments of the populace (especially the minorities) turning to homosexuality, and everywhere people gentling each other toward death and her friends. The more morality that can be linked with personal lethality, the better. If say, a potential suicider can cloak his act in an altruistic "to help society conserve" verbiage, then his passing is more apt to have both personal and social appeal. Voluntarism is preferred. Today's coercive techniques tend to be reserved for the poor and ignorant. But expansion toward the "better folk" is certain. Currently the members of the professional class are permitted almost total voluntarism. And since professionals do a good job of talking up having no or few children, accepting homosexuality and suicide, etc., allowing them to do as they want is okay. Professionals have a solid suicide rate, never fail to have fewer children than would be required to replace themselves, and generally "cooperate." But given the magnitude of the population reduction that will be required to keep our social system afloat, it is highly likely that even professionals will have to be hurried to their graves.

There are few in society who do not recognize, at some gut level, that the system is running out of room, and they are responding by laying their hands to those population-trimming devices at their disposal. The sheer diversity of support for population trimming and the multitudinous means of attaining it inspire attention.

Increasingly the good life will be seen as far more important than the duration of life. In fact, it will be realized that a life extending beyond good or even excellent health is simply not worth living. The dilemma is acute. The choices are plain. Waste either property or people. Only the latter choice rings ethically clear.

Another dimension to population-trimming is added by the mass media. In the past, social systems lumberingly modified their population policies in reaction to changing conditions and/or philosophies. As children were taught by their parents and other adults, lessons tended to the conservatism of habit. Institutionalization of formal schooling permitted more rapid adjustments. Instead of having to modify most adults' cognitions, beliefs of teachers increasingly held key to the minds of children. With the advent of the mass media, especially television, a relative handful holds sway over much of the possibility of change. Where a single substantial change might require centuries in former social systems, the contemporary media-effect permits of many substantive changes within decades. Civilized man has always knowingly labored but a generation from savagery. The next generation has to be trained in the ways of civilization lest it revert. Modern man has lived under the atomic cloud. But no matter what, previous generations have always been able to bank on the sexual fires of youth to replenish the race. The potential of mass conversion to population-reduction raises a new spectre — if the young are diverted from reproduction and/or distaste of childbearing grows sufficiently, we may find the sound of a baby's cry as unusual as the song of a pelican in the desert.

REFERENCES

Kreps, J.M., Ferguson, C.E., Folsom, J.M., Employment of older workers. In *Employment, income, and retirement problems of the aged.* J. M. Kreps, ed., Durham, North Carolina: Duke University Press, 1963, pp. 51–108.

All statistics are from the 1975 and 1976 editions of the Statistical Abstract of the United States, and the Historical Abstract of the U.S. Bureau of the Census, Department of Commerce.